SOCIAL WORK IN CANADA

An Introduction

Third Edition

SOCIAL WORK IN CANADA

An Introduction

Third Edition

Steven Hick

Carleton University

Thompson Educational Publishing, Inc.

Toronto, Ontario

Information on how to obtain copies of this book is available at:

Website:	www.thompsonbooks.com
E-mail:	publisher@thompsonbooks.com
Phone:	416-766-2763
Fax:	416-766-0398

Library and Archives Canada Cataloguing in Publication

Hick, Steven F

     Social work in Canada : an introduction / Steven Hick. -- 3rd ed.

Includes bibliographical references and index.

ISBN 978-1-55077-173-2

     1. Social service--Canada--Textbooks. I. Title.

HV105.H525 2009	361.30971	C2009-900685-5

Cover design: Tibor Choleva, BlueAppleWorks
Cover illustration: Esme Nichola Shilletto, Pink Dog Designs

Every reasonable effort has been made to acquire permission for copyrighted materials used in this book and to acknowledge such permissions accurately. Any errors or omissions called to the publisher's attention will be corrected for future printings. All credits can be found on page 366.

Statistics Canada information is used with the permission of Statistics Canada. Users are forbidden to copy the data and redisseminate them, in an original or modified form, for commercial purposes, without permission from Statistics Canada. Information on the availability of the wide range of data from Statistics Canada can be obtained from Statistics Canada's Regional Offices, its World Wide Web site at http://www.statcan.ca, and its toll-free access number 1-800-263-1136.

We acknowledge the financial support of the Government of Canada through the Book Publishing Industry Development Program (BPIDP) for our publishing activities.

Printed in Canada.

4 5 6   16 15 14

CONTENTS

PREFACE

This book fills a need for an introductory-level text written from a truly Canadian perspective. *Social Work in Canada* is an introductory text in the truest sense, keeping in mind those students who are new to social work and may be considering a career in the field. Unlike many other texts, which tend to emphasize techniques, this book emphasizes the importance of being clear about one's values and world view before beginning to practice social work.

This book does not pretend to provide an easy "ten-step" recipe that can be applied to any particular problem. Social work is a complex field, thus throughout the text there is an emphasis on the need for students to think deeply about issues—particularly controversial ones—before arriving at a theoretical approach or a course of action. In addition to teaching, I continue to practice with people who are suffering deeply, experiencing institutionally based oppression and personal psychological difficulties. Through social activism and policy work, I have also been involved in trying to shift the structures in society toward more justice and fairness. Throughout all of this, I have come to the conclusion that our current social and economic systems are extremely unhealthy, oppressive, and unjust. But, these are only my conclusions. I encourage all students to question and discuss the issues and approaches to social work practice and, with the facts in hand, arrive at their own conclusions. I hope that this book might be a small part of their journey.

Contents

While the chapters are not grouped into units in the third edition of *Social Work in Canada*, there is a clear organizing principle. Chapters 1 to 5 introduce social work to the reader, dealing with social welfare, the history of the field, foundational theories and current approaches to practice, as well as a pragmatic overview of the profession. Chapters 6 and 7 explore the skills and approaches associated with direct practice, considering practice with individuals, groups, and communities in depth. Chapters 8 through 15 relate this acquired knowledge to a variety of contexts, such as practice within the health care and child welfare systems; work with Aboriginal peoples, women, seniors, and persons with disabilities; as well as an exploration of sexual and gender diversity and anti-racist social work. Finally, Chapter 16 introduces the field of international social work.

New to this Edition

Important developments have occurred since the second edition of this book was published. In particular, at the end of 2008, the Canadian and world economy experienced a major setback, and most analysts agree that the recovery will be slow and difficult. Accordingly, the chapters have been updated with new data, where available, that attempt to anticipate some of the implications of these developments for our profession and our clients.

In addition, this third edition contains a completely new chapter on the theory and approaches to social work practice (Chapter 4), and one of the original chapters has been expanded into two chapters, one on social work with individuals and families (Chapter 6) and one on social work with groups and communities (Chapter 7).

Also included are new case studies of social work practice, many of which were contributed by workers in agencies across the country. Each chapter also includes new critical thinking questions in the Exploring Social Work section of the end–of–chapter material.

Acknowledgements

This book began in discussions with Allan Moscovitch at Carleton University and would not have been possible without Keith Thompson's commitment to the work. The primary intention was to give a voice to people who are directly involved in the field. Special thanks to: Gordon Bruyere for his contribution on the history of Aboriginal peoples; Shirley Judge and Judy E. MacDonald for their contributions on social work with women; Bernice Moreau for advice on the history of Black Canadians; and Emily Cronin, Kate Murray, Andrea Johnson, and Andria Samis, graduate students whose hard work made the instructor's manual a possibility.

More and more, this book is becoming a collaborative effort. Special thanks to Purnima Sundar for her assistance with the new theory chapter and to Sarah Todd and Martha Wiebe, authors of the chapter on group and community practice. And, as with the last edition, I must thank Sarah again for writing and updating Chapters 10 and 14, and Roy Hanes for Chapter 15. A special thanks also to Denise Freedman for valuable assistance with material in Chapter 14 dealing social work and sexual and gender diversity.

We are grateful to those reviewers who offered thoughtful suggestions for improvement. Thanks to Jeanine Webber, Anne Martens, and David Boudreau, who reviewed earlier editions of the book, and Ken Barter, Mary Harber, Robert Harding, Nicole Ives, Michael Kennedy, Sandra Preston, Mary Ann Smith, Iris Sokoloff, and Linda Turner, who reviewed this edition. And, of course, we are particularly grateful for the many instructors and students who have used the book in their courses, thereby encouraging us to pursue this new edition. Further suggestions for improvement are always welcome and will be incorporated in future editions.

Special Thanks

Once again, I must express my deep-felt thanks to my family—Vaida, my partner, Justin, my son, and Kristina, my daughter—not only for bearing with me but also for encouraging my work through their support and lively dinner conversations.

THE CANADIAN WELFARE STATE TODAY

Introduction

One hundred years ago private charity was the main recourse for persons in distress (and even then for only a small part of the population). Today, however, public (government-run or government-funded) social programs and services are widespread and affect nearly every Canadian at some point in his or her life. Nevertheless, while the social services are commonplace, Canadians are not very aware of the history of social work in this country or the role it plays in our daily lives.

This book is an effort to redress that imbalance. We hope that you, with the aid of this textbook, will become familiar with the key concepts and issues in social work practice in Canada.

Social Work and the New Economy

With this new edition, we have tried to be attentive to recent developments in the Canadian and world economy. Because of the severity of the economic downturn, and the sheer size of government deficits needed to stabilize the economy, the working environment for social workers will likely become more uncertain over the next period. Exactly by how much things will change, and how quickly, is still hard to say. Social workers need to enter this new period with eyes wide open and with more resolve to serve their clients.

Already there are many more people needing assistance, as wages are being cut, pension security is threatened, large-scale unemployment has raised its ugly head, and social safety nets are eroding at the time when people are losing jobs and need increased support. For those presently using social services, it may be more difficult to turn things around, and there likely will be still fewer services to help them get back on their feet.

A Good Time To Enter the Profession

To be sure, the employment outlook for social workers looks good over the coming period—but, unfortunately, that is not necessarily good news. The caseloads and the cutbacks are likely to be much greater as well, not to mention the personal hardships many people will face.

Nevertheless, while the context is changing, the "content" of social work will not change. It is important to keep that underlying objective in mind—namely, helping people help themselves. Making a difference is what social work is all about, and over the next period there will be ample opportunities to do just that. The overriding goal is creating opportunities for people to discover their power to bring about personal, interpersonal, and political change.

The following points attempt to capture the spirit of social work activism as we go forward in this more uncertain period:

- Keep the ultimate goal in mind—helping people help themselves
- Acknowledge the reality that you are working in, and act accordingly and appropriately, but don't entirely give in to it
- Recognize that you will often be working in a "bureaucracy" but that it is still possible to move things on and bring about change
- Rely on the strength and resilience of individuals, both those you are serving and those experienced professionals you work with
- Do not get discouraged, despite the frustrations, or at least don't stay discouraged for long
- Keep your sense of humour (if you want to be effective)
- Be patient, genuine, and open-hearted
- Remember, your profession is the noblest of all.

A pensioner takes part in a rally on Parliament Hill in October 2009, held to draw attention to the effect of former technology giant Nortel's bankruptcy on pensioners, and terminated and disabled employees.

What Is Social Welfare?

Social Services

Personal or community services provided to help individuals and families improve their social well-being.

Income Security

Financial or material assistance provided to increase the income or other resources of individuals and families.

While this book focuses on social work and the provision of social services, it is important to understand that social services are part of a range of activities that fall more generally under the term **social welfare**. Social welfare includes not only the **social services** proper (that provide personal or community services to help people improve their well-being)—including child care, child protection services, women's shelters, counselling and so forth—but also a range of **income security** provisions—Employment Insurance, Social Assistance, Old Age Security, Workers' Compensation—that provide monetary or other material benefits to supplement income or maintain minimum income levels. Taken together, social services and income security comprise what is known, loosely, as social welfare.

The distinction between social services and income security is an important one, but in real life it is difficult to maintain. This is often a source of confusion for beginning social workers because, frequently, difficulties come in pairs or in even more complex combinations. For example, a man who becomes ill or has an accident may also lose his job and, as a result, his home. A woman who is subjected to violence may be forced to leave her home and may need help obtaining child support as well as personal income support. A man with an addiction may lose his employment and be at risk of becoming homeless, or of ending up in the prison system or mental health system. Thus, social services are often needed to deal with problems that have their roots in economic insecurity and vice versa.

This book deals primarily with the social services and the practice of social work; it does not cover in any depth the complex income security programs in Canada that provide monetary assistance to individuals and families. However, because a basic understanding of the income security system is necessary for effective social work practice, the second chapter in this book provides a quick overview of this vast field. A companion volume, *Social Welfare in Canada: Understanding Income Security*, more fully examines the income security field.

The Welfare State

The range of programs and services available to Canadian citizens is commonly referred to as the **welfare state.** The welfare state is a system whereby the state undertakes to protect the health and well-being of its citizens, especially those in social and financial need. The key elements of the welfare state are the use of state power (government, bureaucracy, the judiciary, political parties) to provide essential social services to citizens, and the use of grants, taxes, pensions, and minimum-income programs, such as Social Assistance and social insurance, to provide basic income security (income redistribution).

The basic goal of the Canadian social welfare system, as it is presently constituted, is simple: to help people through difficult times until they can rebuild their lives. The kinds of difficulties that may arise for individuals and their families are varied. Retirement, unemployment, decreasing income, and rising prices are examples of contingencies that affect *economic survival*. Disability, illness, violence, homelessness, addiction, racism, warfare, and death are examples of contingencies that affect *the integrity of the person*. Separation, divorce, the aging of family members, and additional children are events that threaten the *survival of the family*.

Yet, the role of the state in such situations is still quite controversial. Some people reject the idea that the state has any role to play, even in relation to helping the most vulnerable citizens. Others want to see the state take a larger role in redressing social imbalances and improving the lives of all of its citizens.

These debates over the proper role of social welfare are far-reaching and can be heated at times. In sorting through all this for oneself, as a newcomer to the field, a cool head is a useful asset.

Social Policies and Social Programs

As mentioned, social services are very extensive throughout Canada. They are provided to citizens through social policies developed by various levels of government and they are delivered by means of specific social programs.

- **Social policies** are the overall rules and regulations, laws, and other administrative directives that set the framework for state social welfare activity. For example, universal medicare is a social policy to which the Government of Canada is committed.

- **Social programs** are specific initiatives that follow on from and implement social welfare policies. Continuing with the medicare example, there are special incentives or programs to encourage newly accredited physicians to move to outlying areas, thus ensuring greater equality of access to medical services (in line with the commitment to universal medicare for Canadians).

The network of laws, policies, and programs currently in place around the country is vast. It is through such devices that the Canadian state creates opportunities for individuals experiencing difficulties in their lives and helps them get back on their feet.

This **social safety net** gives Canadians a greater sense of security and, many would say, a greater sense of belonging. In countries where the social safety net is weak or non-existent, there is little or no protection of this kind and individuals are often left to fend for themselves.

Industrial Welfare

Another important source of funding for income security and social services in Canada is industrial welfare, which is not discussed in this text.

Industrial welfare is available through employment and provides everything from dental and optical plans to legal aid services and pension plans. Only people employed by companies offering these services can access these benefits.

In the context of the recent economic downturn, company benefit plans are likely to be one of the first items to be cut.

Social Policies

The rules and regulations, laws, and other administrative directives that set the framework for social welfare activity.

Social Programs

Specific initiatives that implement social welfare policy.

The Provision of Social Welfare

There are several types of welfare services available to Canadians. An important distinction is between public and private welfare programs.

Public Welfare

Public Welfare

Services provided by all three levels of government.

Because Canada is a federal state, **public welfare** occurs at the three levels of government: the federal or national government, the provincial and territorial governments, and the regional and municipal governments.

As well, there are public non-government agencies, such as advisory and appeal boards, which are the creations of government (whether federal, provincial, or municipal) but which consist of members who are appointed from the public by government. The government is ultimately responsible for their activities, but they are either completely independent or semi-independent.

Private Welfare

Private Welfare

Services provided by non-profit and for-profit organizations.

There is also **private welfare.** Here we should distinguish between two types of organizations: private non-profit and private for-profit.

- *Non-profit organizations* are mandated to provide a service or an activity but not to create a profit. In Canada, such organizations are often registered by law, and rules and regulations govern what steps must be taken if a profit is generated. Many of these agencies are incorporated as non-profit corporations; they often receive funds from one or more levels of government and from private sources. At the same time, they can earn money by providing services for other organizations. Governments are moving more and more toward this model to save money. By moving services into non-unionized smaller agencies labour costs are lowered. Liability, should something go wrong, is also limited.

- *For-profit organizations*, on the other hand, are prevalent in certain income security (eg., pensions, insurance) and social service areas (nursing homes, psychotherapy, home care, and child care). These organizations provide services on a fee basis and may often be purchased by the government on behalf of individuals, but their purpose is to generate a profit for the owner of the organization. With government cutbacks in recent years, more and more services are being provided by for-profit or commercial agencies.

These three types of service providers coexist as the backbone of the welfare system in Canada today, sometimes in an uneasy alliance. Advocates of private, for-profit welfare maintain that a for-profit system allows more choice (e.g., private pension and insurance plans). Opponents point out that the private system favours those most able to afford it, fosters social inequality, and undermines the public system.

Debating Social Welfare

The idea of providing income security to citizens in need is no longer a controversial one in Canada. However, major disputes do arise in determining which groups are in need and to what extent they need state assistance. In Canada, successive governments have moved back and forth between two key approaches to social welfare: the *residual view* and the *institutional view.*

- In the **residual view**, social welfare is a limited, temporary response to human need, implemented only when all else fails. It is based on the premise that there are two natural ways through which an individual's needs are met: the family and the market economy. The residual model is based on the idea that government should play a limited role in the distribution of social welfare. The state should only step in when these normal sources of support fail and individuals are unable to help themselves. Residual social welfare is highly targeted to those most in need. Additionally, residual social welfare tends to provide benefits at a low level in order to discourage use and make social welfare appear undesirable. Canadian public social welfare programs, from early history to the Depression of the 1930s, can be characterized as residual in nature. In the past two decades, we have moved back toward this approach to social welfare.

- In the **institutional view**, social welfare is a necessary public response that helps people attain a reasonable standard of life and health. Within this view, it is accepted that people cannot always meet all of their needs through family and work. Therefore, in a complex industrial society, it is legitimate to help people by means of a publicly funded system of programs and institutions. The institutional model attempts to even out, rather than promote, economic stratification or status differences. The period after World War II saw the beginning of the rise of the institutional view.

A third and relatively new approach, the **structural approach,** considers the underlying problems of society to be linked to private concentrations of wealth and power. The welfare state, in the structural view, is one of the "necessary" contradictions of capitalism. While social welfare provides benefits for people in need, it does not directly address the exploitative nature of capitalism. This approach sees social problems and inequalities as a constituent (or built-in) feature of society. The call is for society itself to change. The structural approach has never underlined Canada's social policy, but it is increasingly vocalized by a variety of groups and organizations.

There are additional and more complex ways to distinguish between approaches to social welfare (see Chapter 4). These varied approaches to social welfare capture the political controversy and economic debate surrounding social welfare today. Each conveys a different sense of what social welfare is and how extensive it should be.

Approaching Social Welfare

- **The residual view:** social welfare should be a limited response when all else fails

- **The institutional view:** social welfare should seek to provide reasonable standards of living for all citizens

- **The structural approach:** social welfare should help people in need, and expose and seek to change the underlying inequalities in society that cause these problems

What Do Social Workers Do?

People are often confronted with unforeseen events, such as accidents, illness, incidents of violence, and death. People are also faced with economic contingencies, such as unemployment, retirement, and homelessness. A whole range of welfare services are available to Canadians to help them deal with such circumstances, and it is within this complex web of social welfare institutions (income security programs and social services) that most social workers work or practice.

Those who choose social work as their profession do so for a variety of reasons. In general, they appear to be motivated by a combination of humanitarian and egalitarian values, and by a desire to understand how society works and how to make it better for everyone. Frequently, a person is motivated to become a social worker following exposure to injustice and oppression. Whatever the combination of factors that leads a person into the profession, social work demands more than just the desire to "do good." Social work requires that the practitioner possess the necessary analytical and hands-on skills, as well as the maturity and personal stability, that can allow him or her to bring about effective change.

Social work professionals engage in a wide variety of work with people of different genders, cultures, religions, and economic backgrounds. With the goal of improving the lives of their clients, they may work directly with individuals and families to deal with specific problems, or with groups and communities to bring about social change.

In 2005 the **Canadian Association of Social Workers (CASW)** formulated a new *Code of Ethics* and added a separate document entitled *Guidelines for Ethical Practice,* replacing the 1994 code. The Code's preamble defines social work practice as follows.

> The social work profession is dedicated to the welfare and self-realization of all people; the development and disciplined use of scientific and professional knowledge; the development of resources and skills to meet individual, group, national and international changing needs and aspirations; and the achievement of social justice for all. The profession has a particular interest in the needs and empowerment of people who are vulnerable, oppressed, and/or living in poverty. Social workers are committed to human rights as enshrined in Canadian law, as well as in international conventions on human rights created or supported by the United Nations.

Direct and Indirect Social Work

Often we distinguish between two types of social work. **Direct social work** involves providing services (such as individual counselling, group work, and community development). Most often, social workers who are doing direct social work will be working for public or publicly funded social service agencies and institutions, such as hospitals or child welfare agencies. Some social workers also work on their own or in groups in a private practice. **Indirect social work** also benefits those in need, but is concerned with governments and non-governmental agencies—formulating, analyzing, developing, and evaluating social policies and programs. Indirect practice can also involve social service agencies, advocacy or research groups, and organizations whose purpose is to advocate for people in need and to conduct research. Examples of such organizations are the Canadian Centre for Policy Alternatives, the Canadian Council on Social Development, the Caledon Institute of Social Policy, and the National Anti-Poverty Organization (NAPO).

The different kinds of practice can also be described as being either micro, mezzo, or macro social work. *Micro social work* refers to direct practice with individuals. *Mezzo social work* is social work with groups and communities. Finally, *macro social work* involves working with organizations or communities to improve or change laws or policies in general society. Whether involved directly with citizens or indirectly in research, social workers are above all committed to serving people in need. They are there when circumstances go wrong and people need help.

The traditional notion of the social worker has been that of a **caseworker**—a practitioner doing one-on-one counselling with individuals, usually working as part of a social service agency. However, the idea of social work has now broadened somewhat. Today, social work involves not only attending to individual problems but also changing the social environment and empowering people to improve their situations.

Canadian Association of Social Workers

www.casw-acts.ca

CASW is a federation of provincial and territorial social work organizations that works to advance the social work profession in Canada.

Three Types of Practice

- **Micro:** direct practice with individuals
- **Mezzo:** working with groups and communities
- **Macro:** working with organizations or communities to improve or change laws or policies

Approaches to Practice

Approaches to Social Work Practice

• Locating the problem at the level of the individual

• Locating the problem at the level of social structures

To be effective, the social work practitioner must be able to approach his or her practice from all angles and adapt his or her responses to the specific needs of those they are working with.

In this book, the criterion used for distinguishing the different approaches to social work practice is where, primarily, one locates the cause of the particular problem at hand.

At one end of the continuum are approaches to social work practice that emphasize the personal (or internal) factors. At the other are theories and approaches that view structural (or external) factors as being dominant. Of course, few problems are organized by either internal or external factors alone.

■ **Locating the problems in the individual.** There are a wide variety of approaches within this category. Some locate the problem in the body (the traditional medical model), while others locate the problem in the mind (psychoanalytic approaches such as Gestalt therapy, cognitive-based theories, and behaviour-based theories). These approaches say very little about how to address issues outside of the individual concerned. On the other hand, other theories within this school of thought—such as developmental-based theories, task-centred and problem-solving approaches, and generalist approaches—do take into account the environmental demands and the changes in social systems involved in the problem. In these approaches, the purpose is to enhance the coping and problem-solving abilities of the client, link such people to resources, promote access to services, and contribute to better social policy.

■ **Locating the problems in social structures.** Approaches within this category give emphasis to the wider social factors influencing a particular problem. These factors may include, for example, social class, poverty, racial discrimination, and patriarchal relations. Approaches within this category include structural or critical social work practice, an anti-oppressive approach, radical casework, and feminist, anti-racist, and Aboriginal social work. These approaches vary according to their particular emphasis and clientele, but they are all based on the belief that structural factors have major significance for many types of social work problems.

In the end, to be most effective, the social work practitioner must be prepared to examine their practice from all angles and adopt an approach that works best for their client in the specific situation he or she is dealing with. By remaining flexible, the social work practitioner will be able to help clients overcome the particular difficulties they are facing, whether individual or structural, and help them get their lives back on course.

An overview of the various theories that inform social work practice can be found in Chapter 4.

Defining Social Work

A definition of social work was adopted at the General Meeting of the International Federation of Social Workers (IFSW) in Montreal in July 2000:

> The social work profession promotes social change, problem solving in human relationships and the empowerment and liberation of people to enhance well-being. Utilizing theories of human behaviour and social systems, social work intervenes at the points where people interact with their environments. Principles of human rights and social justice are fundamental to social work.

This definition is important as it represents a broad-based, international consensus as to what social work is all about. It emphasizes four key concepts: (1) social change/social justice, (2) problem solving, (3) person-in-the-environment, and (4) empowerment.

Social Change/Social Justice Mandate

A **social change/social justice mandate** means working in solidarity with those who are disadvantaged or excluded from society so as to eliminate the barriers, inequities, and injustices that exist.

This means that social workers should be at the forefront of promoting policies and legislation that redistribute wealth in favour of those who are less well-off—that is, promoting equal opportunity for women, gays, lesbians, bisexuals, transgendered persons, people with disabilities, Aboriginal peoples and racial and other minorities, and defending past gains made in these areas.

Commitment to social change and social justice is fundamental to social work practice. Reducing inequality of opportunity and seeking ways to redress social imbalances will reduce the need for welfare services.

Four Key Ideas in Social Work

- Social change/social justice mandate
- Problem solving
- Person-in-the-environment
- Empowerment

Problem Solving

Social workers respond to crises and emergencies as well as everyday personal and social problems. They use a **problem-solving process** to identify the problem and formulate possible plans of action. A problem is not usually clearly defined when someone comes to a social service agency. It is therefore crucial for the social worker to explore the person's concerns, to identify the need(s) involved, to identify barriers to meeting need(s), and to carefully determine the goals and possible plans of action.

A key characteristic of the problem-solving process is the inclusion of the client at each stage. The process should also teach clients problem-solving skills so that they can better deal with future problems on their own.

Person-in-the-Environment

A key aspect of effective social work practice is to go beyond the "internal" (psychological) factors and examine the relationship between individuals and their environments. This **person-in-the-environment** approach largely distinguishes social work practice from other helping professions. These "environments" extend beyond the immediate family to include interactions with friends, neighbourhoods, schools, religious groups, laws and legislation, other agencies or organizations, places of employment, and the economic system. Based on this understanding, intervention may focus on the individual, interactions between people and any system or structure, or on the system or structure itself.

Empowerment

In order for the interventions of social workers to be successful, clients must believe that the efforts of the practitioner, as well as their own efforts, will make a difference. This leads to the concept of empowerment. Being empowered means feeling that you have power and control over the course of your life.

Empowerment is the process of increasing personal, interpersonal, or political power so that one can improve one's particular situation. Power can be a personal state of mind, in the sense that one feels one can make a difference and have control and influence over one's own life. It can also be empowerment within an organization in the sense that one has tangible influence and legal rights. Empowerment, then, involves both a personal perception of being in control and tangible elements of power within the various social structures of society. Social workers seek to empower their clients as a way of helping them to focus on, among other things, access to resources and the structures of power.

Empowerment-based social work, therefore, has three aspects:

- making power explicit in the client-worker relationship (to help equalize the relationship between client and worker);
- giving clients experiences in which they themselves are in control (to allow them to see the potential for controlling their lives); and
- always supporting the client's own efforts to understand the power relationships in their own lives as well as their efforts to gain greater control over their lives as a way of promoting change.

Putting an empowerment perspective into practice involves techniques that make power relations between the workers and their clients explicit, thereby equalizing the client–worker relationship. It may entail giving clients—whether they be individuals, families, groups, or entire communities—experiences that put them in a position to exercise power. Voluntary work experiences that allow clients to use their skills to help others can be empowering. Another aspect may be to support clients' efforts to change policies or practices that impinge on their lives and the lives of others.

Community Access Centres

A **community access centre** is a place to get program information and services, fill out applications, and ask questions.

In such centres, individuals can access more than one service, which is then delivered by a service delivery team following a carefully worked-out service plan.

In other instances, an empowering perspective may involve simply focusing on the strengths of the person, rather than on the "pathology" side (or with what is "wrong" with that person). In all relationships, it is generally acknowledged that constructive feedback and positive reinforcement are conducive to helping people make positive changes in their lives. Clearly, it is more helpful for social workers to guide their clients' focus towards the success they have achieved in the past rather than dwelling on points where they have been less successful.

An empowerment perspective is the key to good social work practice. And like other aspects of good practice, it involves not a specific set of skills, but a general orientation on the part of the worker. This orientation is based on helping clients identify their own needs and then helping them to deal with the exigencies of their own particular situation.

Of all the fundamental techniques available to the social work practitioner, the ability to empower the client is perhaps the most critical and the most useful. The key to getting a person, family, or community back on track with their lives is to have them gain some sense of control over the difficult situation at hand and a sense that their actions will lead to positive results. Having the ability to foster a sense of client empowerment in sometimes difficult situations is an important part of the social worker's skill set.

Community empowerment is evident in this demonstration; Sister Elizabeth Kelliher, a member of the Downtown Eastside Association, joins in the protest against the lack of social housing in Vancouver, British Columbia.

Conclusion

The complex field known as social welfare includes two major components: income security (or programs that provide financial or material assistance) and social services (which provide personal and community services to help people improve their well-being).

Social services are provided by a large number of public and private agencies and employ social workers in both direct and indirect practice. Key to comprehending the nature of social work practice are four concepts: social change, problem solving, person-in-the-environment, and empowerment. Using these basic concepts, professional social workers carry out their work at the individual, group, community, and societal levels.

Politicians, and even the general public, do not agree on the extent to which the state should provide income security or social services to people in need. Yet it is within this uncertainty that social work practitioners face real people with real problems, and increasingly with fewer and fewer resources to do so. More and more, social workers are using empowerment to develop the personal, interpersonal, and political power of the people they are helping so that these individuals can gain greater control over their lives.

CHAPTER REVIEW

Key Terms

- Social welfare
- Social services
- Income security
- Welfare state
- Social policies
- Social programs
- Social safety net
- Public welfare
- Private welfare
- Residual view

- Institutional view
- Structural approach
- Direct social work
- Indirect social work
- Caseworker
- Social change mandate
- Problem-solving process
- Person-in-the-environment
- Empowerment

Review Questions

1. What are the main components of the social welfare system in Canada?

2. Define and compare the following terms: (1) social policy and social program, and (2) public welfare and private welfare.

3. Define the different types or levels of social work practice. What is meant by the residual, institutional, and structural approaches?

4. List and describe the four key concepts contained in the International Federation's definition of social work practice.

5. Define empowerment and outline what a social worker can do to put an empowerment perspective into practice.

Exploring Social Work

1. This chapter describes different views of the role of social welfare in our society (residual, institutional, structural). Which "position" do you feel least comfortable with? Discuss your ideas with another student and write up a statement explaining why this approach is inadequate.

2. In 2005 the CASW formulated a new *Code of Ethics* and *Guidelines for Ethical Practice*. Find these documents on the CASW website and see if you can locate a philosophical vision. The 1994 code contained the philosophical statement that social work is founded on humanitarian and equalitarian ideals. Does the new code provide a vision of a society for social work to pursue?

3. Given your knowledge of the *residual, institutional,* and *structural* approaches to welfare, what approach to social welfare best typifies the approach taken within the 2005 *Code of Ethics* and *Guidelines for Ethical Practice*? Support your argument.

4. Empowerment is often mentioned within the context of social work practice. Write a two-page paper on the concept of empowerment and what it means to you and how it may apply in the context of your social work practice with individuals and families.

Websites

Social Work Glossary
www.socialpolicy.ca

This site contains over 600 definitions of social welfare terms. It also includes links to publications and course materials.

Canadian Council on Social Development (CCSD)
www.ccsd.ca

CCSD is one of Canada's most authoritative voices promoting better social and economic security for all Canadians. A national, self-supporting, non-profit organization, the CCSD's main product is information and its main activity is research focusing on concerns such as income security, employment, poverty, child welfare, pensions, and government social policies.

Canadian Social Research Links
www.canadiansocialresearch.net

This is a virtual resource centre for Canadian social program information. The purpose of this site is to provide a comprehensive, current, and balanced collection of links to Canadian social program information for those who formulate Canadian social policies and for those who study and critique them.

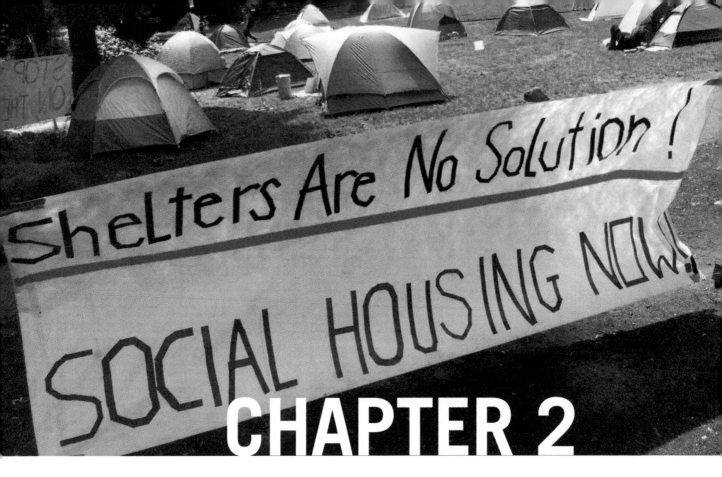

CHAPTER 2

INCOME SECURITY AND SOCIAL WELFARE

Weighing the Benefits

Income security programs are at the core of the welfare state in Canada; however, two myths need to be dispelled. The first is that these programs are used only by the poor. The truth is that every Canadian over the course of his or her life is a beneficiary of Canada's income security infrastructure, whether in the form of a retirement pension, Employment Insurance, Death Benefits, Social Assistance, or Family Benefits. Nor is it true that income programs are in place only to keep the poor from total destitution, another common misunderstanding. They do this, but they also provide the government with key levers over the economy.

Since the post–World War II period, social welfare spending has played a vital role in the macro management of the Canadian economy and labour force. In short, the role of social security is not as simple as it might at first seem.

The Emergence of Income Security

The income security side of the welfare system has income redistribution or income supplementation as its primary aim. Unlike the social services, which involve non-monetary support (child welfare, probation services, women's shelters, etc.), income security programs provide monetary or financial assistance to individuals and families. Without income security programs in place, most Canadians would be even more highly insecure than they already are.

The immediate relief of poverty and of severe destitution sparked the earliest government involvement in social welfare. However, early social welfare was of a "residual" nature in the sense that it was meant to serve those in need only when all else had failed. Following World War I and the Great Depression of the 1930s, a new consensus developed. Canadians began to recognize that hard times could strike anyone through no personal fault. This new consensus led to the development of a comprehensive set of income security programs

The level of commitment to social welfare is based, fundamentally, on what our society values most highly and what citizens believe the role of government is in their lives. Should the risk of unemployment be shared or should those who fall on bad times be left to fend for themselves? Should we be concerned about the social and personal welfare of others, or not? These kinds of questions underlie the income security programs we have in place today.

Four Types of Income Security

Income security programs provide monetary support to individuals or families. They are often called "transfers" because they transfer cash and other benefits from government-funded or government-administered programs to individuals or families. Public income security programs fall into the following four broad categories:

Public Income Security
- Social insurance
- Minimum income
- Demogrants
- Income supplementation

- **Social insurance.** These are programs that follow the insurance principle of shared risk. People contribute to insurance plans with the understanding that not everyone will need to access the benefits. Insurance-based programs are generally linked to employment. All workers contribute, and only those who contribute become eligible for benefits, should the need arise. Employment Insurance, Workers' Compensation, and the Canada/Quebec Pension Plan are social insurance programs.

- **Minimum income.** These are programs that provide monetary assistance to those with no other source of income. They are primarily geared towards those deemed to be living in poverty, and the quantity of assistance tends to be determined by the minimum amount necessary to meet basic needs. Social Assistance, also called welfare or workfare, is a minimum income program.

Seniors protest the government's de-indexing of Old Age Pensions on Parliament Hill in 1985.

- **Demogrants.** These are universal flat-rate payments made to individuals or households on the sole basis of demographic characteristics, such as number of children or age, rather than on the basis of proven need (as in minimum income programs) or contributions (as in social insurance programs). The Old Age Security (OAS) paid to all persons aged 65 and over was a universal program before a clawback was implemented. Now it is considered an income supplementation program. The former 1944 Family Allowance program, benefiting all families with children under the age of 18, was Canada's first widespread demogrant.

- **Income supplementation.** These are programs that, as the name suggests, supplement income that is obtained elsewhere, whether through paid employment or through other income security programs. They are not intended to be the primary source of income. These programs may have a broad entitlement, in that they may be available to everyone within a very broad category, or they may be targeted to those most in need. The National Child Benefit Supplement (NCBS) and the Guaranteed Income Supplement (GIS) are income supplementation programs.

Government participation in income security covers a broad range: cash benefits for people with disabilities and those recovering from occupational injuries and illness, the elderly, the unemployed, and surviving members of families in which the primary earner has died. However, the above list of direct government cash benefits does not reflect the entire spectrum of income security expenditure.

First, income security is provided through the tax system when governments provide tax breaks, forego the collection of taxes, or when income or benefits are taxed differently. While this is not often thought of as income security, it can dramatically affect the income of Canadians. By not collecting taxes from those who have a taxable income, an individual's income is effectively increased. A personal tax exemption for a single parent with income high enough to be taxed provides income for the parent and a foregoing of tax revenue (a tax expenditure) for the state. When the government provides a tax deduction for Registered Retirement Saving Plans (RRSP), it foregoes collecting taxes, which effectively allows a tax break to those with enough money to put some away towards retirement.

Second, income security can be provided by the private sector—both private employers and the voluntary sector. Some countries, such as Norway, the Netherlands, and Denmark, have substantial mandatory employer-paid income security programs. Canada does not. Conversely, Canada has comparatively high amounts—3.5 percent of gross domestic product (GDP)—of voluntary sector income security benefits, outstripping all other developed countries except the U.S. and the U.K. (Adema 1999, 15).

Employment-related policies and legislation can also affect the income of Canadians and therefore should be considered a part of our income security framework. These policies and legislation include labour standards and minimum wage legislation, as well as policies that affect the quantity and distribution of employment and employment equity programs. Employment equity and pay equity legislation attempts to address wage discrimination based on gender, ethnicity, and disability.

Public Income Security Programs

Canada's income security programs are in the newspaper headlines on a daily basis, and the effectiveness and affordability of such programs are frequent topics of discussion. The emphasis is often on the need to cut spending and to reduce the deficit, but the host of benefits that these programs bring to families, society, and the economy are rarely mentioned. Nevertheless, many Canadians rely on the following income security programs to bring some economic stability to their lives, without which they would not be able to participate fully in society.

- **Employment Insurance (EI).** This federally administered program, originally called Unemployment Insurance (UI), dates back to 1941. Since then, UI has undergone numerous changes, including its name change. EI provides a level of income replacement to workers who are temporarily unemployed and meet strict eligibility conditions. Sickness, maternity, and parental benefits are included in this program, as are benefits for some whose livelihood depends seasonal industries, such as fishing. Claimants are eligible for a range of skills development programs. EI is paid for through employer and employee contributions. Recently, the program has become more restricted, providing coverage for fewer and fewer workers. At the time of the last recession in the late 1980s, 84 percent of unemployed workers got benefits. By 2008, only 42 percent of the unemployed received EI benefits, replacing just 55 percent of their usual earnings (CCPA 2009).

- **Workers' Compensation.** Workers' Compensation programs provide provincially administered benefits and are designed to protect individuals against income loss due to workplace injury or disease. Employers fund the programs. In return for participation in the provincial programs, workers waive their rights to sue their employers in the case of a work-related injury or disease. The first Workers' Compensation program was instituted in Ontario in 1914. This was the first social insurance program in Canada.

- **Social Assistance or Welfare.** Social Assistance programs are rooted in early municipal and provincial relief programs designed to provide minimal support to the deserving poor or those unable to work because of age or infirmity. Gradually expanded to include

Public Income Security Programs

- Employment Insurance
- Workers' Compensation
- Social Assistance or Welfare
- Canada Child Tax Benefit/ National Child Benefit Supplement
- Canada/Quebec Pension Plan
- Disability
- Survivor and Death Benefits
- Old Age Security; Guaranteed Income Supplement; Spouse's Allowance
- Veterans Disability Pension
- Occupational Benefits

those in need but without resources, Social Assistance is a program of last resort for those with no other source of income or savings. Social Assistance, also called welfare or workfare, is a provincial responsibility with some funding coming from the federal government. The provinces are free to design their own programs and set the level of benefits. In some provinces, "employable" recipients must participate in work placements (known as "workfare").

■ **Canada Child Tax Benefit (CCTB)/National Child Benefit Supplement (NCBS).** There is a long history in Canada of providing benefits to families with children. Some of these have been and continue to be delivered in the form of tax credits and exemptions, and others have been direct cash transfers. In 1944, a universal benefit called the Family Allowance was instituted; this went to all families with children, regardless of income. Over time, this benefit became targeted towards low- and middle-income families. In 1993, it was eliminated completely. The Canada Child Tax Benefit (CCTB) includes two aspects: the basic CCTB and the National Child Benefit Supplement (NCBS). The CCTB provides a tax credit to those who qualify, based on an income test, as low- and middle-income families with children. Currently, up to 80 percent of families receive some portion of the CCTB. Some low-income families are eligible for the additional NCBS. Interestingly, provinces are allowed to claw back the benefit from families on Social Assistance. Most provinces take all or part of the benefit away from these families, except for Newfoundland and Labrador, Nova Scotia, Manitoba, and New Brunswick.

■ **Canada/Quebec Pension Plan (C/QPP).** The Canada/Quebec Pension Plan is a national contributory and earnings-related pension program introduced in 1966. It provides benefits in the case of retirement, death, and long-term disability. Employees and employers jointly finance the CPP and QPP, with current contributions supporting current beneficiaries. In this sense, the plan is a pay-as-you-go system. Any funds not paid out are invested for the purpose of creating a larger reserve fund. The plan consists of Retirement, Disability, and Survivor's and Orphan's Death Benefits. Eligibility for the retirement benefit begins at 60 years of age, with maximum benefits paid out after age 65. The pension is earnings-related, so there is a maximum amount for which claimants are eligible. Periods of low earnings, because of caring for young children, illness, unemployment, or retraining, are exempt from the calculation. This provision is particularly significant for women, who often take time out of the labour force to provide care. People with disabilities who qualify for C/QPP may also be eligible to receive benefits through provincial Social Assistance programs, Workers' Compensation, and, in some cases, through the Veterans Disability Pension.

- **Disability.** Severe and prolonged disability resulting in the inability to participate in the labour force qualifies one for a disability pension. This consists of both an earnings-related portion and a basic flat-rate portion, which is unrelated to the earnings one had while employed. Recipients may also qualify for supplemental child benefits if there are dependants. Tax credits and exemptions play an important income security role for people with disabilities.

- **Survivor and Death Benefits.** In the case of a contributor's death, surviving family members may be eligible for benefits. These benefits are intended to provide support to both the surviving spouse and dependent children.

- **Old Age Security (OAS); Guaranteed Income Supplement (GIS); Spouse's Allowance (SPA).** Between 1952 and 1989, all elderly Canadians received a universal monthly benefit called Old Age Security—an income security program financed and administered by the federal government. Prior to 1952, this benefit was targeted to the very low-income elderly population. Since 1989, the benefit has again become targeted, with only those who qualify because of low or modest income being eligible for benefits. OAS benefits are quite low in relation to the cost of living. Without another source of income upon retirement, such as C/QPP or Registered Retirement Savings Plans (RRSPs), many seniors would live in poverty. To further assist those who do not have access to these programs, there are two related programs: the Guaranteed Income Supplement (GIS) and the Spouse's Allowance (SPA). The SPA is now called the Allowance. These benefits supplement the OAS for the low-income elderly. Since 1966, the GIS has provided a politically popular add-on to the OAS for those pensioners with little or no other income.

- **Veterans Disability Pension.** A Veterans Disability Pension is available to those who apply to Veterans Affairs Canada, provided they have a service-related permanent disability resulting from an injury or disease. Income and assets are not considered as eligibility criteria; the benefit is based solely on the extent of the disability and the fact that it is military service-related. As is the case with disability benefits, what constitutes a disability and its extent are not always easily determined or agreed upon by all interested parties.

- **Occupational Benefits.** In addition to publicly administered benefits, private occupational benefit plans also exist. These plans may be directly tied to one's workplace and include both retirement plans and other insurance-based benefits such as dental and drug plans, or they may be savings plans with tax-supported provisions, such as Registered Retirement Savings Plans (RRSPs). While individuals save and invest this money for future use, the government foregoes the collection of tax on this saved money.

Selective and Universal Programs

Arguments for Universality

Universal program supporters argue that universal income security promotes a sense of citizenship, solidarity, and nationhood. They claim that selective programs for those in need tend to be punitive and stigmatizing, are more susceptible to cutbacks, and lack necessary mass public support. If services are only for the poor, then they are likely to be poor services.

Many also believe that universal income security programs can fulfill various economic functions, such as economic stabilization, investment in human resources, and development of the labour force.

Over the years, Canada has had a mix of selective and universal programs. Governments have moved away from a focus on citizenship rights and inclusion, to an anti-poverty strategy geared towards promoting attachment to the labour force.

When designing income security programs, a key distinction is made as to whether they are universal or selective.

- **Universal programs** are available to everyone in a specific category (such as people aged 65 and over and children), on the same terms and as a right of citizenship. The idea is that all persons are equally eligible to receive program benefits, regardless of income and financial situation.

- **Selective programs** target those who are found to be in need or eligible, based on a means (or income) test or a needs test. A means test determines eligibility based on the income of the prospective recipient. The benefit is reduced according to income level, and there is always a level at which no benefit is granted. A needs test determines eligibility based on the income and the need of the prospective recipient. Eligibility criteria are used to define need, which is then compared to the prospective recipient's life situation.

In the post–World War II era, universal programs were seen as a way to build national solidarity. More recently, they have been viewed as too expensive and have all but disappeared. The foremost objection to universal programs is their cost. Giving a benefit to everyone, regardless of income, means that even the wealthy get a benefit. On the other side of the issue, universal programs are less expensive to administer, as government workers are not required to scrutinize each person's situation. Selective programs are often viewed as more efficient and less costly, as the government provides benefits only to those most in need. However, identifying eligible recipients using means or needs tests can be administratively complex and costly and take money out of the system that could be directed towards benefits. In some cases, the higher administrative costs are being partially avoided by using the tax system as a method of determining eligibility and dispensing benefits. Increasingly, social policy experts are seeing that some selective programs are necessary for tackling poverty and inequality.

While some programs include aspects of universality, there are no income security programs remaining that can be exactly defined as universal. Health care and education are examples of universal service programs, but they are not income security programs. In the past, there were a number of universal income security programs available to Canadians. Family Allowance, which was available from 1944 to 1993, is the most commonly cited example. All families with a child under the age of 18 were entitled to a financial benefit. Because of the progressive tax system, wealthier people paid much of that back through taxation, but it was nevertheless an acknowledgement of citizenship entitlement and the importance and cost of raising children. In 1993, the Family Allowance was redesigned to become a targeted program, the National Child Benefit, now available to low- and middle-income families.

Selective Entitlements

All of Canada's other income security programs offer selective entitlements. Most have complex selection criteria based on income, work history, or the willingness to find a job. Employment Insurance is based on an insurance principle with eligibility tied to employment and income levels. Everyone within the broad category of "employee" pays into the program, and in this sense it is comprehensive, but a strict set of criteria determines who is eligible to receive benefits. The level of benefits depends on the earnings and contributions one has made. In recent years, eligibility for EI has become more restrictive. With more demands now being placed on the system, the debate over the amount and duration of EI payments is likely to continue to heat up.

Other programs are based on how much money one has and whether this meets one's needs. To be eligible for social assistance, one must prove that income and assets fall below a certain maximum. In provinces with workfare, such as Ontario and Alberta, applicants must also comply with an employment or training placement.

The National Child Benefit is another example of selective programming. If family income falls below a specified level, benefits are paid through the tax system.

Universal Income Security

Programs available to everyone in a particular category, such as seniors.

Selective Income Security

Programs limited to those people who are determined to be in need based on a means test or a needs test.

TABLE 2.1: Minimum Wages in Canada, 2009

	General adult minimum wage		Avg. hourly wage
	$/hour	Date	$/hour
British Columbia	$8.00	November 2001	$21.46
Alberta	$8.40	April 2008	$23.68
Saskatchewan	$8.60	May 2008	$20.34
Manitoba	$8.50	April 2008	$19.24
Ontario	$8.75	March 2008	$22.15
Quebec	$8.50	May 2008	$20.03
New Brunswick	$7.75	March 2008	$17.79
Nova Scotia	$8.10	May 2008	$18.12
Prince Edward Island	$8.00	October 2008	$16.96
Newfoundland & Labrador	$8.00	April 2008	$18.85
Canada	—	—	$21.32

Source: Statistics Canada. 2009. *Labour Force Information—April 12 to 18, 2009*. Catalogue no. 71-001-X. In *Women's Poverty and the Recession*. Canadian Centre for Policy Alternatives. www.policyalternatives.ca.

Poverty and Inequality

Poverty is usually brought on by an unexpected turn of events, such as loss of employment, death, illness or disability, or family breakup. Of course, changes in the economy can also affect family income—fewer hours of work, a decline in the real value of minimum wages, or wages so low that people cannot earn enough to live on. Furthermore, some groups in our society face a greater risk of poverty than others due to discrimination, unequal opportunities, lack of recognition for their work (paid or unpaid), and inadequate income support for those unable to work.

Measuring Poverty

Canada is one of only a few countries without an official poverty line. Since the late 1960s, however, Statistics Canada has produced **Low Income Cut-offs (LICOs)** for different household sizes in different regions. A family is considered to have a low income when it falls below

Low Income Cut-offs

Measure of the poverty rate in Canada; based on average household spending on necessities (plus 20 percent) and varies according to region and family size.

TABLE 2.2: Prevalence of Low Income Family Types in Canada

	2002	2003	2004	2005	2006	2007
	Percent %					
Economic Families (two or more persons)	8.6	8.5	8.0	7.4	7.0	5.8
Elderly Families	2.9 E	2.7 E	2.1 E	1.6 E	2.3 E	1.5 E
Non-Elderly Families	9.5	9.5	9.0	8.4	7.9	6.6
Married Couples	7.1	6.6	6.4	6.4	5.7	4.7
Two-Parent Families with Children	6.6	6.8	6.9	6.7	6.6	5.1
Lone-Parent Families	34.2	34.2	32.1	25.9	24.3	21.3
Unattached Individuals	29.5	29.7	30.1	30.4	29.2	27.4
Elderly Males	15.9	14.7	11.5	13.6	14.0	13.0
Elderly Females	20.7	18.9	16.9	20.3	16.1	14.3
Non-Elderly Males	29.0	30.7	32.0	32.3	31.2	29.7
Non-Elderly Females	39.0	38.1	39.3	37.1	37.1	35.1

Source: "Low Income After Tax (92 LICOs Base), by Selected Family Types, Canada–Prevalence," adapted from Statistics Canada publication *Income in Canada 2007*, Table 13-1. Catalogue 75-202-X (75-202-x2007000-eng.pdf). (E=use with caution.)

TABLE 2.3: Components of a Poverty Reduction Strategy for Canada

Component	Assessment	Recommendation
Good jobs at living wages: Raise living standards for working poor families Ensure full-time full year adult worker at minimum wage can rise above poverty line	**Needs improvement:** Needs federal leadership to reestablish federal minimum wage, ensure labour protection for precarious workers, reform EI, and invest in adult education and lifelong learning programs	Raise minimum wage to $10/hr with inflation index Strengthen Canada Labour Code to cover precarious workers Restore eligibility for EI Address multi-dimensional labour market barriers of excluded groups
Effective child income benefits: Provide income supports to recognize cost of raising a child	**Needs improvement:** No plan to raise Canada Child Tax Benefit beyond 2007 Universal Child Care Allowance is taxable; benefits upper income one-earner couples most	Commit to increase child benefits a maximum of $5,000/child with assurance all low and modest income families retain full payment
Universally accessible system of quality early learning and child care: Support optimal early development of children and enable parents to work or receive training	**Failure:** Cancellation of bilateral Child Care Agreements puts in jeopardy expansion of Canada's fledgling child care services Regulated child care meets the needs of only 15.5% of 0–12 yr olds	Create Pan-Canadian system of Early Learning and Child Care which is accessible, affordable, high quality $1.2 billion/year minimum expenditures to support existing child care agreements with provinces and territories with commitment to increase annually
Expand affordable housing: End adult and family homelessness; enable parents to raise their children in healthy community environments	**Needs improvement:** $1.4 billion of new housing funding allocated to provinces, territories, urban Aboriginal communities—but no comprehensive affordable housing strategy in place	Commit $2 billion/year for new social housing as part of affordable housing strategy Renew and enhance homelessness program (SCPI) and housing rehabilitation (RRAP) Fund new energy conservation program for low income households
Affordable and accessible post secondary education and training: Ensure access to post-secondary education for qualified students from low and modest income families	**Needs improvement:** Tuition fees rising in six provinces	Create separate funding transfer for post-secondary education Increase student financial aid with higher proportion for needs-based grants

Source: Campaign 2000. *Oh Canada! Too Many Children in Poverty for Too Long...: 2006 Report Card on Child and Family Poverty in Canada.* With permission from Campaign 2000, a cross-Canada network on ending child/family poverty. www.campaign2000.ca

the LICO for its family size and community population. LICOs are set by taking what the average household spends on food, clothing, and shelter and adding 20 percent. The process is carried out for seven family sizes and five community sizes. In addition, Statistics Canada produces cut-offs for before-tax and after-tax incomes.

Statistics Canada has another measure of poverty called the **Low Income Measure (LIM)**, which is widely used for international comparisons of child poverty. The LIM measures the relative low-income rates as one-half of the median income of the country. Because it is a straightforward calculation and can be collected in all nations, it allows for simple comparisons between countries.

In conjunction with a federal, provincial, and territorial working group, Human Resources Development Canada (HRDC)—now Human Resources and Social Development Canada, or HRSDC—proposed another measure of poverty called the **Market Basket Measure (MBM).** First published in 2003, the MBM is an absolute measure of poverty based on the cost of purchasing a basket of goods and services in forty-eight different geographical areas. HRDC intended the MBM to represent a level of consumption that was closer to median standards, and it goes beyond the bare minimum of other measures (HRDC 2003). The MBM calculates the amount of income needed by a given household to meet its needs based on "credible" community norms, so the measure will therefore reflect changes in the cost of consumption rather than changes in income. The only issue might be what to include and what not to include in the market basket. Although the MBM is a fairly reliable measure of real poverty, it seems to have fallen out favour with policymakers in recent years.

Child and Family Poverty

In 1989 the federal government declared its commitment to "seek to achieve the goal of eliminating poverty among Canadian children by the year 2000." In November 2007, Campaign 2000, an organization inspired by this commitment, released its annual Report Card on Child and Family Poverty (2006). According to the report, nearly one in six children lives below the Statistics Canada LICO. The report draws attention to the fact that the rate of child poverty today is the same as it was in 1989, the year of pledge to eliminate poverty among Canadian children.

With cutbacks in many income security programs, Canadians are relying on **food banks** and **feeding programs** to survive. In 2008, there were over 700 food banks in Canada. *HungerCount*, the annual national survey of food bank use in Canada, reported that in an average month over 704,000 Canadians used food banks. Food bank use among working people is increasing; 14.5 percent of users reported employment as their primary form of income. Over one-third (37 percent) of those being helped were children under the age of 18 (FBC 2008).

Low Income Measure

Measure of poverty used for international comparisons based on one-half of the median income of a country.

Market Basket Measure

Proposed poverty measure based on the cost of consumption rather than income.

Aboriginal Children in Poverty

According to Statistics Canada's *Aboriginal Children's Survey 2006*, almost one in two (49 percent) Aboriginal children under the age of six (living off-reserve) live in a low-income family.

TABLE 2.4: Before-Tax Low Income Cut-offs (LICOs) 2006

Family Size	Population of Community of Residence				
	500,000+	100,000–499,999	30,000–99,999	Less than 30,000*	Rural
1	$21,202	$18,260	$18,147	$16,605	$14,596
2	$26,396	$22,731	$22,591	$20,671	$18,170
3	$32,450	$27,945	$27,773	$25,412	$22,338
4	$39,399	$33,930	$33,721	$30,855	$27,122
5	$44,686	$38,482	$38,245	$34,995	$30,760
6	$50,397	$43,402	$43,135	$39,469	$34,694
7+	$56,110	$48,322	$48,024	$43,943	$38,626

Note: Table uses 1992 base.

*Includes cities with a population between 15,000 and 30,000, and small urban areas (under 15,000).

Source: Adapted from Statistics Canada publication Income Research Paper Series, Catalogue 75F0002MIE, no. 4, page 23, http://www.statcan.gc.ca/bsolc/olc-cel/olc-cel?lang=eng&catno=75F0002M.

Between August 2008 and August 2009, a period of significant recession, 227,000 full-time jobs were lost in Ontario. During that time, there was a 20 percent increase in the number of Ontarians using food banks each month. Food banks have struggled to meet this increased need, as individual and corporate donations have declined (OAFB 2009).

Feeding programs often operate out of shelters or church basements and provide two meals per day. Such programs are operated by volunteers and by those who use the service. Many are run in conjunction with emergency shelters and provide additional free services, such as laundry facilities, telephone access, newspapers, and clothing. At most times, social workers are available and may even work directly from within the feeding program. There is often difficulty in keeping pace with demand. Almost half (49 percent) of food banks report that they often run out of food. Many believe that the steady unravelling of the social safety net means that access to basic food is in jeopardy.

Prime Minister Stephen Harper sits with a group of children while campaigning at a daycare in Ottawa in October 2008.

Canadian Federalism and Social Welfare

Federalism is a system of government in which a number of smaller states (in Canada's case, provinces and territories) join to form a larger political entity while still retaining a measure of political power. When Canada was formed in 1867, social welfare was largely a private responsibility of the individual, family, and church. Not surprisingly, the *British North America Act* (1867) said little about jurisdiction over income security or social services. The terms, in fact, did not even exist at the time. Political wrangling, informal side-deals between the federal government and the provinces, and constitutional amendments therefore formed the basis for our social security system.

Through this process, income security emerged as an area of federal jurisdiction and the provinces largely prevailed in the delivery of social services. An important point to note, however, is that while the provinces were given this responsibility, the federal government retained its responsibilities for Aboriginal people, as defined by the *Indian Act*. "Indians and lands reserved for Indians" remained within the jurisdiction of the federal government. The provision of social welfare to Aboriginal people (defined as Status Indians by the *Indian Act*) is, therefore, different than for the rest of the population.

Reforms to the Social Welfare System

One of the most significant changes to Canada's social welfare system was the introduction of the **Canada Health and Social Transfer (CHST)** in 1996. Prior to CHST, federal government contributions to social assistance and social services were funded through the **Canada Assistance Plan (CAP)**, established in 1966. Federal government contributions to health care services and post-secondary education had been funded through Established Programs Financing (EPF) since 1977. CAP and EPF were replaced with the CHST. In its first two years, CHST paid the provinces $7 billion less than they would have received under CAP/EPF.

In 2004, the CHST was split into the **Canada Social Transfer (CST)** and the **Canada Health Transfer (CHT)**. Like the CHST, the CST and CHT are federal block transfers to provinces and territories with the CST in support of post-secondary education, social assistance, and social services, including early childhood development, early learning, and child care. The CHT is dedicated to funding health care. The portion of the existing CHST legislated cash amounts and tax transfers apportioned to the CST is 38 percent. Some social policy analysts maintain that this amount is too low and may relegate higher education and social services to a secondary priority. CST cash and tax transfers were $14.9 billion in 2004/05, of which $8.3 billion was cash transfers and $6.6 billion was tax transfers. The CHT transferred $25.1 billion in 2004/05 for health care, of which $14.3 billion was cash transfers and $10.9 billion was tax transfers.

CAP was a 50/50 cost-shared program—the federal government shared 50 percent of the cost of eligible Social Assistance and social services expenditure with the provinces. With CAP, federal transfers rose as provincial social welfare expenditures increased. CAP therefore provided a kind of economic stabilizing function; as federal transfers increased in economic recessions, it helped stimulate the economy through social spending. The CST and CHT, on the other hand, are fixed per-capita or per-person amounts (also called "block transfers") based on the population of the province. Hence, federal transfers are not connected to either the needs of the people or the state of the economy. Many believe that it is the economic stabilizing effect of social spending that has prevented a depression-style drop-off in the Canadian economy since the Great Depression of the 1930s (see Chapter 3). With the CST and CHT, this stabilizing effect is greatly reduced.

The national standards, as set out in CAP, are also largely gone under the CHST. CAP stipulated that the provinces should establish eligibility for Social Assistance based on need (as determined by a means test), make services available for all those eligible regardless of when they established residency in the province, establish an appeal procedure and require no community or other work (also known as "workfare") in return for social benefits. Under the CHST (and now the CHT + CST), the regulations associated with CAP were removed except for the ban on residency requirements, and funding regulations associated with medicare were retained. Many analysts fear that, with the removal of the national standards, provinces will establish very different benefit levels and eligibility criteria.

A subsequent welfare reform was the **Social Union Framework Agreement (SUFA)** of 1999 between the Government of Canada and the provinces and territories. According to the federal government, the objective of the SUFA is to reform and renew Canada's system of social services and to reassure Canadians that their pan-Canadian social programs are strong and secure. So far, several social welfare initiatives have been established under this framework, such as the NCB, the National Children's Agenda, and services for persons with disabilities.

The SUFA was largely a response to the disapproval on the part of provincial governments of the unilateral cancellation of CAP and its replacement with CHST in 1996. The provinces wanted to be notified of and participate in formulating any changes in federal-provincial arrangements. They wanted the federal government to agree that, if it initiated new social programs, even ones for which it paid the total costs, a province could opt out and take the cash instead with virtually no strings attached. In that case, the province would only be required to spend the money in the same general area as the national plan. The provinces also made it clear that they wanted more say about how the federal government acted when stepping into provincial jurisdictions.

Social Welfare Reforms

- Canada Assistance Plan (CAP)
- Canada Health and Social Transfer (CHST)
- Canada Social Transfer (CST)
- Canada Health Transfer (CHT)
- Social Union Framework Agreement (SUFA)

Ideology: Why People Differ on What to Do

Canadians differ in their perception and explanation of social issues or problems and on how they believe these issues or problems should be solved. Opposing views are also held of the role of government in solving or alleviating such problems. As discussed in Chapter 1 (page 7), the two main political approaches to social welfare, residual and institutional, as well as the structural approach, capture the controversy surrounding social welfare today. Indeed, the history of the welfare state is a perpetual controversy over what the boundaries or extent of the welfare state should be.

Underlying the various views of social welfare are broader ideas and values which, taken together, are usually referred to as **ideologies**. Political ideologies can be categorized along a spectrum, with communism on the far left and fascism on the extreme right. The more left-wing views of social democrats hold that social welfare is part of our collective responsibility to our fellow citizens and should be publicly provided within an institutional framework. The more right-wing approach of the neo-conservatives includes the belief that welfare should be an individual responsibility within a residual model and that private-sector provision should be encouraged. The views of liberals tend to focus on the middle ground of these two views, by responding to changing needs and changing situations.

Ideology

The term ideology refers to a broad set of ideas, values, beliefs, and attitudes held by a particular person or group that shapes that individual's or group's way of thinking and acting.

Protesters raise awareness about poverty issues as they participate in a demonstration outside city hall in Peterborough, Ontario.

Workfare

Some provincial welfare programs require applicants to work as a term of eligibility. This is commonly known as **workfare**, and it has drawn criticism. Refusal to participate in the program results in some sort of penalty. For example, workfare could require people to work at specific jobs in order to get a government cheque, or it could mean that people receive a smaller cheque if they refuse to accept work through a government program. It might also require applicants to retrain or pursue self-employment programs. Workfare placements could involve working in a community or social service agency. Applicants may also choose community work placements as a workfare option for the purposes of increasing skills, knowledge, and networks in the labour market.

Critics equate workfare as a return to the "work test" of the Elizabethan Poor Laws. Others cite research to show its failure in other countries—particularly the United States. It has also been criticized for being expensive to administer, and for taking away jobs from the paid labour force. Others feel that workfare unfairly places the blame on individuals for being unemployed, arguing that people want to work but that there are not enough good jobs available.

Social Welfare Economics

Some of these ideological debates have become part of public discourse. This is the case, for example, with the debates among professional economists over the causes of unemployment. In very broad terms, the **Keynesians** (named for John Maynard Keynes, see margin) believe that governments should emphasize policies that combat unemployment in order to maintain the income of consumers. **Monetarists**, on the other hand, believe that governments should keep inflation in check and not worry so much about unemployment. Those adhering to the more radical **political economy perspective** believe that private ownership creates two classes that are antagonistic, and unemployment results when unions are weakened and cannot protect the jobs of the working people.

Keynesians and monetarists have contrasting views on social spending in general. The monetarists believe that social spending stimulates inflation, undermines labour market flexibility and productivity, and distorts the work/leisure trade-off. Keynesians believe that economic efficiency and social equity are compatible; that social spending helps economic recovery, enhances productivity, and keeps the labour market flexible. The political economy perspective holds that the operation of economic markets is tied to private ownership and is essentially exploitative; that social spending is a right fought for by the working class. Canadian government policy has alternated between the Keynesian and monetarist views. The political economy perspective has never figured prominently in social policy, but it has certainly shaped its many critiques.

Fiscal Policy vs. Monetary Policy

John Maynard Keynes (1883–1946) was a British economist responsible for creating *Keynesian fiscal policy*. Influenced by the Great Depression, Keynes argued that to protect the economy, governments should spend money on social programs to avoid economic depression. When a government allocates money to retrain laid-off workers, it is considered fiscal policy.

Milton Friedman (1912–2006) was an American economist of the "Chicago School," which advocated for a *monetary policy*. *Monetarists* argue that governments should safeguard the economy by controlling the money supply. When a government raises or lowers interest rates with the goal of encouraging investment or controlling inflation rates, it is considered monetary policy.

Globalization and Social Welfare

Canada does not exist apart from the rest of the world. This is especially true as the era of "globalization" increasingly takes hold. Whether we like it or not, we live in a highly integrated world economy.

Economic globalization is the growing integration of international markets for goods, services, and finance. It includes the expansion of free trade and investment, the expansion of trade in goods and services between countries, the geographical expansion and increase in power of transnational corporations (TNCs) and the use of agreements between nations and international bodies, such as the World Trade Organization (WTO), to protect the rights of TNCs.

Globalization reflects, perhaps above all, the global expansion of large corporations. Of the roughly 40,000 corporations operating in 2000, 200 control a quarter of the world's economic activity. These top 200 have combined revenues ($7.1 trillion) larger than all the economies of the world minus the largest nine. In other words, these corporations are more powerful than most countries in the world (Rice & Prince 2000).

When these powerful companies fail, as we saw in the fall of 2008, the whole world is affected. When the subprime mortgage crisis erupted in 2007 in the United States, financial institutions and national banks around the world felt the effects. In 2008, several major corporations had to declare bankruptcy, sending the global economy into a tailspin and many countries into recession. This economic crisis clearly outlined the devastating reach of globalization. Realizing that national policies have little effect on corporations with operations in hundreds of countries, there were calls for greater regulation of business practices at the global level.

Less Power to the People

Globalization also means that national and local governments increasingly have less freedom to act on behalf of their citizens, especially on the big economic and social questions of the day. In view of this, in the future, income security provisions aimed at creating greater equality of income and opportunity among individuals will likely become intertwined with the issue of global human rights. Indeed, what might be called **global social welfare**, a concern with justice, social regulation, social provision, and redistribution between nations, is already a part of the activities of various supranational organizations or international governmental organizations, such as the United Nations.

The fight to gain and maintain global human rights in the face of economic globalization is, in many respects, today's epic struggle. Advocacy for equality within and between nations is an integral part of social welfare.

Economic Globalization

The growing integration and expansion of global markets for goods, services, and finances.

Global Social Welfare

A concern with justice, social regulation, social provision, and redistribution between nations.

The economic pressures of globalization will continue to have a direct effect on income security in this country. In many nations, especially poorer ones, economic restructuring and cutbacks to social programs have been imposed by international agencies, such as the World Bank and the International Monetary Fund, in the form of so-called "structural adjustments." The Canadian government is not immune to these pressures and adjusts its own income security programs to meet the new economic order and battle with other nations to be the most "investor friendly."

Unfortunately, the impact of globalization on Canada's income security programs at this point is being felt mainly by the most disadvantaged in our society, and they are also the ones who are least able to fight back. Cutbacks and strict eligibility criteria mean that many are often left without even the bare necessities. The rise in the number of people who are homeless, the growing number of food banks, and the persistence of child poverty are signs of this. But, it is not only the very poor who suffer. The middle class is increasingly finding that high-paying jobs are moving offshore to corporate tax havens or export processing zones. Income security increasingly affects them as well, insofar as welfare cutbacks will mean that ordinary working Canadians may not be able to depend on the traditional social protection offered by such programs as Employment Insurance and Old Age Security.

Activists in Ottawa protest against the G8 Summit meeting in Kananaskis, Alberta, in 2002.

Conclusion

Social welfare is about helping Canadians face difficulties in their lives—whether they be social or economic. It is a way of sharing the risk of events such as poverty, unemployment, disability, and old age among all citizens. Social welfare is also about regulating and stabilizing our economic and social system. A healthy, well-trained, and educated workforce is required for our economy to grow.

Canadians do not always agree on whether social welfare programs should be expanded and strengthened or whether they should be reduced. Politicians agree even less. What is clear is that in recent years the welfare state in Canada has been reformed in ways that weaken overall social equality and social justice. Moreover, the economic forces of globalization seem to be leading to a harmonization of our social welfare system with that of the United States, our largest trading partner, and this will mean a serious deterioration in our welfare system.

Emulating the United States is not the only path open to us. Other countries in Europe, notably Denmark and the Netherlands, have continued to support and even expand their social welfare commitments and continue to have good productivity and economic growth. What is certain is that the debate over the future of the welfare system in Canada will be at the forefront of public discourse in the coming years.

CHAPTER REVIEW

Key Terms

- Social insurance
- Minimum income
- Demogrants
- Income supplementation
- Universal programs
- Selective programs
- Low Income Cut-offs (LICOs)
- Low Income Measure (LIM)
- Market Basket Measure (MBM)
- Food banks
- Feeding programs
- Canada Health and Social Transfer (CHST)
- Canada Assistance Plan (CAP)
- Canada Social Transfer (CST)
- Canada Health Transfer (CHT)
- Social Union Framework Agreement (SUFA)
- Ideologies
- Workfare
- Keynesians
- Monetarists
- Political economy perspective
- Economic globalization
- Global social welfare

Review Questions

1. What are the four categories of income security programs?
2. What is the main difference between a social insurance program and a minimum income program?
3. List five income security programs and describe the level of government responsible for them and who is eligible.
4. Who benefits from income security programs?
5. What are the two primary differences between universal and selective programs? Does Canada currently have any universal programs?
6. How did the discontinuation of the Canada Assistance Plan (CAP) affect social welfare programs?
7. What is the Social Union Framework Agreement (SUFA) and how has it changed social policy in Canada?

Exploring Social Work

1. Why do you think that it might be important for social workers to have knowledge about income security policy and programs? Bring to mind a client that you have had or one that you have read about. As you examine this client's difficulty, explore how knowledge about income security might be useful in assisting this client. Discuss your ideas with another student and write a two-page brief.

2. For better or worse, we live in a period of globalization—in nearly every sense of the word. The global financial crisis that began toward the end of 2008 resulted in governments around the world initiating unprecedented stimulus spending to stave off a further deepening of the crisis. What do you think will be the implications of the deficit spending on social services and income security programs as time goes on? Discuss this with another student and write up a two-page brief.

3. Social workers often work with people that experience oppression in some form from their interaction with power structures in society. Break into small groups and explore what you think might be some of these oppressive structures. How would an understanding of these structures affect how you relate with individual clients? How might it impact assumptions, assessment, and methods of helping?

Websites

- - - - - -

Canadian Centre for Policy Alternatives
www.policyalternatives.ca

The CCPA is a non-profit research organization, funded primarily through organizational and individual membership. It was founded in 1980 to promote research on economic and social policy issues from a progressive point of view. Check out the "Behind the Numbers" section.

Caledon Institute of Social Policy
www.caledoninst.org

The Caledon Institute of Social Policy does rigorous, high-quality research and analysis; seeks to inform and influence public opinion and to foster public discussion on poverty and social policy; and develops and promotes concrete, practicable proposals for the reform of social programs at all levels of government.

Food Banks Canada
www.foodbankscanada.ca

Food banks began 26 years ago as a short-term solution to hunger. They are now a necessary supplement to Canada's frayed safety net. Food Banks Canada is a national charitable organization representing the food bank community across Canada. It represents a national network of food banks, including provincial associations and food distribution centres that serve 85 percent of people who use emergency food programs. Food Banks Canada conducts research, engages in public education and advocates for public policy change to address the causes of hunger in Canada. Food Banks Canada conducts *HungerCount*, Canada's only annual survey of emergency food banks and food programs.

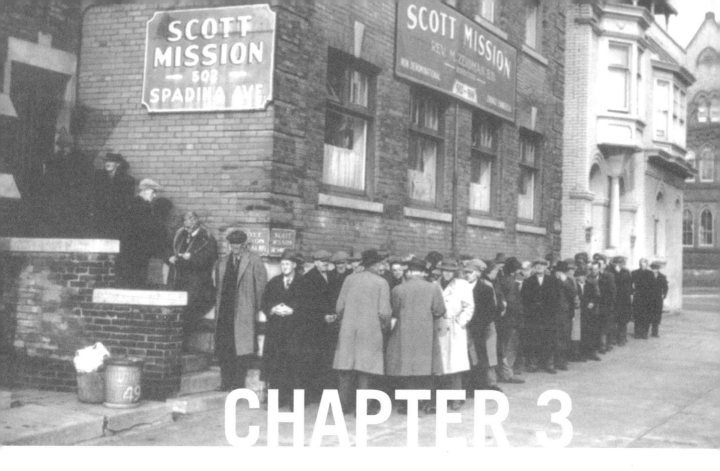

THE HISTORY OF SOCIAL WORK

The Development of a Profession

The systematic giving of charity to the poor coincides, more or less, with the upheaval of the Industrial Revolution and, in particular, with the consolidation of the wage-labour system. The immediate antecedents of Anglo-Canadian social work can be found in such socio-economic changes in Britain and the United States in the eighteenth and nineteenth centuries.

Broadly speaking, relief in the nineteenth century was based on the poorhouse or workhouse. In the twentieth century, it shifted to the provision of food and other necessities to people in need in their own homes, and later to the provision of cash. From the mid-twentieth century onwards, the state came to play an increasingly important role. Following World War II, Canada's economic surplus grew, as did the expectation that the state would ensure the economic and social security of its citizens. As state provision of social welfare expanded, so did the social work profession itself.

PHASE 1:
The Era of Moral Reform—Pre-1890

The pre-industrial phase of the development of social work includes the period from the formation of Canada up to the 1890s. **Private charities** developed during this time, offering material relief and lessons in moral ethics. Many were explicitly associated with religious organizations, and it was religiously motivated individuals working through these organizations who became the early social workers. This period saw the rise of the charity movement, epitomized by the Charity Organisation Society (COS). The roots of casework and the notion of helping people adjust to their environment can be traced to the COS.

The response to urban poverty in Canada during this phase was the result of two types of religious motivation. The explanation by James Leiby of the development of charitable activity in the United States provides some insight into similar development in English Canada as well:

> The early institutional responses to urban poverty came from people who had religious interests and motives. There were two broad types. One was native, Protestant, and missionary. It expressed a concern of pious and rather well-established people for those whom they perceived as strangers and outsiders (and of course unchurched). The other type developed among the immigrant groups as forms of mutual aid and solidarity in a threatening environment (Leiby 1978, 75).

These two religious thrusts underlie the subsequent history of divergent views of social work. The missionary motive led to the COS and, ultimately, to social casework. The solidarity motive led to initiatives such as the settlement house movement and, later, community work and social justice.

Early Charity Organization: The Roots of Social Work

In the nineteenth century, public assistance in English Canada was guided largely by the example of England. Early English legislation, the Poor Laws, required local parishes to provide relief to the deserving poor (those who were elderly, ill, or disabled). Parishes were administrative districts organized by the Church of England. Each had a local council that was responsible for assistance to the poor, known as **poor relief**. The *Poor Law of 1601* and its reform in 1832 carefully distinguished two types of indoor relief: one for the elderly and sick who could receive relief in almshouses or poorhouses, and one for the able-bodied poor who were made to work for relief in workhouses, the purpose of which was to make public assistance cruel and demeaning.

Early in the nineteenth century, "relief," where it was available, was provided primarily by private philanthropic societies founded in the territories that became Canada. Organizations such as the Society for

Private Charities

An early approach to social work that involved private individuals and religious organizations that provided material relief to the poor.

Poor Relief

The Poor Laws signaled an important progression from private charity to public welfare, where the care and supervision of the poor was embodied in law and the responsibility each town, village, or hamlet.

Improving the Condition of the Poor of St. John's (1808), the Society for Promoting Education and Industry among the Indians and Destitute Settlers in Canada (1827), the Kingston Benevolent Society (1821), the Halifax Poor Man's Friend Society (1820), and the Montreal Ladies' Benevolent Society (1832) were preoccupied with the termination of begging and the value of labour. Relief, rarely given in cash, was usually in return for work. These same organizations, however, resisted the introduction of scientific methods of charity that were advocated from the 1830s onwards (Rooke & Schnell 1983, 46–56).

Following a request for assistance, a charity visitor would be designated to visit and interview the applicant in his or her home. Their role was to promote industry, thrift, and virtue among the poor. The visitors were volunteers, generally elite men and women from the upper classes and people from the ranks of the emerging professional and business classes. Their first task was to classify the applicant as either deserving poor or undeserving poor.

People designated as **deserving poor** were seen as being of good moral character and only temporarily out of luck due to no fault of their own. The deserving did not ask directly for help and were clean and tidy. The **undeserving poor** were deemed to be lazy or morally degenerate. Once an applicant was judged to be deserving, he or she had to appear before a committee of trustees who made the final decision to grant aid. The board granted aid in only about half of the cases determined to be circumstances of destitution. While the work required experience and skill, the early boards resisted proposals to hire full-time visitors.

The early relief provided by these volunteers in numerous charities and church parishes was soon deemed disorganized and inefficient, as there was very little regulation or coordination. In Toronto alone, there were 43 different charity organizations by 1894. Over time, the agencies developed their own training programs for volunteers, which, when a shift to a more scientific approach surfaced, formed the basis for the University of Toronto Social Services Program in 1914.

In 1869, proponents of better organization for charitable assistance in England formed the London-based **Charity Organisation Society** (COS) to coordinate the efforts of the various charities. The voluntary work conducted under the auspices of the COS was possibly the most widespread attempt to help the poor. COS brought some order to the chaos created by the activity of 640 charitable institutions. Workers in this organization were expected to cooperate with other charities and with the agents of the Poor Law. The popularity of this voluntary organization partly stemmed from the relief it accorded to local taxpayers; money could be saved if private charities used unpaid volunteers and members of religious orders (Blyth 1972, 21). The Protestant Charity Organization Society arrived in Montreal in 1901, following a similar earlier effort to organize in Toronto. It was primarily directed by businessmen and upper-class women who believed that poverty was the fault of the individual.

Deserving Poor

People who were poor through no fault of their own; considered to be of good moral character.

Undeserving Poor

People who were perceived to be poor because they are lazy or morally degenerate; not deserving of charity.

Charity Organisation Society

In Britain, the Charity Organisation Society advanced the concept of self help and limited government intervention to deal with the effects of poverty. The organization claimed to use "scientific principles to root out scroungers and target relief where it was most needed."

The COS believed that indiscriminate material relief would cause pauperism; relief could lure a person from thrift and hard work into a life of dependency and reliance on handouts. The COS believed that the charity visitors in the homes of the poor could serve as models of the value of hard work and thrift. However, the visitors encountered many difficulties and soon sought out specific training and "scientific methods" to cope with their problems. As these visitors became more familiar with standardized techniques, they began practicing what came to be called social "casework" (Copp 1974, 108–120).

The Settlement House Movement

The aspect of social work concerned with community work has its roots in the **settlement house movement**. The first social settlement house was established in the east end of London in 1884. It was named Toynbee Hall, after an Oxford University historian who had settled in London's East End. (Arnold Toynbee had died in 1883.)

The purpose of the settlement house was to bring the youth of the educated middle class and the charitable gentry to live among the urban residents—a kind of mission to the poor. The term derived from the notion of "settling in," whereby a worker would live in the homes of the poor. As its founder Canon Barnett explained, the idea was simple: "to bridge the gap that industrialism had created between rich and poor, to reduce the mutual suspicion and ignorance of one class for the other, and to do something more than give charity.... They would make their settlement an outpost of education and culture" (Davis 1967, 6).

From the 1880s through to the 1930s, the settlement house movement was a major factor in the emergence of social work as a profession. Young men and women, largely from the middle-classes, volunteered to live and work in converted residential buildings in poor, urban neighbourhoods. With the best of intentions, they hoped to bring about an improvement in the lives of less-well-to-do families. By such means, they provided amenities and services that were not, at that point, widely available to the poor through government agencies—clubs, educational classes, and recreational gatherings, as well as more practical help. The hard-working, committed individuals involved in the settlement house movement saw their mission as sweeping social reform at the community level. These experimental settlements became, in a sense, social work "laboratories" and an arena for training those involved in the emerging field of social work.

The settlement house workers were more inclined to engage in social reform activities than were those involved with the COS, and they tended to advocate for better working conditions, housing, health, and education. Many early workers came to the settlement house movement with radical political ideas, but this radicalism faded out after World War I. It is worth noting that during this period, women began to be involved more actively in work on social and political issues outside the home (Allen 1971).

Goals of the Charity Organisation Society

The COS goals were as follows:

- *Restore people to a life of self-sufficiency, moral rectitude, and Christian values.* Visitors were often rigidly moralistic; the COS was notorious for its rigid moralistic stand. Relief was a matter of Christian uplifting.

- *Restore the bonds of obligation and understanding between the classes.* This was similar to the relationship between feudal lord and serf out of which could come a social and moral contract.

- *Organize and control charity work, aiming for efficiency and communal relations.*

Settlement House Movement

Settlement houses in poor neighbourhoods offered food, shelter, and other basics in the form of charity on the part of wealthy donors, the residents of the city, and scholars who volunteered their services.

The Fabian Society

The Fabian Society, founded in 1884, was (and is still) an influential intellectual movement in Britain. Its aim is to advance the principles of social democracy through gradualist and reformist, rather than revolutionary, means ("Fabianism").

The Fabians laid the foundations for the British Labour Party. Today it is associated with "New Labour" in Britain and continues to represent that gradualist stream of thought and action.

Jane Addams was the most prominent American to transport the idea of social settlements to the United States, founding Hull House in Chicago in 1889 (see Chapter 7, page 123). William Lyon Mackenzie King, later to become prime minister of Canada, worked at Hull House in the 1890s, learning about the charitable work of Addams and others (Addams 1961, viii; Ferns & Ostry 1976, 37). Evangelia, the first settlement house in Toronto, was founded in 1902 by Libby Carson and Mary Bell with the support of the Toronto YWCA. Carson had founded several other settlement houses, including Christadora House in New York in 1897.

Several other settlement houses were established in Canada during this period. In Winnipeg, J.S. Woodsworth (who would later become the first leader of the Co-operative Commonwealth Federation, the forerunner of the present-day New Democratic Party) directed the All People's Mission, which was founded in 1907; in Montreal, the University Settlement House was established in 1909; and in Toronto, the St. Christopher House was founded in 1912, the University Settlement in 1910, and the Central Neighbourhood House in 1911. Most large Canadian cities had at least one settlement house by World War I. The first schools of social work in Canada were connected to, or often were started by, settlement workers (Davis 1967, 3–25).

Social worker Mary Wright hands out Red Cross supplies to wounded soldiers in 1944. Helping to organize and distribute charitable aid has long been an important activity for Canadian social workers.

PHASE 2:
The Era of Social Reform—1891 to 1940

During this period, the notion of helping the needy shifted from private philanthropy, or charity provided by volunteers, to public welfare funded by government bodies and provided by trained and paid workers. This shift in emphasis provided the foundation for the birth of social work as an occupation. The perception that a publicly funded response to poverty was needed arose from middle class fears that increased poverty might result in mob violence and the spread of illness.

In the late nineteenth century, church members involved in charities were motivated by a desire for a more socially oriented church, based on a scientific rather than a moral world view. Recognition grew that skilled and trained workers were required, rather than volunteer, untrained charity visitors.

The notion of **scientific philanthropy** emerged from the early ideals of reform and social progress. These ideals were increasingly influenced by scientific approaches at the time. James Leiby explains that the theory behind scientific philanthropy was that "the scientific spirit pointed toward self-correction and consensus" (Leiby 1978, 91). The purpose of this approach was to depart from moral judgments of deservingness; the client was seen as having an objective problem and the role of the social worker was to help him or her deal with it. To be effective in this role, it was necessary for the worker to have a scientific understanding of human behaviour and social processes. It was assumed that a thorough gathering of information would lead to an understanding of the causes of the person's problem, and that a solution would be found and then applied.

As large urban areas and the number of people in need grew, the poor could no longer be evaluated by a system of charity visitors alone. Charity organizations and the founding of children's aid societies led to the replacement of volunteers with paid and trained staff. Organizations were forced to hire paid workers to efficiently handle the growing demands. During the early part of the twentieth century this transformation was common to many districts in Canada, as well as other parts of the world.

There was a moral as well as a pragmatic concern that poverty might lead to social instability. In the latter third of the nineteenth century, people of the middle and upper classes in England became concerned, either for moral or political reasons, with the unequal distribution of wealth and the poor conditions of the working class. Some also feared that, with an increase in poverty, the working classes might rise up in mob violence, or that the poor might become diseased and spread illness to all members of society. Others took up the more far-reaching critique of capitalism and called for the replacement of capitalism with a socialist system (see sidebar on the next page for more on Karl Marx).

Scientific Philanthropy

An early approach to social work that rejected moral judgments and encouraged a "scientific" assessment of human behaviour and approach to finding solutions.

**Karl Marx
(1818–1883)**

Marx was a German philosopher and political economist who is considered the father of communism and socialism. In 1848 Marx and Friedrich Engels published *The Communist Manifesto*, which outlined a theory of political economy based on the evolution of social classes and argued that capitalism would, like all economic systems that came before it, eventually fail.

Marxist thought has influenced political leaders and scholars for the last 150 years, and is often misrepresented. While Marx never suggested a structure for communism, he was the inspiration behind the communist regimes of the twentieth century.

Marxist thought is also the impetus behind the modern labour movement, especially the concept that as a collective, workers (or the *proletariat*) have power over the traditional power structure and can bring about revolutionary change. By contrast, see the sidebar on the Fabian Society on page 40.

These concerns also emerged in Canada as **social survey research**, which was used to highlight the extent of poverty and inequality in Canadian cities. One of the first social survey research studies was carried out by H.B. Ames in Montreal. Published in 1897 under the title *The City Below the Hill*, it illuminated the conditions of the poorest of Montreal residents. Early studies by other social researcher/reformers, such as J.J. Kelso in Toronto and J.S. Woodsworth in Winnipeg, contributed to the Canadian middle and upper classes' understanding of poverty and what to do about it. Royal Commissions, such as the Dominion Commission on the Relations of Labour and Capital (1889), the Ontario Royal Commission on the Prisons (1890), and the Dominion Board of Inquiry into the Cost of Living (1915), also contributed to increased awareness and a growing interest in social service and social work.

The transition from friendly visitors to paid social workers was not a smooth one. The fact that many workers accepted payment often incurred criticism and disapproval of the upper and middle classes. A willingness to work for nothing, it was considered, was the hallmark of a sincere charity worker (Woodroofe 1962, 97).

The Rise of Trained Social Workers

As the more scientific view of human services emerged, the training of social workers gradually shifted from agency-based volunteer training to a university-based professional education. This shift occurred concurrently in countries such as Britain and the United States.

In 1914, the University of Toronto established a Department of Social Services for the scientific study of society. This program was the first in Canada to undertake the task of training social workers. In 1918, McGill University opened Canada's second English-language social work training program, the School of Social Study and Training. Carl Dawson, the director, was convinced that study and action did not mix well in the university. According to Dawson, the study of social phenomena should proceed separately from its application, which should be left to others. A similar program was begun in 1928 at the University of British Columbia. Several other schools developed after World War II.

Originally based on the concept of charity, social work had evolved from a set of rules to guide volunteers into a philosophy that embodied many of the principles of modern casework and a technique that could be transmitted by education and training from one generation of social workers to another (Woodroofe 1962, 54). Social work in Canada gained a professional prominence in 1927 when the Canadian Association of Social Workers (CASW) was established. In 1947, the first professional social work degree (Master of Social Work) was offered by the University of Toronto. In 1966, the university awarded the first Bachelor of Social Work degree (Armitage 1970).

Social Casework

Modern **casework**—systematic methods of investigation, assessment and decision-making—was strongly influenced by Mary Richmond, who worked for the Charity Organization Societies of Baltimore and Philadelphia and for the Russell Sage Foundation. Her 1917 text, *Social Diagnosis*, was used in the training of workers, and its contents reflect "the strong influence played by medicine in Miss Richmond's conception of social casework" (Coll 1973, 85–86). Richmond felt that the casework technique could approach a "scientific understanding of social dynamics and human behaviour" (Pitsula 1979, 39). In *Social Diagnosis*, she described the social work process as follows:

1. Collection of social evidence, data on family history, and data pertaining to the problem at hand;
2. Critical examination of the material leading to diagnosis; and,
3. Development of a case plan with the involvement of the client.

Richmond used the term *diagnosis*, borrowing the term from medicine. Her work became the source of what would be known as the medical model.

The Social Service Commission in Toronto first introduced the practice of professional casework in Canada. The Commission was appointed by the city in 1911, and employed staff who were paid for their work. It requested that the House of Industry in Toronto hire paid staff to operate their relief program. The distribution of out-of-door relief was coordinated according to modern social work principles, as described in this excerpt from the Commission's 1916 annual report:

> Distress is relieved with care and sympathy, but the emphasis is not placed on mere relief giving. With each family helped the work includes co-operation with other agencies, diagnosis of need, decision as to remedy, application of remedy, subsequent care and tabulation of results. This is not haphazard "tinkering" with human beings but a real effort to render constructive and progressive service (Social Service Commission Annual Report 1916).

After World War I, the emergent social work profession was called upon to assist with the resettlement of war veterans and with others who were not poor but in need of assistance. In 1918, Charlotte Whitton was chosen to assist the Reverend J.G. Shearer at the Social Service Council of Canada and began a period of twenty-five years of intense involvement in social work and in the development of the social services. She subsequently became a successful municipal politician, serving as mayor of Ottawa in the 1950s and 60s.

By 1921, the Social Service Council had become the social welfare division of the Department of Public Health, illustrating the shift from the premise of moral to social reform. In fact, social work gradually became a secular and scientific alternative to moral and religious work. As this replacement occurred over time, religious faith continued to be central to the practice of social work.

During this era of social reform, many families were too poor to afford necessities—such as coal for a fire—forcing them, and their children, to scavenge for their needs.

Casework

The use of systematic methods of investigation, assessment, and decision making in social work practice.

Charlotte Whitton was one of Canada's most influential voices on social welfare matters. She became the first female mayor of a major Canadian city (Ottawa) in 1951.

Psychology and Social Work

The theories of Sigmund Freud, the father of psychology, played an increasingly important role in social work in the 1920s, in tandem with Richmond's text, *Social Diagnosis*. While the latter provided guidance on procedure, Freud provided insight into the inner workings of the individual. Social work shifted from a concern with the societal context to a concern with a person's psychological make-up as the source of problems. Goldstein's comments on American trends apply since the American influence was still very strong in Canada: "Freudian theory overshadowed all other approaches to social problems and orientations about behaviour. By the mid-1920s casework teaching staffs at universities taught psychoanalytic principles as a basis for casework practice" (Goldstein 1973, 31).

Ideas based on **Freudian thought** (see page 67) led to a change in social work, in a sense, supporting a move from a more active to a more passive role for the worker. This was designed to permit social work clients to express themselves. Casework remained the dominant form of social work practice, but social workers began to specialize in such areas as family welfare, hospitals, and psychiatry.

In the 1930s, what became known as functional social work, in which the casework relationship itself would aid the client, began to emerge. Also during this time, group work and community work emerged as different forms of social work (Goldstein 1973, 31–38).

CHARLOTTE WHITTON AND THE CANADIAN COUNCIL ON SOCIAL DEVELOPMENT

The story of the founding of the Canadian Council on Child Welfare, which became the Canadian Welfare Council and is currently the Canadian Council on Social Development, is told in the work of Rooke and Schnell (1983).

A group of social reformers who met at the end of World War I encouraged the founding of a children's bureau in Canada, based on the American model. What resulted was a child welfare bureau in the federal Department of Health, and the founding of a private organization of which Charlotte Whitton became secretary.

Whitton did this work until the late 1920s while she supported herself by working for a Conservative Member of Parliament. She then became a full-time staff member supported by memberships and funds from contracts.

As secretary, she initiated the social survey as a method of modernizing and professionalizing the provision of charity, a task she saw as her mission. She believed that the use of scientific methods had to replace the dated methods of charity visiting.

At the same time, Whitton disagreed strongly with the new breed of social worker/reformer as espoused by Harry Cassidy and Leonard Marsh. She believed in containing and not expanding the role of the welfare state. In *The Dawn of Ampler Life*, a book she wrote at the behest of the leader of the Conservative Party for whom she worked, she explained how charity was a sensitive task requiring the involvement of private organizations and not the involvement of the state.

Writing in 1943, she opposed the development of state social programs in Canada, criticizing the work of Leonard Marsh, who wrote what many consider to be the blueprint for the welfare state in his *Report on Social Security for Canada* earlier the same year (Whitton 1943, 205–221).

Social Gospel, Social Work, and Social Action

During this period of social reform, the **social gospel movement** had a particular influence on Canadian social work. Movements for a more socially oriented church, which would apply Christian ethics to social problems, began to appear within the major Protestant churches in the latter part of the nineteenth century. Within each of the Methodist, Presbyterian, Anglican, and Congregationalist churches, there were movements for a more socially oriented message, or social gospel, concerning justice and social action. The social gospel wings of the churches eventually started many of the settlement houses in Canada. The movement also had strong roots in the prairies.

In 1907, these main Protestant churches established the Moral and Social Reform League. This was the first organization in the country to advocate for social reform. The League was the forerunner of the Social Service Council of Canada, founded in 1914, with the Rev. J.G. Shearer serving as its first director. The Council remained the main social service advocacy organization in Canada for the next 20 years. The name change indicated the shift from a religious and moral perspective to a more scientific one. Not carried out casually, this move was indicative of larger changes in Canadian society, promoting a reform movement that sought to distance itself from a moral base. Several leading members of Canada's trade union movement were active in the Council. After 1925, the Social Service Council declined in significance and was replaced by the Canadian Association of Social Workers in 1927.

J.S. Woodsworth (1874–1942) applied social gospel ideas to his work in social services and later to his political life. Woodsworth was a Methodist minister, born in Ontario and raised in Manitoba, who became interested in social welfare work while studying at Oxford University. Woodsworth returned to Canada, taking a position as minister in Winnipeg, and began working with the city's poor immigrants. He helped develop the work of social workers there, which then spread to other parts of Canada. For example, as part of the settlement house movement he created the All People's Mission, which provided a variety of direct social services. He campaigned for compulsory education, juvenile courts, and the construction of playgrounds. Woodsworth also served as secretary of the Social Welfare League. Social gospel reformers such as Woodsworth were greatly influenced by the labour movement, particularly by ideas concerning worker control of enterprises and workers' direct participation in decision-making.

In the churches, this spirit manifested itself as the social gospel, implying the achievement of justice in this world rather than in the next. For these reformers, service to other human beings was considered a form of service to God. Many Canadian historians, such as Ramsey Cook (1985), view social work as the secular replacement of the social gospel movement.

James Shaver Woodsworth observed industrial capitalism in Canada and Britain and its failure to meet the needs of working people. When Woodsworth was elected to Parliament in the federal election of 1921 as the member for Winnipeg North Centre, his first resolution was one on unemployment insurance.

Social Work and the Great Depression

Great Depression

A worldwide economic downturn that originated in the United States with the stock market crash of October 29, 1929 (known as "Black Tuesday"). The Great Depression lasted until the late 1930s or early 1940s and the onset of the Second World War.

The **Great Depression** of the 1930s was a time of mass unemployment and seriously reduced living standards. In 1933, nearly one-quarter of the labour force was unemployed. This period left an indelible mark on Canadian society. For many Canadians, the Depression shattered the idea that market forces should be left unregulated. They came to see unemployment as a socio-economic problem requiring a national response, rather than as a personal problem to be solved by local charity.

One important outcome was a change in the nature of politics in Canada, which endures to this day. In the 1920s, J.S. Woodsworth began working with the Ginger Group. When the Depression struck, they joined with various labour, farm, socialist, and intellectual groups to form a socialist party, the Co-operative Commonwealth Federation (CCF), with Woodsworth as leader. In 1944, the CCF (based in Saskatchewan) became the first socialist government in North America. In 1961, the CCF came together with the union movement to forge the New Democratic Party, committed to advocating on behalf of farmers and working people.

This period saw remarkable growth in the number of social workers. During the Depression, expanding social service agencies administered relief to a large percentage of the population. The 1941 census recorded 1,805 social workers in Canada, a 65 percent increase over 1931.

For people across Canada, the Great Depression of the 1930s brought great uncertainty and hardship; soup kitchens were often the only recourse for many Canadians.

PHASE 3:
The Era of Applied Social Science—1941 and Beyond

During the war, the federal and provincial governments began to realize that social services were not a luxury, but a vital part of a smoothly functioning economy. They were required to assist the many returning war veterans and their families. The war ended a period of massive unemployment, sped up industrialization and urbanization, doubled the number of women in the labour force and increased and legitimized government intervention in the economy. In the post–World War II period, a period of rapid economic growth and mass consumption, the career opportunities for social workers began to open up. Education and training programs for prospective social workers increased as well.

Following World War II, the federal Liberal government legislated a series of social welfare measures that were, in retrospect, seemingly intended to forestall the election of more CCF party members to the House of Commons. The CCF had achieved considerable popularity during the war with a social reform platform. The Liberals were also concerned with the possibility of a recession, which could cause considerable social unrest. The federal government therefore introduced the Family Allowance, which put more funds into the hands of families, helping to spur more economic growth. In 1951, through a constitutional amendment, the federal government introduced a federally financed and administered universal Old Age Pension. Several years later, they introduced benefit programs for persons with disabilities (see Chapter 2 for more detail).

Many of these programs led to the expansion of employment in the administration of these new services and programs, precipitating a fundamental change in the nature of Canadian social work and the emergence of a profession. Social work opportunities were now shifting from mainly private, volunteer agencies to government departments or government-financed agencies.

The ideas of Freud continued to have an impact on how social workers practiced during this period. Debate occurred between the adherents of the Freudian or diagnostic approach and the newer functional approach. In the **diagnostic approach**, the emphasis was on understanding the condition of the individual by reference to causal events in his or her early life. This approach required a skilled worker who could diagnose the problem and carry out a plan for treatment.

The **functional approach** was based more on the belief in the potential of clients to determine their own direction with the assistance of a skilled worker. The role of the worker was to establish a sound, structured relationship with the client and thereby to facilitate a process of change (Goldstein 1973, 38–39).

Diagnostic Approach

Emphasizes an understanding of an individual's problem by reference to causal events in his or her early life.

Functional Approach

Based on the belief in the potential of individuals to determine their own direction.

TABLE 3.1: Key Events of the Post-War Period and the Implications for Social Work

Canada and World Events	Social Welfare	Social Work
1940s		
War-related state controls Crown corporations End of World War II High labour unrest International revolutions Keynesian economics	Universal social legislation Family Allowance, 1944 Veterans benefits, 1944 CMHC, 1945 White paper on employment, 1945 Hospital construction Organization of provincial departments of social services End of federal relief programs	First social work degree (MSW) awarded Well-paid social work jobs State regulation Men in SW administration Modest growth in employment First social work unionization National Committee of Schools of Social Work established
1950s		
Prosperity High employment Cold War purges of left Liberal government Low level of unrest	Expanded social programs Old Age Pension for all at 70 (1952) Means-tested pension at 65 (1952) Disabled Persons Act (1955) Unemployment Assistance Act (1956) Allowances for blind disabled Hospital care coverage (1957)	Professionalism (CASW expansion) Private agencies dominant Volunteerism Child Welfare Act (Ont) (1954)
1960s		
Grassroots unrest—growth of anti-poverty, Aboriginal peoples, labour, student, and peace organizations Founding of NDP Quebec separatism Economic growth & employment	General Welfare Assistance Act (Ont) (1960) National Housing Act (1964) Canada Pension Plan (1965) Canada Assistance Plan (1966) Medicare Act (1968)	State becomes main employer Grassroots advocacy & social action programs Radical social work Unionization of public sector First Bachelor of Social Work awarded in 1966 CASSW established (1967)
1970s		
Fiscal crisis of state Conservative business strike U.S. influence rises in Canada Rise of women's movement Rise in women's employment	Cutbacks begin in health, education, welfare programs More law and order Rise of contracting out NGO funding of militant groups	Community college SSW programs Contracting out Large growth in schools of social work CASSW begins accreditation of social work degree programs

Canada and World Events	Social Welfare	Social Work
1980s		
Monetarist economics Conservative policies U.S. dominance in Canada Decline in U.S. empire Cold War tensions Third World unrest Waves of refugees Rise in militancy & popular coalitions	Major contracting out, cutbacks, workfare Increases in punitive programs Women's issues (day care, reproductive choice, pay equity, violence) discussed—little concrete progress Rise of food banks, charities Rise of free trade (NAFTA) Young Offenders Act (1984)	Restraint, burnout Cuts of advocacy programs Privatization Short-term training Unionization of NGO workers
1990s		
Economic stabilization Rising militancy of Aboriginal peoples, women, visible minorities, persons with disability, etc. Environmental movement strong Polarization of rich and poor Popular demands for real social justice Rising labour militancy at grassroots Rise of information and communications technology (ICT)	Attempts to dismantle welfare state, and transfer costs to provinces, cities Regressive taxes Cuts in corporate taxes Free trade Privatization of universal programs Cuts to women's, immigrant's, and Aboriginal peoples' rights and programs Move to workfare and privatization (residual model)	Split between professional vs. union and coalition strategies in SW Defensive era Potential for linkages with client groups Continued erosion of social services Rapid expansion of health care spending Concern over the future of public health care
2000s		
Environmental crisis – e.g., global warming Economic globalization intensifies "War on Terror" Aging "Baby Boomers" Indian Residential Schools Truth and Reconciliation Commission Global financial crisis and worst economic downturn since the Depression (1930s) begins in 2008	Global environmental accords not supported by Canada Corporate welfare growth Economic stimulus spending mostly on infrastructure and not social programs Attempts for national child care plan fail Health care spending grows	Job prospects for social workers improve Pressure for licensing exams for social workers Expansion of some social services such as child welfare Increased social work research Information technology increasingly shaping how social work is practiced

In the 1960s, the profession renewed its interest in poverty as a result of anti-poverty measures instituted by the federal government. Community organizing initiatives sprang up in major cities across the country. In Ontario, a second generation of more radical social workers unionized, forming the Federation of Children's Aid Staff in the early 1970s. Several years later, this group of unions joined the Canadian Union of Public Employees, which today represents a large number of social workers who are employed by municipalities across the country.

A range of new models of social work practice also appeared in the 1960s and 1970s, such as the generic or integrated approach, the problem-solving approach, the behaviour modification approach, and the structural approach. The latter was based, in part, on a critique of approaches to individual and family social work that tended to seek explanations for and solutions to problems within the individual alone and not within the institutions or structures of society (see Chapter 4).

The Expansion of Social Services and Social Work

Despite the economic expansion of the post-war years, demands on private organizations for relief grew. The few church and private charities could not keep up. Pressure was put on the federal government by these organizations and by the Canadian Welfare Council, which presented the case for a national program of support for those who were unemployed but not eligible for other assistance. The 1956 *Unemployment Insurance Act* provided federal assistance to the provinces for the so-called unemployed but employable person who did not have access to other income security programs or employment income. A condition of this assistance was that the province could not impose a residency requirement on an applicant.

This federal legislation marked the beginning of modernization of relief administration, which led to the passage of the Canada Assistance Plan in 1966. By offering to share 50 percent of the provincial costs of welfare and social services, the federal government effected key changes in Social Assistance, transforming it into a publicly financed and administered program. This was accompanied by a rapid expansion of social services in child welfare, child care, and other services for people in need.

The period from 1963 to 1973 saw the expansion of income security and social service programs. By the end of this period, Canada had become a welfare state with a public system of health and hospital care and expanded or new income security programs for children, the unemployed, single parents, and persons with disabilities. Public or publicly financed social services, including child welfare and child care, were also expanded, many of which were extended for the first time to meet the needs of the Aboriginal population, including those on reserves. Social workers were required to administer these new programs and deliver the expanded services. The number of persons who identified themselves as social workers in the census rose from 3,495 in 1951 to 30,535 in 1971, with most of that increase occurring in the decade following 1961.

This increased demand for trained social work staff led to increased enrolment in college and university social work programs. The Canadian Association of Schools of Social Work (CASSW) was established in 1967 to oversee professional university-based education programs in Canada. Currently, there are 34 universities and 46 colleges providing social work and social service education. Social workers now earn wages that are comparable to nursing and teaching, with hospitals and child welfare agencies currently employing the largest numbers of social workers.

Conclusion

Social work is a profession with a largely twentieth-century history. In the nineteenth century, charities and settlement houses expanded to provide assistance to the large number of people in need. This later led to the desire to put charity on a more systematic footing. Subsequently, in the late nineteenth and early twentieth centuries, charities received public funds to carry out their work. It was this sequence of events that ultimately lead to the formation of the profession of social work.

The two World Wars and the Great Depression contributed to the need for an expansion of social services and income security programs and an increased demand for social workers. Later, in the 1960s, federal and provincial funding for Social Assistance and social services increased substantially as a result of a national funding program, the Canada Assistance Plan. Consequently, the demand for training also increased, resulting in many new social work programs in colleges and universities.

Social work practice itself has undergone considerable change. At its inception, casework was the predominant form of social work practice, but since that time, both group work and community work have been added. Some universities have recognized social administration and policy as an additional arena of practice. By the 1970s, there was a proliferation of approaches that included both Freudian and functional approaches, as well as the generalist, the problem-solving, the behavioural, and the structural approaches, all testifying to the importance of the field to society and the economy. (Chapter 4 explores the theoretical foundation of these varied approaches.)

The remaining chapters of this book attempt to provide an understanding of the context of social work practice over the past two decades. This context includes the widening gap between the health and welfare of the rich and the poor, the implications of an aging society, the pressures on public health and child care, and the persistent disadvantages experienced by women, Aboriginal peoples, individuals from racialized communities, recent immigrants, and persons with disabilities. In the future, it is likely that this context will include the impact of the economic downturn that began in 2008, as it continues to affect the lives of ordinary Canadians.

During the Great Depression, the large number of unemployed men brought attention to the need for increased social services and income security programs.

CHAPTER REVIEW

Key Terms

- Private charities
- Poor relief
- Deserving poor
- Undeserving poor
- Charity Organisation Society (COS)
- Settlement house movement
- Scientific philanthropy

- Social survey research
- Casework
- Freudian thought
- Social gospel movement
- Great Depression
- Diagnostic approach
- Functional approach

Review Questions

1. What are the historical roots of modern-day social work?

2. What are the three phases of the evolution of social work in Canada, and what are the defining characteristics of each phase?

3. Describe the history of charity organization, the settlement house movement, and social reformers and their influence on social work in Canada.

4. Describe the influence of the social gospel movement on the emergence of social work in Canada.

5. What was the effect of the Depression of the 1930s on the development of social work in Canada?

6. Describe some of the linkages between the social gospel movement, the farm and labour movement, and the New Democratic Party of today.

7. How has casework changed since the days of Mary Richmond?

8. What is the scientific approach to social work and how did it change the nature of social work practice?

Exploring Social Work

1. The social gospel movement had a large impact on the development of social work in Canada. Research this movement, starting with a basic introduction at **www.thecanadianencyclopedia.com**. Write a two-page paper describing the movement and how these ideas may have affected the development of social work.

2. Jane Addams and Mary Richmond were two women who had tremendous impact on social work, but they were very different women. Explore their historic contributions and think about how each of their differing views affected the way social work is described and practiced today. Discuss in small groups or write a two-page paper on the topic. To get started visit the American National Association of Social Workers page on pioneers at **www.naswfoundation.org/pioneers**.

3. One of the underlying precepts of social work in its earliest days was the distinction between the "deserving" and "undeserving" poor. Pair up with another student and discuss whether this key idea persists today and continues to influence current social policy. Write a two-page paper using evidence to support your arguments.

Websites
- - - - - -

Canada's Unique Social History
www.socialpolicy.ca/cush

By going through this website (a project of this text's author, Steven Hick), you will become more familiar with the major concepts and issues in social welfare—what they are, where they come from, how they work, and why they work the way they do.

History of Toynbee Hall
www.toynbeehall.org.uk

Toynbee Hall has been working to combat poverty in London's East End for 120 years, and the organization started an international movement that focused attention on tackling social problems. Toynbee inspired many well-known national organizations and involved eminent people from all walks of life. Toynbee Hall today strives to help the people who live in the impoverished area of Tower Hamlets—an area on the City of London's doorstep.

Information for Practice
www.nyu.edu/socialwork/ip

This vast resource for social workers, produced by Dr. Gary Holden at New York University, offers an eclectic collection of material on social work with a useful search engine, covering many of the topics in these pages. It is particularly helpful for researching a particular topic or locating an international association.

CHAPTER 4

THEORY AND APPROACHES TO SOCIAL WORK PRACTICE

- -

Using Knowledge to Shape Our Work with Clients

with Purnima Sundar

A **social work theory** is an organized way of thinking about the world that guides the way we carry out social work practice. Over the last hundred years, the theories that have informed social work practice have changed, and with them the focus and methods of practice have changed. Traditionally, social workers have been influenced by what is known as the medical model, dealing primarily with the personal problems of individuals, and working to assess or "diagnose" and change or "treat" behaviour. Modern social work theory, however, has shifted to emphasize *assessment* and *intervention*, and takes place at individual, family, social, and structural levels. Today, environmental factors are considered as important as internal factors, and most recently, social workers have acknowledged that social problems are embedded in political, economic, and social structures.

What Is a Social Work Theory?

In social work, theories can be rooted in either *foundation knowledge* or *practice knowledge*. Foundation knowledge comprises general theories about individual personality and behaviour; people in society; and social, political, and economic relations. In social work, this knowledge is drawn from disciplines such as psychology, sociology, economics, political science, and the allied health professions. Examples of foundation theories include behaviour theory, socialization theory, organizational theory, developmental theory, political theory, or critical social theory.

- **Foundation theories** are generalized ideas about the world that provide the basis for practice theories.
- **Practice theories** build on foundation knowledge, making it specific and relevant to the way we practice social work.

While they are influenced by foundation theories, practice theories are focused on what factors are important for practitioners in assessing a client's situation, and how we should intervene, if at all.

Individual- and Structural-Level Practice Theories

Social work practice theories can be classified into two groups: *individual-level* and *structural-level* theories. **Individual-level theories** are varied and complex, focusing on individuals and their interactions. This body of theory concentrates on aspects such as interactions between people or the effect of negative attitudes on people.

Some researchers criticize these theories because they focus on *what* people do rather than on the social structures and policies that *cause* or *influence* what they do. These researchers prefer **structural-level theories**, which emphasize social structures, processes, and systems and how they shape people's experiences. For example, this body of theory would examine the effects of the Canadian economy on people's status or how gender influences the income of Canadians. This approach has been criticized because it minimizes an individual's ability to act and overcome the constraints presented by social structures.

Social workers tend to draw from a range of individual and structural theories depending on the population with whom they work, their personal preferences, and their field of practice. For example, a social worker might use an individual-level approach such as developmental theory when providing support to children, or cognitive theory if they are working in addictions. Or, a social worker may use a structural approach and draw on critical theory while working in child welfare to try and influence public policy on funding child services, or social action theory to advocate for proper housing when working in addictions. Because they deal with specific situations and problems in a variety of contexts, social workers need to draw on a wide range of knowledge and practice skills.

Individual-Level Theories

Theories that focus on individuals and their interactions.

Structural-Level Theories

Theories that emphasize social structures, processes, and systems and how they shape people's experiences.

Specific Theories of Social Work

Social workers are sometimes drawn to clear-cut practice manuals based on the more psychologically oriented approaches. These can be useful, but it is also crucial to have a clear understanding of broad theoretical approaches.

The following theories and approaches are specific to social work. In other words, psychologists and psychiatrists would not normally use them, except perhaps the feminist and functional approaches. They are broad theoretical perspectives that shape overall assessment and intervention, but often do not provide detailed practice guidelines or procedures. This, however, should not lessen their utility for social workers.

Functional Theory

Functional Theory

Problems come from negative experience and can be overcome using one's personal power to effect change.

Functional theory was first introduced in the 1930s by Jessie Taft and Virginia Robinson and was based on the work of Otto Rank, a personality psychologist who had once worked closely with Sigmund Freud (see page 67). While Freud believed that a person's problems were often due to negative childhood experiences, Rank emphasized events taking place in the present.

For Rank, all human beings are engaged in a struggle between a desire to create a unique, individual identity (which is developed through growth and change), and the desire to stay connected to and dependent upon others (which reduces the need to grow and change). Individual problems can only become resolved when a person is assertive and acts as her or his own force for change.

Using these ideas as the foundation for their approach, Taft and Robinson developed a model for social work practice in which the full participation of the client is essential (Taft 1948). With functional theory, the goal of practice is to enhance social functioning in individuals, families, groups, and communities by assessing the problem and using one's personal power to effect change in a structured way. Three particular phases of the therapeutic process were identified (the beginning, middle, and end), each with specific tasks aimed at helping the client move towards change.

The introduction of the functional approach coincided with new ways of understanding the relationship between the client and the social worker. With previous approaches to practice, the therapist was seen as the "expert" who diagnosed a person's problem and developed a course of action to respond to it. Functional theory, however, emphasized the client's role in directing change. This signalled an early move away from the "medical model" or "diagnostic approach" and the beginning of a more egalitarian approach to social work practice where the client and worker together engaged in a "helping relationship" geared towards achieving certain goals.

Strengths-Based Social Work

Currently, many social workers approach practice from an individual-level **strengths-based perspective.** This approach was introduced several years ago by University of Kansas social work professor Dennis Saleebey and his colleagues Charles Rapp and Ann Weick. Saleebey's work with people experiencing serious mental illness helped him to recognize that each person has unique strengths and abilities, and the capacity for growth and change.

In contrast to a problem-based approach such as functional theory, which works from the assumption that the individual has some deficit that needs to be addressed, social workers operating from a strengths-based perspective begin by supporting the client to recognize her or his assets. The worker and client collaborate to understand the situation and draw on available strengths and resources work towards change. These strengths and resources become the building blocks upon which additional strengths can be developed. The therapeutic relationship is an empowering space in which the client recognizes her or his capacity for change. This approach, which can be used in social work with individuals, families, small groups, organizations, and communities, avoids pathologizing people, and helps to create a solid foundation for future growth (Saleebey 2005).

Social Systems Theory

The **social systems theory** places the individual within a series of interdependent systems. This theory is sometimes referred to as the *ecological systems theory*, based on the concept of an ecosystem where every organism is affected by and influences the others within the system. This theory is a reaction to social work practice approaches that locate the cause of problems within the individual. While the idea of the individual as existing within a series of systems had been introduced in previous decades, in the 1980s, social work professors Carel Germain and Alex Gitterman used ideas from ecology and biology to develop the "life model" of social work, which tends to guide much of generalist social work practice today.

According to the social systems theory, people exist in particular environments, and problems arise when there is a lack of "fit" between people and their surroundings. Different "systems" such as the individual, the family, the school, the church, social agencies, the community, and the society interact and relate with one another so that problems at one level can create difficulties at another. For example, if an adolescent is having trouble in school, this may cause disagreements to emerge within the family. This might lead the family to draw on social agencies, which then can change how the youth interacts with the school and family, and perhaps even among his peers. With the ecological or social systems approach, social workers look at what might be causing problems in different areas of a person's life, and work with the client to shape solutions to these problems at different levels.

In a case such as homelessness, a social worker might use crisis intervention to deal with personal issues and social action theory to address the larger systemic issue.

Strengths-Based Perspective

Individual-level approach that focuses on personal strengths and assets.

Social Systems Theory

Based on the idea that society consists of a series of interdependent systems, like an ecosystem, and the individual exists within and is affected by these systems.

When assessing the situation with the client, the social worker decides which system to focus on first. This social systems approach integrates knowledge about human behaviour and knowledge about the influence of social environment on behaviour. The goal of this type of social work practice is to understand how people and their environments influence each other to shape responses at both individual and social levels.

As with other approaches, social workers who draw on social systems theory also incorporate aspects of humanist philosophy into their practice, as their work typically involves a strong element of empathy and reflection.

The Structural Approach

The *structural approach* to social work is largely a Canadian development, and originates in the work of Maurice Moreau, a social work professor at Carleton University. A **structural approach** to practice focuses on the impact of wider social structures on personal problems. It involves a critical analysis of socio-economic structures, which oppress and exploit people, whether based on class, race, age, gender, ability, or sexuality. These can include primary structures—those which shape our society, such as patriarchy, racism, capitalism, heterosexism, ageism, and ableism—as well as secondary structures—those which share our individual experience, such as personality, family, community, and bureaucracy.

The structural approach involves a critical analysis of these structures. While every problem a person experiences is not entirely caused by structures, according to Jan Fook, "there is always a structural element in any experienced problem" (1993, 74–75). Therefore, structural social workers tend to consider all dimensions of personal problems, while being particularly attuned to the less "visible" structural elements.

The skills involved in structural social work are similar to the social systems theory approach. They both draw on the same sense of empathy, reflection, and a belief in the basic goodness of people. It is the way in which the social worker analyzes problems and the type of actions that result from this analysis that distinguishes the structural approach from systems theory. The structural social worker is concerned with helping the individual deal with a difficult problem, but he or she is also concerned with changing the overall situation that is causing the problem, whenever that is possible.

The structural approach requires that the social worker be skilled in casework, family counselling, group work, and community organizing, as well as have a deep knowledge of social policy and social welfare. Structural social work differs from systems theory in that it goes beyond an analysis of the immediate family and community as external factors and looks to the broader analysis of socio-economic factors such as class, gender, and race.

Structural Approach

Focuses on the impact of wider social structures, such as patriarchy, racism, and sexism, on personal problems. It also considers secondary structures such as family, community, and bureaucracy.

TABLE 4.1: Modern Theoretical Approaches to Social Work

Anti-oppressive practice (AOP)	Life model systems approach
Anti-racist social work	Locality development theory
Aboriginal social work	Mediation theory
Client-centred perspectives	Mindfulness-based interventions
Cognitive therapy	Mindfulness-based cognitive therapy (MBCT)
Cognitive-behaviour therapy (CBT)	
Communication theory (communicative-interactive)	Narrative therapy
Crisis intervention theory	Person-centred therapy
Critical theory	Play therapy
Ecological theory	Psychodynamic perspectives
Ego-state therapy	Psychosocial theory
Existential perspectives	Problem-solving theory
Feminist perspectives	Rational-emotive therapy
Functional theory	Social action theory
Generalist practice	Social planning theory
Gestalt therapy	Structural social work
Integrative theory	Strengths-based social work
	Task-centred models

Advocates of structural social work emphasize the links between a person's feelings and behaviour and the larger society. The structural social work approach operates at various levels to deal with an individual's problems as well as work towards a more just and equitable society. It can sometimes be difficult, however, to assess the effectiveness of this approach because social change is hard to achieve and measure, given the interrelated and reinforcing nature of society's systems.

Critical Social Work

Similar to the structural approach, critical social work focuses on the impact of social structures on personal problems.

Critical Social Work

Practice, as conceived from the framework of **critical social work**, must contribute to a transformation of everyday lives, working toward changes in economic, social, and political structures, relations, or organization. The approach is *critical* in that it critiques or unravels the societal relations underpinning our personal problems. In addition, it is concerned with the power imbalance that exists between workers and clients and seeks constructive methods for addressing it.

Both as a strategy addressing the client/worker power imbalance and as an overall strategy, critical social work often draws upon the notion of empowerment. **Empowerment** at an operational level has three aspects: explicitly identified power elements in the client-worker relationship; explicit experience of control by clients; and explicit support by social workers for client's efforts to gain greater control over their lives and promote change.

A social worker may use the social systems approach to work with a troubled individual, such as an adolescent having difficulties socializing at school. By using such an approach, the social worker can shape solutions to the problems at a different level, changing how the youth interacts among his or her peers.

Feminist Social Work Practice

A coherent body of ideas known as feminism has existed since the late 1800s. Historically, the focus of feminism began with efforts to secure legal and property rights for women, and through the 1960s, evolved to address inequality in both private and public spheres. A specific **feminist social work practice** theory emerged in the 1970s along with broader social movements in civil and human rights. The underlying assumption of this approach is that since social categories (like gender) shape the way we understand and interact with others, particular approaches need to be developed to address the unique needs of women.

Social workers using a feminist approach to practice provide support that is women-centred, and which strives to understand their particular experiences of oppression and discrimination both within relationships and in the broader society. Feminist social work practitioners also attempt to understand how social, economic, and political structures create and sustain inequality between genders, while engaging women in consciousness-raising activities to transform these conditions. Mutual support, valuing diversity, and an emphasis on women's lived experiences guide work with clients. This approach is useful in that it considers the role of society's systems in shaping gender relations, and provides constructive roles for both women and men to work towards equality. Feminist social work practice, however, has been criticized for not recognizing the diversity of experiences between women.

Feminist theories offer different ways of asking questions about and understanding women's lives and experiences, the nature of inequality between the sexes, and gender relations in society. Feminist therapies (which draw from feminist theories) have their origins in the women's liberation movement of the 1960s. Self-help-style groups, called consciousness-raising groups began to question gender-based roles and power relations in Canadian society. By sharing experiences, they began to understand how each woman's experience was not unique but had common ground with the experiences of other women. In a manner that is often similar to structural social work, feminist therapy believes that theories of human behaviour must be understood within the broader social context.

Today, feminist approaches to therapy or counselling are based on a recognition that gender is an important factor in many problems presented by clients, and that women constitute a larger proportion of clients than men. In fact, whether workers practice from a feminist approach or not, knowledge of how gender affects a client's situation is important. Some call this "gender-conscious practice" (Orbach 1990); it is based on the belief that ignoring gender issues misses significant aspects of the client's experience, and fails to examine the complexities of the social context influencing the client's life.

Feminist Social Work Practice

Women-centred approach that strives to understand particular experiences of oppression in relationships and the broader society.

SOCIAL WORKERS' GENERALIST SKILLS

Generalist social workers are influenced by different assumptions and viewpoints along a continuum. That continuum includes ecological and anti-oppression perspectives. Using a sample of general social work skills, this chart suggests how workers apply these skills, reflecting different themes, such as adaptation or emancipation.

Social Workers Applying:	Ecological & Systems Perspectives	Structural & Anti-Oppressive & Critical Perspectives
Assessment Skills	Use systems theory and ecological narratives: (1) to explain dysfunctional interactions among different systems (e.g. individual, familial, communal, and formal systems); (2) to explore imbalances between individuals and their environments; (3) to identify areas for reciprocal adaptation by individuals and other systems, to optimize human well-being.	Use structural theory and liberation narratives: (1) to learn how experiences of systemic oppression (e.g. colonialism, patriarchal capitalism, racism, heterosexism, ableism, ageism) are harming the service user's well-being; (2) to identify immediate survival needs; (3) to explore short-term and long-term goals for emancipation.
Empathy Skills	Communicate an understanding and appreciation of the client's feelings and subjective experience (as part of developing trust within a professional relationship). Use this skill in working directly with individuals, as well as with individuals in families, groups, and communities. Develop anticipatory empathy by tuning in, as part of preparing to work with specific client systems.	Communicate efforts to learn about and appreciate the service user's feelings and meanings (as part of trust evolving within a non-elitist professional relationship). Widen focus to include emancipatory empathy: i.e., dialogue about subjective and systemic barriers faced by others similarly oppressed, and about the courage to name and to overcome such barriers.
Reframing Skills	Aim to reduce clients' sense of hopelessness by suggesting new, more hopeful ways of viewing the situation. Congratulate clients for achievements that are ignored or devalued by others. Invite clients to identify unrecognized strengths within themselves and in their interactions with other systems, to help empower alternative, positive, and more hopeful client responses.	Aim to reduce self-blame by co-investigating with service users: (1) external and internalized oppression and (2) external and internalized illegitimate privilege, due to unjustified power over others. Explore new, more hopeful ways of understanding/acting, in light of social justice inspirations, initiatives, and solidarities.

Social Workers Applying:	Ecological & Systems Perspectives	Structural & Anti-Oppressive & Critical Perspectives
Communication Skills (e.g. listening, exploring, focusing, clarifying, encouraging)	Listen. Explore ways that clients and their environments can better adapt to each other. Focus on services/resources, while affirming client strengths. Explore stress reduction among clients, families, and other systems. Respect and support client self-determination. Mediate/guide client systems in their problem-solving and solutions-finding.	Listen. Explore ways that clients may be victims and survivors of oppression. Focus on services/resources, while affirming people's strengths. Model power-sharing with service users. Unmask illegitimate privilege. Support personal/political change to dismantle multiple oppressive practices, while constructing equitable alternatives.
Spiritual Sensitivity Skills	Validate religious/spiritual pluralism. Support spirituality by clients as a strength to cope with stress (e.g. life transitions, crises caused by painful losses). Honour/appeal to spiritual/religious values of compassion and charity within/across diverse communities to encourage more generous help for people in need.	Validate religious/spiritual pluralism. Oppose those religious practices that are oppressive. Learn about/honour spirituality rooted in diverse cultures, including its role in indigenous people's helping and healing. Find spiritual/ religious support for progressive personal and social change within/ across diverse communities.
Advocacy Skills	Work at convincing formal and informal systems to better meet client needs, by mediating between clients and their environments. Active with others in lobbying larger systems for better policies, co-ordination, integration, and delivery of social services. Seek support from private, public, and charitable sectors, for additional resources to alleviate social problems.	Active with others, including service users, to defend human rights (e.g., decent incomes, jobs, social services) by organizing grassroots power upward to deconstruct harmful policies, decisions, processes, and structures. Become allies with social movements, locally and globally, for personal, familial, political, economic, and spiritual emancipation.
Source: "A Teaching/Practice Tool: Generalist Social Work" (draft 27, 2008). Prepared by Ben Carniol, Ryerson School of Social Work. For elaboration, see Ben Carniol. 2005. *Case Critical: Social Services and Social Justice in Canada*, 5th Edition. Toronto: Between the Lines Publishers. Chart appears courtesy Ben Carniol.		

Anti-Oppressive Practice

Anti-Oppressive Practice

Recognizes that people's experiences are shaped by the society in which they live and that many problems are caused by the oppressive structures of that society.

Canadian social work professor Bob Mullaly (2002) defines oppression as "the domination of subordinate groups in society by a powerful (politically, economically, socially, culturally) group" (27). Oppressive relationships exist both at structural and individual levels. Since our identities are influenced by our social interactions with people, oppressive relationships play a key role in how our identities develop and are expressed. The goal of **anti-oppressive practice (AOP)** is to acknowledge the existence of oppression and the complex nature of our identities. This knowledge can be used to overcome oppressive relationships in society, and broadly contribute to social justice. According to social work scholar Donna Baines, AOP is a unique response from social workers to trends taking place in our increasingly globalized society.

The anti-oppression approach is not a single theory; instead, it draws on many traditions that are united in the goal of understanding and responding to oppressive conditions and relationships in society. There are, however, several common ideas:

- Both macro- and micro-level social relations generate oppression.
- Our everyday experience is shaped by multiple oppressions.
- Social work is a contested site.
- Social work is not a neutral, technical profession, but an active political process.
- Social justice–oriented social work assists individuals while simultaneously seeking to transform the forces that generate and benefit from inequity and oppression.
- Social work needs to build allies and work with social causes and movements.
- Social work's theoretical and practical development must be based on the struggles and needs of those who are oppressed and marginalized.
- Participatory approaches between practitioners and clients are necessary.
- Self-reflexive practice and ongoing social analysis are essential components of social justice–oriented social work practice.
- A social justice perspective provides the best potential for politicized, transformative social work practice (Baines 2007, 20–22).

Similar to feminist, structural, and anti-racist perspectives, an anti-oppressive approach to social work practice helps us to acknowledge the existence of structural inequalities and divisions in society that both shape and are shaped by our complex identities. In addition, this perspective highlights the need for social workers to intervene at both individual and structural levels.

Anti-Racist Social Work

Whereas the anti-oppressive approach to social work practice offers a broad approach to understanding oppression and discrimination, what has come to be known as **anti-racist social work** focuses more specifically on how the phenomenon of racism affects the lives and outlook of people of colour. In this context, *race* can be defined as the observable, physical features (like skin colour or hair texture) that a group of people share, and that distinguishes them from members of other groups (Henry & Tator, 2006).

Anti-racist social work examines the effects of racism by means of an economic and social analysis of relations between members of different groups. Although the physical differences that are used to define race may be biological in origin (e.g., skin colour, texture of hair), the way human beings classify and explain these classifications is constructed socially. These differences are used to sustain a system in which some people hold a lot of power and wealth in society and others experience exclusion and marginalization based on their race.

Social workers practicing from an anti-racist perspective work to address racism at structural, organizational, community, and individual levels. A key strength of the anti-racist approach to social work is that it helps us to understand both the individual effects of racism, as well as its broader, structural roots. In addition, it calls for a *deconstruction* of the social systems that function because of racial categorizations, and advocates for a more equitable reconstruction of these structures. An important limitation of the anti-racist approach, however, is that changing something as deep-seated as racism can take a long time. The slowness of the process can easily discourage those social workers and clients who are seeking relatively quick solutions to the immediate and pressing problems that they are facing on the ground.

An illustration of such a deconstruction in Canada can be seen in the circumstances surrounding the Indian residential schools. The residential school system was introduced by the Canadian government in the 1920s to "educate" Aboriginal children according to the standards of education thought most appropriate by the European colonizers. These children were taken away from their families, and forced to speak English or French and ignore their culture and traditions. Physical abuse was a common form of "discipline," and many children were sexually abused by workers at the schools. Although these abuses were first made public in the 1980s, it was not until 1996 that the last federally funded residential school was closed down. Only in the last decade have we, as a society, recognized how much the institution of residential schools and the racist assumptions upon which they were founded injured both individuals and their communities. In 2008, the federal government made a formal apology on behalf of Canada to the Aboriginal peoples affected by these institutions.

Anti-racist social work, which helps us to understand the individual effects of racism and its structural roots, is very important in a multicultural society such as Canada.

Anti-Racist Social Work

Focuses specifically on how racism affects the lives of people of colour.

Psychologically Based Theories

Psychologically based theories are central to social work practice. It is important to explore both the internal (psychological issues) and the external (sociological issues) of our clients. Having said this, it is crucial not to jump to conclusions about psychological issues. Therapeutic labels can be disempowering and can actually work as a barrier to assistance. Medical professionals tend to use the ***Diagnostic and Statistical Manual of Mental Disorders*** (DSM) to ascribe mental disorders to patients. The DSM is maintained by the American Psychiatric Association (APA) and lists categories of mental disorders and criteria for diagnosis. The DSM's primary purpose is to guide mental health professionals in clinical diagnosis; however, the contents of the DSM are often controversial. Social workers can use the DSM's categories to identify concerns, and this is often useful for insurance purposes; however, it's important that practice efforts are not limited to treating the so-called disorder.

The Medical Model

As explained in Chapter 3 (see page 41-44), the social sciences, particularly sociology, were becoming influential in the early 1900s. The *medical model* along with the *scientific method* formed the basis of early social work practice theory. Most social workers engaged in *scientific philanthropy*, an approach that mirrored a medical approach to problems, which involved conducting an in-depth study of a person's situation (resulting in an empirical diagnosis) and then devising a treatment plan that would improve her or his condition. During this period, most social workers located the cause of social problems within the person. For example, if someone experienced poverty, the cause was seen as immorality, laziness, or alcoholism. The typical way of responding to this problem, then, was to attempt to teach the person how to live a more "moral," ordered life. This medical model generally ignored external or society factors, and emphasized internal and eventually psychological causes of social problems.

Psychodynamic Perspectives

The **psychodynamic perspective** was introduced by Freud in the 1920s. Freud argued that the norms and values of a society put limits on the extent to which people can actively pursue fulfilling their basic needs. He suggested that the *id*, the *ego*, and the *superego* work together to fulfill these needs, but only in ways that are acceptable to the people around us. This creates a constant conflict between human desire and the limits set by society. This conflict leads to anxiety, which is upsetting to the person and can cause her or him to act in irrational ways. Early conscious and unconscious experiences that create these anxieties and the ways people manage them, are critical in shaping personality.

Diagnostic and Statistical Manual of Mental Disorders (DSM)

Better known as the DSM, the *Diagnostic and Statistical Manual of Mental Disorders* lists all mental health disorders for both children and adults, as well as known causes of these disorders, statistics related to gender, age, and prognosis, and research pertinent to treatment options.

The manual is published by the American Psychiatric Association and is considered the "bible" for professionals who make psychiatric diagnoses in the United States and many other countries.

Psychodynamic Perspective

Diagnostic approaches to social work (based on the work of Sigmund Freud) that focus on internal sources for individual problems.

From a psychodynamic perspective, the goals of social work are to (1) understand the roots of the anxiety to determine what is fuelling the irrational or troubling behaviour, (2) use specific techniques to expose this source of the problem, and (3) use these insights to resolve the issue, which can then help people manage their anxieties and behaviours. Social workers that adopt this perspective are described as using a "diagnostic approach." A person's troubles are understood to be the result of some internal pathology that likely began in childhood, and the goal of social work practice is to restore normal functioning.

Freud's ideas were critical in shaping much of subsequent social work practice theory. Although today's psychodynamic practice theories (for example, attachment theory and play therapy) have evolved, there continues to be more importance to biological or internal causes for behaviour. Psychodynamic theory and Freud's views are historically important, since they helped to uncover the complexity of our minds and experiences. In addition, these ideas moved social work practice towards a more open, therapeutic approach, rather than teaching people how to live "moral" lives. However, psychodynamic theories remain rooted in white, middle-class, Western judgments as to what is "normal" and "abnormal." In addition, it is hard to gauge the effectiveness of these approaches, since aside from observing behaviours and inferring what might be going on, we can never really know what is going on in the mind.

SIGMUND FREUD

Sigmund Freud (1856–1939), an Austrian physician, is considered the father of modern psychology. Freud's theories permeate our culture, and are referred to often in popular culture (for example, a "Freudian slip"). Social work theory is in part informed by his work.

Freud is best known for his theories about our unconscious mind. He argued that our psyche consists of three parts, the *id*, the *ego,* and the *superego*. The id represents instincts and impulses, the ego represents individuality and the self, and the superego is the conscience. Related to this is the notion that most human behaviour is motivated by a desire to fulfill basic human needs—the id encourages us to act on our needs, and the ego and superego balance our behaviour based on reality and society's norms.

A key Freudian idea is that experiences in our childhood unconsciously influence the adults we become. He identified several key stages through which human beings move as they grow. In each of these stages, people experience certain conflicts and challenges that are resolved and move the person to the next stage. Any trauma that takes place during a particular stage, however, can make us "stuck" in that stage, and unable to move on to the next. Freud believed that this is what lies at the root of adult behaviours.

For example, Freud called the earliest years in a child's life the "oral stage" (from age 0 to 2). At this time, babies have most of their needs met orally, through sucking (either for food or for comfort). A trauma experienced at this stage might result in a person becoming "orally fixated," since she or he never moves on to finding satisfaction in the next stage. This idea could be used to explain negative adult behaviours like alcoholism, since pleasure is derived orally.

Related to this is the notion of repression; often what we say we feel has more to do with repressed desires and needs. Freud is famous for his study of human sexuality, and his theories are often associated with secret sexual desire. However, all of our desires and experiences are relevant, not just those related to sex.

In keeping with Freud's theories of the unconscious mind, when you misspeak, and the incorrect word that you've said seems suggestive of what's "really on your mind," you've made what's popularly known as a "Freudian slip."

Søren Kierkegaard (1813–1855) was a Danish philosopher and theologian. He wrote extensively on faith and the importance of the self. He is considered a father of the existentialism movement, although he never used that term.

Friedrich Nietzche (1844–1900) was a German philosopher well known for many ideas, including the aphorism "that which does not destroy us makes us stronger." Later in life, Nietzsche's writings grew in popularity and provided inspiration for 20th-century philosophy.

Jean-Paul Sartre (1905–1980) was a French existentialist philosopher, playwright, novelist, screenwriter, political activist, biographer, and literary critic. He was one of the leading figures in 20th-century French existentialist philosophy.

Existentialist Approach

Existential therapies are based on the nineteenth century philosophy of existentialism or the search for meaning in life. Existentialists such as Søren Kierkegaard and Friedrich Nietzsche argued that life is essentially meaningless and without purpose, therefore human beings must create meaning and purpose to guide our existence. In the 1960s, French philosopher Jean-Paul Sartre argued that people act according to their goals, the most important of which is to find meaning in their lives.

These ideas offered an alternative to behaviourist and psychodynamic perspectives, which emphasized a person's prior experiences. Existentialists argue that people are intentional and deliberate in their choices to act, and can influence the direction of their lives depending on their goals for the future. With its emphasis on choice and self-determination, existentialists believe that people are inherently capable of controlling and changing their lives. Social workers using an existentialist approach strive to understand what might be causing a person to suffer, and to support people in making and committing to choices to act in ways that will enhance self-awareness and decrease this suffering.

An example of an existentialist approach to social work practice is **Gestalt therapy**. *Gestalt*, which means "shape" in German, refers in this context to a unified whole that is more significant than the sum of its parts. It was first used as a concept in psychology to understand the mind as a whole entity, not just the sum of its individual parts. Gestalt therapy is based on the ideas of psychotherapist Fritz Perls (1893–1970) who believed that human beings are defined by their relationships to others and that it is relationships that influence the way we understand and move through the world. For example, we are not just teachers; we are our children's parents, our parents' children, and siblings to others. We have different roles to play within each of these relationships, and can behave in different ways based on these roles. Perls considered the present to be the most important moment in psychotherapy and advocated the need to "begin where the client is." Social workers practicing Gestalt therapy support clients to develop self-awareness and assume personal responsibility in order to reach self-actualization.

An important strength of Gestalt and other existential therapies is their emphasis on the nature of the relationship between the worker and client. By treating the person as a whole, respecting her or his views and interpretations of reality, and providing non-judgmental, respectful support, social workers can help clients to respond to challenges and reach their goals.

Although a highly important and successful form of social work intervention in the appropriate instances, existential approaches such as Gestalt therapy obviously take time, resources, and patience. Unfortunately, this form of treatment is often discouraged in the more restrictive context of a social service agency working environment.

Client-Centred or Person-Centred Perspectives

The **client- or person-centred perspective** is based on the idea that clients are the experts of their own problems. This approach was introduced by psychotherapist Carl Rogers in the 1950s. Rogers was greatly influenced by the philosophy of *humanism*, and its central belief that all human beings are good, worthwhile, and guided by a search for meaning and purpose in life. When personal growth is impeded—usually by difficulties in relationships with others—people experience problems. Here, the goal of therapeutic practice is to support clients in becoming empowered and in accepting responsibility for making changes in their own lives.

Rogers viewed the therapeutic relationship as central in this process, and believed that the therapist should strive to be genuine, empathize with clients' world views, and provide them with unconditional positive regard (Rogers 1951). He believed that a non-judgmental, non-directive approach, characterized by mutual respect, would help people to tap into their personal power to stimulate change.

As with existential approaches, this type of therapy can sometimes be vague and idealistic, which in turn may result in a lack of consistency among different people adopting this approach. In addition, building the strong therapeutic bond usually requires a time investment that many agencies would not support. While client-centred perspectives undoubtedly can be effective, in reality agencies offering social work services are often pressured to produce measurable results in a relatively short period of time. In an effort to provide practitioners with more practical, time-limited approaches with clearer guidelines, social workers began to draw on cognitive-behavioural approaches (see page 70). These approaches are used to modify behaviours by changing the way we understand the world.

> ### Client- or Person-Centred Perspective
>
> This approach centres on the idea that individuals can, through the therapeutic relationship, effect change in their own lives. It is rooted in "humanist" philosophy, which sees people as having a "free will" and the ability to make reasonable, meaningful choices.

NARRATIVE THERAPY

Narrative therapy views storytelling as an integral part of the way we communicate with one another and make sense of our experiences (McLeod 2006). According to narrative therapy, which was developed in the 1980s by therapists Michael White and David Epston (1990), the way people tell stories reveals how they understand the world and their relationships within it, and provides insights into their values, morals, and beliefs.

These stories are also shaped by broader culture, as we draw on typical narrative conventions and forms in relaying our own stories. The goal of the social worker using narrative therapy is to provide opportunities for an individual to share her or his life narrative in order to reflect upon and process the meanings ascribed to specific events and experiences. This process helps to reveal how our problems are expressions of oppressive stories about ourselves and our relationships. By collaboratively "re-authoring" such narratives, the client and worker can point future experiences in a more positive direction.

This approach is considered empowering for clients and is encouraging given its focus on the opportunity for change. Further, communication is not only verbal; social workers using this approach are trained to attend to non-verbal cues while focusing on the client's narrative.

Rational-Emotive Psychotherapy

Rational-emotive psychotherapy (RET) was the earliest form of a cognitive behaviour approach to inform social work practice. This approach, introduced by psychologist Albert Ellis in the mid-1950s, blended ideas from two key areas in psychology: cognition and behaviourism. Ellis believed that the way we think (our cognition), how we feel (our emotions), and how we act (our behaviour) interact together (Ellis & Dryden 1987).

Ellis viewed the client as active in the process of identifying the emotional and practical problems in her or his life and working actively to change these. The goal of the therapist is to help a client to see that the negative emotions experienced are due to a flawed perception of reality. For example, if an individual believes that she is not likeable, she might experience a level of anxiety that makes it impossible for her to meet and socialize with others. With help, the client is able to gain a more accurate perception of reality, and is therefore able to challenge these troubling emotions, and work to change the undesirable behaviours such thoughts and emotions have produced. This process should take place in a supportive, nurturing relationship that is directed largely by the client.

Many social workers are drawn to this approach, since it encourages clients to exercise control and effect change in their lives. In addition, clear guidelines direct the therapeutic process, which can establish consistency among practitioners. The rational-emotive approach is limited, however, since these types of theories tend to discount the importance of the conditions in which such problems and solutions exist and largely ignore the structural or systemic context within which individual problems occur.

Cognitive-Behaviour Therapy

Another shorter-term approach is **cognitive-behaviour therapy (CBT)**, which views behaviours as learned and shaped by our interpretations of the world (our cognitions). When flawed or inaccurate, these interpretations can lead to irrational or maladaptive behaviours. Therapists using this approach work with clients to understand the thought patterns that bring about certain behaviours, as well as what is sustaining these patterns or behaviours. The next step is to help the client re-interpret events in her or his environment and reshape the conditions that are sustaining the negative behaviours. The focus of CBT is on problem-solving and promoting more accurate ways of understanding the world.

These therapies are particularly useful when working with people experiencing anxiety disorders, phobias, and mood disorders like depression. CBT focuses on the client's specific behaviours, and so does not view her/him as inherently pathological or flawed. The approach is guided by a series of well-articulated, technical procedures that make practice relatively uniform across practitioners. CBT has a strong record of effectiveness, which makes this a preferred practice approach for many agencies.

Mindfulness-Based Interventions

Mindfulness is often associated with Mindfulness-Based Stress Reduction (MBSR)—a group intervention. But it can be central for social workers in training to develop their capacity for empathy and compassion. Mindfulness is a way of paying attention, on purpose, to the present moment in a non-judgmental way. It can be cultivated using various exercises and with meditation.

Task-Centred Model

Developed in the 1980s, the **task-centred model** is a short-term therapy with a measurable outcome and proven effectiveness. This approach is based on the assumption that people experiencing particular problems typically have the resources and motivation to resolve them (Reid & Epstein 1977). Critical to a person's success is the extent to which personal, family, and environmental contexts support or impede the problem-solving efforts.

The task–centred model is particularly helpful in dealing with persistent problems like interpersonal or relationship conflicts, problems with role performance, difficulties in making decisions, and reactive emotional stress. Social workers assess and clarify the target problem and desired outcome, and create a list of tasks that must be accomplished in order to resolve the problem. The process of engaging with these tasks is as important as the eventual outcome, and so the support of the worker is essential.

TABLE 4.2: Practice Theory Timeline

Time Period	Emerging Practice Theories	Time Period	Emerging Practice Theories
Early 1900s	Scientific Philanthropy	1961–Mid-1970s	Generalist Practice Existential Therapy Gestalt Therapy Ego Psychology Cognitive Behavioural Therapy Crisis Intervention Problem-Solving Approach Integration Theory Communication Theory Mediation Theory Social Planning Theory Locality Development Theory Social Action Theory
1920s	Psychodynamic Perspective		
1930–Mid-1940s	Functional Theory	Mid-1970s–1990	Narrative Therapy Task-Centred Model Feminist Social Work Practice Ecological/Life Systems Theory Structural Approach Anti-Racist Social Work
Mid-1940s–1960	Client/Person-Centred Perspective Rational-Emotive Therapy Attachment Theory	1991–Today	Strengths-Based Social Work Mindfulness-Based Interventions Cognitive Therapy Anti-Oppression Approach Aboriginal Social Work

Toward a Personal Approach to Social Work Practice

Some social workers use the task-centred model to assist individuals who have persistent problems like emotional stress and interpersonal conflicts.

Often social work students, and even veteran practitioners, think they must adhere to *one* theoretical approach. This is not necessary or even desirable. All approaches to social work practice have something to offer. Look seriously at all approaches, for one or more is likely to resonate with your own experience and may fit better with your outlook on social work practice.

What Works for You?

It is not necessary to adhere strictly to one approach or another. Taking what you deem to be the best of each approach may make more sense to you in the context in which you find yourself.

When combining various theoretical perspectives, practitioners often take either an *integrative, eclectic,* or *dialectical* approach.

- With an **integrative approach** you, as a practitioner, would select concepts and methods from various sources and theories and build a unified system that fits you and is appropriate for the particular setting in which you work. This approach tends to draw theories together that are compatible (i.e. not containing opposing assertions).

- In contrast, an **eclectic approach** involves selecting concepts and methods, but it does not attempt to unify or integrate the pieces. It merely selects various concepts and methods as deemed appropriate. In this sense, an eclectic approach is extremely flexible.

- The **dialectical approach** involves a synthesis or combination of opposing assertions within theories. This approach incorporates concepts from differing approaches by holding in awareness the competing aspects of each differing theory. The dialectical approach encourages the drawing together of theories that may appear on the surface to contain opposing assertions. For example, Gestalt therapy addresses primarily inner personal dynamics, whereas critical social work emphasizes societal-level dimensions. Opposing contentions are recognized and held in awareness so that the practitioner can address all dimensions of a particular problem or situation in a coherent and reasoned manner.

Theory is important, to be sure, and a good grasp of social work theory is vital. But the determining factor in selecting a point of view should be what works for you, the social work practitioner, and especially what works for your clients. The overriding goal is to help them overcome the particular set of difficulties they are encountering at that moment in time to allow them to get on with their lives.

Conclusion

According to social work scholar Jan Fook, "a theory of practice consists of the general guidelines [that are used] to help translate broad theoretical concepts so that specific practice strategies and techniques can be devised" (Fook 1993, 40). Typically, practice theories include a way of understanding a person's personality and behaviour, a way of assessing the causes of the presenting problem, a way of establishing goals to guide helping, and strategies for reaching those goals.

There are dozens of theories or approaches to social work practice that appear in the literature today. An overview of these is provided in this chapter and summarized in Table 4.1. In a world that is so rapidly changing, and with a knowledge base that is always growing, it is only natural that such a range of methods for doing social work exists.

By its very nature, boundaries of concern in social work are wide, encompassing individual psychology, community development, political change, and so forth. In general, social work practice is considered "eclectic" with respect to theory, since we draw from an entire range of theoretical frameworks to inform the way we practice. The presenting needs and concerns, as well as our own foundation knowledge and practice knowledge, will shape how we respond to a particular issue that presents itself to us.

The chapters that follow examine social work with various groups in society and within social service agencies. As you work through these chapters, and as you encounter specific casework situations, keep in mind the range of theories and approaches that have been surveyed in this chapter, and how these theories might be helpful in shedding light on, and ultimately in finding solutions to, different types of problems.

CHAPTER REVIEW

Key Terms

- Social work theory
- Individual-level theory
- Structural-level theory
- Functional theory
- Strengths-based perspective
- Social systems theory
- Structural approach
- Critical social work
- Empowerment
- Feminist social work practice
- Anti-oppressive practice (AOP)
- Anti-racist social work
- Diagnostic and Statistical Manual of Mental Disorders
- Psychodynamic perspective
- Mindfulness-based interventions
- Existential therapies
- Gestalt therapy
- Client- or person-centred perspective
- Cognitive behavioural approaches
- Narrative therapy
- Rational-emotive psychotherapy
- Cognitive-behaviour therapy (CBT)
- Task-centred model
- Integrative approach
- Eclectic approach
- Dialectical approach

Review Questions

1. What is the difference between individual- and structural-level practice theories in social work? Why is each type important?

2. Select three of the social work practice theories discussed. What are some of the strengths and limitations of these theories?

3. Consider the similarities and differences between a client-centred/person-centred approach and rational-emotive psychotherapy. How might each explain the social problem of alcohol addiction and propose solutions to address this issue?

4. Use the main ideas of ecological/systems theory and the structural approach to analyze the growing problem of homelessness among youth. What are the similarities and differences between these perspectives?

5. Review the theories discussed in this chapter and describe which approach to social work practice feels most natural to you at this point in time, and why. If more than one theoretical approach appeals to you, explain why a combined approach seems better suited to your style of social work intervention. Give examples of how your approach might be applied to a specific social work problem.

Exploring Social Work

- - - - - - - - - - - - - - -

1. Use the Internet to look up some current approaches to social work practice that are based on the psychodynamic perspective and the ideas of Sigmund Freud (e.g., attachment theory, play therapy). How have these contemporary theories built on Freud's ideas about anxiety and the unconscious?

2. Imagine that you are a practitioner working in a community health centre located in an economically disadvantaged part of the city. Recently, you have noticed that there is an increase in the number of older women of colour seeking services for anxiety and depression. Using an AOP approach, what might be some of the issues you should consider when assessing and working with these clients?

Websites

- - - - - -

Association for the Development of the Person-Centered Approach
www.adpca.org

The Association for the Development of the Person-Centered Approach is an international network of individuals who advance the person-centered approach. The site offers an excellent collection of articles on this approach, which seems to be making a comeback among social workers.

Critical Social Work
www.criticalsocialwork.com

An online journal with articles on how social work can contribute to social justice. In part, the goal of the Critical Social Work site is to assist in collectively recognizing the current potentials for social justice as well as the future possibilities. Theorists propose that through dialogue there exists the possibility of refining our ideas about the individual and community, clarifying the relationship between interpersonal relations and institutional structures, and identifying actions that promote both individual and community well-being.

CHAPTER 5

SOCIAL WORK AS A PROFESSION

People Making a Difference

According to available census data, there were 1,056 self-described social workers in 1931, the first year for which data is available. Thirty years later, in 1961, there were 10,854 social workers. As a result of the funding made available after the passage of the Canada Assistance Plan in 1966, there was enormous growth in the number of social workers in the following years. By 1991, the number of workers had reached 61,135. In 2004, the combined total number of social workers and community and social service workers was 121,800 (43,000 social workers and 78,800 community and social service workers). Of the 43,000 social workers, 28,689 registered with their provincial regulatory bodies in 2004 (CIHI 2006a, 231).

According to www.jobfutures.ca, a website maintained by Service Canada, approximately 80 percent of social workers and 75 percent of community and social service workers are women.

The Growth of the Profession

Of course, this growth in the number of social workers reflects the expansion of social services and income security programs over this period, particularly in the 1960s when significant new money was put into child welfare and income security (see Chapter 3, page 50). As the importance of social welfare programs increased, and as more and more people were involved in providing these services, a higher level of organization and a greater degree of professionalization were required. Also, important legislation was passed by provincial legislatures to meet the increasing demands for social services, and provincial associations were created to help train and organize social workers at the local level. Training and professional programs were introduced to accommodate this expansion, and codes of practice were elaborated to ensure quality service.

Social Work Associations

The profession of social work in Canada is regulated by ten provincial associations and one territorial organization, each with its own name, policy, and regulations. Each association is mandated by provincial legislation to regulate and monitor professional social workers and social work practice in their jurisdiction. Each province has established regulatory bodies (sometimes referred to as *colleges*) to govern the profession in accordance with the legislation. Social workers become registered or licensed by becoming members of the regulatory body in the province where they work.

The associations come together under the umbrella of the *Canadian Association of Social Workers* (CASW), which provides national leadership in strengthening and advancing the social work profession. The education of social workers is monitored by the national *Canadian Association for Social Work Education* (CASWE).

The Canadian Association of Social Workers (CASW)

The **Canadian Association of Social Workers** was founded in 1926 after close to 60 social worker representatives from Winnipeg, Toronto, Ottawa, Halifax, and Montreal met and agreed to form a Canadian association. On September 1, 1926, the constitution for the Canadian Association of Social Workers was approved. Initially, social workers joined individually; there were 197 initial members. Today, the CASW is a federated organization with member organizations across the country. The first edition of its professional journal, *The Social Worker*, appeared in 1932. A simple code of ethics was adopted in 1938 and a significantly revised code was adopted in 1956 (revised or amended in 1963, 1983, 1994, and 2005). The 2005 *Code of Ethics* is discussed later in this chapter and is included in the Appendix to this book (beginning on page 357).

Job Futures

www.jobfutures.ca

This Service Canada website provides an overview of occupations in Canada, including employability prospects.

The Canadian Association of Social Workers (CASW)

www.casw-acts.ca

CASW is a national professional organization of social workers.

The CASW has jurisdiction over some issues, while the provincial associations maintain jurisdiction over others. Because social services are a provincial responsibility in Canada, the provincial associations assume great importance in the development and administration of social work. The CASW assesses foreign social work credentials to evaluate equivalency with Canadian standards; Quebec and British Columbia have separate provincial evaluations.

Data on the membership of the CASW is an indication of the rapid growth of the profession: in 1939, CASW had 600 members; by 1966, it had 3,000; and by 1986, there were 9,000 members. Today, there are about 16,000 CASW members across the country, all with some formal credentials in social work.

CASW supplies members with relevant professional documents, a national journal, activities and events, access to benefits, representation nationally and internationally, and an opportunity to participate in professional development panels and organizations. CASW also influences governments through consultations, position statements, and the presentation of briefs. The main benefit of belonging to the CASW is being part of a group of like-minded people who share the same goals and who work together to improve their profession.

All provinces have introduced legislation that will give more control over the title and practice of social workers. Employers frequently ask that their employees be members of CASW or their provincial association. Social workers, in turn, have supported this move as a way to protect the public and to guarantee a level of professionalism. Like the provinces themselves, the associations vary in terms of their level of organization, their activities, and their priorities.

The Canadian Association for Social Work Education (CASWE)

Canadian Association for Social Work Education

www.caswe-acfts.ca/en

This is a voluntary organization of universities and colleges offering social work and social service workers programs in Canada.

The Canadian Association of Schools of Social Work (CASSW) was established in 1967, replacing the National Committee of Schools of Social Work, which, since 1948, had been the forum for programs offering professional education in social work. Since 2008, CASSW has been called the **Canadian Association for Social Work Education** (CASWE). The CASWE is a national association of university faculties, schools, and departments offering professional education in social work at the undergraduate, graduate, and post-graduate levels. There is not a specific association representing college-level social service work education.

The purpose of the CASWE is to advance the standards, effectiveness and relevance of social work education and scholarship in Canada and, through participation in international associations, in other countries. The CASWE is responsible for reviewing and approving social work education programs. It also publishes a quarterly journal entitled the *Canadian Social Work Review* and undertakes research studies of relevance to the profession.

The International Federation of Social Workers (IFSW) and the International Association of Schools of Social Work (IASSW)

The **International Federation of Social Workers** is a successor to the International Permanent Secretariat of Social Workers, founded in Paris in 1928. In 1950, the IFSW was created, with the goal of becoming an international organization of professional social workers. Today the IFSW represents over half a million social workers in fifty-five countries. The IFSW promotes social work as a profession, links social workers from around the world, and promotes the participation of social workers in social policy and planning at the national and international levels.

The **International Association of Schools of Social Work** is an association of educators and institutions involved in social work education worldwide. It helps to promote social work education, facilitate mutual exchanges, and represent social work educators at the international level. The IASSW adheres to all UN Declarations and Conventions on human rights, while recognizing that respect for the inalienable rights of the individual is the foundation of freedom, justice, and peace.

Regulating the Social Work Profession

Each Canadian province or territory has extensive legislation governing the practice of social work, most of which has come into effect in the last 30 years. Manitoba was the first to enact legislation, in 1966, and Ontario was the last, passing social work legislation in 1998.

In general, each Act governs who can call themselves a social worker, the qualifications required to use the title, and penalties for contravening the Act or for unethical behaviour. For example, in British Columbia, the *Social Workers Act* (1979) provides for the control of the use of the title Registered Social Worker and stipulates that whoever contravenes these provisions commits an offence and is liable to a fine of not more than $1,000. It also specifies that a Board of Registration be appointed by the Lieutenant Governor in Council to enforce the Act. Similarly, the *Manitoba Institute of Registered Social Workers Incorporation Act* (1966), provides for voluntary registration and control of the designation Registered Social Worker. The Board of the Manitoba Institute of Registered Social Workers requires either a BSW or an MSW from an accredited institution or the equivalent as they determine.

In 1998, the Ontario government enacted the *Social Work and the Social Service Work Act*, which stipulates that any practitioner wishing to use the title Social Worker/Registered Social Worker or Social Service Worker/Registered Social Service Worker must be a member of the Ontario College of Social Workers and Social Service Workers. The College's regulatory functions include a complaints and disciplinary process that can result in suspension or revocation of a license to practice.

International Federation of Social Workers

www.ifsw.org

IFSW is an international organization for social work professionals based in Switzerland.

International Association of Schools of Social Work

www.iassw-aiets.org

IASSW is an worldwide network of social work educational institutions based in Ethiopia.

The Roles of the Social Worker and Social Service Worker

The roles of social workers and social service workers as defined by various provincial regulatory bodies are largely the same. The exception is the provision of diagnostic services which are generally only the purview of social workers. For example, the Ontario College of Social Workers and Social Service Workers specifies the scope of practice of the profession of social work as the assessment, diagnosis, treatment, and evaluation of individual, interpersonal, and societal problems through the use of social work knowledge, skills, interventions, and strategies, to assist individuals, dyads, families, groups, organizations, and communities to achieve optimum psychosocial and social functioning. When they specify the scope of practice for social service workers, they use exactly the same words but omit "diagnosis" and "psychosocial."

Qualified social workers (not social service workers) may diagnosis a mental illness and provide psychotherapy.

Community centres like Trefann Court in Toronto (pictured here in 1973), are increasingly used as a way of effectively delivering coordinated services to whole communities.

A practitioner may assume a number of different *social worker roles*, depending on the nature of their job and the approach to practice that they use. The role that is selected and applied should ideally be the role that is most effective with a particular client in the particular circumstances.

Social Worker Roles

- Enabler
- Broker
- Advocate
- Initiator
- Mediator
- Negotiator
- Activist
- Educator
- Coordinator
- Researcher
- Group facilitator
- Public speaker

- The role of *enabler* involves the worker in helping people organize to help themselves; for example, helping a community identify problems, explore and select strategies, and organize and mobilize to address the problems.

- A *broker* links individuals and groups who need help; for example, linking a woman who is abused by her spouse to a shelter for battered women.

- In the role of *advocate*, the worker provides leadership in advocating on behalf of a person or in challenging an institution's decision not to provide services.

- The *initiator* calls attention to problems or the problems a particular policy or program may cause.

- The role of *mediator* involves participating as a neutral player in a dispute between parties to help them reconcile differences or achieve mutually beneficial agreements.

- As a *negotiator*, the social worker is allied with one side in a dispute and tries to achieve agreement by bargaining on his or her client's behalf.

- The *activist* seeks to change institutions and structures in society, helping to organize people to shift power and resources to oppressed or disadvantaged groups.

- As an *educator*, the social worker is providing information and awareness of problems and solutions.

- The social worker is frequently a *coordinator*, bringing all the pieces together in an organized manner to accomplish a task.

- As a *researcher*, the social worker provides resources for clients and stays abreast of her or his field.

- The *group facilitator* may lead a group activity as part of group therapy, a self-help group, or any other type of group.

- The social worker may be engaged as a *public speaker* at schools, for service organizations, with police, or within related agencies.

Whatever the particular context that social workers find themselves in, they must apply themselves at all times in a professional manner, using all the knowledge and skills they have at their disposal and taking into account the specific needs of the client and the range of interventions currently available.

Comparing Social Work, Psychology, and Psychiatry

Canadian Psychiatric Association

www.cpa-apc.org

The Canadian Psychiatric Association is the national voluntary professional association for Canada's 4,000 psychiatrists.

Canadian Psychological Association

www.cpa.ca

The association's goals are to improve the health of Canadians, and to promote both excellence and innovation in psychological research, education, and practice, and the development, dissemination, and application of psychological knowledge.

There is significant overlap between the three helping professions—social work, psychology, and psychiatry. However, the focus of attention of each can be quite different, with social work emphasizing the individual within the context of a broader social environment and the interaction between the two.

Psychology tends to focus on individual behaviour and internal thoughts and feelings. Psychiatry, on the other hand, focuses on mental illness (and psychiatrists are qualified to prescribe medications). Social workers and psychologists will use similar counselling or psychotherapy methods, but social work tends to focus more on family, community, and other systemic or structural factors.

The profession of social work is unique in the way that it views and treats people. Its dual focus on the individual and the environment and structures (which include family, community, school, economic, and social structures) casts a wider net in identifying the roots of individual social problems. This is not to say that social workers do not provide services directed at the individual. They certainly do and in some cases this may be the focus of intervention.

Integrated Service Delivery (ISD)

Increasingly, social and health services are being provided to Canadians using **integrated service delivery (ISD)**. The ISD model recognizes that individuals or families coming to an agency for help often have a variety of needs. It is therefore important that programs coordinate effectively so that all needs are met.

Integrated Service Delivery

Integrated service delivery is a team-based and client-focused model. This approach enables people to access services in one location but from a variety of service providers.

Social workers are playing a key role in these integrated service delivery systems. With their multi-disciplinary and collaborative skills, they act as case managers and service planners and provide direct services to those members of the community who are in need.

In Manitoba, for example, a long list of services—including child and family services, child daycare, children's special services, mental health, employment and income assistance, home care, housing, and supported living—can be accessed in a **community access centre**. A community access centre is a place to get program information and services, fill out applications, and ask questions. In such centres, individuals can access more than one service, which is then delivered by a service delivery team following a carefully worked-out service plan.

Similarly, in Ontario, Community Care Access Centres are funded and legislated by the Ministry of Health and Long-Term Care, and are connectors to home care, long-term care destinations, and other services in the local community. The centres provide innovative, cost-effective ways to provide people with high-quality services and health care.

CASW's *Code of Ethics*

The CASW has a code of ethics and guidelines to help guide social workers in the course of their work. The 1994 code was replaced by two documents in 2005: the *Code of Ethics* and the *Guidelines for Ethical Practice*. These documents should be studied carefully by those entering the profession. The *Code of Ethics* is reproduced in the Appendix to this book (beginning on page 357).

Core Values

The **Code of Ethics** sets out values and principles to guide social workers' professional conduct. It does not provide a set of rules that prescribe how social workers should act, but its contents can be used to formulate more specific standards of practice. According to the *Code of Ethics* (2005) social workers uphold six core values:

- Value 1: Respect for Inherent Dignity and Worth of Persons
- Value 2: Pursuit of Social Justice
- Value 3: Service to Humanity
- Value 4: Integrity of Professional Practice
- Value 5: Confidentiality in Professional Practice
- Value 6: Competence in Professional Practice

Code of Ethics, 2005

The CASW *Code of Ethics* lays out a set of six guiding principles that form the basis of ethical practice. It does not prescribe how social workers should act, but provides guidance that can be used to formulate specific standards.

The *Guidelines for Ethical Practice* (CASW 2005b) are a companion document to the *Code of Ethics*, providing guidance on ethical practice by applying the values and principles in the *Code* to common areas of social work practice. Whether dealing with **voluntary clients** (people who have chosen to seek the services) or **involuntary clients** (those who are legally obligated to accept services, such as prisoners on parole or children in care), social workers have a responsibility to address their clients' needs while respecting their dignity and self-worth.

According to C.S. Levy (1993), codes of ethics focus typically on three broad types of principles. Identifying these three dimensions can help one gain a better understanding of the various aspects of professional ethics.

- *Normative standards* identify what the expected standard should be.
- *Aspirational ethics* identify the principles that professionals should attempt to reach.
- *Prescriptive ethics* refer to behaviours to which professionals are held accountable to uphold.

The CASW code (referring to values and principles) is concerned with the first two aspects of ethics (normative and aspirational). Prescriptive ethics are contained in the *Guidelines for Ethical Practice*—a breach of these may form the basis for disciplinary action. These correspond to what are referred to as *Ethical Responsibilities* in the CASW *Guidelines for Ethical Practice*.

Child welfare workers attend to the child's best interests above all else.

As with other professionals, and arguably more so given the nature of their work, social workers regularly face situations that demand a clear understanding of ethical obligations and responsibilities. For this reason, social workers must have a comprehensive and solid understanding of the CASW *Code of Ethics,* the *Guidelines for Ethical Practice,* and any provincial code, if they are different. But even this is not enough. Practitioners also need to know workplace and legislated guidelines and obligations and how these apply in any given context.

Ethical codes and guidelines for practice try to define values and acceptable behaviour, but they can only provide very broad guidelines for resolving dilemmas and not specific answers to localized problems. Ethical dilemmas exist when there are conflicts between different values. More often than not, the situation is complex and the ethical issues are not easy to unravel, let alone act upon.

An often-cited example of this is the potential conflict that arises if a client voices an intention to hurt someone. This presents a clash between a client's right to confidentiality and the rights of society to protection from harm. Situations like this are not uncommon in the field.

The Ambiguity of Social Work

The **ambiguity of social work** refers to the fact that the social worker frequently has to balance urgent and practical intervention measures with more difficult ethical and sometimes "political" questions. In the course of their work, for example, social workers are inevitably confronted with situations in which the policy and regulations of the agency conflict with what they, as experienced social workers, see as being in the best interests of their client. As well, the standards and ethics of the profession may be inconsistent with the established procedures and practices of a particular agency. Balancing one's beliefs, professional standards, and agency rules can be difficult. In this context, the social worker's place of employment can be either a source of empowerment or a source of distress.

For example, ethical dilemmas often arise in income support and child custody cases. Based on their assessment, welfare workers often refer clients to particular services for which they qualify. However, part of the mandate of welfare organizations is to spend public money wisely. Therefore, welfare workers must ensure that the client is genuinely in need and eligible for assistance, while representing the client's interests as fairly as possible. Striking a balance is often easier said than done.

Similarly, in child custody cases (where a child welfare worker is expected to act in the best interest of the child), the social worker may be criticized for leaving a child in the home or for taking the child away from its family prematurely. Such dilemmas are obviously aggravated when there are large caseloads or tight budgets that make it difficult for social workers to provide services in a way that is consistent with their professional and personal beliefs.

Many introductory texts present the delivery of social services in an idealized form, assuming that the professional's relationship with the client will always be governed by an exclusive concern for the client's well-being. Unfortunately, this is not always the reality. While staffed with the most dedicated and hard-working people, many social work agencies may enforce rigid rules and regulations, engage in excessive paperwork, and enforce computerized control over the client–social worker relationship. And too often, such rigid controls are at direct odds with the needs of the client.

The working life of a social worker is very much a mix of the "ideal" and the "practical," balancing the profession's high ideals with the reality of institutions and laws that can limit the capacity of an individual to deliver on such ideals. In the face of many difficulties, individual social workers make judgments based on their knowledge and experience and, in the end, that is all they can be expected to do. Then again, those entering the profession normally do so hoping the journey will, on the whole, be satisfying, but knowing that it will not always be simple or easy.

Ethical Decision-Making

Social workers often confront ethical issues. For example, a client may present a gift to show their appreciation. Or, they may tell you something that is (or is not) questionable under the law. In many cases a social worker may be legally obliged to pursue a course of action (e.g., with respect to privacy and access to information). How does one react in such situations? To deal with ethical issues, consider the following five-step process.

First, identify the key ethical issues in the situation. Second, the relevant ethical guidelines within your province's social work code of ethics or any employer-based ethical guidelines must be identified. Third, identify which ethical principles are of major importance in this particular situation and which are not. This is the rational and straight-forward part of the process.

Then, you should acknowledge and examine your own emotions and values. This is where virtue-based ethical decision-making may be helpful. Virtue ethics takes the stance that social workers are motivated to be virtuous and caring because they believe it is the right thing to do (see Table 5.1). Using this approach, there is no step-by-step method but the following five questions may help in ethical decision-making:

1. What are my feelings and intuition telling me to do?
2. How can my values inform my decision? Will they hinder or help?
3. How will other people be affected by my decision?
4. How would I feel if this decision was made public?
5. What decision would best define who I am as a person?

Finally, in the fifth step the social worker determines a concrete action plan that will be most helpful in the situation.

The Ambiguity of Social Work

By virtue of their close working relationship with clients in a caring context, social workers often must face balancing an urgent and practical intervention that might help to remedy a difficult situation with more difficult ethical concerns.

The Education of Social Workers

Whatever type of work is pursued, some post-secondary education is required in order to practice in the field of social work. In general, a university-trained person is referred to as a "social worker," whereas a community college-trained individual is called a "social service worker." In some provinces, and in everyday contexts, this distinction is often ignored, though obviously university-trained individuals will have more years of training behind them.

The first trained Canadian social workers graduated from the University of Toronto's Department of Social Services in 1914. Until the early 1970s, social work schools in Canada were accredited by the American Council of Social Work Education. There are now thirty-five universities offering social work degrees and forty-six community colleges offering diplomas, which are accredited by the CASWE. According to Canadian Institute for Health Information data, 2,856 students graduated from undergraduate and graduate programs in 2004, and over 400 faculty are employed to teach them (2006b, 230).

A Bachelor of Social Work (BSW) normally requires four years of university study. At least one additional year of graduate study is required for the Master of Social Work (MSW) degree. A Diploma in Social Service Work from a community college requires at least two years of training. Those holding a non-social work undergraduate degree normally must complete two years of study for a Master of Social Work degree. There are currently twenty-nine MSW programs offered in Canada.

Post-graduate study leading to a doctoral degree in social work is normally pursued by those who wish to teach at a university or those involved in high-level research, social policy, or large-scale administration. Seven Canadian universities offer PhDs in social work.

Employment Opportunities in Social Work

The career opportunities for qualified social workers today are quite diverse, ranging from various public institutions to private practice and within many different fields of experience.

- **Health and social services.** Job settings in this area include family and child welfare agencies, hospitals and other health care facilities, group homes and hostels, addiction treatment facilities, and Social Assistance offices.
- **Government services.** A large number of social workers work directly for some level of government, although this setting is declining as more and more services are devolved to community agencies. These services include planning and administration of programs, correctional facilities, and the justice system.

- **Communities.** Community organizers work out of community health centres, resource centres, and other grassroots organizations and provide counselling and support to local communities.
- **Research.** The federal, provincial, and local governments frequently call upon social workers to conduct surveys and carry out research that affects social work practice in various settings.
- **Self-employment.** A small but growing number of social workers are self-employed, offering services directly to the public for fees or contracting their services to large organizations.

TABLE 5.1: Values, Beliefs, and Attitudes that Influence Social Work Practice

Values that Hinder Social Work	Values that Help Social Work
To accept help from others is a sign of weakness.	To accept help is a sign of strength.
Some people are just not deserving of our respect or caring.	Everyone has intrinsic worth and the capacity to be productive.
People are inherently evil. Unless you are careful, they will take advantage of you.	People are essentially good.
I know what is best for my clients.	People are capable of finding their own answers and making decisions.
It is essential that my clients like me.	The purpose of counselling is to help clients exercise choice, not to make clients like me.
I've been there myself, so I know what my clients are feeling.	I can't know what my clients are feeling until I take the time to let them teach me.
People are incapable of changing.	People can and do change.
My religion/culture/viewpoint is the best.	I can accept a wide variety of cultures, religions, and viewpoints.
In this world, it's survival of the fittest.	We depend on one another and we have a responsibility to help others.
Counsellors have a right to impose service when it is in their client's best interest.	Clients have a right to refuse service.

Source: Bob Shebib. 2007. *Choices: Interviewing and Counselling Skills for Canadians.* 3rd Ed. Toronto: Pearson Education Canada. page 57. Reprinted with permission by Pearson Education Canada, Inc.

Newfoundland and Labrador social workers, who are members of the provincial NAPE union, protest increased workload and chronically low wages.

Unionization and Salaries

Today, most Canadian social workers are members of **public sector unions**. Indeed, the social work profession was part of the wider unionization of the public sector during the 1960s and 1970s, when, for the first time, public sector employees were permitted to join a union.

Of course, there was some debate over whether social workers should join trade unions, because social workers had their own professional associations, and trade unions were traditionally associated with industrial workers (not those who were professionally trained). This matter was resolved, in the end, by a division of labour. The associations represent social workers in issues pertaining to the development of the profession, the education of their members, and in discussions of social issues and social policy. The unions represent them in the areas of pay or working conditions. The professional association and the union in effect complement each other and both have mandates to act as voices for those they represent.

According to 2008 Service Canada data, 69 percent of social workers belong to unions, compared with 32 percent for all occupations. Forty-five percent of community and social service workers are unionized. The largest unions representing social workers in Canada are the Canadian Union of Public Employees (CUPE) and the Public Service Alliance of Canada (PSAC). CUPE members are represented by provincial level divisions and sectors. For example, the membership of CUPE Ontario is broken down into five principal sectors: municipal, health care, school boards, university and social services. Social workers in children's aid societies, associations for community living, children's care centres, municipal social services, community agencies (such as women's shelters), and municipal and charitable homes for the aged are all unionized.

Salaries of Social Workers

Social workers have benefited from unions in ways similar to other workers. Unions have helped to raise salaries, improve working conditions, and enhance job security. Pressure from female social workers and from the broader women's movement has encouraged the unions to address issues important to women, such as equal pay, child care, maternity leave, pensions, and sexual harassment.

Unions in social work agencies have also played another important role that is less well recognized. Labour unions have, throughout history, advocated for improved social programs, income security, and social services. Programs such as Employment Insurance and medicare would not exist today without pressure from the labour sector. As these programs come under increasing pressure from funding cuts, the unions are again playing a key role in opposing cutbacks.

Social workers are generally among the lowest-paid service workers. Two main reasons have been advanced to explain why this is so. First, social workers are paid less because they work with underprivileged people who are themselves not highly respected and have little power. Second, the profession has always been seen as female-dominated (and since women in general are paid less than men, social work tends to pay less than male-dominated professions). Unfair as this may be, both explanations are undoubtedly a large part of the reason for the low wages (and, of course, beg even larger questions).

Cutbacks continue to affect the income of social workers. As well, all levels of government are moving towards "contracting out" the delivery of social services to the private sector, arguing that it will save money. Accordingly, social workers increasingly find themselves working for non-unionized, underfunded private agencies, and the wages of social workers are squeezed. With the likelihood of even deeper funding cutbacks in the near future, there will be an ever greater need for social workers, their associations, and their unions to be more forceful in demanding just compensation for their efforts.

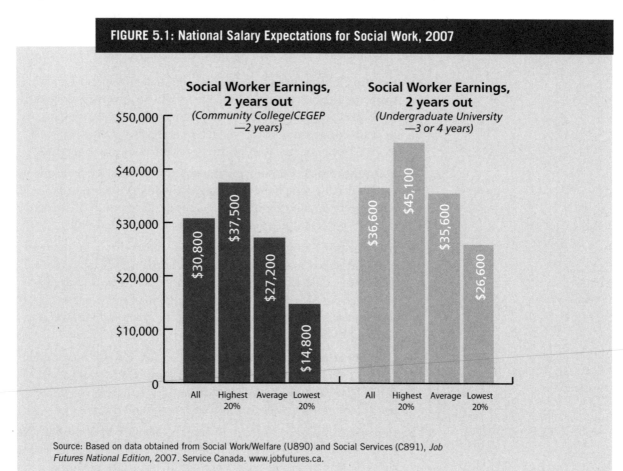

FIGURE 5.1: National Salary Expectations for Social Work, 2007

Social Worker Earnings, 2 years out (Community College/CEGEP —2 years)

	All	Highest 20%	Average	Lowest 20%
	$30,800	$37,500	$27,200	$14,800

Social Worker Earnings, 2 years out (Undergraduate University —3 or 4 years)

	All	Highest 20%	Average	Lowest 20%
	$36,600	$45,100	$35,600	$26,600

Source: Based on data obtained from Social Work/Welfare (U890) and Social Services (C891), *Job Futures National Edition*, 2007. Service Canada. www.jobfutures.ca.

The Future of the Profession

In Critical Demand: Social Work in Canada

www.casw-acts.ca

The most recent sector study of the profession was in 2000. It examined labour market trends, relevant demographics, and the social service sector. A copy of the executive summary can be found on the Canadian Association of Social Workers website.

The profession of social work currently finds itself facing a dilemma: there is an unprecedented demand for the skills and knowledge of social workers, but at the same time there is a devaluation of social services and of those providing them.

The devolution described above is causing shifts in the types of jobs and earnings of social workers. Social workers are increasingly finding jobs in community-based and non-institutional social services where they earn less, have fewer benefits, and have less security than government and hospital social workers.

Doing More with Less?

As a result, it seems likely that social service workers in the next period will be expected to do more with less funding, resulting in increased caseloads and a higher level of work-related stress. Moreover, as the use of computer and communications technology for case management and file recording intensifies, workers will need to be aware of the implications of this for judgments about client needs as well as client privacy.

The profession of social work will face significant challenges in the future. Several factors contribute to these challenges.

- **Funding cutbacks.** There is decreasing financial support and a weakening of public support for the work social workers do and for those they serve. Rising federal and provincial deficits will have to be reduced sooner or later, which will lead to substantial cutbacks in social service areas and ever more reliance on private services.

- **Demographics.** Demographics and, therefore, service demands are rapidly shifting. The population is growing older; common-law and lone-parent families are increasing, as is the proportion of children living in poverty; and immigration is creating cultural shifts.

- **Immigration and multiculturalism.** Canada is one of the most multicultural nations in the world. As Canada rightly continues to welcome people to this country, the difficulties, as well as excitement, associated with new families integrating into Canadian society, changing Canadian society as this process unfolds, will continue to dominate the field.

- **Globalization.** Social workers and social activists will increasingly confront the seemingly relentless integration of our world at the global level—economically, politically, and socially—over which local communities will seem to have less and less power.

- **Privatization.** There is trend toward the devolution of health care services from direct government delivery at the federal, provincial, and local levels to third-party community or private provision.

- **Technology.** Technology is good, for it enhances our ability to act, but social work is also a hands-on, caring profession where personal interaction is particularly important. Computerized, matter-of-fact solutions to difficult individual problems, in the absence of a caring social worker, can make a bad situation even worse.

- **Interdisciplinary practice.** Interdisciplinary teams that pool resources (social workers, psychiatrists, addictions counsellors, family-care workers, etc.) provide obvious advantages and economies of scale. Nevertheless, social workers and others will need to be attentive to the potential dangers, perhaps inherent in large-scale practice settings, of a lack of attention to the often very specific and complex needs of individuals and families.

- **Evidence-based practice.** There will be increasing pressures for social workers to show measurable results in relation to the kinds of interventions they use to help their clients. They will also need to keep in mind, as will their superiors, that resolving the most intractable personal and family problems usually takes time and patience and often requires various attempts and creative approaches.

Conclusion

There has been a tremendous increase in the number of practicing social workers and social service workers over the past fifty years. This reflects not only the need for their services but the complex nature of Western societies today. Certainly, without the efforts of committed social work practitioners, the day-to-day lives of a great many Canadian individuals and families would be much worse.

Increasingly, the task of the social work practitioner is legally defined or mandated and guided by professional standards. More often than not, however, situations arise for which there are no clear law or precedents. This is why values, training, and approach are so important and why there has been a significant expansion in the accreditation of social workers at colleges and universities.

The task of the social worker is to simultaneously act in the best interests of their clients and adhere to agency policies and procedures. These objectives are sometimes at odds with each other, and the social worker is left using all of his or her knowledge, experience, and skill to resolve the conflict. While ethical codes of practice are in place, none can address every particular complex situation as it arises. Inevitably, a great deal of discretion resides with the practitioner.

Above all, social work requires an commitment to the welfare of people, to the development of resources to meet individual and group needs, and to the achievement of social justice for all.

CHAPTER REVIEW

Key Terms

- **Canadian Association of Social Workers (CASW)**
- **Canadian Association for Social Work Education (CASWE)**
- **International Federation of Social Workers (IFSW)**
- **International Association of Schools of Social Work (IASSW)**
- **Integrated Service Delivery (ISD)**

- **Code of Ethics, 2005**
- **Community access centre**
- **Voluntary clients**
- **Involuntary clients**
- **Ambiguity of social work**
- **Public sector unions**

Review Questions

1. What are the main associations to which Canadian social workers belong?

2. Define the ambiguity of social work, and discuss its implication for direct practice.

3. Social work has its own code of ethics. What is the purpose of the code, and what are three of the key elements contained in the code?

4. Define and describe the various roles that social workers may take on in the course of their work.

5. How are the employment patterns of social workers changing and what are the implications for social workers?

6. What challenges do social workers in Canada face, and how will these challenges affect social workers and social work practice?

Exploring Social Work

1. The 2005 *Code of Ethics* contains a section that explains what is meant by Value 2: "Pursuit of Social Justice." Social justice has always been a key tenant of the social work profession. Read the section over twice and then meet in small groups to discuss the conception of social justice espoused in the *Code*. Is it a conception that advocates redistributive justice, equal access style justice, or social change oriented justice? How does this conception of social work fit with your personal values and beliefs?

2. Read more about the IFSW definition of social work at **www.ifsw. org** and compare this with the CASW definition as contained in the Preamble of the *Code of Ethics*. From your reading, are there any key differences in the two definitions. If so, what are the implications of the differences?

Websites

- - - - - -

Canadian Association of Social Workers
www.casw-acts.ca

The CASW website contains useful information about how the CASW represents Canadian social workers, information about the profession, and the status of professional legislation in each province.

Canadian Association for Social Work Education
www.caswe-acfts.ca/en

CASWE-ACFTS is a voluntary national charitable association of university faculties, schools, and departments offering professional education in social work at the undergraduate, graduate, and post-graduate levels. Check out their research reports, news, and school information.

International Federation of Social Workers
www. ifsw.org
The federation is a global organization striving for social justice, human rights, and social development through the development of social work, best practices, and international cooperation between social workers and their professional organizations.

CHAPTER 6

SOCIAL WORK WITH INDIVIDUALS AND FAMILIES

Applying Direct Practice Skills

Social workers may find themselves working in social policy and administration settings, but it is important to understand the processes and activities of direct practice or intervention. There are three main categories of direct practice: (1) social work with individuals, (2) group work, and (3) community work. These specializations or fields of direct intervention emerged in the 1940s. Today, many schools of social work use this breakdown for purposes of social work training.

Most social workers and social service workers will find themselves involved in one of these three forms of direct practice in their careers, and more likely they will be involved in all three. This requires that social workers have multiple skills and a broad-based perspective on social work practice. This chapter introduces the first of these fields and discusses the main activities a social worker is likely to encounter.

Introduction to Direct Practice

Social work practice essentially consists of a series or process of interventionist actions. The worker calls upon his or her repertoire of helping knowledge, skills, and values and applies it in particular ways in specific situations to achieve purposeful change. While each situation will require different interventions, the process or steps are essentially the same.

A useful analogy is that of a skilled dancer who knows the steps involved in a particular dance, but to be truly excellent, must re-combine the moves into new patterns. Social work requires this kind of artful improvising, or the ability to "think on one's feet."

Regardless of the approach taken to social work, it is important to have an understanding of all three fields of direct practice. Figure 6.1 indicates how each field influences the other and reveals that a primary intervention in one field may involve some level of intervention in the others.

Working with Individuals and Families

The process of helping individuals is sometimes called *social casework*, although this term is now infrequently used. A majority of social workers spend their time working with individuals in private or public agencies and increasingly in private practice, although this is still rare. Even though other types of social work are increasing, the practice of social work with individuals still predominates.

Individual social work is aimed at helping people resolve their problems or situations on a one-to-one basis—that is, helping unemployed people obtain work or training, providing protective services for abused children, providing counselling for mental health, providing parole or probation services, supplying services to the homeless and poor, coordinating services for people with AIDS, and coordinating discharge services for a person being released from hospital.

Social work with families involves working with a couple, or a child and a parent, or entire families to help them address specific situations or achieve purposeful change. Often the work focuses on communication or relationship difficulties, or on transitions or family crisis situations. Examples include: violence within the family, relationship breakdown, care for family members with disabilities or the elderly, issues at school, help for immigrant families, and families facing economic crisis.

The profession of social work has a long history of working with the needs of families and family members, predating that of many other professions. Social work models tend to emphasize empowering family members and developing more secure relationships between family members. When working with vulnerable families, such as families in transition (e.g., immigrant families, divorcing parents) and families living in poverty, the emphasis is on stabilizing connections with social institutions such as schools, churches, child welfare agencies, and hospitals.

Mapping Family Relations

It may be useful to visualize family relationships using a *genogram* (a graphic illustration of at least three generations). *Ecomaps* may also be used to illustrate the relationships between family members and institutions and to assess the social support and requirements for the family.

FIGURE 6.1: The Three Fields of Direct Practice

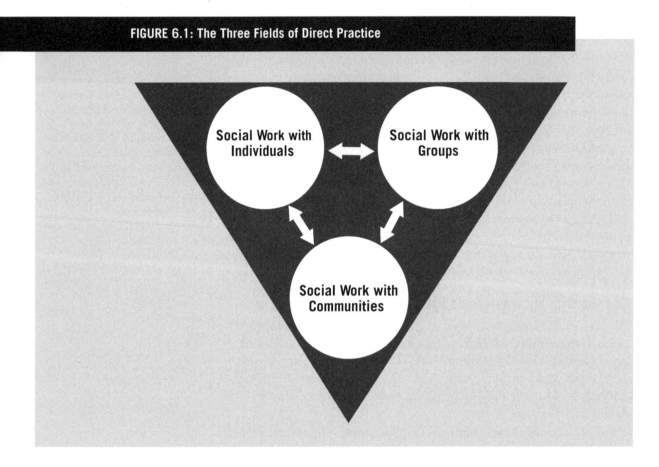

Beginning social work students may become confused by the wide array of ways to introduce social work practice with individuals and families. Some texts outline a series of steps, others emphasize a set of skills, and still others stress theories or models of practice. This text does not focus on one or another of these, but rather introduces all of them—stressing the helping relationship as a core element.

In general, social work practice involves a number of steps and within these steps different skills and theories are appropriate, as is a constructive relationship between client and workers. These steps are common to most social work interventions with individuals and families. Although assessment precedes intervention, and intervention precedes termination, the process can be cyclical. For example, during intervention the client and worker may discover new information that raises the need for more planning. In fact, each process is taking place throughout the intervention, but at each step, one or more is emphasized. The steps are guideposts that involve combining and re-combining actions into new ways of looking at things—that is, a process of **reflection–action–reflection**.

The Role of Critical Self-Reflection

Social work scholars, such as Bob Mullaly (2002), emphasize the importance of what is sometimes called "critical self-reflection" or "knowledge about oneself." This self-reflection helps social workers understand how their own identities, beliefs, and their professional and personal lives are shaped by forces in society such as the media, parental influence, educational institutions, and social structures.

Many beginning social workers find it useful to write a short description of themselves and then reflect on where they think these views come from and how these views might influence their perceptions of the people with whom they may eventually be working.

Clinical Social Work

When the term **clinical social work** appeared, critics equated it with casework and psychotherapy. Many viewed it as a means of treating personal pathologies while ignoring systemic factors. They viewed it as an effort to promote private practice with middle-class clients, and an attempt to achieve greater status.

The majority of social workers work with individuals and families in private or public agencies, and sometimes in private practice.

Since those early days, clinical social work has emerged to encompass a varied range of approaches and is not wedded to one theoretical perspective. Nowadays, critical, feminist, and structural social workers all use the term "clinical social work" to describe their work with individuals.

Throughout social work's history two key themes have distinguished it and have provided coherence to the professional activity of social workers: the person-centred perspective and the importance of the helping relationship. The first was discussed at length in Chapter 4 (see page 69) and the helping relationship is explored at the end of this chapter. Both ideas are part and parcel of all forms of clinical social work today.

Social work has been criticized by other therapy-oriented professions for not having extensive empirical research that demonstrates the effectiveness of various forms of intervention. (See page 108 for more on this "evidence-based practice" debate within social work.) Social work practitioners have largely turned a blind eye to this criticism. Instead, practitioners and scholars continue to distinguish themselves by focusing on vision- or values-based interventions, while emphasizing the ideas of client empowerment and supportive relationships.

Beginning students may find it a little disconcerting that social work as a profession appears not to have gone out of its way to justify its existence or to continuously validate its methods of intervention. However, social work practitioners are clearly very effective at what they do. Moreover, they perform an indispensable role. In the end, it may be that attitude and approach are as important, or even more important, to success than any particular technique that is used.

The Social Work Process

- - - - - - - - - - - - - - - - - - - -

The social work process outlined below consists of four broad stages: *intake, assessment and planning, intervention,* and *evaluation and termination.*

Intake

Intake is usually the first step taken by a worker when a client or family seeks help. Intake is a process whereby a request for service is made by or for a person, and it is then determined whether and what kind of service is to be provided. The social worker attempts to gather initial information in order to determine what assistance is needed, and whether the agency and worker is the appropriate provider. If it is mutually determined that the agency can be of service, then some sort of agreement or contract is made. When it is determined that the needs cannot be met by the agency, then a referral to a different service is made or a decision is made that no social work service is required.

During the intake phase, the client makes a personal request for help or someone from the community directs the client to a particular social work agency. The social work relationship can be either *voluntary* or *involuntary*. The intake step is voluntary when a client willingly seeks help from a social work agency. For example, a parent who recognizes the difficulties of caring for a child may approach a child welfare agency for assistance. By contrast, an involuntary client is ordered to see a social worker or is required to do so by law. For example, a social worker is required by law to assist a child in danger when, for example, the child's situation has been reported as unsafe by a physician, hospital worker, police officer, or school-teacher. In such cases, families are often uncooperative, especially if allegations of child abuse are reported.

In the intake step, the social worker acknowledges the client's need for help, collects information from the client, assesses the client's problem or situation and, based on the agency's resources, determines if the social work agency can help the client. In essence, when they first meet, both the worker and client want answers to specific questions. The applicant or potential client wants to know: Can I get the help I need here? Can this person help me? How can I get the help I need at this agency or with this person? The worker will ask: Can I help this person or would it be more appropriate for someone else to help? How can I help this person?

It is important in this phase for the social worker to clarify his or her role and purpose and the agency's role. The context of practice is particularly important during the intake phase. In some cases an agency mandated intake form or checklist is used. The social worker should ensure that there is some congruence between the mandate of the agency and the issues that are important to the client. In the case of an involuntary client this is assumed. Finding this congruence forms a kind of contract between client and agency, with the worker as the intermediary. The worker's function in this initial phase is a form of mediating an engagement between client and agency—a finding of common ground.

The social worker might start with an opening statement as follows:

> *My name is Ms. Harris, and I am a social worker here at the social work department. Your doctor has asked me to see you regarding your recovery from your operation and difficulties you might be having. This can be a difficult time and, if you wish, I could provide some assistance here.*

This straightforward statement sets the groundwork and then leaves it open to the client to clarify what the role of the worker might be from his or her perspective. Often it is preferred that the social worker does not specify what the client *should* be working on, but instead to explore what the client is *already* working on. This is both empowering for the client and builds on strengths.

This approach is rather different from the more traditional method of social casework, whereby the worker would administer diagnostic scales to determine the illness for which the worker would then provide treatment. This is not to say that these latter scenarios do not happen nowadays, just that it is probably better not to start this way.

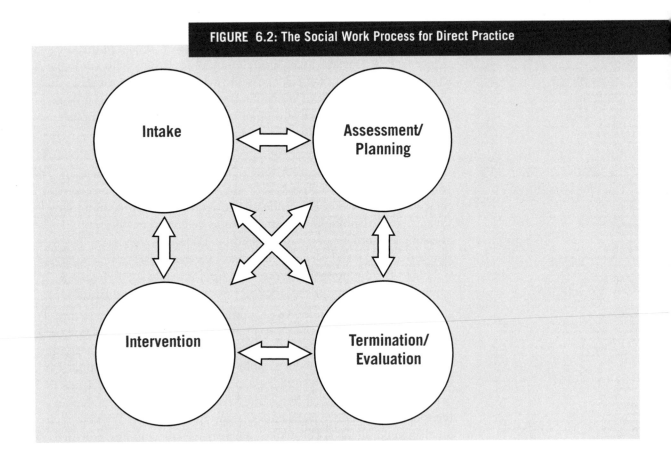

FIGURE 6.2: The Social Work Process for Direct Practice

Assessment and Planning

The assessment and planning step includes two processes. In the assessment process, the social worker and the client analyze what help is needed based on the client's ideas, thoughts, and feelings. Once the assessment is complete, the social worker formulates a plan in collaboration with the client that is designed to help the client with the particular problem. The plan is not set in stone but provides an initial course of action, and the client is a partner rather than simply a consulted party.

Many social work textbooks describe a process that involves problem definition, data collection, and "objective" recommendations. This type of model flows more from a management or bureaucratic approach to social work where the worker knows best and can rationally plan the optimal course of action. In this section, we are emphasizing a social work process that stresses reflection-action-reflection in which the social worker continually thinks things through while acting on the problem at hand *and always in consultation with the client.* She or he adapts the intervention based on dialogue and reflection on experiences of and feelings about past actions. **Assessment** is both a process and a product of understanding on which action is based (Siporin 1975, 219). It involves gathering relevant information and developing an understanding. How a social worker selects and analyzes information is accomplished with reference to the assumptions that underlie a particular social work theory or approach, and by one's own experience of the world. In order to form a plan in the assessment phase, the social worker also relies on other people who know the client personally. For example, in cases in which a client is provided with social services as a result of an involuntary intervention, the social worker may initially rely on information provided by a teacher, doctor, police officer, or elder as in a First Nations community.

Assessment involves the art of asking questions. Purposeful and well-timed questions are the cornerstone of the assessment phase. Social workers may used a structured interview whereby they ask a predetermined set of questions. This is the case in agencies (i.e. most child protection agencies) that require specific forms to be completed as part of the assessment. In other cases, unstructured interviews are the norm. This type of interviewing is still focused, but it takes a more conversational tone and is flexible. Beginning social workers must pay attention with the latter approach and ensure that the interview does not wander too far off topic.

Planning is based on sets of decisions made by the worker and the client that are shaped by the worker's analysis of the information collected in the assessment phase. The planned actions may be at a wide variety of levels: individual, environmental, multi-person, systemic, or structural. For example, they might involve therapeutic, educational, and social action-oriented approaches. What frequently varies between practice models is the focus of attention. A behaviour therapy approach would tend to focus on changing individual behaviours, whereas a social action or structural approach may focus on examining behaviours within their context, perhaps exploring how they might be changed, and working towards changing systems or structures in society in order to shift power relations. In any event, the social worker assesses the client's problem with the client and negotiates a plan with the client that includes:

- the type of actions or interventions
- the length of the intervention
- the frequency of their meetings and the desired effects
- the intervention plan (where a contract is made with the client)

The concept of empowerment is crucial in the planning phase. Chapter 1 defined and discussed this concept (see page 12). Here we examine how this is actually implemented in practice.

The foundation of empowerment is the notion that clients have the right to self-determination and are capable of discerning their best course of action. Often clients come with negative self-image and a feeling of powerlessness. Sexism or racism may have fed into this. This poses a challenge in taking an empowerment attitude. One response is to use a *mindfulness* approach to engage with clients to explore their thoughts, feelings, and body sensations. Clients are able to see self-deprecating thoughts as just thoughts and not who they are. They are able to learn that they have an effective intuitive sense that can be called upon to face life's difficulties. Other approaches might use *consciousness-raising* to initiate empowerment. Consciousness-raising encourages people to gain insight into their circumstances with a view to changing them. This notion is often associated with progressive, feminist, or structural approaches to social work (see Chapter 4), but it is increasingly becoming part of many other approaches. Consciousness-raising can involve one or more activities, including the provision of information concerning the social structures implicated in the person's situation, reflection based on the client's lived experience, sharing of common experience of the workers (if this is the case), or awareness exercises that cultivate insight. Part of the consciousness-raising process is *normalization*. Normalization highlights the notion that any particular difficulty that a person experiences is universal and not unique to any individual—that it is a normal part of being human or being part of a particular social grouping that is oppressed.

Intervention

The worker, the client, or both may undertake the **intervention** stage. The actions may be directed at the client, other individuals, family members, groups, communities, institutions, social policies, or political and social structures. Intervention is not always directed at the treatment of the individual alone. For example, where the social worker is using a structural or feminist approach to practice, the intervention will usually include some kind of organizational, community, or social action measures.

Self-Disclosure

Social workers often struggle with the appropriateness of sharing personal feelings with clients. This is usually discussed within the context of boundaries and there is no one answer. There are definitely times when beginning social workers should be careful in spontaneously expressing personal feelings. It is also important to understand the triggers and underlying issues that lead social workers to do so. On the other hand, such sharing can help demonstrate that it is common to have particular feelings. In the feminist approach, workers often share to illustrate common experience and draw the link to social structures. Workers will make mistakes and these mistakes form the basis of professional experience. What is frequently ignored is that clients can often forgive a mistake more easily than they can deal with a worker who seems perfect.

It is through the process of intervention that the worker and client implement the assessment and plans. The intervention undertaken is directed at meeting the client's needs as determined by the worker and client. In the intervention stage, the client shares with the social worker any information regarding what progress has been made in resolving the problem or situation. During this step, the social worker:

- establishes a rapport with the client.
- accompanies the client in the intervention.
- provides advice and support to the client.
- adjusts the intervention based on the client's information.
- helps the client to resolve the problem or situation by providing new knowledge and skills that assist in solving the problem or shift the relationship to the problem.

The intervention phase should focus on creating a dialogue between the client and worker and perhaps others involved in the situation. In situations where the uncertainties are large or numerous, it would be advisable to take small, cautious steps and then reflect on the experience. This will allow for an enhanced understanding of the situation and altering the course of action.

Evaluation and Termination

In the final step, *evaluation and termination*, the client and the social worker work together to assist the client to achieve a resolution to the original problem or situation, and to prevent the situation from occurring again. In this step, the social worker evaluates the following items with the client and the social work supervisor.

- the choice of the intervention
- the length of the intervention
- the frequency of their meetings
- the outcomes
- the need for any follow-up
- when to terminate the intervention

Evaluation is an ongoing part of the social work process. Evaluation should identify the rationale for the actions chosen, whether or not needs were met, the expected and unexpected effects, and alternative courses of action that may need to be taken.

Clients are usually not involved in the evaluation process because it is believed that specific skills are required and evaluation is focused primarily on issues of accountability. Increasingly, however, there is a recognition of the benefits of client participation: clients can have an insider's perspective on agency functioning, information can be validated, issues of confidentiality can be discussed, plans and contracts can be adjusted, knowledge and skills can be gained, the client–worker relationship may be strengthened, and clients can be empowered.

Intervention can take many forms, including dealing directly with an individual, or with communities and institutions, such as schools.

Termination, or the ending of the client–worker relationship, occurs ideally when the action plan is completed and the client's goals have been met. In the termination stage, essential records relating to the case are organized and stored.

The use of records raises concerns about the confidentiality of sensitive information: What constitutes the ethical disclosure of information about a client? In addressing this question, social workers are obligated to follow the guidelines of the agency or organization employing them. They must also obey legislation and association policy. The CASW Code of Ethics stipulates, at length, the requirements for collecting, recording, storing, and accessing client records.

Social workers must ensure that appropriate supports are in place before the intervention is ended. A client who has become reliant on assistance and interaction with the social worker may have difficulties with termination. Helping clients build their own support network is crucial. Such support may come from family and friends, informal helpers, self-help groups or through community or voluntary activities. If an empowerment perspective is taken, termination is often smoother.

The helping relationship requires empathy—without judging or even liking the person, a social worker tries to understand. This requires deliberate effort on the part of the social worker to be aware of his or her own emotions, assumptions, and reactions.

Direct Practice Skills

Interviewing vs. Dialoguing

The term *dialogue* may prove more useful than interview, as it denotes the two-way nature of the "interviewing" process. The etymological Greek origin of the word dialogue is diá (through) and logos (speech), denoting a coming together through speech. In addition, it is crucial to acknowledge that clients are interviewing us as much as we are interviewing them.

Social work practice with individuals and families involves a set of skills; while not mechanical in application, they can nevertheless be practiced. Often social work students will engage in role-playing exercises whereby one student takes the role of the client and another student acts as the social worker. This is an effective way to practice these skills.

The skill set for direct intervention should include the following techniques:

- **Listening.** Some say this is the first and most important skill, since it underlies many of the other skills. Without genuinely listening, the social worker cannot fully appreciate the message and feelings of the client.

- **Validating feelings.** A social worker validates a client's feelings by conveying an understanding of them. This builds a rapport and helps the client to identify and sort out a variety of feelings. The social worker must also consider non-verbal emotional responses in developing this understanding.

- **Interviewing or dialoguing.** Open-ended and closed-ended questions are used in an interview or dialogue to elaborate information. Open-ended questions give the client the opportunity to discuss in more depth the aspects of the problem that they see as important. The questions often begin with "how" or "what." Closed-ended questions give the social worker the opportunity to clarify details of the client's narrative. They are often used late in a session to check for accuracy.

- **Paraphrasing.** Paraphrasing is a basic social work communication skill. With paraphrasing the social worker re-states what the client has said in her or his own words. Social workers use paraphrasing to confirm that the meaning the worker has attached to a client's message is indeed the meaning intended by the client. It also provides feedback to the client. Beginning social workers need to be aware that overuse of paraphrasing can give the client the impression of being mimicked.

- **Clarifying.** This skill is used to determine if the worker and client are on the same "wavelength." You may, for example, pull together the essence of a situation in the form of a mini-summary, which can be used to compare your understanding of the particular situation with that of the client. It is often used to probe an issue that is not understood by the social worker. It involves asking for specific details about an event. Clarification often becomes a reciprocal process between the social worker and client as each tries to understand the true meaning of what the other is saying.

Direct Practice Skills

- Listening
- Validating feelings
- Interviewing or dialoguing
- Paraphrasing
- Clarifying
- Giving information
- Summarizing
- Interpreting
- Building consensus

TOP TEN DIALOGUING SKILLS

1. Being open to the client's lived experience, especially at the beginning.

2. Exhibiting warmth, empathy, and genuineness.

3. Listening and speaking in a way that benefits the client.

4. Ability to define "problems" from a wide perspective.

5. Ability to maintain a non-judgmental and accepting attitude.

6. Ability to reflect on sociological dimensions of an apparently individual problem.

7. Ability to elicit required information and feelings.

8. Ability to relate to client's and one's own emotions.

9. Ability to develop an egalitarian relationship as opposed to an authoritarian relationship.

10. Ability to let silences between the words be a part of the dialogue.

- **Summarizing.** This skill is used in attempts to capture or pull together the most important aspects of the problem or situation. It provides focus for the next interview and can assist in planning. Both the feelings and content of the client's message should be used. It is also useful when the social worker believes that it is time to move on to another topic.

- **Giving information.** Without overwhelming people with too much information at one time, the social worker often shares information about resources in the community (e.g., women's shelters) or information that shows that the client is not alone in experiencing the problem. Be sure the client realizes that they can refuse the information, and provide pamphlets or brochures where possible.

- **Interpreting.** This skill enables the social worker to delve into the presented problem and "read between the lines." By using this method, you may be able to "re-frame" the issue, giving it your own unique angle. The worker's insights may help the client develop a deeper understanding of what is really going on, and not just what appears to be happening. It may provide an alternative way of looking at the problem or a new frame of reference. Always check both verbal and non-verbal responses of the client to your interpretation.

- **Building consensus.** Consensus building attempts to work out an agreement on what should be done to address a problem. It may be easily attained or there may be discrepancies between what a client says they want and their behaviour, or between separate messages given by a client. Confrontation may be used to challenge a client to examine discrepancies. It should be non-adversarial, respectful, and used only when a safe and trusting relationship exists.

SOCIAL WORK IN A RURAL HEALTH CENTRE
A Role with Limitless Boundaries

As part of expanded services in community health centres, the River Valley Health Region of New Brunswick piloted two social work positions in 2003, one of which was in the Boiestown/Doaktown area known as Central Miramichi. When I arrived in Doaktown in the summer of 2004, the pilot project was complete, the position permanent, and the role of social work ready to unfold.

The primary concern in the two communities was the alarming increase in opiate drug use among youths. Within a few weeks, I was invited to attend public meetings of the Community Against Drug Addiction (CADA) and to help local parents lay the groundwork for a support group. We spent six months discussing topics and compiling a reference manual for future groups, and the following year the Community Health Centre staff agreed to pilot the first satellite methadone program in the region.

Currently, our team offers weekly service to twenty-two methadone clients. As the resident social worker, I am also a representative of the "Community Mobilization Pilot Project," a federally funded, joint program involving the University of New Brunswick, Addictions Services, and the Central Miramichi community.

A large percentage of social work intervention involves crisis management, and it is no different in a rural health centre. Suicide intervention, domestic violence, protection issues, and homelessness are part of my day-to-day involvement with the centre's clientele. Three and a half days are devoted each week to scheduled appointments in the local Doaktown community, and one afternoon and evening in the Boiestown community. Counselling referrals are made by my colleagues at the Health Centre—physicians, nurses, and practitioners in other disciplines—as well as by outside agencies or the clients themselves. Counselling addresses finances, coping, grief and loss, relationships, and addictions issues, to name a few.

The prevention and education component for this role is made possible through the annual PARTY (Prevent Alcohol and Risk-Related Trauma in Youths) Program. Each year, I make a presentation, along with practitioners from fellow disciplines, to grade 8 students bused in from Blackville, Doaktown, and Boiestown schools. As part of prevention, I designed and piloted a "Managing Emotions" program for teens in the local area; introduced an annual pumpkin give-away contest in the elementary school; and co-chaired a focus group for students in grades 10–12 on sexual health needs. I am also a member of the School Health Advisory Committee in the Boiestown/Doaktown Schools.

For two years I have offered one-on-one counselling services one morning a week to Doaktown School students, and last fall I was able to expand social work involvement to include weekly visits to the Boiestown School.

The Health Centre staff in this community has always offered public education sessions. With the expanded space available in our new facility, to which we moved in the winter of 2005, we have been able to increase the programming, and my role has been to organize, advertise, and help mobilize the monthly evening education programs. From these sessions evolved a regular following of about seven to ten seniors, and for four months (January–April) the nurse practitioner and I catered to topic requests from this particular audience.

I also manage to maintain a larger community connection with St. Thomas University through placement monitoring of students and as an annual presenter to the Gerontology Program. I have been guest speaker for Heart and Stroke sessions in several communities, and for three years was a guest speaker at the Community College LPN program in Fredericton. I was also pleased to be invited to speak to the first NICHE Geriatric Resource Nurse Course offered at River Valley Health last fall.

A great personal and professional opportunity arose in 2005, when I was asked to train as a facilitator in a Department of Health project called "Building a Better Tomorrow Initiative." I joined a team representing all the Atlantic Provinces involved in the design and implementation of five educational modules to be offered, as an initial step, to all Heath Centre personnel. As a trainer, I facilitated a series of education sessions on "Team Building" and "Community Development" among my colleagues from River Valley Health Region.

In March 2007, I celebrate twenty-four years in my career as a social worker. After years of searching, labelling, and adjusting, I find my role in this rural health centre setting to be the truest definition of "my kind" of social work. This role has limitless boundaries, leadership opportunities, team commitment modelling, community development initiatives, education/prevention programming, and counselling. I am a generalist, and to my way of thinking, I have arrived.

Source: Written by Nora Watson (RSW). Originally published by the Canadian Association of Social Workers. www.casw-acts.ca/practice/rural_e.pdf. Used with permission of the author.

The Helping Relationship

Often students are taught skills and theories of intervention and there is little discussion of the helping relationship. There is a renewed interest in this relationship in social work education due, in part, to recent research findings. Research has shown that this relationship accounts for as much as 30 percent of positive client outcome compared with only 15 percent attributable to the intervention model (Norcross 2002, 5). The helping relationship is at the heart of change. Students should not take this to mean that social work is merely a "go with your gut" or "common sense" approach to helping. Rather, it highlights the fact that the "intervention" model is only one dimension of effective practice.

The **helping relationship** refers to a partnering relationship between a client and a professional social worker in which it is expected that the client will confide personal information toward the attainment of specific goals and the practitioner will listen and become involved in a manner that benefits the client. The relationship involves a number of elements: deep listening by the practitioner, a sense of emotional bond between client and workers, and an agreement on treatment goals and tasks.

Psychologist Carl Rogers emphasizes three attributes: warmth, empathy, and genuineness.

- **Warmth.** Nowadays social workers rarely believe that they should keep clients at a distance. Too much emphasis on diagnostic labels and professional objectivity can interfere with developing a warm relationship. Social workers need to learn that it is safe to express their warmth and to let clients know that they care. Warmth is especially important during the early stages of intervention as trust and acceptance develop. *Warmth* communicates to the client that you are approachable and kind and genuinely care about them. This might involve simple courtesies such as offering a comfortable seat or a beverage or conveying warmth with eye contact. It does not imply that social workers engage in a lot of small talk. It is not a social visit. It does mean that we take the time to care about the client's physical needs and their state of mind, even if we are busy.

- **Empathy.** *Empathy* is the capacity to understand another person's subjective experience and their personal frame of reference by means of listening and curiosity directed at a deeper understanding. It is described as the ability to "put oneself into another's shoes." Such an understanding can generate powerful bonds of trust and rapport. Often it begins with acceptance and the suspension of judgment. Without judging or even liking the person, the social worker tries to understand. To be non-judging requires an intention on the part of the social worker to be aware of their emotions, assumptions, and reactions. It can take time to hone this kind of

The Helping Relationship

The relationship or partnership between a client and a professional social worker, in which the worker exhibits warmth, empathy, and genuineness toward the client.

attitude. Research studies have shown that a mindfulness practice (see sidebar on page 70) can help in facilitating this. Additionally, it is important not to become trapped in the suffering of the client. We need to be able to perceive and be open to the pain of the client, but at the same time be able to recognize an identification of or reaction to the pain.

- **Genuineness.** To be *genuine* is to be real and authentic in the helping relationship. It means not being phony, putting on false fronts, or hiding behind professional masks or roles. Central to this is self-awareness. Being aware of how you are feeling, what you are thinking, and even how your body might be reacting helps a social worker be genuine. In action, genuineness means that we are trustworthy and honest with clients. It is, however, important to recognize that doing no harm is also paramount. We need to be truthful, do no harm, and be timely in our communication.

Social Work as Art and Science

Beginning social workers may be inclined to look to science to validate their actions and choices. Referred to as **evidence-based practice**, this approach asks social workers to locate empirical studies to determine how best to relate to a situation presented by a client or family.

Evidence-Based Practice

A broad trend or movement that seeks empirical evidence to validate alternate kinds of social work practice interventions.

The evidence-based practice movement is based on the belief that the most important question is which theory or intervention is most effective with which particular problem or diagnostic category. But that belief has been challenged by research findings. For example, studies have found that different therapies produce similar positive therapeutic outcomes (e.g. Luborsky 1976). Other studies have found that very little of the variance in therapeutic outcomes is due to the treatment model that is used (e.g. Lambert & Barley 2001). Social work researcher Hugh England noted,

> that the practice of social work is simply too complex an activity, and one embedded with particular meanings, to be described only as a science: An assessment of the nature of social work must necessarily include an examination of social work as art as well as social work as science; both are clearly integral and essential parts of the whole. (England 1986, 115)

Historically, social work practitioners have emphasized an experiential understanding rather than the findings from large-scale empirical studies. In contrast, psychologists and psychiatrists have tended to focus on empirically validated treatments and pharmacology. More recently, however, many therapists and helping professionals have gravitated toward a more holistic and artistic understanding of practice.

Conclusion

Social work practice with individuals and families moves from intake, assessment and planning to intervention. The intervention is the action stage in which the issues and concerns of the client are addressed. These interventions will not only be directed at the individual client, but will often include actions at the group, community, institutional, policy, or political level.

The evaluation and termination phase terminates the intervention and determines whether or not it was effective. It also includes a review of clients' records. Keeping accurate records according to agency policy and the *Code of Ethics* is critical to ensuring continued care and protecting the individual client and families should his or her records be subpoenaed for a court case.

To be successful, a social worker requires knowledge and a variety of skills as well as a commitment to certain basic social work values. All types of social work share a body of knowledge, skills and values that involve a commitment to humanitarianism and egalitarianism aimed at empowering people and building on their strengths.

CHAPTER REVIEW

Key Terms

- **Social work practice**
- **Clinical social work**
- **Intake**
- **Reflection-action-reflection**
- **Assessment**
- **Planning**

- **Intervention**
- **Evaluation**
- **Termination**
- **Helping relationship**
- **Evidence-based practice**

Review Questions

1. What are the three fields of social work practice and how do they differ?

2. What steps does a social worker usually follow in providing help to an individual or family? Identify and describe each step.

3. Select four direct practice skills and describe their importance for working with individuals and families.

4. Why is the helping relationship important?

5. Briefly describe the three attributes identified by Carl Rogers which are needed to develop the helping relationship. Why are these important?

Exploring Social Work

1. Families are complex. Sometimes "graphic organizers" can be helpful in beginning to understand family dynamics. For practice, plot a genogram and an ecomap (see sidebar on page 95) of your own family, showing the complex relations between your family members—today and over generations—and how you and various members of your family interact with people and institutions in ways that might be relevant to a better understanding of your family today.

2. Social work with individuals and families involves the skill of listening. You have the opportunity to practice this skill every day. Choose a period of time in your week when you are in dialogue and consciously practice deep listening. Notice how your listening shifts when you consciously listen. How is it different from your usual form of listening? How would this benefit your work as a social worker or social service worker? Record your experience in a two-page report. Be sure to indicate how this technique might be employed in a practice setting.

3. Is social work art or science (or both)? Discuss this issue with a small group of your fellow students and develop a "position paper." Be sure to address whether the evidence-based practice movement has a place in the evaluation of social work interventions.

Websites
- - - - - -

Success and Innovation in Social Work Practice
www.casw-acts.ca/celebrating/innovation_e.html

The Canadian Association of Social Work (CASW) shares stories from across Canada of creative and innovative practice. By sharing these stories the CASW hopes to facilitate further innovation and to celebrate the social work practice of our colleagues.

Information for Practice
www.nyu.edu/socialwork/ip/

IP's mission is to help social service professionals throughout the world conveniently maintain an awareness of news regarding the profession and emerging scholarship. It is sponsored by the New York University School of Social Work; the Division of Social Work and Behavioral Science, Mount Sinai School of Medicine; the Institute for the Advancement of Social Work Research, and the Society for Social Work and Research.

The Vanier Institute of the Family
www.vifamily.ca

The Vanier Institute of the Family is a national, charitable organization dedicated to providing leadership on issues affecting the well-being of Canadian families. Its work includes: collecting and analyzing information on changing patterns of family formation and function; advocating social change to create more supportive environments for families; and advising government, corporations, and religious organizations on matters of family policy.

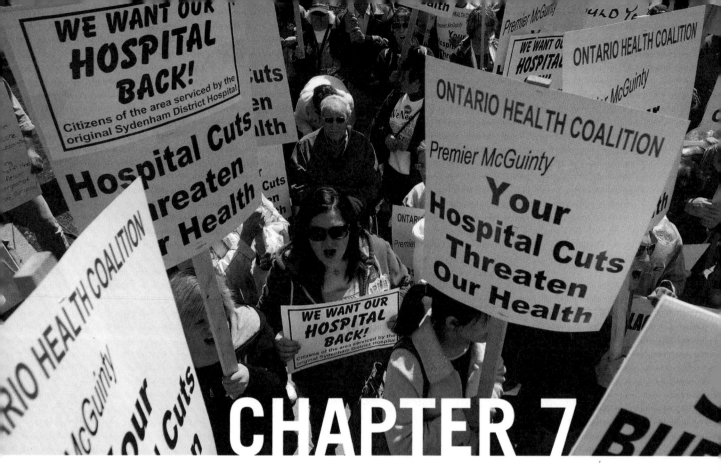

CHAPTER 7

SOCIAL WORK WITH GROUPS AND COMMUNITIES

Applying Direct Practice Skills

by Sarah Todd and Martha Wiebe

While the theories behind social work with groups and social work with communities differ, there are many obvious connections between the two. The skills used in group practice are often important for work with communities, as they offer strategies for helping a collective of people develop trust and communicate more effectively with each other. Understanding how group members are linked to wider communities can be very important in group-based practice.

This chapter focuses first on groups and then explores a variety of approaches to working with entire communities. The final sections explore the various stages of community work, which in many ways are similar to those involved in group work.

Social Work with Groups

Groups have long been an important part of the work that many social workers do. Both group work and community work have their roots in the settlement movement of the 1800s that resulted from rapid industrialization and increasing urbanization. In Canada in the early part of the twentieth century, churches were establishing a chain of settlement houses in the country's largest cities. As was explored in Chapter 3, the social gospel movement had a deep commitment to collective action and to the development of good citizenship (see page 45).

While casework was defined as a methodology by the early twentieth century, *group work* and *community work* or community organizing were latecomers to the profession. Group work was basically seen as an informal and unstructured activity and not part of the profession (Goldstein 1973, 26). The focus was on helping people participate collectively in dealing with common problems. Ellen Mesbur (2002) notes that it was not till the 1930s that group work was considered a method of practice. It was during the Great Depression that social action came to be a significant and accepted part of the social work profession, and involved helping and supporting destitute farmers, unemployed labourers, and orphaned children. This was also the period when self-help groups started to develop; people dealing with similar issues came together to support and aid each other.

Since that time, **group work** has undergone a number of iterations, with attention paid to developing a theory base. Over the past forty years the profession has identified it as one of the models of practice in social work, with a growing body of literature and research on the subject.

Kinds of Groups

There is a wide range of groups operating in most communities. Groups can be categorized as generally falling into the following five categories; self-help, educational, support/therapeutic, task, and social action groups.

- **Self-help groups.** Self-help groups are ones that do not have a professional facilitator and may be either leaderless, have a rotating leader, or designate a leader from within the group. Alcoholics Anonymous is one of the most well-known and longest running self-help groups. Many others have been established such as PFLAG (Parents, Families and Friends of Lesbians and Gays) and CanSurmount, a peer group for cancer patients and their families. There is also a growing number of web-based support groups, which can be useful for people who are not able to connect with a community group. However, online groups do have limitations—for example, health information online is not subjected to the same scrutiny as information in printed medical journals. There are also privacy concerns related to Internet groups.

Defining Group Work

Group work can be defined as assisting a collection of people who are dealing generally with a similar problem or issue. Groups can be peers, a family, or a therapeutic group. Group work approaches range from therapeutic to educational to activist. Similarly, some communities want to take a healing or therapeutic approach to their problems, others want to learn skills, and some want to head to the streets in protest. Whether a group considers itself a community or not, the approaches that are described in this chapter are helpful for working with any collective of people as they try to create change in their lives.

- **Educational groups.** Educational groups have a primary focus on education, but might also have a support aspect. Examples are groups for heart and stroke victims, parenting groups, and groups for families where there has been a recent diagnosis of diabetes. These groups usually have a leader with expertise on the topic.

- **Support/therapeutic groups.** In support/therapeutic groups the primary purpose is supporting people dealing with specific problems. They are groups that have a professional facilitator. Examples are groups for victims of sexual abuse, women empowerment groups, and groups for people dealing with mental illnesses.

- **Task groups.** With task groups, the primary focus is to accomplish a specific mandate. Although social support may be a side benefit it is not the primary purpose for which the group was designed. Some examples are a group that coordinates settlement services for newcomers in a community or a personnel committee charged with the task of hiring an executive director.

- **Social action groups.** Social action groups tend to focus on broader social issues, though they may well have a personal dimension to them. For example, a group organized to ban the use of pesticides on lawns may have been sparked by the personal concern around a child's cancer diagnosis. These groups are part of community organizing. A premise for social action groups is often the need to equitably distribute resources, locally or globally.

While task groups and social action groups share common aspects with self-help, educational, and support/therapeutic groups and many of the skills are similar, the focus and the emphasis are different.

Group Dynamics

Although there are many similarities between helping people in a group setting and assisting them one-on-one, there are some significant differences. These elements are sometimes referred to as group dynamics. **Group dynamics** include how people talk and interact with each other in the group (communication and interactive patterns), a sense of belonging to the group (cohesion), and the influence that a group has on individual members to conform to certain behaviours, practices, and beliefs (Toseland & Rivas 2005, 65). The purpose for which a group is established will in large measure influence its dynamics.

- **Communication patterns.** Depending on the overall objectives of the group, a facilitator will want to establish a certain communication pattern. For example, in an educational group the facilitator will have a central role in conveying information to the group; in many parenting groups the facilitator will systematically present course materials followed by group discussion; in a support/therapeutic group the facilitator generally aims to have free-floating communication rather than the group being leader-centred.

- **Cohesion.** Cohesion is an important component to be aware of in working with a group. When group members are attracted to the group and feel connected to the other members in the group they are more likely to benefit from the group experience. The sense of cohesion in a group provides safety and sets the stage for group members to interact in an authentic way with each other. This sense of connectedness is possibly the most important ingredient in making a group a valuable experience for its members. It is also what motivates people to continue participating in the group.

- **Group influence and conformity.** Group influence and conformity will affect how well a group will function and be able to achieve the purpose for which it was established. Groups where members have many common characteristics and hold shared values and expectations are groups that tend to move more quickly forward on achieving group goals. For example, a group of parents of adolescents who have dropped out of school might have many similar goals and are thus able to be supportive to one another. However, part of the strength of groups also lies with the member differences. Different experiences and different backgrounds can provide perspectives and insights that are new to other group members. The balance between homogeneity and heterogeneity in the membership will effect the functioning of the group and how influential the group is on the individual members.

Group Dynamics

The communication and interaction between group members, members' sense of belonging, and the degree to which a group influences its members.

An understanding of group work is a critical part of social work practice knowledge, since group dynamics can help to shape individual behaviours, practices, and beliefs.

The Stages of Group Development

Group Stages

- **Forming**—planning and creating a group

- **Storming**—conflict emerges within the group

- **Norming**—roles are defined and trust begins

- **Performing**—work towards the goal begins

- **Adjourning**—conclusion of group

Different writers have described the stages of a group in various ways. While defining group stages provides a useful template for looking at and anticipating various behaviours in a group it is important to note that groups do not proceed systematically or in a linear way through these stages but rather will move back and forth. For example, while conflict is usually associated with the early stages of group development, major conflicts may arise during the later phases of the group when members challenge each other and challenge the basic framework of the group.

Different theoreticians have conceptualized group development in various ways although there is substantial agreement. Shulman, for example, has outlined group development as having three general phases: beginning, middle, and end. Others have suggested that groups go through five or six stages basically consisting of orientation, conflict, negotiation, functioning, and termination (Toseland & Rivas 2005, 87). Bruce Tuckman's (1965) early work on group stages continues to be useful. He outlined the stages in an easy-to-remember way: forming, storming, norming, and performing, and later he added adjourning to that list (Tuckman & Jensen, 1977).

Forming Stage

The **forming stage** has two primary components: planning the group and getting the group started. In planning the group it is vitally important that the purpose is clearly defined (i.e., whether it is to provide support, to educate, or to accomplish a specific task). The purpose should be broad enough to attract sufficient numbers of people with somewhat varying needs, and yet specific enough to define the common nature of the group. The facilitator should also want to think about whom the group is intended to attract. In other words, who is the group designed for?

Part of planning also includes issues like the length of the group meetings, the frequency with which the group meets, and the duration of the group. It is also important at this stage to consider whether the group will be open to new members along the way or whether it will be a closed group.

The following criteria should be considered when selecting group members:

- common experience/common problem
- motivation
- age, gender, and socio-cultural factors
- expectations that the group will help

It is important to remember that homogeneity increases possibilities for closeness and cohesiveness, and heterogeneity fosters learning and a wider assortment of choices and problem solving skills.

The optimum group size depends on the following criteria:

- age of clients
- type of group
- problems/issues to be explored
- needs of the members
- experience of social worker

In starting the group, the facilitator generally takes an active role in establishing the structure and format of the group. It is at this stage that ground rules are discussed and established and that group members make some type of commitment to the group.

Storming Stage

The **storming stage** is where conflict emerges in the group. Differences in understanding of the group's purpose and the group members' roles and expectations can lead to friction. If it is a voluntary group, members may decide not to return at this stage. This is also the time when members test and challenge the authority of the facilitator. Although this can be a difficult phase in the life of a group, it is also a time when growth can occur and when relationships are established. By anticipating conflict, group leaders can help members to view it as a natural or helpful part of group development and as an opportunity to gather information and share views and opinions rather than as personal attacks. It is at this stage that the facilitator can be very useful in establishing a tone for the group and operationalize the ground rules by encouraging members to own their statements, listen without interrupting, ask questions before reacting, and deal with each other in a respectful manner.

Norming Stage

In the **norming stage** group norms (or expectations, standards, common practices) and roles become more clearly defined and members establish a beginning trust with each other. Group cohesion increases and the group moves toward working on the agreed upon objectives. One example of a useful norm to establish is that everyone has a right to be heard. It is also useful to encourage members to talk directly to each other rather than communicating through the facilitator.

Performing Stage

In the **performing stage** the group members work toward achieving the outlined goals. Trust and a sense of confidence with each other are evident. Members might disclose painful personal issues from their past and seek assistance and support from each other. Group cohesion is strong and group participation is good, with attendance at sessions generally high. Individuals might at this stage consider other group members as friends

Bertha Reynolds was a social work educator and social activist. Her book *Learning and Teaching in the Practice of Social Work* influenced both clinical and community social work practice.

Just before her death in 1978, she was asked what message she would give to young people entering the social work profession today. Her response was: "Do not get locked into traditional moulds."

Daily Strength

www.dailystrength.org

Daily Strength is a repository of online support groups, founded by Internet veterans in the U.S. and moderated by experts; individuals can find online support on a number of health and social issues.

and feel a sense of closeness and connectedness to each other and to the group facilitator. The role of the facilitator is largely one of maintaining a safe and supportive environment for the group members. The facilitator continues to be cognizant of group process and will refocus the group when members get off track. The performing stage is where both the members and the facilitator feel rewarded for their efforts.

Adjourning Stage

The **adjourning stage** is where the group moves towards terminating. Group members may start disengaging from each other. Some members may express increased anxiety about the group ending, while others might deal with the ending by participating less actively or attending more sporadically.

Groups come to an end for a variety of reasons. For example, some groups have a very fixed timeline and when the eight or twelve sessions are completed the group is finished. This is frequently the case with educational groups. A group may also terminate because the goals of the group have been met and people are ready to move on. A group may also fall apart and disintegrate because members are no longer committed to the purpose for which the group was established.

One of the tasks of terminating is evaluating the group experience. This can be done in either a formal way, where the facilitator systematically collects information at the beginning, middle, and end of the group or it can be done informally, where, for example, group members might be asked in the last session to identify what was valuable about the group and what they found to be less helpful.

PFLAG CANADA
There for people when it seems no one else is

PFLAG is a volunteer organization dedicated to providing support, education, and resources to parents, families, and individuals who have questions or concerns about sexual orientation or gender identity. The family and friends of lesbians and gays support movement started in the 1970s, and spread across Canada; in 2003 several grassroots organizations and chapters formally joined under the name PFLAG Canada.

This group is designed to support people in gaining an understanding of sexual and gender diversity. It reaches out to people who are gay, lesbian, bisexual, transgender, transsexual, two-spirited, intersex, queer, or questioning, and to family and friends who care about someone who is dealing with these issues.

PFLAG also provides educational tools for teachers to assist them in confronting homophobia in the classroom and works with employers on ways of making the workplace an accepting and safe environment for sexual minorities. PFLAG promotes the development of stronger, safer communities by challenging prejudice through education and outreach. PFLAG has approximately seventy chapters in Canada.

To learn more, visit the website at www.pflag.ca.

THEORETICAL ORIENTATIONS IN GROUP WORK

The theoretical orientation of a practitioner is a key variable in determining the way a group functions, its activities, and its process. Although there are many theoretical models for group practice (see Chapter 4), the following classifications represent a vantage point from which to look at group behaviour and how change happens.

Cognitive Theories

Groups based on cognitive theories subscribe to a fundamental belief that when people change their thinking or their ideas, other changes will follow.

An example of a program that is based on cognitive theories is the Ottawa New Directions Program that works with men who abuse women. The men in these groups are challenged to rethink their concepts of women as property or their notions of men as the superior human beings. The assumption is that the men will make behavioural changes when their thinking changes.

Behaviour Theories

Behaviour theories have as a starting point the objective to change group members' behaviours with the understanding that changed behaviour will lead to a change in feelings and thinking.

A behavioural approach is frequently used in adolescent facilities where appropriate behaviours are reinforced in a group. Reward tokens are given to the youth if they change their behaviour. This is premised on the belief that a change in behaviour will result in an improved sense of self and this in turn will promote continued improvements in behaviours and a change in thinking.

An example of the use of a behavioural approach is the work done with children suffering from fetal alcohol syndrome at Bosco Homes in Edmonton—various social reinforcements are employed to help these children change their destructive behaviours. Behavioural theory is also the basis of a range of desensitization therapies used in helping people deal with anxiety disorders and phobias such as a fear of flying or of small spaces.

Affective Theories

The focus with affective theories is on feelings. The belief is that a change in feelings is fundamental to other changes. Being affirming to the person will result in improved self-esteem, more positive thinking, and a change in behaviours. Most treatment groups use elements of affective theories, helping group members examine and deal with feelings.

Structural Theories

As discussed in Chapter 4, the primary premise of structural theories is that personal problems are linked to public issues and require intervention at a number of levels. Structural or social change is based on concepts of social justice.

Within these theories, oppressive elements are examined and issues of privilege are considered. Examples of this approach include ecological systems theory, feminist theory, and anti-oppressive practice. Consciousness-raising groups and many women's groups use a structural framework.

The theoretical approach used in a group tends to be related in large measure to the ideology of the particular practice setting and to the facilitator's particular belief system regarding the causes of the distress. A key variable to how a group will operate is the facilitator's personal and professional values, beliefs, and experiences rather than the issues that members bring to the group.

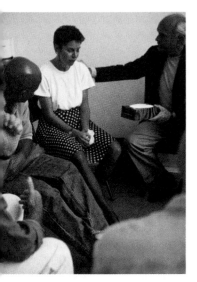

The sense of cohesion in a support/therapeutic group provides safety, which allows the facilitator to encourage group members to interact in an authentic way and offer support and encouragement to each other.

Group Facilitation Skills

The skills mentioned in Chapter 6 for working with individuals are also the types of skills required when working with groups: active listening, expressions of empathy, questioning, paraphrasing, reflecting, summarizing, providing information or suggestions, building consensus, and interpreting or reframing. In addition to these skills, however, there are specific group facilitation skills that are important to learn.

Connecting

This skill involves linking what one person is saying or doing to what another member in the group is experiencing. The facilitator listens for common themes in people's specific stories. For example, one person's story about losing a job may lead to a discussion of how others in the group have dealt with losses they have experienced. This skill is important in terms of building group cohesion. Part of the effectiveness of groups lies in the support that people get from recognizing that they are not the only ones dealing with a particular concern. It dispels the sense of isolation and helps build group cohesion, moving the group toward mutual aid.

Focus on Process

Process is critical in group work, but it can get overlooked when the facilitator gets too engaged in the content of the discussion. While the content may be very interesting, it is frequently the process that is the most important issue to attend to in a group. Groups are a microcosm of the larger society. How members react to one another can serve to reveal how they treat others outside the group. Helping people to examine their interactions and reactions in the here-and-now can provide an opportunity for gaining insight into the self. Focusing on process includes pointing out the pattern to the group and re-framing issues. Shulman (1992) notes that the group facilitator has to consider two clients at all times, both the individuals in the group and the group as a whole. This requires the worker to use the microscopic lens and the wide-angle lens simultaneously.

Cueing

Cueing is another skill that is specific to group work. Here the facilitator scans the group, takes its pulse, and becomes directive in inviting silent or non-participating members to engage. This might be done non-verbally through body language (e.g., by making eye contact with the person you are inviting into the conversation). Other times it is done verbally by specifically inviting someone to comment. When one member is dominating the discussion, it might be useful take the time to invite each member to contribute to the discussion.

Supporting

The facilitator's judgment is required to determine when to support a group member. Jumping in too early might prevent the member from fully exploring a situation and learning from it. This skill also incorporates encouraging group members to support each other. For example, many people come to treatment groups because they feel powerless or isolated. The phenomenon of feeling like you're "in the same boat" is one of the curative aspects of a group. In a cohesive group, members will frequently support each other by sharing similar feelings, thus making the feelings less frightening or overwhelming. The worker can also encourage empathic statements by asking the group, for example, "Has anybody else in the group had similar feelings?" or "Can anybody relate to what was just said?"

Blocking

In addition to supporting, a facilitator must also decide when to challenge a group member. Harmful things can be said in groups and as much as possible the group facilitator must try to block certain comments or activities in order to maintain the safety of the group. This requires sensitivity and the ability to use power effectively without dis-empowering group members. Situations when the facilitator should block discussion include: if a member is breaking confidences; making racist, sexist, homophobic, or other discriminatory comments; or being abusive and disrespectful. It is the responsibility of the group facilitator to ensure the safety of all members of the group.

Social Empathy

While expressing empathy means understanding and validating a client's feelings, **social empathy** takes this a step further. The facilitator makes links between personal troubles and structural issues. These statements are ways of joining on an emotional level as well as on an intellectual level. Connecting the personal and the political can be very affirming to clients. For example, introducing the fact that there is a serious shortage of afford-able child care services can be assuring to a young mothers' group. By providing a social and political context to their experience the facilitator reframes their issues from a sense of worthlessness and feelings of frustra-tion with not being in the workforce to one of empowerment. Generally, the facilitator will not make direct statements that link structural barriers to personal experience, but rather will ask questions that help group members make those connections in their own lives. Questions such as "in whose interest is it that women stay at home and care for their children?" or "what gets in the way of you getting what you want?" The expression of social empathy highlights various oppressions but also acknowledges that there are differences in group members' experiences. It is important to recognize that the same context may impact individuals in the group in different ways.

Talking Stick

The "talking stick" is often used by First Nations to ensure that everyone's message and opinion is heard by the group, but it can be used in a variety of social work groups.

One stick or feather (or almost any object) is required, and the group usually positions itself in a circle without obstructions in the middle. Each group member can speak only when he or she has the stick. The speaker passes the stick to the next person who wants to speak.

The method ensures that everyone can contribute without interruption, and encourages shy members to participate.

Group Facilitation Skills

- Connecting
- Focus on process
- Cueing
- Supporting
- Blocking
- Social empathy

Social Work with Communities

In social work we generally think about **community** as a group of people who share either a geographic space (e.g., a neighbourhood), an identity (e.g., people with disabilities), or an interest (e.g., social activist communities) (Lee, B. 1999). Communities also require a consciousness of themselves as a community. For example, while people may share a geographic space or an identity, if they don't think of themselves as a community, then generally we think of them as a group of people who lack a sense of community.

In social work we are very interested in helping people organize into communities because we know they are often helpful for decreasing isolation, sharing resources, and facilitating a sense of self-efficacy, and they are often an effective defense against oppression and exploitation. People who have a greater sense of community tend to have better overall sense of health and well-being.

As you read in Chapter 3, one of the first and most well-known community organizers was Jane Addams, who helped to introduce the idea of the settlement house to the U.S. from the U.K. Those involved in the settlement house movement helped to ensure that social work included social activism and bringing people together to more effectively meet their own needs. Jane Addams's work at Hull House in Chicago reflects much of what continues to be integral to community practice today. The women of Hull House created a community space where people could come together, share their concerns, and begin to develop solutions to their problems. The work of Hull House also included research with communities to obtain empirical evidence regarding their challenges, which was in turn used to pressure politicians and city officials to create change and to more effectively meet people's needs. Many of the programs at Hull House focused on meeting the needs of women and children who were considered the heart of the community. When traditional pathways for creating change were not available, the women of Hull House worked with the citizens of east downtown Chicago to hold public protests calling for legislative and policy changes.

Today, this balance of program development, creating community space and resources, completing research, and agitating for political change remains central to community work. It often takes place in community health centres, within city governments, or out of various non-profits in a community. Even larger bureaucracies such as Children's Aid Societies often employ a community worker to help build more effective community relations.

There are a number of different approaches to community development. Each tends to work better in particular situations, with particular people, and around specific issues. It is helpful to know what approaches are available so that you can find one that fits with your personal style and the community with which you are working.

A Framework for Group Work

An approach to working with groups should be framed by exploring these questions:

- How do people change?
- What is my philosophy of human nature and how will I incorporate this into my group work?
- How much responsibility for the group's work lies with the leader?
- How much responsibility lies with the members?
- Should the primary focus be on personality change, attitude change, behaviour change, or social change?

Rothman's Model of Community Work

In the 1960s Jack Rothman summarized community work as fitting into three distinct types:

- **Locality development.** Locality development typifies those approaches to community organizing that focus on organizing around issues that are relevant to a particular neighbourhood or geographic space. Its focus is on community building by engaging a wide number of community participants in the organizing process. Consensus is built between members by trying to establish their common interests. Community members themselves are encouraged to become leaders in the process. This approach is exemplified by the settlement house movement and is continued in many community health centres. The focus of change tends to be municipal governments, external developers, and sometimes provincial and federal governments. The concerns that this type of community work tends to address are often about quality of life. Social workers who use this approach often see their role as one of educating people, facilitating conversations, and organizing community members.

- **Social planning.** Social planning is an expert-driven approach to community work, which can often be found in social planning councils and city planning departments. While community members are involved to varying degrees in making this process work, the experts (social workers, public health workers, or social planners) tend to facilitate meetings and write any reports that come from the process. This approach focuses mainly on the technical aspects of achieving tasks and allocating resources. It is not about changing society, but about how to meet immediate needs. Social workers in this type of community work are often taking on the role of researcher, proposal writer, and communications manager.

- **Social action.** Social action is an activist approach to community work. It can be seen in many social movements such as the anti-corporate globalization movement, the feminist movement, and the anti-racist movement. This social action approach often uses public confrontation and social protest to challenge what are seen as injustices. A social action approach to community work aims to redistribute power, resources, and decision making. Generally, it involves organizing people who are marginalized from the decision-making process, but it can also focus on the general public. The aim of this type of organizing is to build political power and to create institutional change. Social workers who engage in this type of community work are often advocates, facilitators, organizers, and researchers.

Jane Addams founded the social settlement Hull House on Chicago's Near West Side in 1889. She devoted her life to helping the needy and distressed, most of them immigrants, until her death in 1935.

Saul Alinsky's Approach to Community Activism

Saul Alinsky

Saul Alinsky was born 1909; in the 1930s he organized the stockyard workers of Chicago and founded the Industrial Areas Foundation (IAF), which now has affiliates across North America, Germany, and the U.K. Alinsky helped organize Mexican-Americans after World War II, and is credited with inspiring the grassroots movements of the 1960s. Alinsky's most famous work, *Rules for Radicals*, was published just before his death in 1972.

Saul Alinsky was an American organizer in the 1930s and beyond. He is sometimes called the father of community organizing. Alinsky was very effective in organizing communities in the 30s, 40s, 50s, and 60s. He even came to Canada to work with Aboriginal peoples.

Alinsky's approach is confrontational and strategic. Alinsky was largely concerned with strategies to win battles for marginalized communities. He spoke of community organizing as a process of going to war (Alinsky 1971). This masculine language often alienated women and peace activists, but many groups have successfully adapted his methods to fit their own agendas. Alinsky was not only concerned with battling the power holders to demand distribution of resources, he was also very effective at building community organizations, which he saw as instrumental in making community work sustainable. So, his approach is a balance between building long-term activist organizations and planning short-term, exciting challenges to power holders.

One of the most helpful insights that Alinsky brought to organizing is the notion that community work needs to be fun—people only like to get involved with tactics that are enjoyable and do not drag on too long (Stall & Stoeker 1998). He was also well aware that an organizer needed to plan tactics that were in the experience of the community members and outside the experience of those people who you are organizing against. He understood how powerful the element of surprise was for communities who challenged power holders.

Alinsky did not feel that democratic capitalism itself needed to be challenged, but he did believe in creating confrontation to redistribute resources within that system (Alinsky 1971). He was disdainful of idealistic approaches to community work, feeling that it was important to start where people were at, and to create a vision that was fundamentally built within the existing social structures. His approach to organizing is still widely used in North America today.

THE ALINSKY METHOD
Making Activism Fun While Getting Results

One of Saul Alinsky's most famous actions was carried out while working with a group of people living in poverty who were unable to get authorities to follow through with a redevelopment project that they had been promised. As part of his action, Alinsky threatened to shut down O'Hare Airport in Chicago. He leaked to his adversaries that he was going to have the activists occupy all the restrooms in the airport, making it unusable for the thousands of passengers arriving at the airport.

The threat worked and city officials called a meeting to recommit to their promise to the group with whom he was working. This is a perfect example of Alinsky's commitment to fun, simple actions that are within the experience of the people he is working with, but outside the experience of the opposition (how *does* the city deal with no access to restrooms at a busy airport?). It is also an example of one of his rules of community activism— the threat is always more terrifying than the thing itself.

Paulo Freire's Approach to Community Mobilization

Paulo Freire was an educator in Brazil in the 1950s and his work is significant in the shaping of contemporary community work. In Brazil he worked to develop a national educational system at a time when the poor in Brazil were starting to realize that they needed to challenge the oppression they were facing. In this revolutionary context, Freire developed a radical approach to education which is applicable to community practice.

He criticized the "banking" approach to education where an educator stands in front of a group of people who stay silent and quickly copy down everything the educator says. Freire argued that this makes people into passive objects. Instead, he developed an approach to education in which the educator asks the community members questions about their lives; in critically exploring their lives, people also learn to read and write. When the questions asked by a facilitator are relevant to people's lives, they learn easily. At the same time, they develop a collective, critical consciousness of their lives and the challenges that they are facing. Freire's education system was very effective, but was perceived as a threat to the country's power holders, many of whom relied on the peasants' acquiescence to being exploited. As a result, Freire was exiled in 1964 after a military coup.

A Freirian approach to community work begins with a listening survey. The community organizer goes into the community and talks to people, knocking on doors, visiting people at bus stops, in laundromats, etc. When doing this, an organizer tries to find out what community members feel strongly about—either positive aspects of their lives or negative ones. The organizer and a small group of community members—called a learning group—gather together and go through the findings of the listening survey, making *codes* from the ideas they have heard. Codes can be pictures, films, images, or plays that represent the issues the community feels strongly about. These codes are then presented to the community to stimulate discussion about what is going well or badly in the community and to stimulate action planning to create change (Hope & Timmel 1984).

What is integral to a Freirian approach to social change is a process of reflection and action called **praxis**. Freire believed that a successful action for social change must be reflected upon in advance and afterwards, thereby creating new and more effective actions, which are also then reflected upon. He argued that this approach would encourage thoughtful actions rather than reactive responses to injustice, which are often contradictory and difficult to sustain. For example, when some revolutionary movements achieve power, they can be just as oppressive as the power holders they overthrew. Freire's approach to community work and community education is fundamentally committed to people being empowered to create a social justice revolution.

Paulo Freire

Born in Brazil in 1921, Freire studied law and philosophy, but worked as a teacher. In the 1940s, he worked with the illiterate poor. In 1962, while working for Recife University, he was able to apply his educational theories, teaching 300 sugarcane workers to read and write in 45 days. In the 1960s and 70s, Freire taught at universities in the U.S. and U.K. and helped with education reform in former Portuguese colonies in Africa, returning to continue his work in Brazil in the 1980s. He published several works on the philosophy of education and educational theory.

Women-Centred and Feminist Approaches to Community Work

Feminist and women-centred approaches to community development are not linked with a particular person, but rather a way of organizing that has been identified with feminist and women's organizing throughout the twentieth century. This style of organizing was developed by working-class women, black women activists, lesbian activists, and middle-class white women. While it does not necessarily exclude men, it often focuses on women as key to their communities and the notion that meeting their needs impacts positively on families and the community more broadly (Stall & Stoeker 1998).

Feminist or women-centred approaches to community organizing tend to rely on consensus decision making, shared leadership, and a process orientation (Adamson et al. 1988). The activist group uses methods to achieve its ends that are consistent with their goals. For example, one of the reasons that women-centred processes use consensus decision making is because the groups are often struggling for more inclusive processes at the government or society level. This model tends to be focused on creating concrete changes in the experiences of women and communities and is often used to establish community kitchens, playgrounds, co-operative childcare, shelters for abused women, and sexual assault centres.

This approach usually involves a great deal of peer education, or consciousness raising. One of the limits of this approach is that it can take some time, so it is not always the most appropriate approach when decisive action is needed. It is also geared to more long-term changes involving small groups of citizens coming together.

Community Capacity Building

Community capacity building is an approach originating in the U.S. and spearheaded by John McKnight and John Kretzmann. It is a contemporary approach to community organizing that is currently quite popular both nationally and internationally. McKnight and Kretzmann believe that it is vitally important to develop an approach to community work that builds upon the strengths and assets of a community rather than focusing on the community's needs. They also argue that communities should develop their own resources to meet their needs rather than relying heavily on state programs, which are stigmatizing and create a destructive dependency (McKnight & Kretzmann 1993).

This approach involves assessing the strengths and resources in the community in terms of social relationships, people's gifts and skills, local businesses, churches, and community space. Generally organizers using this approach create a map of these resources, which is the foundation from which community members work to further develop their assets. This approach is particularly powerful for communities in which people need to become more aware of their potential.

Communities: A Licence to Exclude?

While a lot of good things come with a sense of community, communities themselves are neither entirely good nor bad. While communities can offer members a sense of inclusivity, they also rely on excluding those who are not seen as fitting inside the community boundaries. This can result in communities being quite oppressive. For example, certain geographic, social, and religious communities can be quite hostile to lesbian, gay, bisexual, or transgendered persons when they "come out."

Thus as we think about creating communities it is important to always remain aware of who are included and excluded in the communities we are organizing and to work to develop a notion of community that embraces diversity and difference, while at the same time bringing people together around their commonalities.

One possible limitation of this approach is that there are some communities that are so resource-poor, they are unable to deal with their problems without state support. Some argue that a more rights-focused approach to community work is necessary, one that demands state institutions be accountable to meet the needs of marginalized communities, rather than simply encouraging communities to meet their own needs (McGrath et al. 1999).

Community Work as Healing

Another approach to community work looks at the building of community as a healing practice (sometimes linked to spirituality). From this perspective, community members draw on community traditions and values as part of a process of healing. This reconnection to traditional values and practices is seen as an important way to deal with problems such as family breakdown, suicide, addiction, and histories of abuse. This approach is often used by Aboriginal groups and spiritual communities. The community members are encouraged and supported to find a path to wellness. This approach to community work is useful in helping people remove internal obstacles to meaningful participation and in bringing about genuine healing for the individuals involved, but tends not to focus on structural inequalities that may also exist in a particular context.

Since 1985, Evergreen, a division of Yonge Street Mission, has offered Toronto's street youth a safe haven. Evergreen provides counselling and programs specific to the needs of street youth, encouraging health and spiritual well-being, aiding those they help to view the world as a place of opportunity.

Phases of Community Work

Bill Lee (1999) breaks down community work into a series of discrete phases. While these phases do not always occur in a linear fashion, they give you some idea of the process that constitutes community work. The following phases are similar to those outlined by Lee in his book, *Pragmatics of Community Organizing.*

Pre-Entry

The work of a community worker begins even before they enter the community, in a process identified as pre-entry. Often before having contact with a community, a social worker is hired by a funder to complete a project. While it is preferable to begin work at the community's direct request, it is rare that communities have sufficient resources to do this. As a result, there is work that the social worker can do to help prepare to work effectively with community members.

A social worker who is hired by a funding organization to work in a local community needs to spend time learning the general history of the community and its relationship with the funder, before entering the community. They also need to have a sense of the politics of the community, how the community's problems are perceived by a diverse group of its members, and whether this differs from the funder's understanding of the problems. A social worker also needs to understand the length of time available to do the work and what outcomes are expected (and whether the community has any input into these outcomes). This type of preparation work is vital to ensuring that an organizer is able to create a helpful beginning for the community process.

Contact and Engagement

The next stage of community work is contact and engagement. It is in this phase that the community organizer starts to meet community members, listens to how they feel about their community, and begins to engage them in a process of change. Engagement is often a long and challenging process in which the organizer works to build trusting relationships with as representative a sample of the community as possible. In this phase the worker also tries to support people in developing a sense of hope that things can change.

The most challenging part of this, and future stages in community practice, is that rather than doing all the work necessary to organize and create change, a social worker is always trying to support the *community* to do the work themselves. This often requires that the worker take a slow and often winding approach to reaching goals.

The key issues in contact and engagement are significantly shaped by whether the community worker is perceived as an insider or an outsider to the community and the amount of trust that develops between the organizer and community members. Being a community outsider presents a different set of challenges in this phase than those presented when one is a community insider. In either situation the building of trust, broad participation, and hope that change is possible is key.

Community Analysis

Since the days of the settlement movement, it is clear that in order to create change, a community must understand itself and develop a process to gain information about what is happening to its members. The most common approach used to achieve this is **participatory action research** (PAR), where community members are involved in deciding the research question, the research process, and analyzing the data. Through this process two important things happen: first, community members develop skills, and second, the community gets the evidence they need to encourage power holders to listen to their demands and create change. It is far harder to ignore a community group armed with data to support their position, than it is a group that is simply presenting opinions or their perspective.

Organizational Development

The next important phase of community work is to help the community get organized and develop roles and responsibilities that people can take on to facilitate change. This requires establishing processes to guide how group members work together. For example, a community association may elect board members through biannual elections in which anyone who lives within certain community boundaries can vote. Sometimes communities hire a part-time staff person to help develop community programs. Other communities rely on a large number of volunteers who make decisions as a collective. In either situation, the roles, responsibilities, and decision-making processes need to be clear and agreed upon.

It is important in this, and all phases of community practice, that social workers work *with* people, not *for* them. Community workers are not helping communities if they go in and do all the work for people. If instead we support community members in doing the work to create change, they learn skills, and become more confident, and this can often help build solidarity. If a community worker does everything, then all the community learns is to be dependent on that worker. Despite the benefits, working with people, not for them, can be difficult. It requires patience and sometimes we have to let people make their own mistakes. It can be quite painful to watch communities make mistakes, but it is only by doing so that those communities can do the learning that helps them become more confident in their decisions and processes.

Phases of Community Work

- Pre-entry
- Contact and engagement
- Community analysis
- Organizational development
- Action planning and mobilization
- Conflict resolution
- Evaluation

Action Planning and Mobilization

After a group has a bit of organization, it is time to begin to plan actions and mobilize. The most important predictor of success at this stage is the amount of community support for any action. Any plan for action relies upon people building consensus around a clear plan in which *everyone* knows what is being achieved, how long it will take to achieve these goals, and how the community is going to achieve these goals. If a community is deeply divided, it is difficult to have a successful action. As the stakes rise, so do the divisions—often power holders are able to remain unaffected by actions because the community members are too busy fighting among themselves. There are usually three approaches to action planning; the first involves co-operating with power holders. Then, if that is unsuccessful, groups launch various types of issue-raising campaigns. If such campaigns don't effect change, the third approach is confrontation.

Key to any successful action is media coverage. Again, this requires substantial work prior to an action. Relationships need to be built with the media and care has to be put into ensuring that the action is, in itself, media worthy. Are there visuals for television cameras? Does the group have a clear message that is easy enough for an audience who is unfamiliar with the issue? Are your community members prepared to speak to the media? Does everyone know how to stick to the message? Do you have information for reporters so that they have the facts and the background?

Conflict Resolution

Another key component of community work is trying to mediate conflicts either within the community or with those outside of the community. In this process, a community worker needs to be aware of what is at stake in a conflict in terms of process, emotions, and content. To resolve conflict an impartial person may need to be brought in to help each side clarify their positions and search for possible compromises. There are many different resources, workshops, and certificate programs to help social workers develop their conflict resolution skills.

ANTI-POVERTY SOCIAL ACTION GROUPS

The OCAP (Ontario Coalition Against Poverty) is an example of a social action group. For many years they have taken a public and confrontational approach to the government's inaction towards ending poverty. They have erected tents in Toronto parks to draw attention to the problem of homelessness, helped organize doctors in health centres to support people living on Social Assistance, and have organized some of the most significant street protests in Toronto. OCAP deals with all aspects of—and populations living in—poverty, including immigration, First Nations, homelessness, welfare rates, and minimum wage. OCAP protests the system and advocates for policy changes, but it also provides activist casework. For example, it works with individuals and families who are having trouble navigating the Social Assistance system. OCAP helps write letters to officials and representatives and will even attend appointments to help people negotiate with their caseworkers. This combination of broad social action and individual advocacy has proven very effective in organizing the poor. See www.ocap.ca for more on the organization.

Evaluation

One of the final stages of community practice involves evaluation, which allows a community to reflect upon whether they were able to achieve the goals that they set for themselves. A final evaluation is most effective when evaluation has been an ongoing component of the community work. Sometimes it is driven by a funder who wants a report of outcomes, but evaluations can also provide a useful opportunity for communities to reflect upon what they have achieved and to enhance their enthusiasm and confidence for future projects.

Social work with communities often addresses the same problems that individual- or family-focused counsellors deal with, but they take a slightly different approach, looking at problems as something that a group of people experience. They work hard to find the common experiences that people have and build from those to create effective community groups able to achieve change for themselves. As they do so, community groups often gain valuable skills and are more able to affect change. Increasingly they have a sense that they can influence their environment and improve their lives. And with this, they are armed with the skills and the confidence to challenge those who exploit them and to imagine and create a better future for themselves.

Conclusion

Group work has gained respect and prominence in the profession of social work. From an organizational perspective, group work is frequently seen as a more appropriate and more economically efficient approach to helping individual work. From a client's perspective, there are many advantages to dealing with issues in a group context. Groups can provide a feeling of belonging. They also provide a context for interpersonal learning. By listening to others' experiences, group members' gain new insights and learn different coping strategies. Groups also provide an opportunity for altruism not available in individual counselling. Personal affirmation comes with group members sharing their own experience and knowledge in order to help others in the group.

The study of group work is being revitalized in schools of social work. Groups that focus on treatment, as well as those that are task oriented, will continue to be an important part of the roles of social workers. Groups play a vital part in the delivery of social services and are fundamental building blocks for society.

Photography as Research for Change

In 2004 and 2005 a group of youth in Toronto's Malvern neighbourhood, as part of a larger community youth arts project, used disposable cameras to document what it was like to be young and living in poverty. These photographs provided "data" about poverty and youth in Toronto, which in turn raised the issue's profile and was used to advocate for more recreational and employment programs.

CHAPTER REVIEW

Key Terms

- Group work
- Self-help groups
- Educational groups
- Support/therapeutic groups
- Task groups
- Social action groups
- Group dynamics
- Forming stage
- Storming stage
- Norming stage
- Performing stage
- Adjourning stage

- Cueing
- Social empathy
- Cognitive theories
- Behaviour theories
- Affective theories
- Community
- Locality development
- Social planning
- Social action
- Praxis
- Community capacity building
- Participatory action research (PAR)

Review Questions

1. Name five kinds of social work groups and discuss how they differ.
2. What is meant by group dynamics?
3. Identify and explain the main stages of group development.
4. What are some criteria that should be considered when selecting members for a group?
5. What is a community and what different kinds of communities exist?
6. What is the role of a community worker when organizing a community to create change?
7. What are the phases of organizing a community?
8. What is unique about Paulo Freire's approach to community work?

Exploring Social Work

1. There is a plethora of self-help groups in most urban communities. Many deal with specific medical ailments or genetic abnormalities. There are also a range of groups designed for addressing specific age-related issues such as parenting teens. Discuss the self-help groups with which you are familiar or have had involvement; you may need to do some research. What do you identify as the strengths of these groups?

2. While educational, self-help, and therapeutic groups can provide support and assistance to many, not all people benefit from groups. Discuss the limitations of group work and situations where you would decide not to work in a group context. When is a group counter-indicated?

3. Another challenge in community practice is that the boundaries between the role of the worker and community members can be a little less clear than they are in more traditional counselling contexts. The social worker often attempts to work collaboratively with community members, letting them take the lead in much of the work. Workers are often in people's homes and participate in community activities. Sometimes this can make it difficult for community members to see the social worker as a worker and not a friend. In small groups, discuss what boundaries might be important to keep rigid, what ones might need to be more flexible, and how you can decrease power imbalances while also keeping roles clear.

Websites
- - - - -

Self-Help Resource Centre
www.selfhelp.on.ca

The Self-Help Resource Centre is a charitable organization based in Toronto that provides information on starting and maintaining a self-help group. It outlines ideas and questions to bear in mind when thinking about starting a group and fourteen steps for organizing a self-help group.

Canadian Directory of Genetic Support Groups
www.lhsc.on.ca/programs/medgenet/

Operated by the London Health Sciences Centre, this website provides a directory for genetic or rare medical conditions and accompanying support groups. Increasingly people are turning to the web for information and support in dealing with medical ailments.

Tamarack: An Institute for Community Engagement
www.tamarackcommunity.ca

Tamarack is a Canadian organization that fosters citizens and institutions to address community challenges through engagement. The website offers ideas for engaging a broad range of community members and discusses a variety of issues related to creating progressive change in communities.

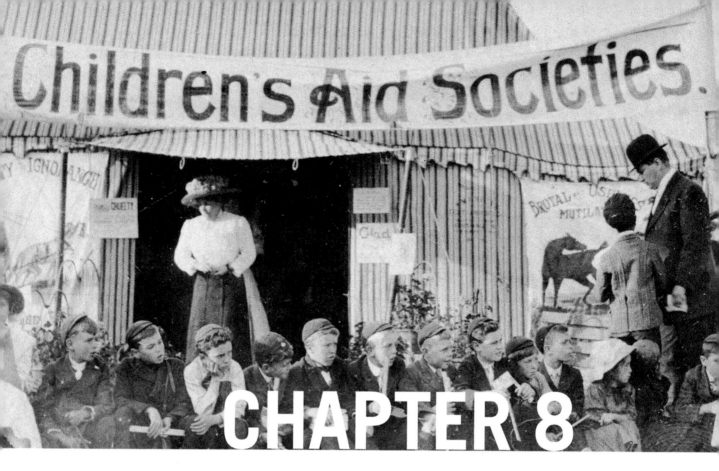

CHAPTER 8

SOCIAL WORK WITH CHILDREN AND YOUTH

- -

Child Protection and Family Support

Across the country, governments and non-profit agencies are responsible for providing a range of indispensable services to children and families. These services include child protection, foster care coordination, group homes, and a variety of family support services. Collectively, they are what is known as the child welfare system, and social workers play a major role in it. For example, in Ontario child protection and family support, over 7,000 social workers provide services through fifty-three Children's Aid Societies (CASs) with an annual budget of over $1 billion.

Despite determination and hard work, however, the lesson of the past two decades is that child welfare practitioners across the country cannot make good on their commitment to help families and children unless there is adequate government funding to back them up.

The Organization of Child Welfare

Child welfare is a major area of employment for social workers today. It is also one of the most difficult areas of work for practitioners in terms of the heart-wrenching cases that can arise and the often complex ethical issues involved. Much of the social worker's daily activity involves complex and sensitive issues and decisions surrounding children and their families. Over 76,000 Canadian children are currently under the protection of various provincial child and family service agencies.

The work of child welfare involves much more than simply removing children from unsafe home environments. Child welfare is highly regulated through laws and regulations and involves five key activities:

- **Family support.** Providing a range of family programs and services in order to maintain healthy families, support families at risk, and protect children.
- **Child protection.** Protecting children at risk by removing them from their families and finding substitute care.
- **Child placement.** Finding temporary substitute care, such as foster and group homes, for children who cannot continue to live with their parent(s) or guardian(s).
- **Adoption.** Finding permanent homes for children who cannot live with either of their parents.
- **Foster care.** Recruiting foster care providers, providing training and support, as well as monitoring foster homes.

Acting in these many ways through provincial agencies and non-profit centres, social workers intervene on behalf of children and their families—without them, the lives of a great many Canadian families and children would be much more tenuous.

Children from an Ottawa daycare protest the government's cancellation of early learning and child care programs in 2006.

In-home and Out-of-home Services

Canadian social workers also provide a wide variety of related services for children and youth, in the form of in-home and out-of-home services.

In-home services are provided to help a household or family members live together harmoniously in a secure and safe environment. The main categories of in-home services include family counselling services, parenting supports, in-home child care, homemaker services, and family educational services. **Out-of-home services** are implemented when the home situation becomes unsuitable for the child. These services include foster care, adoption, daycare centres, community supports (e.g., the Community Action Program for Children and Aboriginal Head Start), group homes, institutional care, parenting self-help and empowerment groups, and family housing assistance.

Centre of Excellence for Children's Well-Being

www.cecw-cepb.ca

The CECW encourages collaborative projects that integrate prevention and interventions across a variety of sectors. The Centre's four main functions are fostering research, disseminating information, developing policy, and forging networks.

Provincial Agencies and Programs

Each of the ten Canadian provinces and three territories has different organizations and legislation governing child welfare. Provincial services for children and youth may be provided by a branch of the provincial government or by a private or non-profit agency.

Besides child protection agencies, there are a variety of youth/child agencies across the country. The Ottawa-based Youth Services Bureau (YSB), is one example. It provides programs that work with families in the home as well as individual counselling. It also has a residential program for girls under 16 years of age to help build their self-esteem, as well as a six-month transitional residence program for youth 16 and older who are not ready to live on their own and require skills development.

Provincial Legislation

Provincial legislation and policy in this area change frequently. An overview of some current systems is provided below.

- First Nations child welfare services are provided by either the provincial agency on behalf of the federal government or directly by First Nations agencies as negotiated under the federal government's policy on Aboriginal self-government. Arrangements must be negotiated individually with each First Nation, and generally involve federal and provincial representatives. In Ontario there are three Aboriginal-specific children's aid societies.

- In British Columbia, child protection services are provided by the Ministry for Children and Families, under the terms of the 1996 *Child, Family and Community Service Act*. The Ministry states that its role is to ensure a child-centred, integrated approach that promotes and protects the healthy development of children and youth while recognizing their lifelong attachment to family and community (BCMCF 1999). The 2002 *Child, Family and Community Service Amendment Act* expands the options available for placing children once they have been taken into custody. Now children can be placed in the custody of extended family, friends of the family, and other community members shortly after removal from the home.

- Alberta child protection services are provided by Alberta Family and Social Services, which is run by the provincial government and is governed by the *Child, Youth and Family Enhancement Act* of 2000 and the *Child Welfare Amendment Act* of 2002.

- Saskatchewan has the *Child and Family Services Act* (1990). Bilateral agreements continue to be negotiated between Saskatchewan Social Services and First Nations bands for the control and delivery of child and family services on reserves.

- In Manitoba, child protection services are provided through the non-governmental Child and Family Services Agencies, which are mandated under the *Child and Family Services Act* of 1985. These are overseen by the provincial Ministry of Family Services.

- In Ontario, child protection services are delivered through fifty-three separate Children's Aid Societies (CAS). These organizations are legislated under the *Child and Family Services Act* (1990), *the Children's Law Reform Act* (2002), and the *Family Law Act* (2002) to investigate allegations of abuse and neglect, provide services to families for protecting children, prevent circumstances requiring the protection of children, and provide care or supervision for children and provide adoption services. As of 1998, the provincial Ministry of Community and Social Services assumed 100 percent funding of Children's Aid Societies.

- The New Brunswick provincial government provides child protection services through its Family and Community Social Services (a department of the Ministry of Health and Community Services) under the *Family Services Act* of 1983.

- The Children's Aid Society of Halifax provides services in Nova Scotia. Under the *Children and Family Services Act* of 1990 (amended in 2002), child protection workers and designated social workers in child welfare agencies investigate all reports of alleged child abuse and neglect. There are twenty child welfare offices throughout the province—six are offices of the government, fourteen are privately run agencies. The Mi'kmaq Family and Children's Services Agency provides services for families living on reserves. Adoptions are regulated by the *Adoption Information Act*, 1996.

- In Prince Edward Island, the 2003 *Child Protection Act* made major changes in child welfare practice, including lowering the age for defining a child (from 18 to 16 years), introducing progressive and preventive approaches, and tightening time frames, particularly for younger children.

- In Newfoundland, the *Child, Youth and Family Services Act of 1999* replaces the *Child Welfare Act*. The new Act represents a shift in the way child welfare services will be provided in the province. The legislation supports a move away from remedial approaches towards prevention and early intervention strategies, with services delivered by community-based agencies.

- The government of the Northwest Territories provides child protection services through its Department of Health and Social Services. The 1997 *Child and Family Services Act* and the *Adoptions Act* define "best interests of the child" with the recognition that differing cultural values and practices must be respected. Under the legislation, applicable Aboriginal organizations must be informed whenever someone who is, or is eligible to become, a member of

Aboriginal Head Start Program

An example of an innovative out-of-house program for children up to age 6, is the *Aboriginal Head Start* (AHS) program. Through Health Canada AHS funds early childhood development programs for First Nations, Inuit, and Métis children and their families. There are over 120 AHS sites in urban and northern communities across Canada. AHS emphasizes a holistic approach by fostering the spiritual, emotional, intellectual, and physical growth of the child. Many attribute the success of the program to its focus on Aboriginal self-determination. Aboriginal communities designed the program and continue to control its operation and evaluation. Programs are controlled locally and are based on traditional community beliefs and cultural practices. AHS illustrates how an approach that uses self-determination and participation can succeed, especially for Aboriginal people.

the organization has a child protection case proceeding to court. This creates an opportunity for the organization to provide input, particularly with respect to any unique customs and traditions that may be important in the development of a case plan for the child and family.

■ Like the Northwest Territories, the government of Nunavut provides services through its Department of Health and Social Services. The *Child and Family Services Act* is the primary legislation providing for the protection and well-being of children. The *Aboriginal Custom Adoption Recognition Act* specifically provides for the well-being and adoption of Aboriginal children that respects cultural traditions.

History of Child Welfare

Over the years, each province accumulated its own imposing array of child welfare legislation. Nevertheless, certain patterns can be discerned in the history of child welfare legislation and practice in Canada.

Pre-industrial Child Welfare—Pre-1890

The problems of child abuse and neglect did not suddenly appear in the twentieth century. The children of rural settler families typically worked at farming along with other family members and household employees. Often the work was difficult and a strict division of labour was enforced. The mother was responsible for family care needs, such as cooking, cleaning, and nursing. The father was responsible for the economic survival needs of the family. The wife and children existed as economic dependants of the family patriarch: the husband and father. Patriarchal authority was reinforced by the state through a variety of laws and practices.

By contrast, Aboriginal communities had rather more inclusive ideas concerning the raising of children. First Nations believed that a child belonged to his or her people, and that a child was a gift from the Creator. They believed that this connection of child to community was non-discretionary—he or she simply belonged to the nation and it was the responsibility of all to meet the child's needs.

In 1792, The Province of Upper Canada proclaimed that the Common Law of England would be in force for the new province. This body of law was exceedingly harsh towards children. For example, Upper Canada introduced the first Act concerning children in 1799. It was called the *Orphans Act*, and it gave town wardens the power to bind a child under 14 to an employer as an apprentice. In 1827, this Act was replaced with the *Guardianship Act*, which allowed guardians to be appointed by the court. The guardian then had the right to bind the child as an apprentice. The role of the family in the early laws in Canada did not extend beyond its value as an economic unit. Therefore, families that were poor were viewed as moral and economic threats, and their children were to be "bound out" to proper self-supporting families who would not taint the children with parental failure.

The period from 1867 to 1890 saw the introduction of new laws that changed the exalted position of husbands and fathers. The legislative right of men to inflict arbitrary and severe punishment on their wives and children was beginning to be challenged. These new laws also affected the treatment and rights of children in general. The period began with amendments to Ontario's *Apprentices and Minors Act* (1874) and saw the introduction of compulsory education, regulation of work hours, the right of women to hold property, and the rise of new and improved social agencies. For the first time, courts would decide whether a child's best interests would be better served with his or her family, one parent, or an employer. Until this time, children generally were not seen as needing special care or nurturing; their needs often were ignored and severe punishment was meted out to enforce rules.

It should also be noted that, in relation to Aboriginal peoples, the system of child welfare became part of an orchestrated campaign to dismantle communities and assimilate Aboriginal children into mainstream Canadian society. *The Indian Act of 1876* exemplified the colonizer's views towards First Nations and their children. Beyond outlawing traditional ceremonies, such as the potlatch, the laws of the day attempted to eradicate Aboriginal culture by taking children out of First Nations homes and communities and placing them in residential schools administered by a number of Christian churches in association with the government. (For more on the residential schools, see Chapter 11, page 225.)

In the 1890s, legislation was passed to regulate working conditions and hours of work for children.

A New Era in Child Welfare Legislation—1890 to 1940

There was a marked increase in government involvement in children's issues in the late nineteenth and early twentieth centuries. In particular, legislation was enacted that allowed the state to remove children from the care of their parents or guardians. The federal *Juvenile Delinquent Act* of 1908 and the Ontario *Act for the Prevention of Cruelty to Children* of 1893 were both aimed at the protection of children. The legal mandate for promoting the "best interests" of children was given to the state, and the state could decide whether parents were good or bad. It had the authority (through legislation and the courts) to remove children from homes and put them into care.

In the 1890s, Canadian provinces also began to establish commissions to inspect the working conditions for children in factories. Many children as young as 8 and 9 years of age were employed, and inspections often revealed a callous disregard for the welfare of these children by factory owners. For example, there were repeated reports of poor ventilation and a lack of sanitary equipment. As well, the children were receiving no

J.J. Kelso

J.J. Kelso (1864-1935) was an Irish immigrant to Toronto, a crusading journalist, and a child welfare pioneer. He helped found the Toronto Humane Society in 1887, which at the time concerned itself with the prevention of cruelty to children and animals. He was appointed Superintendent of Neglected and Dependent Children in Ontario until his retirement in 1934. During this time, he was instrumental in helping to establish Children's Aid Societies throughout Ontario—sixty by 1912— and in British Columbia, Manitoba, Prince Edward Island, and Nova Scotia during the first two decades of the 1900s.

His influence led to the Ontario *Children's Protection Act*, the first in Canada. He was a skilled organizer and a tireless promoter of children's rights who firmly believed that wide community mobilization is required for social change. His fresh and new ideas on children are exemplified in his presentation to the Social Service Congress in 1914 in which he said, "The child is the central figure in all social reform."

education while working in the factories, which contributed to the large number of illiterate adults across the country. As a result, new legislation was passed to regulate working conditions and hours of work. For example, Ontario passed the *Factory Act* and the *Regulation of Shops Act*. Eventually, the age of those considered to be children was raised to 16 years.

Several important women's organizations emerged in the late nineteenth century that affected the rights of children. The Women's Missionary Societies, which originally had an evangelical approach, began addressing the needs of women and children. The Women's Christian Temperance Union, founded in 1874, emphasized the prohibition of the sale of alcohol. Their broader social goals were helping children and included ensuring child protection, establishing reformatories for juveniles, and building cottage-style homes to replace institutional care. The Young Women's Christian Association (YWCA) addressed the needs of urban working women, including assisting them with their children. The National Council of Women, formed in 1893, was an alliance of women's organizations aimed at coordinating policies at a national level. They considered many women's issues to be "mothering" issues, and their goal was to bring private mothering practices to public and national attention.

In Toronto, J.J. Kelso, a journalist who had himself been raised in a single-parent family, began organizing meetings to address the problem of street children and their abuse. He was critical of the care provided by many of the private charities and orphanages. He believed children in such institutions suffered from careless policies, lack of supervision, and a lack of inspection or visitation.

Kelso's work resulted in numerous changes to child welfare services in Ontario and in Canada. The Toronto Children's Aid Society was incorporated in 1891, with Kelso serving as its first president. In 1892, the name was changed to the Children's Aid Society of Toronto, and a charter was granted to carry out the administration of the *Act for the Prevention of Cruelty and Better Protection of Children*. Kelso also played a pivotal role in the formation in Ontario of a Royal Commission on Prisons and Asylums in 1890, the creation of an office for the protection of children, and the *Children's Protection Act* of 1888, which is the forerunner of the current *Child and Family Services Act*.

The passing of the 1893 *Children's Protection Act* in Ontario ushered in a new era of modern child welfare legislation protecting children from abuse and neglect. The notion of neglect, which is still controversial today, stated that a child found sleeping in the open air was considered to be neglected. Those found guilty of mistreating a child were sentenced to three months of hard labour. The idea of foster homes, supervised by Children's Aid Societies, also originated with this Act. In 1908, the *Child Welfare Act* repealed some of the more draconian aspects of the previous Act and provided for procedures to rehabilitate mistreated children.

Between 1891 and 1912, sixty Children's Aid Societies sprang up in Ontario. In 1912, they joined together as the Associated Children's Aid Societies of Ontario, now known as the Ontario Association of Children's Aid Societies (OACAS).

The obligation on the part of society to protect children began to crystallize during this period and a new notion of "childhood" emerged. Prior to this, children had been regarded essentially as adults. Now children were beginning to be seen in a different light and the period of childhood itself was viewed as having great bearing on the later development of the person. This was a fundamental shift in thinking.

Modern Child Welfare Policy—1940 to Present

Since 1940, literally hundreds of provincial laws have been passed that affect child welfare. Across the country, while each province has distinct and separate legislation, several trends have emerged:

- A shift from a volunteer to a professional service system.
- The development and implementation of risk-assessment models and standardized record-keeping.
- Provincial governments' acceptance of direct responsibility for the delivery of child welfare services through public financing, as well as agency reporting and provincial supervision.
- A shift from institutional and protection-oriented services to non-institutional and prevention-oriented services.
- A shift towards legislation that emphasizes the "best interests" of the child over a model that stresses keeping children in their families.
- An improvement in the capacity of Aboriginal agencies to provide services under Aboriginal leadership.

Within this broad framework, a number of new developments and shifts of emphasis have occurred. During the mid-1950s and 1960s, the near total reliance on foster homes and large-scale institutions such as orphanages and training schools came under scrutiny. Increasingly, child welfare agencies dealt with older children. These older children had emotional problems and exhibited more troublesome behaviour. Social workers were spending a lot more time with foster parents, families, and the children themselves. By the end of the 1960s, the number of foster homes was also declining.

In response, two alternatives to foster homes and large-scale institutions emerged. First, treatment regimes were emphasized. This involved many different kinds of treatment, ranging from strict discipline to a more permissive approach that concentrated on free expression and creativity. Second, group homes were launched. Reformers noted that children were being shuffled from foster home to foster home. One out of every three permanent wards of the court could expect to be placed in the care

J.J. Kelso was instrumental in the creation of the Toronto Humane Society for the Prevention of Cruelty to Children and Animals, and in 1891 he founded the first Children's Aid Society.

of various foster parents five or more times. The children were simply not able to adjust. Both the government and social workers believed that group homes would be less stigmatizing and impersonal than the large institutions of the past and more able to meet the adjustment needs of the children. They hoped that group homes would provide the children with the remedial help they needed.

In the 1970s there was increased concern about the damaging effects of child welfare agencies on children in their care. A new generation of reformers argued that children were coming out of the child welfare system more damaged than when they went into it. Some of this concern was reflected in a new 1978 *Child Welfare Act* in Ontario, which defined child abuse for the first time. However, it wasn't until Ontario's *Child and Family Services Act* of 1984 that this concern was expressed in legal language. The 1984 Act begins with a statement of principles that includes: "The least restrictive or disruptive course of action should be followed, keeping the child in the home, if possible. Social workers can no longer 'apprehend' a child unless imminent risk can be shown."

In 1990, new legislation in Ontario shifted to stating that the paramount purpose was "to promote the best interests, protection and well-being of children." Many similar sentiments can be noted in provincial child welfare legislation across the country around this time. The provincial Acts of the 1970s and early 1980s had stressed the least disrup-

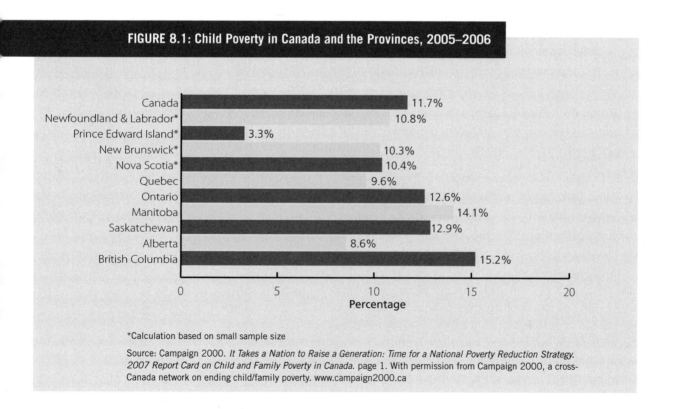

FIGURE 8.1: Child Poverty in Canada and the Provinces, 2005–2006

*Calculation based on small sample size

Source: Campaign 2000. *It Takes a Nation to Raise a Generation: Time for a National Poverty Reduction Strategy. 2007 Report Card on Child and Family Poverty in Canada.* page 1. With permission from Campaign 2000, a cross-Canada network on ending child/family poverty. www.campaign2000.ca

tive course of action in addressing the abuse and neglect of children—the child was to remain in the home if at all possible. The more recent provincial Acts have swung back somewhat to the notion of acting in the best interests of the child. Several widely publicized deaths of children who were left in the home caused a reaction on the part of some provincial governments. The legislation now allows for quicker removal of children who may be in danger. As well, the expansion of the notion of neglect has increased the likelihood that social workers will determine that a child needs to be removed and placed in care.

The Ontario proclamation of Bill 210 in 2006 amended the *Child and Family Services Act* (CFSA) to provide more flexible services and responses, to reduce court delays and encourage alternatives to court, and to provide a broader range of care options for children and youth that support long-term and permanent homes. **Differential response (DR)** enables a new flexible intake and assessment model that assesses eligibility for service, safety, and risk, while allowing for greater engagement with families. **Alternative dispute resolution (ADR)** intends to streamline court processes and uses alternatives to court. Child and Family Services in Ontario will also emphasize two options for care with respect to placement with kin: **kinship service** is for children who are not in care and **kinship care** refers to children in care.

Members of the Aylmer Church of God pray and protest as they await a court ruling in St. Thomas, Ont., in 2001. The Children's Aid Society had removed seven children from their home amid allegations that the parents refused to promise not to spank their children.

The Dilemma of Child Protection

The primary response to child abuse and neglect in Canada is provincial child protection systems. The provincial child welfare laws require that all cases of suspected abuse and neglect be reported and investigated. Various actions or interventions occur if an investigation indicates that a child is in need of protection. Responses range from the provision of counselling and support services to the family, to the temporary or permanent removal of the child from the home, to the removal of the abuser or abusers from the home. In the most serious cases, abusers may be convicted of a crime if the abuse can be proven under the *Criminal Code of Canada*.

CHILD POVERTY IS FAMILY POVERTY
Some Families Are More Vulnerable Than Others

Persistent social and economic inequality in Canada based on gender, race, length of time in the country, and ability is reflected in disproportionately high child poverty rates among families that face systemic discrimination. Lone mothers and children are one of the most economically vulnerable groups with almost one in every two female lone parent families (47 percent before tax) living in poverty. Women earn approximately 71 percent of what men earn for full-time, year-round work, and are more likely to be found in low-wage work.[1]

Low income rates among new immigrants are more than three times higher than for people born in Canada.[2] One in two children in recent immigrant families (49 percent) lives below the poverty line, according to the 2001 Census. Despite the highest educational credentials and skills of arrivals to Canada, newcomers experience a sharp decline in living standards when compared with immigrants from past decades. Valuable skills are squandered when Canadian employers fail to recognize international work experience and credentials.

Barriers to employment for immigrants of colour are compounded by discrimination faced by racialized communities.[3] One in three children in racialized families (34 percent) lived in poverty in 2001. Compared to people of European background, racialized people experience are more likely to be unemployed or in low-paying occupations.[4]

Canada's Natives are also at risk. According to Statistics Canada's *Aboriginal Children's Survey 2006*, almost one in two Aboriginal children under six (living off-reserve) lives in a low-income family.

The poverty rate for children with disabilities is 28 percent. Families with a parent or child with a disability are more likely to rely on social assistance as a primary source of income. They face barriers to full inclusion and encounter immense financial, social, and emotional stresses. For adults with disabilities, employment rates are low, with 51 percent of working age adults with disabilities employed.[5] We need a guaranteed income system for persons with disabilities equivalent in adequacy and design to that in place for seniors.

Along with a broad national poverty reduction strategy, we need specific policies and investments that address systemic barriers and promote equity.

Notes:

1. Canadian Research Institute for the Advancement of Women. (2005). *"Women and Poverty."* Ottawa: CRIAW. After-tax data indicates 33 percent of female lone parent families live in poverty.

2. Picot, G., Hou, F., & Coulombe, S. (Jan. 2007). *Chronic Low Income and Low Income Dynamics Among Recent Immigrants*. Ottawa: Statistics Canada.

3. "Racialized persons" refers to people who face systemic discrimination based on socially constructed concepts of race and includes those born in Canada as well as newcomers.

4. Teelucksingh, C. & Galabuzi, G.E. (May 2005). *Working Precariously: the impact of race and immigrant status on employment opportunities and outcomes in Canada*. Toronto: Canadian Race Relations Foundation.

5. Human Resources Development Canada. (2003). *Disability in Canada: A 2001 Profile*. Ottawa: Human Resources Development Canada.

Source: Campaign 2000. 2007. *It Takes a Nation to Raise a Generation: Time for a National Poverty Reduction Strategy. 2007 Report Card on Child and Family Poverty in Canada.* page 2. With permission from Campaign 2000, a cross-Canada network on ending child/family poverty. www.campaign2000.ca

Child protection agencies have long grappled with the dilemma of deciding when children should be brought into the care of the state and when they should be left in the home. The social worker operates with the knowledge that she or he must obtain and assess as much background information as possible and use the information to make judgments regarding the parents' and the child's best interests, all the while knowing that the process is not an exact science. As one CAS administrator put it, "The work is not for the faint of heart. It is not a vocation for those who are just 'well-meaning.'" The work requires knowledge, stamina, exceptional versatility, and an ability to find common ground with parents in order to secure safety for children.

It is sometimes stated that social workers must "desensitize" themselves when they work in the child welfare field. Of course, in practice this is nearly impossible since, in order to do their jobs effectively, social workers must be very sensitive to the needs and feelings of the children and families they are involved with.

The "Best Interests" of the Child

Throughout the history of modern child protection legislation in Canada, the terms *best interests* of the child and *least restrictive intervention* have been debated, and Acts have been passed that move between the two approaches. The **best interests approach** emphasizes the protection and well-being of the child, whereas the **least restrictive approach** emphasizes the course of action that will cause the least change for the child, leaving him or her with the family if at all possible.

Deciding what is in the best interests of a child is difficult. A social worker makes the initial decision to remove a child from the home, but the case must go before a judge for a final decision. When provinces have "best interest" legislation, the number of children taken from their families generally increased, sometimes dramatically. A few high-profile cases in which children have been harmed as a result of being left in a dangerous situation have led several provinces to change their "least restrictive" legislation. Of course, the state must also consider the damage that may be caused by removing children from their families and placing them in group homes.

In Nova Scotia, for example, the following factors are considered in deciding which criteria are to be used by social workers and the courts when trying to decide on the best interests of the child:

- the child's physical, mental, and emotional needs and the appropriate care or treatment to meet those needs

- the child's cultural background and religious faith

- the importance for the child's development of a positive relationship with a parent and a secure place as a member of a family

---

UN Convention on the Rights of the Child

The United Nations Convention on the Rights of the Child spells out basic human rights that children everywhere have. These include the rights: to survival; to develop to the fullest; to protection from harmful influences, abuse, and exploitation; and to participate fully in family, cultural, and social life.

The convention is a universally agreed upon set of non-negotiable standards and obligations. It was developed in 1989, when world leaders decided that a special agreement that specifically addressed the care and protection of those under eighteen years of age was necessary.

Best Interests Approach

Emphasizes the protection and well-being of the child.

Least Restrictive Approach

Emphasizes the least disruptive course of action in child protection, advocating keeping children with their families.

- the child's relationships by blood or through an adoption order

- the importance of continuity of care; whether it is likely that the child will be moved from one agency or home to another

- the child's views and wishes, which must be respected

- the risk that the child may suffer harm through being removed from or kept away from the care of a parent

- the degree of risk, if any, that justifies the finding that the child is in need of protection

(Nova Scotia Department of Community Services 1990)

For example, section 22 (j) of Nova Scotia's *Children and Family Services Act* of 1990 (amended 2002) states that a child is in need of protective services when he or she "has suffered physical harm caused by chronic and serious neglect by a parent or guardian…the parent or guardian does not provide, or refuses, or is unavailable or unable to consent to services or treatment to remedy, or alleviate the harm" (NSDCS 1993, 17), or when "the child has suffered physical harm, inflicted by a parent or guardian of the child or caused by the failure of a parent or guardian to supervise and protect the child adequately." The Act does not provide specific directions as to what a social worker must do; rather, it provides general guidance on what a social worker or judge must consider when deciding what to do.

More recent Ontario legislation, on the other hand, is directive in declaring what a social worker must do to protect the best interests of the child. In 2000, the Ontario government stiffened its previous legislation with the *Family Services Amendment Act*. The words "least restrictive" were removed to ensure that the "best interests" clauses were clearly paramount. It also expanded the reasons for finding a child in need of protection. For instance, the word "neglect" was specifically included, and the threshold for risk of harm and emotional harm to children was lowered. In 2006 the *Child and Family Services Statute Law Amendment Act* placed emphasis on engaging with family and kin to work toward keeping children within permanent family structures.

Children in Care

Consistent with the hopes of the 1978 and 1984 Ontario legislation, there was a decline of children in care between 1971 and 1988. In this period, the CAS reported an increase of 160 percent in the number of families served, but the number of children in care decreased by 45 percent (Trocmé 1991, 63). However, the trend subsequently changed. The 1994 and 2000 changes in legislation emphasized the best interests of the child, and the number of children in care has again increased. In 2004, 19,105 children required substitute care in Ontario. This represents an increase of nearly 34 percent from January 1995 (OACAS 2006). By 2006 this number had increased dramatically to 29,385 which resulted in significant legislative changes (OACAS 2008).

The Need to Monitor the Quality of Out-of-Home Care

As remarkable as it may seem, over 200,000 children and youth come into contact with child welfare authorities every year across Canada, and on any one day of the year over 67,000 children and youth are living in out-of-home care. Although this group is clearly one of the most high-risk groups of children in Canada, there is no accepted framework for tracking how well these children are doing. In an effort to address this issue, Nico Trocmé and his colleagues have put forward an "outcomes matrix" that could be used by child welfare managers and policy makers to track trends and evaluate programs and policies (Trocmé et al., 2009).

In the absence of any national benchmarks, the proposed indicators can be used to measure the degree to which child welfare services are working on behalf of Canadian children and families. The National Child Welfare Outcomes Indicator Matrix (NOM) takes into account the balance between a child's immediate need for protection, a child's long-term need for nurturing and a stable home, a family's potential for growth, and the community's capacity to meet a child's needs. The framework consists of four nested domains that capture the key indicators—the child's safety, the child's well-being, permanence, and family and community support (see adjacent graphic).

The National Child Welfare Outcomes Indicator Matrix (NOM) provides a framework that can be used to track outcomes for children and families receiving welfare services.

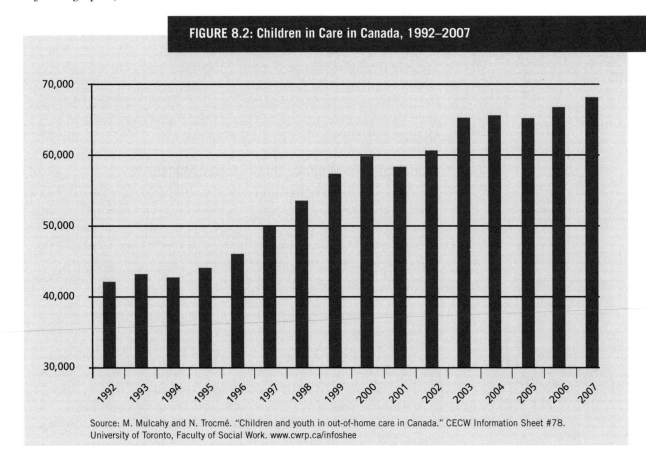

FIGURE 8.2: Children in Care in Canada, 1992–2007

Source: M. Mulcahy and N. Trocmé. "Children and youth in out-of-home care in Canada." CECW Information Sheet #78. University of Toronto, Faculty of Social Work. www.cwrp.ca/infoshee

Aboriginal Children in Care

Information about the number of Aboriginal children in care across Canada is not readily available. In 2006, the National Council of Welfare contacted all provincial and territorial child welfare authorities and asked for the total number of Aboriginal and non–Aboriginal children in care. Some provided the information, some were reluctant and others were unable or unwilling to do so. The results are shown in Table 8.1.

As the table indicates, Aboriginal children are grossly overrepresented among children in care. Moreover, provincial data show that the percentage of Aboriginal children in care is increasing. In British Columbia, for example, Aboriginal children made up 37% of children in care in 2000/01, compared to 50% in 2005/06. In 1997 in Manitoba, about 70% of children in care were Aboriginal, compared to 85% in March 2006. The increase is too great to be explained by population growth.

According to Phil Fontaine, National Chief of the Assembly of First Nations (AFN) at the time, the situation facing First Nations children and their families today has never been worse. "There are more than 27,000 First Nations children in care today. This represents three times the number of children who were in residential schools at the height of their operations." This dire state of affairs has prompted any First Nations people to argue that the "sixties scoop" never ended, rather it increased.

There is evidence that the majority of the children taken from their homes are removed because of neglect brought on by poverty. Without adequate housing, child care, and employment, Aboriginal families face great difficulties in raising their children. But experience tells us that the state makes lousy parents and additional efforts need to be made to keep Aboriginal children with their kin and communities.

Aboriginal Controlled, Culturally Based Models

The failure of provincial/territorial child welfare agencies to make a meaningful difference in the health and well being of Aboriginal children supports the need for Aboriginal controlled, culturally based models ("First Nations, Métis and Inuit Children and Youth: Time To Act," 2007). What is needed is a rethinking of the mainstream colonial approach to Aboriginal children in which the dominant culture perceives that it knows best. Structural reasons why Aboriginal children are being taken into care must also be dealt with—poverty, lack of education, unemployment, housing, and many other interconnected factors.

"Aboriginal peoples are best positioned to make decisions about Aboriginal children and youth," the National Council of Welfare notes in its report. "In the spirit of reconciliation and restoration, there is a need for adequately funded, Aboriginal controlled, culturally based models of childcare while also tackling the myriad interconnected factors such as poverty that facilitate Aboriginal children ending up in care."

TABLE 8.1: Aboriginal Children in Care by Province and Territory

	% of children (0-14) who are Aboriginal	Number of Children in Care			
		Total	Total Aboriginal	Percentage Aboriginal	Date
Nfld & Labrador	6				
PEI	2				
Nova Scotia	3	2,000	310	16	2006
New Brunswick*	4	1,445	191	13	Sept. 2006*
Quebec	2	11,135			March 2006
Ontario	2	19,035			March 2006
Manitoba	23	6,629	5,627	85	March 2006
Saskatchewan	25	3,050	2,135	70	2005
Alberta	9	8,565	4,880	57	March 2006
British Columbia	7	9,157	4,542	50	March 2006
Yukon**	33	252			Sept. 2006
Northwest Territories	63				
Nunavut	95	311	311	100	Oct. 2006

*New Brunswick: Data includes 178 First Nations children on-reserve served by First Nations Child and Family Services Agencies as of July 2007.

** Yukon: An estimate from the grand chief of the Council of Yukon First Nations put the share of First Nations children in care at over 80%. (CBC News "CYFN withdraws from Children's Act review," March 24, 2006.)

Source: National Council of Welfare. 2007. *First Nations, Métis and Inuit Children and Youth: Time to Act.* Ottawa: National Council of Welfare. www.ncwcnbes.net. page 86. Reproduced with the permission of the Minister of Public Works and Government Services Canada, 2008.

Addressing the Problem of Child Poverty

Social workers are presented with a persistent dilemma in their daily practice; namely, to what extent they and their agency should take into account the broader social context of individuals, families, and communities. Strong arguments have been made for having children's agencies do more work as child advocates on prevention programs and on combating widespread child poverty. In fact, critics argue that when government finances are strained, prevention programs are the first to be cut. Consequently, child welfare and protection programs can become increasingly reactive and crisis-oriented.

However, others argue that child welfare agencies should be involved only in straightforward protection issues, such as neglect or abuse. Only when there is an immediate danger should the state intervene. This viewpoint rests on the belief that child welfare agencies are already sufficiently intrusive and that they should not be concerned with broader social issues as well. Both sides firmly maintain that what they are advocating will be in the best long-term interests of children and their families. By and large, governments have pursued a short-term perspective, dealing with emergencies at hand, and the overall trend seems to be away from proactive intervention that seeks lasting solutions to underlying causes.

Demonstrators march through Vancouver's Downtown Eastside during the Poverty Olympics in February 2009, held to draw attention to poverty and homelessness in the city.

The Incidence of Child Abuse

Child abuse entails the betrayal of a caregiver's position of trust and authority over the child. Child abuse can take many forms:

- **Neglect** is the sustained deprivation of food, clothing, hygiene, shelter and other needed care so as to cause, or potentially cause, physical, emotional, developmental, or psychological harm.

- **Physical abuse** includes physical assaults, such as hitting, kicking, biting, throwing, burning, or poisoning, that cause, or could cause, physical injury as well as behaviours or omissions that cause, or could cause, physical injury to a child.

- **Sexual abuse** includes any sexual exploitation of a child, whether consented to or not. It includes touching or other behaviour of a sexual nature towards a child.

- **Emotional abuse** consists of emotional attacks or omissions that cause, or could cause, emotional injury, including the behaviour of parents or guardians who do not take an interest in their child.

Age of Consent

In 2008, the federal government increased the age at which youth can consent to sexual activity from 14 to 16 years of age. To protect teenagers from prosecution, the legislation includes close-in-age exceptions. A 14- or 15-year-old can engage in consensual sexual activity with a person who is less than five years older. The close-in-age exception for 12- and 13-year-olds is two years.

TABLE 8.2: Child and Youth Victims of Assault by Family Members in Canada, 2006

	Female		Male	
	Number	**Rate***	**Number**	**Rate***
Sexual assault				
Total family	3,257	102	832	25
Parent	1,257	40	311	9
Sibling	896	28	245	7
Extended family	1,083	34	273	8
Spouse/ex-spouse	21	1	3	0
Physical assault				
Total family	4,232	133	3,877	116
Parent	2,756	87	2,682	80
Sibling	701	22	680	20
Extended family	485	15	489	15
Spouse/ex-spouse	290	9	26	1

*Rate per 100,000 population for the geographic areas policed by respondents to the Incident-based Uniform Crime Reporting Survey, which collected data from 149 police services representing approx. 90% of Canada's population in 2006.

Source: Adapted from *Family Violence in Canada: A Statistical Profile*. Table 2.4. Statistics Canada 2008. Catalogue No. 85-224-X.

Attitudes towards discipline and punishment of children are changing in Canada. Parents have a great deal of discretion but some forms of punishment are clearly abusive and against the law. Many Canadians believe that physical force is an unacceptable means of disciplining children.

The law currently allows parents to use "reasonable force" to discipline children. What's considered reasonable depends on the situation, but judges have indicated that forms of physical punishment that were acceptable in the past may no longer be permitted.

Clearly, any injury that requires medical attention is not reasonable discipline. Also, physical discipline that results in bruising, welts, or broken skin would almost certainly be considered abuse.

The Ontario Association of Children's Aid Societies also provides the following statistics on child maltreatment and neglect on their website, www.oacas.org.

- The incidence of child maltreatment is estimated to be one in five children.

- Thirty-three percent of sex offenders experienced some form of sexual trauma as children.

- Eighty percent of women in correctional facilities were victims of child physical or sexual abuse.

- Eighty percent of people with eating disorders experienced some form of abuse or witnessed violence between their parents as a child.

- Children with a history of sexual abuse are seven times more likely to become alcohol or drug dependent.

- Suicide prevention programs find that children with a history of sexual abuse are ten times more likely to attempt suicide.

- Child prostitution prevention programs for ages nine and up find that 99 percent of child prostitutes have a history of child abuse.

- Eighty-five percent of runaways served by Covenant House in Toronto have been sexually abused.

- Children with a history of child abuse are more likely to have psychiatric and other health problems, commit crimes, drop out of school, or be unemployed.

The Problem of Under-Reporting

Over the past two decades, there has been a dramatic increase in both reports of suspected abuse and neglect and in the number of children found to be in need of protection. But many cases of child abuse are still not reported.

People working with children, including social workers, may not report abuse because they do not recognize its signs and symptoms. They may also resist admitting that it is happening or convince themselves that it is not serious enough to report. Other factors inhibiting voluntary reporting are the nature of family problems related to child abuse and neglect, the sense of secrecy and shame surrounding child maltreatment, the possible consequences of intervention by child protection authorities or police, and the fact that many of the victims are young and relatively dependent.

Children may want to disclose their abuse, but they are often afraid that no one will believe them. They may also be afraid of what will happen. Abusers frequently warn children not to tell anyone about their actions. They may convince the child that the abuse is the child's fault and that telling someone will only get them into more trouble.

Risk Assessment

A key component of child protection services is risk assessment. A discussion paper on best practice in child welfare assessments issued by the Children's Aid Society of Toronto gives a fairly complete overview of the process of assessment and the principles for service. **Risk assessment** is used to estimate the likelihood that a child will be maltreated, based on a careful examination of pertinent data, so that action can be taken to prevent it.

Research has identified the risk assessment factors that correlate with the abuse of children. Of course, such risk assessments are not foolproof and must be used in conjunction with worker judgment. Such research helps in supporting casework judgment, standardizing decision making, providing a teaching tool, focusing service plans on risk and demonstrating accountability. Workers therefore require a sound knowledge of the risk factors to enable them to make judgments that are supported by credible information.

A Duty to Report

It is important to note that it is not only child protection workers who have a responsibility to report suspected instances of child abuse or neglect. Every member of society has a responsibility to report child abuse or neglect when there are reasonable grounds for believing a child may be in need of protection. People in professions that bring them into contact with children have a particular responsibility to ensure that young people are safe. In the course of their duties, they have a professional **duty to report** if they have reasonable grounds to suspect that a child is or may be in need of protection. If professionals do not report their suspicions of child abuse or neglect, they can be convicted and fined up to $1,000. This legal obligation affects the following persons:

- health care professionals, such as physicians, nurses, dentists, pharmacists, and psychologists
- teachers and school principals
- social workers and family counsellors
- priests, rabbis, and other members of the clergy
- operators or employees of daycares
- youth and recreation workers (but not volunteers)
- police officers and coroners
- solicitors
- service providers and employees of service providers
- any other person who performs professional or official duties with respect to children

Duty to Report

The professional obligation to report reasonable suspicions of abuse or neglect to the proper authorities. Failure to report can lead to criminal charges and fines.

Steps in Providing Child Welfare Services

Child welfare service procedures are outlined in detail in the various provincial standards manuals. Specific criteria for determining whether or not a child is in need of protection are found in provincial child welfare Acts. These Acts outline the conditions under which children are considered to be in need of protection. The general steps for providing child welfare services in Canada are outlined below.

Initial Response to Reports of Abuse and Neglect

The person receiving the report of child abuse and neglect must exercise careful judgment. Workers should collect accurate information from various sources, such as the child, other family members, anonymous neighbours, and other callers; from persons with well-meaning intentions as well as from persons intending to make malicious accusations. Even though decision-making may be difficult and emotional, workers must make decisions in the best interests of the child. The response steps are as follows:

- receiving the report
- obtaining complete information from the informant
- assessing the motivation and credibility of the informant
- checking records
- determining if investigation is necessary
- developing an initial investigation plan
- documenting the reported abuse

Investigation

The social worker should obtain detailed and complete information using interviews, observations, and assessment and service reports from professionals, and by checking available records. All decisions must be based on detailed, accurate, and documented evidence. Crucial decisions must be made at this juncture in response to the following questions:

- Has the child been abused?
- What are the immediate safety needs of the child?
- Is there a risk of future harm?
- What is the capacity of the family to protect the child?
- What services are required by the child and family?

All provincial child welfare Acts empower child protection workers to enter premises to remove children whom they deem to be in need of protection. Workers will frequently interview children at school, as this is considered a safe and familiar environment. Interviewing children requires considerable skill.

SACYHN: A SHARED RESPONSIBILITY FOR CHILDREN AND YOUTH

The Southern Alberta Child & Youth Health Network (SACYHN) brings together parents, child-serving government ministries, provincial agencies, regional authorities, First Nations, universities, and not-for profit agencies to work together to enhance the health and well-being of children, youth, and families.

SACYHN was established in 2001 in recognition that the well-being of children and youth is a shared responsibility. Participants in the Network collaborate to establish links among services and across regional boundaries, set priorities, develop new services, and build family and community capacity to address the needs of children and youth.

SACYHN accomplishes its goals through a variety of activities. Examples of its work include:

- literature reviews on topics of interest to Network participants such as family centred care, Aboriginal child health, network development, and evaluation (knowledge building and mobilization).

- development of outreach services to bring care closer to home (facilitation of service delivery).

- development of an Outreach Services Framework (policy development and implementation).

- professional and community (including family) education, creation of a SACYHN website, and preparation and distribution of newsletters (communication, information provision, and building awareness).

Social workers provide direct service and leadership through many of the organizations in SACYHN, in sectors such as health, education, and child welfare. Social workers have a special role as change agents within any inter-organizational network for children and families. Educated to view the person within their environment, social workers are taught to take a strengths-based, capacity-building approach and to look beyond the individual or family to the role and impact of surrounding systems on client outcomes. The fundamental social work value of respecting the right to self-determination is particularly suited to a network environment where multiple actors have varying agendas, needs, and capacities to participate, such is the case in SACYHN.

Source: Prepared by the Southern Alberta Child & Youth Health Network. Copyright © 2008. Printed with permission.

As discussed, the assessment of risk to the child is increasingly seen as the key component of child welfare practice. While each province and, indeed, each local agency has its own policies and procedures, general investigative guidelines are common. A typical investigation would include the following steps:

- Conduct a telephone interview with the person who reported the alleged abuse and any other individuals who have information.

- Search existing agency records for any present or past contact with the family, the alleged abuser, or the child.

- Contact the Child Abuse Register to ascertain if the alleged abuser was registered in the past and, if so, what the details were of that registration. Contact any child welfare authorities that previously registered the alleged abuser.

- See the child who is alleged to have been abused and conduct an interview using methods appropriate to the child's developmental stage and ability to communicate.

- Ensure that the alleged abuser is interviewed by the police or an agency worker pursuant to the protocol established between the agency and the police.

Child Abuse Registries

A child abuse registry is a list of known child abusers. In most cases it is only available to professionals such as child welfare agencies and law enforcement officials. Individuals who work with children are often subjected to a child abuse registry check, much like a police check. Unlike a sex offender registry, individuals listed on a child abuse registry have not necessarily been convicted of a crime.

In Manitoba, there are three reasons a person may be listed:

- He or she has been found guilty of abusing a child.

- A child in his or her care has been deemed to be in need of protection.

- Child protection authorities have formed an opinion that he or she has abused a child.

In 2006, the United States passed a federal child protection law that created a national child abuse registry to prevent children from being adopted by convicted child abusers.

■ Interview the parent or person having charge of the child, if they are not the alleged abuser.

■ Interview other potential victims (for example, siblings, other children in the home, classmates).

■ Gather evidence from other professionals involved in the investigation (for example, medical, law enforcement, educational).

■ Gather information from other witnesses.

Assessing the urgency of a response is critical. The child who is the subject of a report of abuse must be seen as soon as possible, but generally not later than twelve hours after the report is made. To assess urgency, the social worker should consider the child's age, the nature of the alleged abuse, the known injury to the child, the potential for the child to suffer physical harm, the availability of possible evidence (for example, visible marks), and the immediate need for counselling or support. The worker should ensure that a medical examination by a qualified medical practitioner is performed when there is a need to document the child's condition.

A medical examination may also be necessary in certain situations to ascertain whether the child has been harmed. This can be arranged by obtaining the cooperation of the parent. However, if the parent's cooperation cannot be obtained, the social worker may need to apprehend the child and authorize the medical examination without parental consent.

Verification

Agencies generally have established policies and procedures outlining the process and factors to be considered when a protection verification decision is made. The verification decision must be made at a formal meeting in consultation with the social worker's supervisor or higher authorities. The worker should record the process of verification and the standards of proof for making the decision in the case file.

There are generally four possible investigative outcomes:

■ The complaint is not verified and the child protection concern does not appear to exist.

■ A protection concern is verified but the child remains in the home. This outcome occurs when the abuse has been perpetrated by a non-family member.

■ A protection concern is verified and the child remains in the home, but may be in need of protection. With this option, a plan must be developed to ensure the child's safety, including a schedule of visits and restricted access by some family members. This approach is consistent with the philosophy of taking the "least restrictive" course of action necessary to protect the child.

- A protection concern is verified, and the child is removed from the home. The child welfare agency must decide on, and seek from the court, an order that it believes to be the least restrictive or disruptive. Options include the placement of the child with some other person subject to the agency's provision, child welfare agency wardship, Crown wardship, or consecutive child welfare agency wardship and supervision order.

Assessment Report and Service Plan

If abuse is verified, the law requires a complete assessment and plan of service for the child and family. The assessment report should address numerous issues, including the nature of the abuse, precipitating factors, the nature of the dispute, family dysfunction, family background, parental capacity, family relationships, family strengths, service needs, child development, and the risk of further abuse. The service plan should include the specific risk factors, service needs, strategies and service providers, ongoing care responsibility and coordination, expectations, review dates, and client involvement in the service plan.

Case Management

Careful record-keeping is mandatory in child welfare agencies. If called upon, a worker must be able to substantiate the decisions made. Supervision, consultation, review, and decision making occur frequently during the management of all child abuse cases. All agencies have strict documentation requirements.

FAMILY VIOLENCE IN CANADA—A STATISTICAL PROFILE

Offenders

- Police-reported data in 2006 indicate that children and youth under 18 years of age are most likely to be physically or sexually assaulted by someone they know.

- For every 100,000 young persons, 334 were victims of physical or sexual violence by a friend or an acquaintance, 187 experienced violence by a family member, and 101 were victimized by a stranger.

- When children and youth are victims of family violence, parents are the most commonly identified perpetrators. In 2006, 107 per 100,000 children and youth were physically or sexually assaulted by a parent.

- The rate of physical assault by a parent was more than 3 times higher than the rate of sexual assault (83 compared to 24 victims per 100,000 children and youth).

Gender Factors

- Girls (under the age of 18) experienced somewhat higher rates of physical assault by family members than boys (133 compared with 116 incidents per 100,000 population). The rate of sexual assault committed by family members was 4 times higher for girls compared to boys (102 vs. 25 incidents per 100,000 population).

- About 4 in 10 child and youth victims of family violence sustained a physical injury in 2006, compared to 5 in 10 when the perpetrator was a non-family member. The majority of injuries sustained were considered to be minor injuries.

- Boys were more likely to sustain physical injuries resulting from family violence (46% compared to 35%).

For more information, see Family Violence in Canada: A Statistical Profile, 2008. Catalogue No. 85-224-X.

Social Services for Children and Youth

Many families and individuals experience stress due to problems that are not restricted to the poor, the uneducated, or the unmotivated. These difficulties may take a number of forms, such as addiction or substance abuse, partner assault, and eating disorders. Some of these problems involve children and youth. There are a number of programs, agencies, and organizations that exist to assist these families and are, in the broad sense of the word, concerned with child "well-fare." These include youth services agencies, crisis intervention and residential treatment centres, youth addiction centres, shelters for homeless youth, and income support programs.

Services for Young Offenders

Prior to the *Juvenile Delinquents Act* in 1908, young offenders were treated as "little adults." They were sentenced as adults, and were incarcerated with adult prisoners. In 1892, Canada's *Criminal Code* contained measures to supposedly protect children in the justice system. It established a minimum age of seven for charging a child, and a child under the age of fourteen could not be charged unless he or she was competent to understand the nature of the crime "and to appreciate that it was wrong."

In 1894, the *Youthful Offenders Act* legislated the separation of youth from adults both in trials and in prison facilities. Alternatives to imprisonment were also enacted and encouraged in this Act, including placing young offenders in foster care or sending them to reformatories. The reforms had little impact, and young offenders were often still given sentences equivalent to those of adults and incarcerated in adult facilities. In practice, however, the 1908 *Juvenile Delinquents Act* (JDA) provided a separate justice system for youth. For the first time youth were treated within a different system and in youth-specific facilities.

In 1984 the JDA was replaced with the *Young Offenders Act* (YOA). Due to outcries from the public regarding youth crime, the YOA was amended three times. It was criticized on many counts: for being too soft on the offender, for lacking a clear philosophy on youth justice in Canada, for inconsistent and unfair sentences, for not properly addressing serious and violent offences, for an overuse of the court system, and for not giving enough recognition to the victims. Prison-reform advocacy groups, such as the John Howard Society, were highly critical of the YOA. The more punitive approach of the YOA resulted in the increasing use of custody sentences for juvenile offenders. Under the YOA, youth were more likely than adults to be sentenced to custody for all offences and, in particular, for minor offences. Youth were serving longer sentences than adults for the same crimes and were being incarcerated at a much higher rate than in other western nations (John Howard 1999).

Over-Diagnosing/ Labelling

Attention disorders are an issue social workers encounter with young people, especially in school settings.

Attention Deficit Disorder (ADD) and Attention Deficit Hyperactivity Disorder (ADHD) are patterns of behaviour that appear most often in school-aged children. Children who are inattentive, overly impulsive and, in the case of ADHD, hyperactive are given these labels, and are often prescribed medication.

Such children may have difficulty sitting still and attending to one thing for a long period of time, and may seem overactive. But, we must consider the consequences of attaching a firm psychiatric label to what may be an essentially "normal," though classroom-disrupting, behaviour (or the possibility that the behaviour may have other, more obvious explanations).

In other words, it is important to ensure children receive proper attention when needed, while at the same time avoiding any unnecessary use of labels or medication.

The Youth Criminal Justice Act

In 2002, Parliament replaced the YOA with the *Youth Criminal Justice Act* (YCJA). The Act was implemented in 2003. The YCJA sought to emphasize the rehabilitation and re-entry of a young offender into society. It also addressed the criticism that the youth justice system lacked a clear philosophy. Among other things, the *Youth Criminal Justice Act* (YCJA) sought to end transfers of youth to adult court, although it enabled a judge to impose an adult sentence on a youth from within youth court. The YCJA also lowered the "age of presumption" to 14 years. Whereas under the YOA, it was presumed youths aged 16 and over convicted of a serious offence such as murder would be transferred to adult court, the new act lowered the age to 14 (individual provinces can adjust the age to 15 or 16).

On the sentencing and custodial side, the YCJA was also an attempt to lower the number of youth in prisons by placing less emphasis on custody as a sentence for non-violent or less serious offences. The new Act also emphasized alternative sentencing, such as referrals to community programs, letters of warning to parents, and meetings with police.

In 2008, the Harper government attempted to change the YCJA. The proposed changes included allowing courts to try and sentence youth over age 14 in adult court when they are charged with serious violent crimes, and removing the obligation to protect the identity of young people involved in criminal activity. In a 5-4 split decision, the Supreme Court ruled that these changes are unconstitutional. In the October 2008 federal election, Prime Minister Stephen Harper made youth justice a campaign issue, suggesting that 14 year olds convicted of violent crimes should lose the right to anonymity and be subject to life sentences, if warranted. Many felt the Conservative party was pandering to the public's fear of gang violence.

Youth Crime Today

Public concerns regarding youth crime (or juvenile delinquency, as it was previously called) began in the late 1950s. This early concern reflected a real increase in youth crime at the time. Table 8.3 illustrates the increase during this period. This trend in rising youth crime rates continued during the 1970s. The government responded by completely reviewing the youth justice system (resulting in the 1984 *Young Offenders Act*). The federal government hoped the YOA would ease public concerns, but the 1980s witnessed a continued increase in youth crime, particularly violent crimes. Public criticism of the legislation reflected the rising statistics.

However, in the 1990s, the pattern began to reverse with a steady drop in youth crime. Youth court cases related to *Criminal Code* offences decreased 29 percent between 1991 and 1992, and 2002 and 2003 (after the YCJA was enacted). Nevertheless, during this time, there has been a

TABLE 8.3: Total Convictions of Juvenile Delinquents, Ages 7–15 (1957–1966)

Year	Convictions
1957	9,679
1960	13,965
1964	16,608
1966	20,310

Source: Adapted from Owen Carrigan. 1998. *Juvenile Delinquency in Canada: A History.* Concord (ON): Irwin Publishing. page 160.

Review of the Roots of Youth Violence

The Review of the Roots of Youth Violence was established by Ontario's provincial government to examine youth violence and its underlying causes and to make recommendations to continue building safer communities.

In a report released in 2008, the review found that poverty, racism, a lack of decent housing, an insensitive education system, and limited job prospects create hopelessness, alienation, and low self-esteem among youth that can lead to violence.

The report went on to recommend that the government focus on using its resources to improve conditions in the province's most disadvantaged communities.

For more on the report, go to: www.rootsofyouthviolence.on.ca

widening gap between public perceptions of youth crime (that it is high and growing) and the actual statistics (declining). Overall rates of youth crime have decreased since 1992, while violent youth crime rates have been steadily decreasing since 1995 (Robinson 2004, Savoie 1999).

Fighting Root Causes

Given the reduction in youth crime, many argue that alternative approaches are needed. Front-line social workers in correction facilities, child welfare services, and youth service have advocated for an approach that recognizes the many factors that are at the root of youth crime:

- *Societal factors* include poverty and unemployment, substandard housing, high urban mobility, racism, homophobia, and lack of resources in the community.
- *Family factors* include abuse of children, the witnessing of violence (usually against the mother), lack of supervision by parents, excessive discipline, spousal conflict, the father's absence, alcohol or substance abuse, and parental and sibling psychiatric problems.
- *Individual factors* include poor school performance and learning disabilities, poor attendance and dropping out, low self-esteem, rejection by peers, association with a delinquent peer group, alcohol or substance abuse, and psychiatric problems (CWLC 1995, 8).

Social workers point out that the courts and prisons often fail to combat the youth crime problem because its roots lie outside the reach of these institutions (Waller 1989). The late Solicitor General Herb Grey summed it up best when he said that if the answer to youth crime was longer sentences, then the United States (with its punishment-oriented approach to crime) would be the safest place in the world.

Early Childhood Education and Care

There is wide consensus that high quality early childhood education and care (ECEC), together with supportive policies and programmes for working families, are hugely important for all aspects of children's development. ECEC also brings major social and economic benefits for individuals, families, and society, reducing the workload on social workers and other care-giving professions. In the United Kingdom, for example, 60 percent of young children are in regulated care; in Denmark, 78 percent.

Canada, on the other hand, is lagging behind. There is a shortage of regulated child care spaces—only enough for less than 20 percent of children under six with working parents. *Starting Strong* (2006), a report by the Organization for Economic Co-operation and Development (OECD) offers cross-national insights about best practices as well as international comparisons for ECEC. The data show Canada's low ranking internationally with respect to spending on families and children overall, and on spending for ECEC programs and access.

Although Canada is one of the most affluent industrialized countries (by GDP), we invest relatively little in the earliest years—a critical period of development that lays the foundation for each child's potential. Canada invests about 0.2 percent GDP in early child care and education (for 0-6 years). According to the OECD Canada Review (2006), investing in quality services for all children who need them would cost about 1 percent of Canada's GDP.

Provincial Variations

Fourteen jurisdictions—the federal government, ten provinces and three territories—are involved in delivering ECEC programs in Canada. Because child care and kindergarten are under separate mandates across the country, each jurisdiction has multiple child care, early childhood education and "child development" programs. Kindergarten programs tend to be more consistent across Canada, although there is variation in amount of provision (full or part-day), age eligibility, curricular approaches, and educational expectations. (This section is adapted from "Early Childhood Education and Care in Canada, 2006," by Martha Friendly, Jane Beach, Carolyn Ferns, and Michelle Turiano, 2007.)

Generally, Canadian ECEC programs are either not sensitive to parents' labour force schedules (for example, the need for all-day kindergarten) or are inaccessible to many families because fees are too high or services unavailable (child care costs). The research also shows that the quality of much of Canada's regulated child care is less than it should be. Moreover, many young children are in private unregulated care arrangements while their parents are at work. This unfortunate state of affairs negatively affects children, parents and families and it puts Canada at a disadvantage relative to other advanced economies.

How Does Canada Fare in Early Childhood Care?

Canada achieves only 1 of 10 international benchmarks of minimum standards for early child care and education.

X Parental leave of one year at 50% of salary

X A national plan with priority for the disadvantaged

X Subsidized and regulated child care services for at least 25% of children under three years old

X Subsidized and accredited early education services for 80% of four-year-olds

√ 90% of all child care staff trained

X 50% of staff in accredited early education services tertiary educated with relevant qualification

X Minimum staff-to-student ratio of 1:15 in pre-school education

X 1.0% of GDP spent on early childhood services

X Child poverty rate of less than 10%

X Near-universal outreach of essential child health services

Role of the Federal Government

While Canadian provinces/territories have jurisdictional responsibility for developing and maintaining ECEC programs, federal funding and leadership has over the years played a significant role. The federal government is involved in ECEC in four ways:

- Delivering ECEC services to specific populations (Aboriginal people, military families and new Canadians);
- Providing cash or tax benefits—for example, maternity/parental benefits under Employment Insurance, the Child Care Expense Deduction, the Universal Child Care Benefit (UCCB);
- Financing ECEC programs through transfer payments to provinces/territories. (This began in 2003 and continues through payments specifically designated for provincial/territorial ECEC programs.)
- Providing federal leadership, for example, through the Multilateral Framework Agreement (2003); Foundations (2004); the UCCB (2006).

More recently, child care advocates have been critical of federal policy, arguing that little progress is being made with regards to increasing funding and introducing new initiatives.

Full-day Kindergarten Programs

In June 2009, the Premier of Ontario accepted a report calling for school boards to provide optional, full-day learning for four-and five-year-olds beginning in September 2010 and available province-wide within three years.

British Columbia's attempt in 2009 to create a similar program faced temporary setbacks owing to difficulties finding classroom space and qualified teachers.

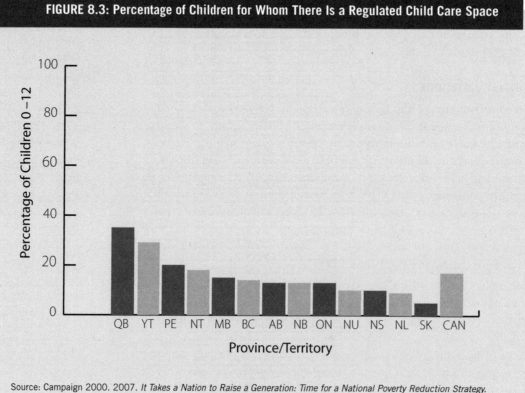

FIGURE 8.3: Percentage of Children for Whom There Is a Regulated Child Care Space

Source: Campaign 2000. 2007. *It Takes a Nation to Raise a Generation: Time for a National Poverty Reduction Strategy. 2007 Report Card on Child and Family Poverty in Canada*. page 5. With permission from Campaign 2000, a cross-Canada network on ending child/family poverty. www.campaign2000.ca

Recent Policy Reversals

Between 2004 and 2006, there were several significant shifts in ECEC policy at the federal level. In 2004, recognizing the need for leadership in early childhood education and care, the federal government proposed the Foundations program to "ensure that children have access to high-quality, government-regulated spaces at affordable cost to parents." Five billion dollars (in new funds) over five years were committed for this purpose. In 2005, bilateral agreements between the federal government and provinces/ territories were executed to put this in place by transferring funds to each province/territory upon completion of an early learning and child care plan and ongoing reporting.

Following another federal election (January 2006), the subsequent government introduced a different approach. They said: "The best role for government is to let parents choose what's best for their children, and provide parents with the resources to balance work and family life as they see fit— whether that means formal child care, informal care through neighbours or relatives, or a parent staying at home."

In 2006, the nascent ECEC program was terminated through cancellation of the federal/provincial agreements. Beginning in July 2006, the Universal Child Care Benefit, a $100/month payment to parents of all children aged 0-6, began. In addition, the 2006 federal budget committed ECEC transfer payments to provinces/territories totaling $250 million per year and a tax credit to businesses to create new child care spaces in the workplace.

Quebec's Universal Child Care Program

Since its inception, Quebec's universal child care program has been an exceptional model and the standard to which other provinces should aspire.

The best-known feature of the Quebec model is the $7-a-day daycare program, attended by about 130,000 children. Quebec also provides full-day kindergarten for five-year-olds and after-school care for kindergarten and primary school children.

It is estimated that a similar Canada-wide child care program would cost in excess of $10 billion annually.

TABLE 8.4: Federal Transfer Payments Designated for ECEC Programs 2003-2008 (millions)

Program	2003/04	2004/05	2005/06	2006/07	2007/08
Multilateral Framework Agreement	25	150	225	300	350
"Foundations" Bilateral Agreements		200	500	650	
Child Care Spaces 2007 Federal Budget					250
Total Transfer $ Designated for ECEC	25	350	725	950	600

Source: J. Beach et al. "Table 31: Federal transfers designated for early learning and child care. Total breakdown by federal program by province/territory by fiscal year 2003/2004–2007/2008 ($ millions)" *Early Childhood Education and Care in Canada 2008* 8th Edition. Toronto: Child Resource and Research Unit. 2009. page 209.

Signs and Symptoms of Stress in Child Welfare Workers

In a study of 175 child welfare workers for the Children's Aid Society of Toronto, 82.7% reported that they had been exposed to at least one critical incident at work (including the death of a client, threats, and assault). Seventy percent reported experiencing stress as a result.

Symptoms of stress or trauma among child welfare workers include:

- Intrusion symptoms, such as recurrent dreams and repetitive thoughts.

- Avoidance symptoms, including social isolation and avoidance of high-stress situations.

- Arousal symptoms, such as anxiety and irritability.

Source: L. Lambert and C. Regehr. 2004. "Stress, Trauma, and Support in Child Welfare Practice." Research Institute for Evidence-Based Social Work

Compassion Fatigue

Child welfare social work is a noble profession to be sure, but a disconcerting phenomenon in this field has recently received considerable attention—the extent of worker burnout among dedicated child welfare workers. As "burnout" can happen to anyone in a stressful occupation, it may be more accurate in the social work context to refer such a phenomenon as "vicarious trauma" or "compassion fatigue."

The term **compassion fatigue** refers to the anxiety resulting from dealing with emotionally difficult cases under increased workplace pressure and increased workloads. This type of stress occurs among social workers and others who are faced with increasing responsibility and less and less control over how the work is to be completed. Across Canada, where increased workloads are compounded by distressing cases of child abuse and dire family circumstances, this condition seems to have become the norm for child welfare workers.

Paperwork and Cutbacks

A recent study found that social workers employed by the Children's Aid Society of Toronto showed traumatic stress scores "considerably higher" than those of workers in other emergency services, such as firefighters and ambulance paramedics (Philip 2001). The study, conducted by the Ontario Association of Children's Aid Societies, found that mounting caseloads and a mismatch between the time allotted by provincial regulations for investigation and assessment (12.5 hours) and the actual required time of 19.3 hours are causing undue stress and the departure of many workers. Workers who successfully remain in child welfare tend to artfully manage the paperwork. For example, they may choose to compile all the paperwork only on cases that have a high potential for problems in the future. While this may be common, it is not standard procedure.

In response to a number of high-profile inquests into the deaths of children in care, provincial governments are mandating new administrative requirements. It is quickly becoming impossible for the workers to comply with the mounting paperwork within the time allotted. And, of course, a failure to comply with administrative requirements places the onus for any mistakes on the worker. When combined with larger caseloads and the significant emotional stress of the work, it should not be surprising that worker burnout results.

The ultimate victims of this state of affairs are the children themselves. Dedicated individuals enter this area of the profession with the intention of doing good work and helping children and families as best they can. If they are to remain, and if others are to be attracted to this important field of social work practice, working conditions must be improved. The current round of government cutbacks is taking a severe toll on these social workers and, in turn, on the children they are seeking to help.

Conclusion

Only recently has child maltreatment received recognition as a significant social problem, although child abuse and neglect have a long history. In 1893, the passing of the *Children's Protection Act* in Ontario ushered in a new era in modern child welfare legislation protecting children from abuse and neglect. The following years saw a range of provincial legislative Acts, as child welfare was, and still is, defined in the Constitution as a provincial jurisdiction. Modern child welfare work has continued to struggle with dilemmas such as protection versus family preservation, or the "best interests" of the child versus the "least restrictive" measures of intervention.

Child welfare work is one of the most common fields of work for graduating social workers today. The field is changing rapidly and workers continually need to update their skills and learn new techniques. For example, research has been done to identify the risk assessment factors that correlate with the abuse of children, and workers are expected to apply knowledge of this in their practice. The first step in the overall process of child protection is to obtain and record the initial response from a variety of sources. Next, the worker determines if the child has been abused, any safety concerns, future risk, the capacity of the family to protect the child, and any services that will be required. Verification decisions are critical in today's litigation-filled society, so the worker must document both the evidence of abuse and the standard of proof. Finally, the social worker needs to complete a plan of service for both the child and the family and keep careful records of the implementation of the plan.

Doing social work on behalf of, or with, children and youth includes more than child protection work. Social workers work with children and youth in a variety of roles. Other social work settings include daycare centres, schools, foster care, adoptions, residential group homes, youth corrections, and various income security programs, to name a few. In all these settings, social workers have always been at the forefront in advocating for improvements in policy and services for children and youth.

Social workers continue to enter the child welfare field, despite its difficult conditions and high attrition rates. While working with abused children and their abusers may not be pleasant, this work is indispensable in a civilized and just society.

CHAPTER REVIEW

Key Terms

- In-home services
- Out-of-home services
- Differential Response (DR)
- Alternative Dispute Resolution (ADR)
- Kinship service
- Kinship care
- Best interests approach
- Least restrictive approach
- Child abuse
- Risk assessment
- Duty to report
- Early Childhood Education
- Universal child care program
- Compassion fatigue

Review Questions

1. Identify and discuss the three main phases in the history of child welfare.

2. Explain what is meant by the "least restrictive" and the "best interests" approaches to child protection cases.

3. What is the extent of youth in care in Canada and how does this match up with government policy in this area?

4. What is the extent of child abuse today in Canada?

5. What are the steps to be followed in providing child welfare services?

6. What are some of the issues that trouble youth who are in care?

7. Briefly describe the current state of the youth criminal justice system. How does public perception of youth crime affect the welfare of children?

8. How has provincial child welfare legislation changed in the past few years—both positively and negatively?

Exploring Social Work

1. According to an article in *New Internationalist* magazine, 52,390 child runaways were reported to police in Canada in 2002. While more than 75 percent return to their homes within a week, the rest remain on the streets. It works out to about 1,300 children joining the ranks of homeless street youth each year. Visit the *New Internationalist* website and read the profile on Nicole in Issue 377, April 2005 (**www.newint. org/issue377/nicole.htm**). Consider why some people would leave their families for a life on the streets. What are the societal conditions that make this possible? What can social workers do both at the practice level and the policy level to help prevent this?

2. Stigma is a big problem for youth living with mental illness. It undermines young people's self worth, their relationships, their well-being, and their prospects for recovery. Visit the Centre for Addiction and Mental Health website (**www.camh.net**). In the "Education and Courses" section, under Resources for Teachers and Schools, read the "Talking about Mental Illness" page and answer the following questions: What is stigma? Why do we stigmatize mental illness? How does it affect people's lives?

Websites

- - - - - -

Child Welfare League of Canada
www.cwlc.ca

The CWLC is an organization active in Canadian policy, research, and advocacy. The site contains an issue-specific search engine for those doing research in the child welfare area.

The Ontario Association of Children's Aid Societies
www.oacas.org

The voice of child welfare in Ontario, dedicated to providing leadership for the achievement of excellence in the protection of children and in the promotion of their well-being within their families and communities.

Southern Alberta Child and Youth Health Network
www.sacyhn.ca

This organization brings together parents and youth, ministries, regional authorities, First Nations, universities, and not-for-profit agencies to focus on optimizing the health and well-being of children and youth.

CHAPTER 9

SOCIAL WORK AND THE HEALTH OF CANADIANS

Medicare at Risk

Social workers play a key role in the provision of health services in Canada. In hospital settings, social workers are often part of multidisciplinary teams that provide a unique holistic perspective to health care. This holistic perspective is not only concerned with the treatment of illness, but also with the promotion of wellness and the consideration of the social, economic, spiritual, and cultural needs of the health services client. This chapter provides an overview of the history of public medical care. Several key issues are discussed, including universality, privatization, extra billing, and user fees. The chapter also looks at the recent agreement between the federal government and the provinces to restore federal funding to the health care system and the role of social workers in medical social work, community health centres, and social work with people who have contracted HIV/AIDS.

Health and Inequality

- - - - - - - - - - - - - - - - -

Despite the availability of public health care across the country, there is a serious **health gap** between the rich and the poor in Canada—the rich are healthier than the middle class, who are in turn healthier than the poor. The well educated are healthier than the less educated, the employed are healthier than the unemployed, and so on.

A 2006 Canadian Institute for Health Information report showed an association between low income and poorer health outcomes (CIHI 2006c). Higher-than-average median income neighbourhoods were more likely to report excellent or very good health and be physically active.

Household Spending on Health

Statistics Canada's recent "Survey of Household Spending" offers more evidence of the gap between the rich and the poor in terms of health spending. Problems with health care, particularly items not covered by public health insurance, were featured in the data (see table below). The average out-of-pocket spending on eye care was relatively scarce in the poorest quintile at 36 percent of households, whereas spending on eye care reached 72 percent in the richest quintile. Dental care was "even worse"— only 29 percent of the poorest households reported going to the dentist, compared to 64 percent of the richest households (Kerstetter 2009).

In other words, the health gap in Canada is serious. Moreover, there is evidence that new immigrants and visible minorities are at an even greater disadvantage when it comes to health care. And, located as they are in the lowest quintile of the Canadian socio-economic hierarchy, Aboriginal peoples have the poorest levels of overall health.

Obesity Levels

According to Statistics Canada, in 2005, 12% of adults were obese and 27% were overweight. Obesity is defined as a Body Mass Index (BMI) score of over 30, whereas overweight is a BMI of over 25. (BMI is calculated using height in metres divided by weight in kilograms squared.)

The obesity rates for Aboriginal people are higher than for the Canadian population as a whole. A study of Aboriginal people aged 19 to 50 in Ontario and the western provinces (excluding reserves) found that, in 2004, they were 2.5 times more likely to be obese or overweight as their non-Aboriginal contemporaries.

TABLE 9.1: Spending on Health by Income Quintile, 2007

	Poorest 20%	Second 20%	Middle 20%	Fourth 20%	Richest 20%
Eye Care	$265	$323	$359	$406	$537
% of Households	36%	49%	57%	61%	72%
Dental Care	$516	$569	$696	$729	$935
% of Households	29%	48%	57%	61%	64%
Health Insurance	$554	$682	$757	$847	$981
% of Households	22%	33%	27%	24%	24%

Source: Statistics Canada. 2007. "Table 7: Spending on Health by Income Quintile, Households with Actual Spending Only." *Survey of Household Spending*. Cat. No. 62FPY0032XDB.

History of Health Policy

Universal Public Health Care

Publicly funded health care that is available to all who meet requirements of eligibility.

Universal public health care involving publicly funded quality health care for all Canadian citizens, took some time to evolve. Prior to the late 1940s, access to health care was based solely on one's ability to pay. Access did not become a concern of governments until illness threatened to hamper the supply of workers for industry, and even then, the road to state-funded health insurance plans was not smooth.

Early in Canada's history, doctors and barber-surgeons served the European populations in towns and military forts, while women provided in-home care as midwives and caregivers. Within First Nations communities, healers and shamans undertook the curing of illness. By the late 1700s, increasing numbers of immigrants and growing towns meant that doctors provided more "complete" health care services to the European population, while First Nations communities were confronted with new European illnesses for which their traditional methods were not equipped. The first Canadian medical school was founded in 1824, and in 1869, legislation gave allopathic practitioners (doctors who provided diagnosis, surgery, obstetrics, and whatever else was needed) control over medical education (Clarke 1990). At the time, women were excluded from access to medical schools by the male-dominated medical associations.

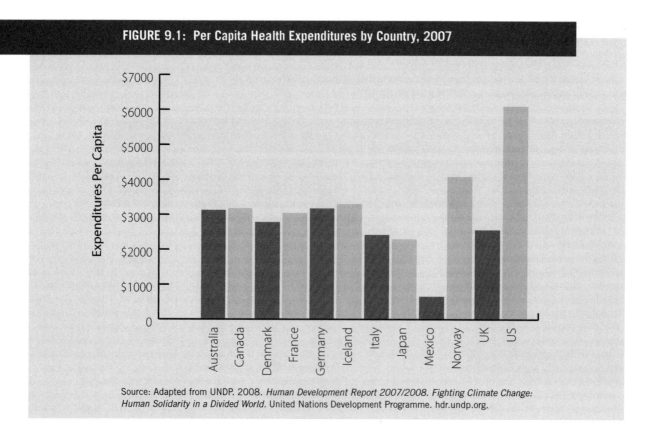

FIGURE 9.1: Per Capita Health Expenditures by Country, 2007

Source: Adapted from UNDP. 2008. *Human Development Report 2007/2008. Fighting Climate Change: Human Solidarity in a Divided World*. United Nations Development Programme. hdr.undp.org.

One of the first pieces of government health care regulation was a directive in 1832 by the Upper Canada Sanitary Commission and Board of Health pertaining to the quarantine and sanitation of immigrants infected with cholera. More extensive public health measures were introduced later in the nineteenth century (Clarke 1990). The *British North America Act* of 1867 established the jurisdictions of the federal and provincial governments in delivering health services. The management and maintenance of health institutions fell to the provinces. The larger tax base of the federal government allowed it to exert a strong influence on Canadian health delivery, as it continues to do today.

From 1880 to the 1950s, there were a variety of **pre-payment health plans** in place, sponsored by local governments, industries, and volunteer agencies (Vayda & Deber 1995). By 1934, there were twenty-seven hospital-sponsored pre-payment plans in six provinces. An example of such a plan is a payroll-deduction plan for miners in Nova Scotia and Ontario. The Municipal Doctor System, which paid physicians on an annual contract basis, was established in Saskatchewan in 1914. Medical associations and hospitals also developed health insurance plans in Ontario, Manitoba, and Nova Scotia. In 1939, the first Canadian Blue Cross plan was formed in Manitoba, with most provinces following suit in the 1940s. These voluntary insurance plans did not cover all medical services, and they were available only to those who could afford to pay the premiums.

Provincial governments were slow to take action under pressure from the medical profession. For example, in British Columbia, relief workers, the One Big Union, and the Co-operative Commonwealth Federation (CCF) put intense pressure on the Pattullo government to institute comprehensive health insurance in the 1930s. In 1933, the Pattullo government included health care as a key component of its election platform. Health care legislation passed a third reading, but because of opposition from doctors, T.D. Pattullo refused to enact it. Health insurance plans were also blocked in Alberta by the powerful Medical Association.

Debates about health insurance also occurred within the field of social work. The 1942 Heagerty Report and the 1943 Marsh Report both recommended comprehensive state-funded health insurance. The more conservative Social Service Council, led by Charlotte Whitton (see Chapter 3, page 44), opposed state-funded health insurance.

The Marsh Report was a crucial report in the history of social welfare. It detailed the need for comprehensive and universal social programs. The report suggested that the country should establish a "social minimum," a standard aimed at protecting the disadvantaged through policies such as social insurance and children's allowances. The study didn't attract much attention from policy-makers at first, but by 1966, most of Marsh's recommendations had become law. University of Toronto historian Michael Bliss described the Marsh Report as "the most important single document in the history of the Welfare State in Canada."

Pre-payment Health Plans

Health plans sponsored by local governments, industries, and volunteer agencies from 1880 to the 1950s. These voluntary insurance plans did not cover all medical expenses and were available only to those who could afford to pay premiums.

T.C. (Tommy) Douglas (1904–86)

The impetus for comprehensive public medical care that included coverage for visits to, and services provided by, physicians outside of a hospital began in Saskatchewan.

The CCF government in that province—under the leadership of T.C. (Tommy) Douglas—considered more comprehensive medical coverage to be a necessity and, in the end, won the day in a major confrontation with the powerful medical establishment.

Tommy Douglas was voted "The Greatest Canadian" of all time in a nationally televised contest organized by the Canadian Broadcasting Corporation in 2004.

Federal Involvement

Several factors precipitated more active federal involvement in medical insurance. When the issue of public medical insurance first arose in the 1920s in British Columbia, it was considered to be a provincial matter. But in the 1930s, working Canadians were devastated by the Great Depression, and political unrest was widespread. Because many people were unable to pay medical expenses, some doctors found the idea of public medical insurance attractive—at least their bills for medical care would be paid.

In 1942, the Heagerty Report proposed a federally funded, two-stage health insurance scheme. The report had wide agreement including the support of the labour movement and the Canadian Medical Association, but the plan foundered because of federal-provincial disagreements.

In 1945, the Royal Commission on Dominion Provincial Relations produced a series of proposals and called for the federal government to help finance health and social services programs in return for the provinces' renouncement of their claim to income and corporate taxes. The provinces, particularly Ontario and Quebec, turned down the offer, because they thought the tax-sharing formula represented federal interference in provincial matters, such as health care (Cumming 1985, 51).

By the end of World War II, however, children's allowances and unemployment insurance were in place. In 1947, the first public insurance plan for hospital services was instituted in Saskatchewan. The scheme did not provide funding for care received in a doctor's office, but it did provide for emergency services, curative medicine, and surgery in hospitals.

In 1957, the *Hospital Insurance and Diagnostic Services Act* was passed. Under the Act, the federal government agreed to finance 50 percent of the cost of provincial acute and chronic hospital care (although mental hospitals, tuberculosis sanatoria, and custodial care institutions, such as nursing homes, were excluded, and patients still had to pay a daily user fee for hospital services). This legislation encouraged the development of hospital insurance plans, and by 1961, all provinces and territories had signed agreements with the federal government for limited, in-patient hospital care that qualified for federal cost sharing.

In 1964, Conservative Prime Minister John Diefenbaker appointed Justice Emmett Hall to chair a Royal Commission on Health Care. In 1964, the **Hall Report** disclosed that 7.5 million Canadians did not have medical coverage and recommended that a comprehensive, publicly administered universal health service plan be implemented.

Women's organizations and organized labour were particularly positive about national medical insurance. The Liberal minority government that followed Diefenbaker's Conservative government was supported by the newly established New Democratic Party, which advocated universal health care. The physicians threatened to strike but were unsuccessful in reversing the tide, and the *Medical Care Act* was passed in 1968.

The Medical Care Act (1968) and Canada Health Act (1984)

The *Medical Care Act* (1968) provided for equal federal–provincial cost sharing of non-hospital medical services. By 1972, all provinces and territories had extended their plans to include physicians' services. Funding was made available to provinces if their services met the criteria of comprehensiveness, accessibility, universality, portability, and public administration. Under the new legislation, physicians were permitted to opt out of the plan and extra billing was permitted.

The *Canada Health Act* (1984) changed the funding structure, introducing conditions that provincial health systems must meet. These conditions included the stipulation that the provincial systems must be "universal" and cover all "medically necessary" hospital and physician services. The primary objective of the Act is "to protect, promote and restore the physical and mental well-being of residents of Canada and to facilitate reasonable access to health services without financial or other barriers" (Section 3). Meeting this objective will be critical to maintaining and improving the health and well-being of Canadians.

Former Prime Minister Paul Martin, first ministers, and Aboriginal leaders meet in Ottawa in September 2004 to discuss health care.

Medicare Under the Microscope—From Hall to Romanow

- - - - - - - - -

In 2001, Allan Rock, the federal Minister of Health, announced the formation of the Commission on the Future of Health Care in Canada, under the leadership of Roy Romanow. Its mandate was to engage Canadians in a national dialogue on the future of health care and to make recommendations to preserve the long-term sustainability of Canada's universally accessible, publicly funded health care system.

Romanow Commission

Led by Roy Romanow, the Commission on the Future of Health Care in Canada made recommendations in 2002 to preserve the long-term sustainability of Canada's universally accessibly, publicly funded health care system.

In 2002 the final report of the **Romanow Commission** was released. In his work, Romanow said he was guided by two things: Canadian values of fairness, equity, and solidarity, and by the evidence. This approach led him to recommend expanding public, not-for-profit medicare, to include home care and pharmacare, and to introduce a genuine system of primary health care. "In the coming months, the choices we make, or the consequences of those we fail to make," declared Romanow in his final report, "will decide medicare's future. I believe Canadians are prepared to embark on the journey together and build on the proud legacy they have inherited" (Romanow 2002, 247). The Romanow report has been the backdrop for the major debates and disagreements between the federal and provincial governments over health care in recent years.

Main Recommendations of the Romanow Commission

The Commission's final report, *Building on Values: The Future of Health Care in Canada*, comprises forty-seven detailed, costed recommendations that include implementation time frames.

Romanow explained that the recommendations were premised on three main themes: that strong leadership is needed to maintain Medicare, that the system should become more efficient and responsive, and that both short-term and long-term strategies are needed (Romanow 2002).

Report highlights include:

- Establishing a Canadian Health Covenant and updating the *Canada Health Act*.
- A new Health Council of Canada to foster collaboration between governments, providers, and citizens.
- Achieving the goal of adequate, stable, and predictable funding.
- Integrating home care services into the *Canada Health Act* to make the system more comprehensive.
- Improving prescription drug coverage.
- Improving access and reducing wait-list times through efficient management and increased services.
- Creation of an electronic health record system and amending the *Criminal Code* to protect patient privacy.

The Commission's report also addressed, among others, such diverse issues as Aboriginal health care, culturally sensitive access, and the impact of globalization and applied research. It is worth noting, as well, that the Romanow Commission set something of a new standard for transparency in commissions of enquiry of this type. It released, in advance of its final report, all of the submissions it had received, all the research it had commissioned, and summaries from all of the consultative activities in which it had been engaged.

Based on the Romanow report and federal provincial discussions, health care reform is focusing on the following themes (CIHI 2000):

- decentralization of authority and the regionalization of service delivery through the creation of Regional Health Authorities (RHAs), such as Ontario's recently created fourteen Local Health Integration Networks (LHINs)
- increased emphasis on evidence-based decision making and the development of a more cost-effective and accountable health system
- a shift from institutional care and a focus on illness, to community-based services and a focus on wellness
- integration of agencies, programs, and services to create a seamless continuum of health services and to reduce duplication and overlap
- a move toward client-centred services
- an emphasis on health promotion/disease prevention, and promoting individual responsibility for health

Roy Romanow (speaking at a rally in Edmonton) headed the Commission on the Future of Health Care in Canada in 2002, which made recommendations to preserve the country's publicly funded system.

Canada's Health Care Spending

Total health expenditure was $160.1 billion in 2008, up from $131.4 billion in 2004. After adjusting for inflation, health care spending grew at an average annual rate of 3.8 percent between 1975 and 1991. From 1991 to 1996 total spending on health care edged up by a rate of 0.8 percent per year. It increased by 5.0 percent from 1996 to 2004. Real growth is expected to have been 3.7 percent in 2005 and 2006. Total health expenditure per capita was estimated at $4,109 in 2004, $4,333 in 2005, and $5,170 in 2008. Canada's public share of total health spending is smaller than most countries'. In 2005, public funding accounted for 70 percent of total health care expenditures in Canada, 44 percent in the U.S., and about 85 percent in Denmark, Norway, and Sweden (OECD Health Data, 2006). The other 30 percent of Canada's health spending was funded through private insurance and directly out-of-pocket by Canadians.

Funds from private insurance support health services such as dental, eye, and chiropractic care, as well as prescription drugs. Household out-of-pocket spending typically includes over-the-counter drugs, hospital expenditures (for a private room, for example), and residential care facility fees. Spending on private health care has grown more rapidly than spending within the public system. From 1975 to 2005, public spending increased an average of 3.5 percent per year compared to a 4.4 percent increase in private spending (Armstrong & Armstrong 2008).

Medicare

Publicly funded and universal health insurance in Canada delivered through hospitals, private physicians, and other health care providers.

Five Principles of Medicare

Today, Canada has a health care system—called **medicare**—that is funded by government insurance, and is publicly delivered by hospitals and privately delivered by physicians (who are self-employed or employed by physician-owned corporations). Each province must meet the following *five principles of medicare* to receive funding from the federal government:

- **Public administration.** Pursuant to section 8, the health care insurance plan must be administered and operated on a non-profit basis by a public authority responsible to the provincial government, and be subject to an audit of its accounts and financial transactions.
- **Comprehensiveness.** Pursuant to section 9, the plan must cover all insured health services ("medically necessary services") provided by hospitals, medical practitioners, or dentists, and, where permitted, cover services rendered by other health care practitioners.
- **Universality.** Section 10 requires that 100 percent of the insured persons of a province be entitled to the insured health services provided for by the plan on uniform terms and conditions.
- **Portability.** In accordance with section 11, residents moving to another province must continue to be covered for insured health services by the home province during any minimum waiting period imposed by the new province, not to exceed three months.

■ **Accessibility.** By virtue of section 12, the health care insurance plan of a province must provide for: (a) insured health services on uniform terms and conditions and reasonable access by insured persons to insured health services unprecluded or unimpeded, either directly or indirectly, by charges or other means; (b) reasonable compensation to physicians and dentists for all insured health services rendered; payments to hospitals in respect of the cost of insured health services.

Commitment to these "five principles" was reaffirmed, after intense negotiations, in the Social Union Framework Agreement (SUFA) of 1999 between the federal government and all provinces and territories (except Quebec). The Agreement, entitled *A Framework to Improve the Social Union for Canadians*, attempted to define how power and responsibility would be divided. It also attempted to smooth relations between the federal government and the provinces following the fallout from the unilateral federal changes to funding in the *Canada Health and Social Transfer Act* (CHST). As of 2004, health care falls under the *Canada Health Transfer* (CHT). (See Chapter 2.)

FIGURE 9.2: Total Health Expenditures by Use of Funds, Canada, 2006 (billions of dollars)

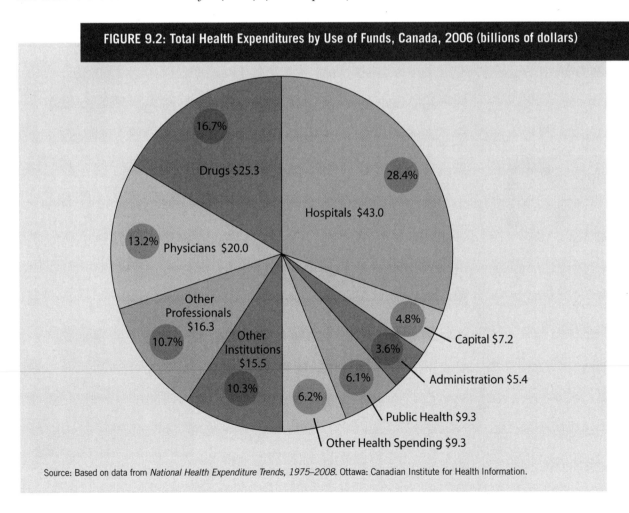

Source: Based on data from *National Health Expenditure Trends, 1975–2008*. Ottawa: Canadian Institute for Health Information.

Universal Public or Privatized Health Care?

Today, the case for publicly funded health care is accepted by most countries in the world. The major exception to this is the United States, where health care is essentially privately funded and privately delivered, with forty million citizens not having any coverage.

Canadians often debate the merits of our public health care system, but few believe that it should be privatized along the American model. The Americans themselves, under the Obama administration, are looking for workable public health care models. The U.S. system has been found to be more expensive and deliver less and lower quality services. Research here also supports this; for example, a recent *Canadian Medical Association Journal* article found that for-profit hospitals result in higher payments for care than not-for-profit hospitals (Woodhandler & Himmelstein 2004).

Nevertheless, our public health care system is not entirely secure. An aging population and ever-spiralling costs will require defenders of universal care to be even more alert to the dangers outlined below.

A team of health care professionals—two doctors, a pharmacist, and a social worker—display their concerns for improving medicare during the 2004 First Ministers' Conference on Health.

Privatization. One the biggest threats to our public system of health care is the current movement to privatize care in some provinces, particularly in Alberta and Ontario. Several trends indicate increased privatization in our health care system:

- the "de-listing" of services covered by medicare (e.g., specific medical procedures, support services, and drugs)
- the transferring of care out of areas covered by medicare (e.g., acute care in hospitals) to areas that are not (e.g., home care)
- the contracting out of "non-core" medical services (labs, ambulances, and rehab services) to private companies
- the contracting out of services (laundry, meal preparation, cleaning and maintenance, materials handling, information management, and disposal services) to private companies
- the contracting in of management services, leading to the redesign of management practices in accordance with private sector criteria

Comprehensiveness. Some provinces have attempted to reduce costs by reducing comprehensiveness—that is, the range of what are considered to be "medically necessary" services. Because the *Canada Health Act* states that the provinces should determine which services are "medically necessary," there is some room for provinces to limit the range of "necessary" services.

Contracting out. There are also concerns regarding the administration of hospitals. Governments are **contracting out** the management of some hospitals to private companies. If the company generates additional funds for the hospital, it can claim those funds as profit. For example, in Alberta, Bill C-11 of 2000 encourages the establishment of private, for-profit hospitals. Also, some services, such as catering, laundry, and cleaning, have been contracted out to private, for-profit organizations. While not contrary to the letter of the *Canada Health Act*, the Alberta legislation threatens universal health care as it builds into hospital care the concept that patients can be charged privately for non-insured services while they are receiving an insured service. It may also activate troublesome provisions under the North American Free Trade Agreement (NAFTA) by binding succeeding Alberta governments to deal with for-profit hospitals and by allowing foreign companies to claim that they should be allowed into other provinces.

Apart from being more effective as a delivery method, public medicare has important advantages over a private health care system. First, public financing spreads the cost of health care across society, rather than only to those who are unfortunate or sick. Second, financing health insurance through taxation is efficient, since it does not require the creation of a separate collection process. Third, medicare encourages Canadians to seek preventive care services and to treat problems before they worsen and treatment becomes more costly. Fourth, the government can cut costs, as it is largely a single buyer of health care supplies and services.

Housing and Health

According to the Canadian Institute for Health Information (2006c), there is a clear connection between health and adequate housing, which is defined by the Canadian Mortgage and Housing Corporation as affordable, suitable in size, and in good condition. The 2001 Census indicated that only 70 percent of Canadians live in adequate housing. The adverse health issues related to housing, which are more common in the highest-need neighbourhoods, are caused by various biological, chemical, and physical hazards and range from chronic issues such as respiratory problems to injury caused by falls and unsafe structures.

Many Canadian businesses also recognize and support Canada's universal medicare system, since it provides a competitive advantage with other countries. Lower employee benefit costs and a healthy and mobile workforce are advantageous. Also, the portability principle of medicare ensures that workers can move from province to province and still be covered by health insurance. Provincial governments have also begun to address preventive medicine and community-based care and have considered experimentation with community-based health and social service centres, such as the community health centres in Ontario.

Cost Reduction and Containment

Medical care costs in Canada have been rising steadily because of the aging of the Canadian population, the emphasis on curative and high-technology medicine, the rising cost of drugs, the increasing demand for hospital services and for expensive equipment, and the increasing fees of medical personnel. Cost containment has become an area of major concern and will certainly be a focus of attention in the coming years.

The issue of spiralling costs is one that advocates of public health care take very seriously. Nevertheless, they insist that keeping operating costs under control should not be used as a justification for greater privatization. For example, under pressure to meet overall provincial budgets without raising taxes, many provincial governments have attempted to lower hospital costs by reducing the range of services or by approving smaller budgets. They have also permitted hospitals to introduce cost-cutting measures, such as fees for emergency care, fees for use of ward beds, contracts with private companies to manage hospitals, and contracts for services such as food or laundry. In practice, such measures are counterproductive, as they undermine public confidence in medicare and open the door to even wider privatization.

In his report on the future of health care, Roy Romanow recommended a $15-billion cash infusion to stop the growth of private medicine.

Community Health Centres

In the 1970s, the federal government recommended the establishment of a network of **community health centres** (CHCs) with the intention of providing primary care, health promotion, and prevention services using salaried primary health care professionals.

The idea of community-based health centres as a serious alternative to individual physician care has existed since early in the twentieth century, with the first examples appearing in the United Kingdom and the United States. Canada's first CHC—the Mount Carmel Clinic in Winnipeg—opened over 80 years ago, in 1926, and is still in operation. Ontario's first CHC opened in Sault Ste. Marie in 1963.

Once considered the "poor cousins" of the mainstream health care system (because of their association with low-income and disadvantaged populations), CHCs have grown in number and size as provincial governments recognize their role in preventative medicine and health promotion. Since the mid-1980s, they have offered an ever-broadening range of client services to the general public, as well as to specialized client groups such as parents, seniors, and ethnic and immigrant populations.

Community Control

CHCs tend to network with other health and social services agencies and are accountable to their communities through community boards. They operate on the premise that communities should work together to "own" health care services. They frequently address issues affecting health, such as violence, housing, literacy, and poverty through programs and social action.

An important advantage of the CHC model is the focus on prevention, education, community development, social action, and health promotion. CHCs tend to address four determinants of health: living and working conditions, social support, individual behaviour, and genetic makeup. Located as they are between the patient and the medical practitioners, social workers are central to the provision of both direct care and community development in the CHC model of health care delivery.

CHCs are funded primarily by provincial grants. Additional funding is often obtained from the United Way, other foundations, and federal government programs. Funding is allocated either through a global budgeting process, based on services directed at populations, or through capitalization funding, where fixed sums are established for each registered client based on need as a reflection of age, sex, key demographic factors, and prevalence and severity of chronic illness. The use of CHCs (centres locaux des services communautaires) is most widespread in Quebec. Ontario is second highest. There is, however, a growing interest in the CHC model across the country, both as a way to cut costs and as a community-based approach.

Community Health Centres (CHCs)

Centres that provide primary care, health promotion, and prevention services using salaried primary health care professionals.

Medical Social Work Practice

Medical Social Work

The role of social workers in health care is of vital importance and is increasing along with the understanding that illness is greatly affected by social and environmental factors, and that preventive and educational approaches are both effective and cost-efficient.

One of the chief settings for **medical social work practice** (also referred to as health care social work) is the hospital. Almost every hospital in Canada has social workers in its departments, including emergency services, oncology, pediatrics, surgery, intensive care, rehabilitation, gerontology, and orthopaedics. The type of work performed by social workers in hospitals is wide ranging and includes direct casework, group work, discharge planning, family consultation, advocating for patients, counselling terminally ill patients, training other professionals, and policy and administration. Medical social workers generally have a graduate degree in the field, such as a master's degree in social work (MSW).

One of the primary roles of social workers in hospitals is discharge planning. Ensuring that patients are discharged in a timely manner with appropriate supports in place requires numerous skills. Social workers must work cooperatively with other staff as part of a multidisciplinary treatment team, have good analytical and assessment skills, communicate clearly with patients and staff, quickly initiate a therapeutic relationship with the patient, process paperwork, and be willing to advocate for the patient. Discharging a patient may involve ensuring that home care services are set-up. The discharge can become complicated, such as with a previously homeless person with multiple psycho-social and addictions issues. Sometimes even simple issues need attention; for example, a patient's discharge could be delayed because they have do not have a winter coat.

Interdisciplinary Teams

Interdisciplinary Teams

Teams of health care professionals (that may include doctors, nurses, occupational therapists, social workers, etc.) that work to holistically address health care and ensure that each patient's physical, psychological, social, and cultural needs are met.

When working in a hospital setting, the social worker is often a member of an **interdisciplinary team** that includes members of other health professions (such as medicine, nursing, and occupational therapy). The team approach is increasingly used to ensure that each patient's needs are being met. The role of social workers is becoming more central in this holistic approach to health care, which involves taking into account not only the physical aspects of health, which have commonly been addressed by physicians, but also the social, cultural, mental, and spiritual aspects.

In addition to hospital work, social workers are also involved in other health care settings, such as hospices, local medical clinics, community health centres, and specialized care agencies (such as HIV/AIDS clinics, addiction treatment centres, family planning, prenatal care, long-term care, home care, nursing homes, and services for people with disabilities). Social workers are also active as health promoters, community developers, and policy advocates in the health field. For example, a social worker may work with a community health centre to promote an aspect of healthy living in the community. Through this work, social workers are at the forefront in addressing primary health care prevention, health promotion, and self-care.

Hospice Care

Increasingly social workers are working in hospice care. **Hospice or palliative care** concentrates on reducing the severity of disease symptoms, rather than providing a cure, to those at the end of life. It can also include bereavement support or relieving the distress of family members and other caregivers.

Generally hospice social work includes one or more of the following services.

- **Pain management.** Often life-threatening illness causes pain. Social workers often work with other health care providers to determine what is causing the pain and the best ways to relieve it. Pain may be managed with narcotics and other drugs, but also by other means such as massage therapy and relaxation exercises, including mindfulness meditation.

- **Symptom management.** A variety of symptoms such as loss of appetite, nausea, weakness, difficulty breathing, bowel and bladder problems, and confusion may need to be addressed.

- **Social, psychological, emotional, and spiritual support.** Social workers will often focus on the well-being of the person in the final days of living. People in such circumstances confront a variety of psychological and spiritual issues. Different kinds of support to both the individual and family may be helpful in these instances.

- **Caregiver support.** Social workers work closely with family and other caregivers, providing necessary support, not only during the patient's last stages, but also to family members during the bereavement process.

Hospice or Palliative Care

Providing comfort and relief to patients living with terminal illnesses.

EXAMPLE OF A COMMUNITY HEALTH CENTRE

The Safe People Project at Pinecrest-Queensway Health and Community Service Centre in Ottawa is an excellent example of a health centre that is involved in community work. The Safe People Project emerged when community members came to the health centre because they were concerned about addictions in their community. The health centre staff worked closely with community members to develop a program that could support the entire community. It included training community members to be "safe people" who their neighbours could approach with problems. These people went through an extensive training session where they learned about addictions,

mental health, community engagement etc. The project also included running community events and creating clearer pathways to traditional addiction support programs. In the end, the process focused on supporting everyone in the community, not just people who were struggling with addictions and through this, community members were able to come together and help one another. As community members received more effective support from one another, fewer people needed to rely on substances and those who already relied on substances were able to get support and help.

Mentail Health and Social Work

Canada is second last compared to other developed countries when it comes to spending to treat mental illness, with Ontario and Saskatchewan spending the least. According to the May 2008 issue of the *Canadian Journal of Psychiatry*, Canada spent $6.6 billion on mental health in 2003/04 (Jacobs 2008). This represented 4.8 percent of the total health budget and just $197 per person. The breakdown for each province is:

- BC: 6.4% or $285 per person
- NB: 6% or $242
- PEI: 5.8% or $231
- Alberta: 5.6% or $242
- Manitoba: 4.6% or $219
- NS: 4.9% or $203
- NFLD: 4.8% or $200
- Quebec: 4.5% or $166
- Ontario: 4.3% or $185
- Sask: 3.5% or $146

The World Health Organization (WHO) defines mental health as "a state of well-being in which the individual realizes his or her own abilities, can cope with the normal stresses of life, can work productively and fruitfully, and is able to make a contribution to his or her community." The Public Health Agency of Canada (PHAC) has also adopted a broad definition: "Mental health is the capacity of each and all of us to feel, think and act in ways that enhance our ability to enjoy life and deal with the challenges we face. It is a positive sense of emotional and spiritual well-being that respects the importance of culture, equity, social justice, interconnections, and personal dignity" (PHAC 2006, 2). According to a 2002 Statistics Canada survey, nearly seven out of ten Canadians (67.1 percent) believe their mental health is excellent or very good. About one-quarter (26 percent) perceive their mental health to be good (Statistics Canada 2003a).

Mental illness is the term used to refer to a variety of diagnosable mental disorders. Mental disorders are health conditions that are characterized by alterations in thinking, mood, or behaviour (or some combination thereof) associated with distress or impaired functioning. Mental illness implies significant clinical patterns of behaviour or emotions associated with some level of distress, suffering, or impairment in one or more areas of functioning (school, work, social, and family interactions). At the root of this impairment is biological, psychological, or behavioural dysfunction, or a combination of these (CPA 1996). The terms mental health problems, mental illness, and mental disorder are often used interchangeably. Diagnosis criteria and treatment protocols for mental disorders are contained in the Diagnostic and Statistical Manual of Mental Disorders, DSM (IV), published by the American Psychiatric Association.

It is estimated that one in five Canadians will be affected by a mental illness in their lives. The WHO considers mental well-being an integral part of the general definition of health. In the WHO Constitution, for example, health is defined as "a state of complete physical, mental and social well-being and not merely the absence of disease or infirmity."

Social workers are playing an increasingly important role in promoting the mental health of Canadians with respect to prevention, treatment, and rehabilitation. Social workers may specialize in one of these areas or work across all three. Prevention aims to reduce the number of people with mental illness through awareness, standards development, and avoidance of risk factors. Treatment aims to reduce the prevalence (number of existing cases) of mental illness through counselling, intervention, or therapy and advocacy. Rehabilitation intends to reduce the after-effects of a mental illness and maximize the use of remaining capacities by the individual. Rehabilitation activities may focus on clients who are disabled by mental illness and include building knowledge and coping skills or the provision of specialized residential, vocational, and leisure services.

Social work in the mental health field requires the ability to work collaboratively with family members and the community. Social workers in the mental health field may deliver any of the following services:

- **Direct services**—available to individuals, couples, families, and groups in the form of counselling, crisis intervention, advocacy, and management of resources.

- **Case management**—the coordination of interdisciplinary services to a specified client, group, or population.

- **Community development**—working with communities to identify mental health needs and issues as well as the development of capacity to deliver services.

- **Administration**—putting systems in place and directly supervising to maintain effectiveness of mental health.

- **Program management**—development, implementation, and evaluation of a mental health program.

- **Teaching and research**—providing university and college courses or other workshops, conferences, and professional in-services.

- **Policy analysis**—analysis of mental health policies.

- **Social action**—organizing people to change mental health policy or advocate for system or program changes.

Social workers have contributed two key ideas to the mental health field. First, they have expanded the understanding of mental health. Social work has highlighted the influence of social and economic factors, family and other relationships, and the physical and organizational environment on individual mental health. The role of physiological processes, human biology, and experience are now viewed within the wider social context.

Secondly, social workers have worked to avoid labelling those with mental illness. Although social workers must understand and often refer to the DSM (IV), they avoid over-labelling. Using labels such as depressed, schizophrenic, manic, or hyperactive in a negative way can lead to branding and indignity. Stigmatizing labels are a barrier and discourage individuals and their families from getting the help they need.

The Canadian Mental Health Association (CMHA) exists to promote the mental health of Canadians, and employs an increasing number of social workers. Each year, CMHA provides direct service to more than 100,000 Canadians through the combined efforts of more than 10,000 volunteers and staff in locally run organizations in all provinces and territories, with branches in more than 135 communities. Each region, city, or province has a CMHA that has social workers providing services to the local community. They operate on the principles of empowerment, peer and family support, participation in decision-making, citizenship, and inclusion in community life.

Canadian Mental Health Association

Social workers in CMHA-run programs assist with employment, housing, early intervention for youth, peer support, and recreation services for people with mental illness, as well as stress reduction workshops and public education campaigns for the community.

In addition, social workers act as advocates to encourage public action and commitment towards strengthening community mental health services and towards legislation and policies affecting services.

RIGHTS OF INDIVIDUALS WITH MENTAL HEALTH PROBLEMS

The Canadian Mental Health Association, Winnipeg Region, is part of a nation-wide, charitable organization that promotes the mental health of all and supports the resilience and recovery of people experiencing mental illness, so that they can be full participants in society. A core objective of the CMHA Winnipeg Region office is to advocate for the interests of individuals with mental health problems. One of the ways that this is accomplished is through our Rights Consultation Service, the only dedicated mental health advocacy service in Winnipeg. The aim of the service is to help people with mental illnesses to be heard in the way they wish to be heard when there are issues with the services they are using. Grace Weinfortner has been our rights consultant for four years.

When a person has a problem or complaint about the services they are receiving, the place where they are living or working, or a system they are involved in, Grace can explain the choices that are open to them and guide them through a complaint process. This can include assistance in drafting letters, accompanying people to meetings about the complaint, and providing information about rights under the *Mental Health Act* and other Manitoba laws. The focus of the rights consultation work relates to treatment, income support, housing, and access to service issues.

Assisting people who have been admitted to a psychiatric unit who wish to challenge their involuntary patient status is a common issue. The process of assisting a person in this situation typically starts with receiving a phone call from the individual. During the initial phone call(s), it is important to determine how the person was admitted and what happened leading up to being admitted, confirming their status as either voluntary or involuntary, and providing information on the sections of the *Manitoba Mental Health Act* that apply to their situation.

Once it is determined that the person does want to challenge their involuntary status, Grace will then provide information on the Mental Health Review Board and the hearing process. This includes how to appeal their involuntary status, the timeline for scheduling the hearing, the names and contact information of people involved in setting the hearing, the make up of the hearing panel, and who can attend the hearing with the individual making the appeal. A person can hire a lawyer or apply through Legal Aid to have a lawyer represent them, they can attend the hearing on their own, or they can have someone other than a lawyer attend the hearing. Sometimes this may be Grace.

When the hearing has been scheduled (which can take up to twenty-one days), Grace will arrange time to assist the person to prepare for the hearing. This can take place over the phone or in person at the psychiatric unit of the hospital. During this meeting, Grace will help the person determine what they want the board to hear and coach the person through questions that will likely be asked at the hearing.

During the actual hearing, Grace will assist the person, if necessary, to communicate what they have determined is important for the board to hear. When the hearing has ended, Grace will ensure that the person understands the possible outcomes of the hearing. After a decision has been made, Grace will follow up with the person to ensure they understand the decision and the options available at that point.

During this process, Grace encourages the person to make the best of the time that they will spend in the hospital while waiting for the hearing. This can include enlisting nurses and hospital-based social workers as supports both in the hospital and in planning for eventual discharge. Grace works with the person to do as much as they can for themselves, to the extent of their capacities. The focus is often on ensuring that the person understands their rights and to support the person to have some control over the outcome of this process.

In discussing her role as the rights consultant, Grace stated, "It is gratifying to see that when armed with information, and perhaps some guidance, people can and do solve problems on their own. This can be empowering for the person and builds confidence and skills."

Social Work and HIV/AIDS

The human immunodeficiency virus (HIV) is a sexually transmitted and blood-borne retrovirus that undermines a person's immune system. Acquired immune deficiency syndrome (AIDS) is the stage of HIV in which the immune system is destroyed.

HIV/AIDS is a worldwide pandemic. According to estimates from the UNAIDS 2008 Report on the global AIDS epidemic, around 30.8 million adults and 2 million children were living with HIV at the end of 2007. During that year, some 2.7 million people became newly infected with the human immunodeficiency virus. That year also saw 2 million deaths from AIDS—a high global total, despite the introduction of anti-retroviral (ARV) drugs, which have helped to reduce AIDS-related deaths.

The overwhelming majority of people with HIV, some 95% of the global total, live in the developing world. However, the number of people living with HIV continues to rise in high-income countries as well. It is estimated that 1.2 million people are living with HIV in North America and 730,000 in Western and Central Europe. The Public Health Agency of Canada estimates that 58,000 people had HIV/AIDS in 2006 and that every two hours someone in the country becomes infected with HIV.

Helping Individuals and Communities

People diagnosed with HIV/AIDS face a great many difficult issues. Upon detection, an individual must first deal with the illness itself and the possibility of impending death. He or she must also confront social and economic problems, such as dealing with social stigma, rejection by friends and relatives, maintaining a work life, health insurance and medication costs, and maintaining interpersonal relationships. Women face special challenges, as often services do not exist specifically for them and they must frequently deal with child care concerns.

The services that social workers deliver for people with HIV/AIDS include prevention initiatives, primary care, hospital care, home care, hospice care, support groups, family support, and advocacy. Social workers also provide information and public education, make referrals to community resources, and prepare discharge plans.

In a hospital setting, social workers play a pivotal role as part of the wider health care team. In many cases, the social worker is the only person in the hospital who deals with non-medical or non-physical needs. They also work with family members and friends to provide both information and support after leaving the hospital.

In the community at large, social workers continue to advocate on behalf of those living with HIV/AIDS through community organization and policy initiatives in relation to HIV/AIDS prevention, public education and health promotion.

It is estimated that one in five Canadians will be affected by mental illness at some time in their lives. Social workers are playing an increasingly important role in dealing with mental health issues.

Canadian Centre on Substance Abuse

www.ccsa.ca

The CCSA's 2004 Canadian Addiction Survey (CAS) is the first national prevalence survey dedicated to alcohol, cannabis, and other drug use since 1994.

Addictions and Social Work

The treatment of addictions is a growing concern and, increasingly, social workers and social service workers are being called upon to address problems of this kind. **Addiction** can be defined as a compulsive need for, or persistent use of, a substance known to be harmful. Nearly one in ten adult Canadians (9.2 percent) have problems with excessive alcohol consumption. Others experience problems with narcotics, tranquilizers, sleeping pills, cocaine, LSD, and cannabis.

Harm Reduction Approach

Social workers are at the forefront in developing innovative ways to help people with addictions. Increasingly social workers and others in addiction treatment programs are taking a **harm-reduction approach** instead of an abstinence approach to treatment. Just over one-half of the Ottawa-area programs, for example, list abstinence as their treatment goal, while the other agencies list reduced consumption as the treatment goal. Social workers using a harm-reduction approach believe that people can overcome an addiction in incremental steps. The focus may be on safer use patterns for addicts rather than on immediate suspension of use.

Harm reduction was originally developed in response to the spread of HIV among injection drug users. Basically anything that reduces injection drug use, or makes it safer, can be considered harm reduction. Such programs also facilitate contact between drug users and social workers or other service providers, making it easier to offer education, counselling, health care, and access to treatment. More recently, harm reduction has spread to helping those with other substance addictions and gambling.

Insite—The First Legal, Supervised Injection Site in North America

A well-known, if somewhat controversial, example of the harm reduction approach in action is Insite, North America's first legal, supervised injection site located in Vancouver, BC. Insite is operated by Vancouver Coastal Health in partnership with Portland Hotel Society Community Services. The facility is accessible to injection drug users who may not normally be well connected to health care services: men and women who use more than one drug; those experiencing both addiction and mental illness; those with a history of trauma; the homeless and those living in shelters or in substandard housing; men and women of Aboriginal descent; and people who have tried in the past to beat their addictions but were unsuccessful.

Since opening in 2003, Insite has been a safe, health-focused place where people can go to inject drugs and connect to health care services —from primary care to treat disease and infection, to addiction counselling and treatment.

DRUG TREATMENT FOR OFFENDERS IN THE JUSTICE SYSTEM

The Centre for Addiction and Mental Health (CAMH) in Toronto helps people on the journey from addiction to recovery. CAMH's Toronto Drug Treatment Court (TDTC) program provides alternative intervention for offenders in the justice system.

In most cases, clients in custody apply through their lawyers to the TDTC—a joint collaboration between CAMH and the Ontario Ministry of the Attorney General. The program is not available to violent offenders, so most applicants are charged with crimes such as trafficking or simple possession, prostitution, or petty property crimes.

Specifically, the TDTC looks for people whose criminal behaviour is directly linked to their need to support their addictions to cocaine, crack, or opiates. TDTC focuses on harm reduction by providing treatment for the underlying cause of illness, something that would be ignored within the prison system.

The first step is a 30-day assessment. Throughout the client's stay with the program they attend a specific TDTC session twice a week, while simultaneously receiving treatment three days a week at CAMH. The program encourages honesty and unlike many treatment programs, doesn't punish early stage relapse, because program proponents believe relapse is part of recovery.

Once the client is stable, and a reduction in substance use is evident, the intensive stage—overcoming addictions—begins. Clients are either directed to the Structured Relapse Prevention Program or to the Women's or Youth Program. Those who really struggle are sent to a residential treatment facility.

In phase two, clients meet with CAMH caseworkers once a week; at this point clients are expected to be abstinent from their drug of choice (crack, cocaine, or opiates) and to be working on reducing use of secondary substances such as marijuana or alcohol. Clients often discuss the root causes of their pain, such as childhood abuse, institutionalization, and child welfare experiences. They also attend a drug treatment course once a month.

Caseworkers prepare clients for re-entry into school, work, and long-term housing. When the client is closer to graduation, they come to a support group one evening a week. To graduate from the program, clients must be drug free for three months, in school, working, or volunteering and in stable housing.

The goal is to reduce the rate of recidivism among this population, and to avoid the "revolving door" of crime and addiction when incarceration is used to deal with addictions issues. CAMH's recovery model allows for more success because it keeps clients where they belong: in the TDTC.

As one TDTC worker put it: "We're helping our clients to recover in their communities by facing real issues and pressures and walking with them as they struggle."

Source: Adapted from the Centre for Addiction and Mental Health website, www.camh.net.

Since it opened in September 2003, however, Insite has been variously praised and criticized. Peer-reviewed studies in reputable medical journals suggest that the facility has been highly successful in reducing the spread of disease through needle sharing, in preventing deaths by overdose, and in helping to link people in need to counselling services, treatment centres, and affordable housing.

On the other hand, there have been attempts to close down the Insite facility. For its part, the federal government has moved to a more enforcement- and treatment-based approach. The 2007 National Anti-Drug Strategy includes three action plans: preventing illicit drug use, treating those with drug dependencies, and combating the production and distribution of illicit drugs. This is a sharp departure from the holistic approach based, in the first instance, on harm reduction and helping people overcome chronic addictions rather than be punished for them.

Aboriginal Health

Health Canada has a special responsibility for the delivery of health care services to First Nations and Inuit communities. The federal government is obligated through treaties to fund 100 percent of the cost of First Nations health care.

In general, the health status of Aboriginal people is much worse than that of the average Canadian, and the Assembly of First Nations (AFN) states that the health gap between First Nations people and the general population is widening.

Holistic Healing

While improvements in health care services have eased this situation somewhat, they have also contributed to the gradual erosion of traditional Aboriginal **holistic approaches to health and healing**. Generally, First Nations leaders wish to see an integrated, holistic, interdepartmental, and inter-organizational strategy to address the inequities in health and social service delivery. They believe that jurisdictional issues between the federal and provincial governments with respect to responsibility for First Nations health care need to be removed, particularly in light of provincial health care reform (AFN 2000).

The AFN's Health Secretariat, the National First Nations Health Technicians Network (NFNHTN), and the Chiefs Committee on Health (CCOH) have identified seven health priorities: sustainability, health research, jurisdictional issues, mental health, children's health/gender health, smoking, and environmental health and infrastructure (AFN 2000).

Crowded Housing

While the housing conditions of some Aboriginal people have improved in the past decade, others are living in overcrowded conditions and in homes needing major repair. This is particularly true of First Nations people on reserves and Inuit in the North.

Inuit live in some of the most crowded living conditions in Canada. (Crowding is defined as more than one person per room in the dwelling.)

Most Inuit live in Inuit Nunaat, the northern region spanning the Northwest Territories, Nunavut, Quebec, and Labrador. In that region, more than 15,000 Inuit—38% of the total Inuit Nunaat population—lived in crowded conditions in 2006, down from 43% in 1996.

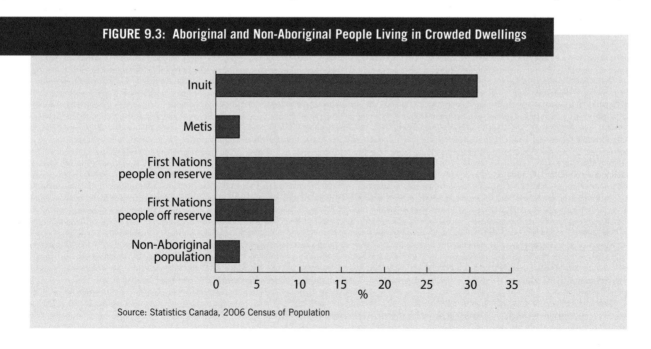

FIGURE 9.3: Aboriginal and Non-Aboriginal People Living in Crowded Dwellings

Source: Statistics Canada, 2006 Census of Population

Conclusion

- - - - - - - - - -

The *Canada Health Act* (CHA) of 1984 laid the foundation of the current Canadian health system. The CHA establishes the federal government's commitment to transfer money to each province and territory, to enable them to deliver universal, accessible, comprehensive, portable, and publicly administered health insurance.

Recent provincial trends indicate that equal access to the same health care services is diminishing and that the gap between the rich and poor is increasing. Several provinces are trying to move towards user fees, extra-billing, and the privatization of some services. This movement has the potential to lead to a two-tier health care system in Canada. The experience in the U.S. shows us that this type of system increases the disparity between the rich and poor and leads to a more costly, wasteful, and inefficient system of delivery.

On a positive note, our public system enables all provinces to shift away from an emphasis on health treatment towards a more comprehensive and integrated view of health. All levels of government are looking at ways to adapt our current system. The emphasis within the health care system is moving increasingly towards a community-based model that focuses on health promotion and prevention. Social workers are often at the forefront in advocating for, and providing, primary, community-based, and preventive health care.

In the health field, social workers work in a variety of capacities. While the primary setting for medical social work is the hospital, social workers also provide direct services in community centres, specialized facilities, and alternative care settings. While social workers in hospitals frequently feel that their role is not respected, it is quickly becoming more central as health care becomes more holistic in its approach. The holistic approach is one that takes into account not only the physical aspects of health that are commonly addressed by physicians, but also the social, cultural, mental, and spiritual aspects of the patient.

The wide skill set of social workers ensures that they will continue to be an essential part of multidisciplinary health care teams in Canadian health care settings.

CHAPTER REVIEW

Key Terms

- **Health gap**
- **Universal public health care**
- **Pre-payment health plans**
- **Hall Report**
- *Medical Care Act* **(1968)**
- *Canada Health Act* **(1984)**
- **Romanow Commission**
- **Medicare**
- **Public administration**
- **Comprehensiveness**
- **Universality**
- **Portability**

- **Accessibility**
- **Privatization**
- **Contracting out**
- **Community health centres**
- **Interdisciplinary teams**
- **Medical social work practice**
- **Hospice or palliative care**
- **HIV/AIDS**
- **Mental illness**
- **Addiction**
- **Harm-reduction approach**
- **Holistic approaches to health and healing**

Review Questions

1. What is the *health gap* in Canada, and why should it concern us?

2. Canada's health care system is publicly financed but largely privately delivered. Explain.

3. Briefly outline the history of Canada's health care system.

4. What are the five fundamental principles of medicare in Canada?

5. What are some signs that universal public health care is being eroded in Canada?

6. Describe the social worker's role in palliative care.

7. Explain the harm-reduction approach to addictions treatment.

8. What are some the key challenges facing medical social workers today?

Exploring Social Work

1. It seems that health care in Canada is one area that is subject to a variety of myths. Go to the myth busters website of the Canadian Health Services Research Foundation at **www.chsrf.ca/myth-busters/index_e.php.** Write a paragraph each about three myths, reviewing the empirical evidence in each case.

2. We are exposed daily to radio, television, and newspaper accounts that present people with mental illness. Write a two-page report on how the media portrays mental illness. Do the media portray people with mental illness unfavourably as violent, criminal, dangerous, comical, incompetent, and fundamentally different from other people or favourably as competent productive members of society? What is the impact of the portrayal that you found? You can begin with information from **www. withanopenmind.com.**

3. Harm-reduction programs for drug users have been controversial in Canada. Investigate either a needle-exchange program or another harm-reduction program. Evaluate the research behind the program. Does the program increase drug use? Does the program decrease health risks and costs? Outline your findings in a report.

Websites

- - - - - -

Health Canada Online
www.hc-sc.gc.ca

Health Canada is the federal department responsible for helping the people of Canada maintain and improve their health.

Canadian Health Coalition
www.healthcoalition.ca

The Canadian Health Coalition is dedicated to preserving and enhancing Canada's public health system for the benefit of all Canadians. Founded in 1979, the coalition includes groups representing unions, seniors, women, students, consumers, and health care professionals from across Canada.

World Health Organization
www.who.int

World Health Organization (WHO) is an agency of the United Nations and is based in Geneva. WHO was established in 1948 and is "the directing and coordinating authority on international health work."

Public Health Agency of Canada
www.publichealth.gc.ca

The Public Health Agency's website contains information about the health of Canada's population, including the government's response to the WHO Commission on the Social Determinants of Health. Key determinants of health include income/social status, education and literacy, and the physical and social environment.

CHAPTER 10

SOCIAL WORK WITH WOMEN

- -

A Feminist Approach

One of the defining social characteristics of the second half of the
twentieth century was the increased labour force participation
of women. Indeed, the participation rate for Canadian women
more than doubled from 29 percent in 1961 to 60 percent in 1991. The
social implications of this economic fact were phenomenal (Gunderson
1998). Among other things, it gave rise to the dominance of the two-
earner family. It precipitated a marked increase in the demand for child
care, part-time work, flexible work arrangements, and in social pressure for
legislation that would foster and ensure greater equality between men and
women.

What feminist author Betty Friedan referred to in the 1950s as "the
problem with no name" very soon received a name and a solution—
women's inequality and women's liberation.

Social Work Beginnings

In Canada, the movement for greater participation of women in public life arose at the end of the nineteenth century. It had a number of major strands, including the temperance movement, women's missionary and charitable activities, and the suffragette movement. The temperance movement focused on the prohibition of alcohol (because of its devastating effects on male breadwinners and therefore on women and children); missionary and charitable activities were an opportunity for women to become involved in public life beyond their role as caregivers in the family; and the **suffragette movement** sought to establish the voting rights of women. Women became involved in the Women's Christian Temperance Union, the National Council of Women (founded by Lady Aberdeen), the Young Women's Christian Association (YWCA) and church missionary societies and charities such as the Protestant Orphans Homes, homes for unmarried mothers, homes for the aged, and settlement houses.

Women were also involved in campaigns to improve conditions for nursing mothers through the provision of pure milk, in organizations that provided care for victims of tuberculosis and other illnesses, and in providing assistance to families of veterans during and after World War I. When the federal government agreed to pay an allowance to support the families of men who died in the war, a group of Manitoba women (including suffragette leader Nellie McClung) campaigned for a similar benefit for the widows and children of men who died in peacetime. The Mothers' Allowance established by the Manitoba government in 1916 was the first legislated welfare program, and it soon became available in all Canadian provinces.

These early women's organizations were the forerunners to the profession of social work. Participation in these organizations, as well as wartime employment in jobs vacated by men at the front, led to an increased role for women in public life, and to the acquisition of the vote. Together these political and social changes opened the door for women who wanted to participate in public affairs.

In the early period, women in social work were typically **maternal feminists**. They felt that women's nurturing and caring qualities and their understanding of children were critical in the reformation of society. The Child Welfare Council, for example, was composed of early feminists who entered social work because of their primary concern for families, mothers, and poor children in particular. Although they brought women into public life and social work, these early activists now tend to be viewed as quite conservative in outlook, insofar as they supported more traditional conceptions of the family in which women were expected to stay in the home.

Nellie McClung (1873–1951) was a leading Canadian feminist who is remembered most for her role in winning women the right to vote, and arguing the "Person's Case" which saw women in Canada declared as persons in 1929.

Helen Levine is a radical feminist social worker. In her writings, she challenged traditional views of mothering, critiqued psychiatry for defining women through a patriarchal lens, and offered an alternative way of working with women through feminist counselling. At the School of Social Work at Carleton University, Levine pushed the parameters of structural social work to include a feminist analysis.

Given the expectations on women to maintain family life, it is not surprising that it was largely single women who sought employment in social work and in other helping professions. Moreover, at this time, women's salaries were low compared to men with similar qualifications: "excluded in large part from the male-dominated fields of business, government, and the professions, a new generation of college-educated middle class women after the turn of the century provided a large pool of available labour for the emerging fields of nursing, teaching, library science and social work" (Struthers 1991, 128). Delegates to a 1929 conference on equal pay pointed out that "the same salary which will attract superior women will interest only mediocre men" (Struthers 1991, 128).

The ensuing economic crisis of the 1930s did little to change this situation. It was only later, in the 1960s, that the salaries and make up of the profession began to change dramatically with the wholesale expansion of employment in the social services sector.

Equal Pay and Employment Equity

Although more and more Canadian women entered the labour force from the 1950s onward, they seldom did so on equal terms with men. The industries and occupations initially open to women were generally less prestigious. Women's incomes were far inferior to those of men in the same occupations, and justifications for this fundamental inequality seemed to be readily available. In addition to economic inequality, patriarchal family and social relations were still in force. In many households, women were expected to tend to their children, husband, and household affairs as well as earn an income outside the home.

Nevertheless, many legislative changes and important policy initiatives in the post-war period were aimed at fostering greater equality for women at work. These included: (1) equal pay policies (including pay equity or equal pay for work of equal value) designed to improve women's income; (2) equal employment policies (including employment equity) designed to help women's employment and promotion opportunities; and (3) other facilitating policies (such as child care and parental leave) designed to put women on an equal footing in the labour market. (For a more complete discussion of women and the labour market, see Gunderson 1998.)

- **Equal-pay policies.** During the 1950s and 1960s, every Canadian province enacted legislation requiring equal pay for similar or substantially similar work (**equal-pay policies**). During the 1970s, both Quebec and the federal government introduced pay equity legislation that required equal pay for work of equal value (allowing comparisons between occupations). In the 1980s, most jurisdictions followed suit, at least with respect to public sector employment. In Ontario, most establishments are required to have a pay equity plan in place, regardless of whether there has been a complaint.

- **Equal employment and employment equity.** All Canadian provinces now have **equal employment** legislation in place, usually as part of their human rights codes. This legislation prohibits discrimination on the basis of race, age, religion, nationality, and sex. The prohibition of discrimination on the basis of sex was generally added during the 1960s and 1970s. **Employment equity** legislation, which requires or encourages proactive hiring practices in regard to identified groups, such as women, was not introduced in Canada until the 1980s. The first legislation took effect in 1986 and applied only to Crown corporations and federally regulated employers with 100 or more employees. In 1996, it was expanded to include the federal public service. Employment equity is also required of federal contractors. Employment equity may also be required by cities and municipalities. One study, reported by Morley Gunderson, found that only slightly more than one-third of firms where employment equity was required had effective procedures in place to administer the policy (Gunderson 1998).

- **Facilitating policies.** Many other changes have been introduced to help put Canadian women on an equal footing with men in the labour market. These include changes in divorce laws, policies against sexual harassment at work, expanded maternity leave, policies to protect part-time and temporary workers, and policies designed to ensure women have equal access to higher education.

Such policies have undoubtedly helped to equalize the situation for women, though there is still the overriding concern that women leave work at the end of the day only to find that they have still to assume the main burden of work at home and in the family.

Equal Employment

Legislation that prohibits discrimination on the basis of race, age, religion, nationality, and sex.

Employment Equity

The use of hiring policies and programs to increase employment opportunities for groups previously denied advancement.

Thousands participated in the Quebec Federation of Women march for equality and social justice in Montreal in October 2000.

Persistent Problems

While new legislation and strategic policy initiatives have undoubtedly helped to improve the position of women in Canadian society, there is a growing realization that employment legislation in itself has not resolved many of the underlying problems. In many areas of economic and social life, women are still vulnerable.

Even with advances in labour force participation, women dominate the ranks of those living in poverty. An examination of the situation reveals persistent problems for women in many areas of economic life.

- **Poverty.** Women constitute a substantial segment of the working poor. High poverty rates (based on after-tax LICOs) are concentrated in three family types: unattached women under 65 (37.1

TABLE 10.1: Reasons for Part-Time Work by Women, 2008

Reason	Percentage			
	Total	15-24	25-44	45 and Over
Own Illness	3.6	0.7	2.9	6.7
Caring for Children	14.6	1.5	37.8	5.6
Other Personal or Family Responsibilities	4.3	0.8	5.4	6.5
Going to School	27.0	75.3	8.6	0.8
Personal Preference	28.3	5.6	17.2	57.9
Other Voluntary	0.6	0.4	0.8	0.6
Other[1]	21.6	15.6	27.3	21.9
Total Employed Part-Time (thousands)	2,135.9	679.1	681.8	774.9
% Employed Part-Time[2]	26.4	52.6	18.9	24.2

Notes:
1. Includes business conditions and unable to find full-time work.
2. Expressed as a percentage of total employed.
Source: Statistics Canada. "Reasons for Part-Time Work for Women." CANSIM, table (for fee) 282-0014 and 282-0001 and Cat. no. 89F0133XIE. Adapted from the Statistics Canada website www.statcan.gc.ca.

percent, compared to 31.2 percent for men), unattached women 65 and older (16.1 percent, compared with 14 percent for men), and single mothers with children under 18 (28.2 percent, compared to 7.2 percent for men) (Statistics Canada 2007).

- **Part-time work.** Women still constitute a large proportion of part-time workers in Canada and, as such, are usually earning less and therefore are particularly vulnerable to economic downturns. Part-time employment as a percentage of total employment has grown steadily and in 2007 over a quarter (26.1 percent) of employed women were employed part-time. Seventy percent of all part-time workers are women. Over 20 percent of these women are not voluntarily taking part-time jobs and would take full-time employment if it was available (see Table 10.1, page 198)

- **Minimum wage legislation.** Because women hold 64 percent of minimum wage jobs, they are the group most in need of minimum wage legislation. For example, although Ontario's minimum wage was recently increased, it had been fixed since 1995. In addition, providing a living wage for women can be a policy instrument by governments for promoting greater wage equity and anti-poverty policy goals.

- **Maternity and parental leave.** Women still perform a double duty—even if they work outside the home, women are most often the primary caregivers for dependent children and relatives and therefore have to work another "full shift" with the family. Employment Insurance (EI) benefits can play a significant role in addressing this issue, if women are eligible for the benefits. EI was expanded in 2000, allowing parents to receive benefits for up to one year while caring for a child, but many women find that they are not eligible.

- **Dependent care.** Because women are most often the primary caregivers of dependent relatives, Canada's lack of universal daycare (child care) programs is a significant barrier to women's full participation in the labour force. Daycare is a necessity for many employed mothers. According to the Ontario Association of Food Banks 2008 report, 66 percent of lone-parent mothers with at least one child under six fall below the Statistics Canada LICO.

- **Free trade and globalization.** These global trends, involving competition from low-wage countries, particularly affect women who find themselves in low-wage jobs.

- **Pension programs.** These programs are of special significance to women, because women are often employed in jobs that do not give them access to private pension plans.

The Poorest of the Poor

Women on their own are the poorest of the poor, especially women raising children in lone-parent families, who are almost five times more likely to be poor than those in two-parent families.

Older women on their own are also thirteen times more likely to be poor than seniors living in families.

Women are also among the poorest of the poor within Canada's most vulnerable populations: Aboriginal people, people from racialized communities, recent immigrants (many of whom are also from racialized communities), and persons with disabilities.

Source: Excerpted from Monica Townson's "Canadian women on their own are poorest of the poor." Canadian Centre for Policy Alternatives Editorial, September 8, 2009. www.policyalternatives.ca/editorials/2009/09/article2301

- **Recessions.** Economic downturns affect women disproportionately. Forty percent of employed women hold part-time, casual, or temporary jobs, which are the first to be cut during recession (CCPA 2009).

- **Employment insurance programs.** Programs designed to assist workers can place women at a disadvantage. Increases in the required eligibility periods make it more difficult for women than men to collect Employment Insurance; for example, women who work part-time because they care for children may not have worked enough hours to qualify for EI.

Despite all the changes in the area of pay equity and employment equity, there is a continuing need for policy-makers, social work practitioners, and others to be aware of the economic problems that women still face.

In short, the problems Canadian women face in (and out) of the labour market are widespread and persistent. The economic and psychological stresses resulting from these inequalities take a toll on women and their families, and social workers are often called upon first to deal with the unfortunate consequences.

FIGURE 10.1: Equity a Long Way Off: Women's Wages as a Percentage of Men's Wages

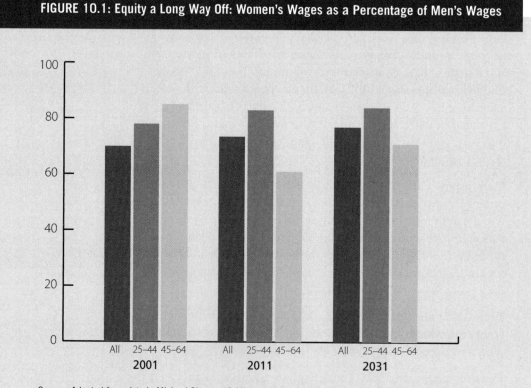

Source: Adapted from data in Michael Shannon & Michael Kidd. 2001. "Projecting the Trend in Canada Gender Wage Gap 2001–2031." *Canadian Public Policy.* XXVII(4): 447–467.

Sexism and Gender Equality

Before going on, it may be useful to distinguish several key terms.

- **Gender** has come to refer to the characteristics that identify the social relations between men and women or the way that this relationship is socially constructed. Gender is a relational term similar to the concepts of class and race, and it is an analytical tool for understanding social relations and processes.

- **Gender equality** means that women and men live in an environment that affords them equal opportunity to realize full human rights; to contribute to national, political, economic, social, and cultural development; and to benefit from the results. In this context, *gender equity programs* refer to measures taken to compensate women for the historical and social disadvantages they have suffered, which lead to gender equality. Gender equity and gender equality form the basis upon which the principles of a feminist social work practice are based.

- **Sexism** refers to prejudice or discrimination based on a person's sex. It is a system of discriminatory interrelated physical and social controls, derogatory beliefs, and institutional- and societal-level policies. Sexism can be both blatant and subtle; it can take the form of derogatory language and put-downs or result in the denial of job or career opportunities based on a person's sex. Sexism can be so extensive, commonplace, and internalized that it is not initially visible. Acknowledging that sexism can and does have a significant impact on the daily lives of women in Canada can be a difficult process for many individuals. It is sometimes easier to accept traditional roles and norms, which are comfortably familiar. Sexism is rooted in the patriarchal family system.

- **Patriarchy** literally means "rule by the father" but, in a broader sense, it has come to mean the domination of society by men. Men are still the major stakeholders in Canadian society, men continue to be represented in higher numbers in positions of authority, and male interests continue to take precedence over those of females.

Given the deep-rootedness of the patriarchal family system—and with it sexism and gender inequality—the prospect of eradicating widespread sex discrimination in Canadian society may seem a little daunting. However, while one should not minimize the difficulties ahead, it is important to note that great strides have been made by the women's movement. Without wishing to diminish the obstacles, the future looks brighter than ever and social workers and others have every reason to be optimistic as they join this long struggle for full gender equality.

Gender

How we identify as male, female, or transgendered and adhere to cultural norms of femininity and masculinity; in contrast to sex, which is biological.

Principles of Feminist Practice

Social work, like many other fields of study and practice, was greatly influenced by the women's movement of the 1960s and 1970s. Students demanded that social work schools look more critically at social problems and develop programs that would be more responsive to women's issues. The feminist movement dramatically changed social work thinking, as well as social work practice. Feminist theories offered different ways of seeing and understanding women's lives and experiences, the nature of sexual inequality, and gender relations. Feminist therapy, for example, has

WOMEN HELPING WOMEN

The Women's Centre of Calgary is every woman's place for support, connections, and community. It is a street-level storefront, an accessible gathering spot for all women. The heart of the Women's Centre is a large open room with comfortable seating and a welcoming atmosphere. Women can simply drop by for a cup of coffee, talk with other women, and seek help with any concern.

The Women's Centre is a place where women from all walks of life can feel safe to get and to give help, without waiting lists, time restrictions, cost, or judgment. Services include peer support, information and referral, legal advice, groups, workshops, basic needs assistance, computer and equipment use, and community events.

The work of the Women's Centre is founded on a peer support model of service delivery, whereby women are supported and trained to help other women. This means that all services are provided by and for women with the backup and support of staff. As women talk, work, and help each other at the Centre, it is often difficult to distinguish between service user, volunteer, and staff member. The peer support model also reflects our feminist, anti-oppressive, and community development approach.

We work to recruit a diverse base of staff and volunteers, conduct ongoing diversity training, and develop inclusive policies and practices. Programs are based on the requests of women who use the Centre, and deliberate efforts are made to offer programs that will engage a wide range of women as well as promote their participation in the community and on issues that affect them. We have community kitchens for women in poverty and women with disabilities, practice English groups, book clubs, and girl power camps. We participate in coalitions, organize community events, and contribute to social action initiatives.

While we do not keep individual client files, the Women's Centre keeps track of program contacts and aims to assess its work in various ways, such as through focus groups and surveys. For example, one recent survey of women who use the Centre found that 86 percent of the 689 women who responded said they had made new friends and increased their support networks. "I feel like I belong to a strong community. I've been able to meet many women from different walks of life," one woman explained.

The Centre recently celebrated its ten-year anniversary by organizing a grassroots conference to create and support connections and community for women. We worked with grassroots community groups to help them define and present their issues. Women presented at the conference, shared their stories, discussed issues relevant to them, and made new connections. More than 200 women participated who were in unions, athletics, the corporate world, as well as living with mental health issues, living in poverty, living on the street, in conflict with the law, experiencing domestic violence, and working as live-in caregivers. We discussed issues like immigration, child care, literacy, sexuality, global issues, and activism. We also celebrated together with an evening of dinner, dancing, and artistic performances. The conference was a great success.

With incredible support from the community, funders, over 350 volunteers, and six staff, the Women's Centre continues to be a place for support, connections, and community for thousands of women. As one woman said, "sometimes I feel like the Centre is my second home."

Source: Prepared by the Women's Centre of Calgary. Copyright © 2008. Printed with permission.

its origins in the women's liberation movement of the 1960s and 1970s. Women's **consciousness-raising groups** began to question gender-based roles and power relations in society. By sharing experiences, women began to understand how their own experiences were not unique.

There are different definitions of feminism and numerous formulations and debates within feminist theory. There is, however, a common core belief that sex-role stereotypes and social structures perpetuate women's subordination. Fundamentally, many feminist principles and concepts are similar to those of social work practice, such as the empowerment of the individual and the examination of society through a critical lens. In her 1995 book *Feminist Practice in the 21st Century*, Helen Land, a University of Southern California professor and accomplished feminist clinical practitioner, outlines the following thirteen components of feminist social work practice:

- **Validating the social context.** Feminist approaches emphasize the effect social context or structures have on the client; and the client and the worker jointly assess them.

- **Re-valuing positions enacted by women.** Social workers see the activities and stances assumed by women, such as nurturing, cooperating, and caregiving, as vitally important and valuable. Society and mainstream psychotherapies, however, are considered to place more value on the activities of men, such as competition and upward mobility.

- **Recognizing difference in male and female experiences.** Feminist social workers maintain that mainstream theories are gender-blind and ignore the different experiences of women and men. To understand the emotional worlds of women, therapists must understand how the oppressive structures in society affect women.

- **Re-balancing perceptions of normality and deviance.** The need for re-balancing perceptions of normality refers to the fact that what is considered abnormal or dysfunctional is often the normal behaviour of less-privileged groups. For example, feminine behaviour, such as expressing emotion, is seen as a weakness in male-dominated society. This is also true for people of colour and gay men and lesbians.

- **Taking an inclusive stance.** This enables feminist counsellors to challenge narrow assumptions and to include the experiences and values of all, regardless of ethnicity, class, sexual orientation, age, or ability.

- **Paying attention to power dynamics in the therapeutic relationship.** This aspect ensures that the therapist works towards an egalitarian relationship between client and worker. It also serves to empower the client and thereby fosters lasting solutions.

Thousands of men and women participate in the Quebec Federation of Women march for equality and social justice in 2001.

- **Recognizing how "the personal is political."** This important component acknowledges that very personal difficulties faced by clients may reflect historical and political contexts (for example patriarchy). Such wider structures and ideologies influence how we think, feel, and experience events.

- **Taking a deconstructive stance.** The deconstructive stance attempts to uncover and examine how social relations of patriarchy support and perpetuate a male-dominated world. The feminist approach therefore continually questions commonplace notions of what is "right" and "wrong," "normal" and "abnormal."

- **Taking a partnering stance.** This refers to the belief that disclosure of personal experiences by a therapist is helpful to a client, especially if common experiences are apparent. This practice is quite contrary to traditional psychotherapy, which holds that professional distance between the therapist and client is required.

- **Fostering inclusive scholarship.** In challenging the traditional notions of objective science, feminist scholarship frequently emphasizes both qualitative (such as interviews or case studies) and quantitative (such as numerical frequencies and statistics) research methods. As well, it stresses beginning with women's experience and what actually happens in the world, rather than with abstract theoretical models that claim to represent reality.

- **Challenging reductionist models.** *Reductionism* refers to the practice of reducing behaviours to simple cause-and-effect models, which often amount to stereotypes and severely limit one's ability to understand complex issues. For example, there is a stereotype of women as naturally more emotional, and men, more objective. Feminist social workers resoundingly challenge such views.

- **Adopting empowerment practice.** Empowerment practice means that the worker and client develop goals together with a focus on empowering the client to change structures and environments, rather than on helping the client adapt to and cope with existing oppressive structures.

- **Countering the myth of value-free psychotherapy.** In general, feminist therapists reject the idea that a person can be value-free in their practice, and they believe that therapists must be explicit about their own biases and values. As well, they would assist clients in discovering and taking ownership of their own beliefs and values.

Regardless of the particular emphasis, these components of feminist social work practice offer a way of seeing and understanding women's lives that will help individual clients *and* begin to change wider structures and policies that foster gender inequality and oppression. Indeed, these principles are so important that gradually they are becoming an accepted part of standard social work practice.

Incorporating Feminist Principles

Incorporating feminist principles into one's social work practice is not an easy task. To begin, it is important to value women's experience and identity, and to recognize that women have been subjected to unfounded negative stereotypes. Myths, such as "women are the weaker sex" and "a woman is nothing without a man," must be rejected, and the important contributions women have made must be stressed. Social workers who incorporate these principles value the diverse experience of all their clients—women and men.

In addition, social work practice informed by feminist principles seeks to identify power differences and examines how they affect both the therapeutic relationship and the client's life, thereby linking the "personal" and "political." For example, while a client is recounting a bad experience, the worker may ask, "How does this experience relate to the fact that you are a woman?" or "How is your situation similar to that of other women?" This type of question may help a client analyze their situation or experience. Identifying and critically analyzing behaviours, rather than labelling them, enables women to replace powerlessness and helplessness with strength and determination. This fosters self-esteem and an egalitarian client–therapist relationship.

Another process that encourages self-esteem and egalitarianism is worker self-disclosure. Sharing relevant personal information with a client allows the client to see that she has a common experience and faces many of the same problems as others. This helps women to differentiate between individual and social problems and thereby eliminates some of their self-blame. Listening and validating the experiences of women is one of the most important aspects of applying feminist principles. This voicing of her experiences begins the process of healing.

There are obviously many occasions when it is only appropriate that a female worker, rather than a male, work with a woman in need. This is the case, for example, when working with women who have been sexually abused or raped, where the presence of a male social worker is clearly inappropriate. It is widely recognized that women should counsel such individuals. This work normally takes place in settings such as rape crisis centres and women's shelters, where an experienced staff is equipped to deal with emergency situations and provide support and assistance.

However, male social workers can, should, and do incorporate feminist principles into their practice. Male practitioners working with the New Directions program in Ottawa, for example, use feminist principles to help men who have abused women. The program helps men take responsibility for their behaviour and helps them see their abusive behaviour within the wider social context of a male-dominated society. The history of abuse that many of the men themselves may have experienced is also addressed and common experience between the men is explored.

Implications of Record Keeping

As in all types of social work practice, social workers must keep case records or written documents that detail the client's situation, the intervention, and the outcomes. However, practitioners who follow feminist principles and who work with abused women increasingly find the requirements of case records to be troublesome: they find it difficult to keep accurate records knowing that they might be entered as evidence in court proceedings.

For example, Bill C-46, the Rape Shield Law, is intended to protect women from character attacks by defence lawyers and restricts the questioning of women regarding their sexual histories. To compensate for this restriction, lawyers might subpoena women's counselling and medical records. Social workers need to be mindful of this when writing case notes and be careful not to write things that might be misinterpreted. Subjective comments and judgments should be avoided.

Violence Against Women

While wife-beating has never been a legal act in Canada, historically, women who were financially dependant on their husbands found that they had little recourse if their husbands should become abusive. In fact, the view that men should have complete authority met with general acceptance, in part because men held economic power in the marriage. It was not until the late nineteenth and early twentieth centuries that women were recognized as having legal and political rights.

Meanwhile, the status quo prevailed with respect to domestic violence—what happened behind closed doors was considered to be no one else's business. Police were reluctant to respond to domestic disputes, and the courts did not take the matter seriously. As a result, many assaults on women were not reported to the authorities. It was not until the 1980s that mandatory charging policies took effect across Canada. Formal training was established in Canadian police forces to assist officers in determining a proper course of action when responding to domestic disputes, as well as to help them recognize chargeable assaults.

Victimization Survey

Many social workers take exception to the phrase "family violence" or "domestic violence." They believe these more general terms gloss over the fact that it is usually men who are violent against women. The facts are certainly clear. According to Statistics Canada, in 2004, 653,000 or 7 percent of women aged 15 and over (in either a current or previous marital or common-law union) experienced spousal violence in the previous five years. This was unchanged from 1999. Statistics on violence reported to police also show women being much more likely than their male counterparts to be victims of spousal violence (85 percent versus 15 percent). Young females aged 25 to 34 experienced the highest rates of spousal violence (CCJS 2000).

A victimization survey carried out in 2003 by the Canadian Centre for Justice Statistics underlines these facts. At the time, there were 606 victim service agencies in Canada. Of these, 41 percent were police-based, 19 percent were community-based, 17 percent were sexual assault centres, 10 percent court-based, and 8 percent system-based. A survey conducted on one day in 2003 demonstrated that over 75 percent of the individuals who sought help from these agencies were victims of violent crime, and the majority were female.

In fact, of the 4,400 individuals helped on the day of the survey, almost three-quarters were women or girls. Even when sexual assault centres are removed from the total, women seeking assistance still represent 70 percent of those who seek help. Of the 4,400 individuals surveyed, more than 1,300 females were victims of violence by a spouse, ex-spouse, or intimate partner.

SHELTERS, TRANSITION HOUSES, AND ADVOCACY FOR ABUSED WOMEN

Transition houses are responsive to the needs of the abused woman and her children, are sensitive to the power relations within traditional family structures, and emphasize social change. Because of their success, the number of transition houses or shelters is growing. While they are becoming a primary resource for women and their children, they face serious funding problems.

The women's movement in the 1970s struggled hard for the funding and development of shelters. Today they are the primary resource for protecting assaulted women from violent partners and to assist women in moving on with their lives. Services dedicated to responding to the abuse of women include transition houses and shelters, second-stage housing, safe houses, and family resource centres. Each province and territory has a unique array, with varied funding arrangements and availability.

All of the services are residential, meaning that they can provide accommodation for abused women and their children as required. The services provide counselling and other support programs, such as safe and secure emergency housing, crisis intervention, emotional support, information and referral, food, shelter, advocacy, a crisis telephone line, and children's programs. Some centres provide services to former residents and non-residents with newsletters, walk-in services, or support groups.

Research has shown that an effective shelter provides the following kinds of services:

- emergency access to a safe place (including emergency transportation and overnight accommodation, particularly for those in rural and isolated areas)
- counselling and emotional support (immediately following a crisis and through follow-up and outreach on a residential or non-residential basis)
- information and referral
- access to affordable and safe housing, and to legal and medical services
- employment and income support
- mental health and addiction services where required
- child care, child support, and counselling for children to overcome trauma
- safety planning
- assistance with the family law system (spousal maintenance, custody and access, child support, and accommodation)

Source: Adapted from Statistics Canada. 2001d. "Shelters for Abused Women." *The Daily*. 28 March 2001. Ottawa: Statistics Canada. www.statcan.gc.ca.

Women commemorate the deaths of 236 women and 35 children who were murdered in Ontario since 1995, during a "Step It Up" campaign.

Sexual Assault and Sexual Harassment

Sexual Assault

Unwanted sexual activity forced upon a person without consent, including physical and non-physical acts; falls under the Criminal Code.

Sexual Harassment

Any unwanted behaviour, comment, gesture, or contact of a sexual nature; falls under civil law.

Canadian Association of Sexual Assault Centres

www.casac.ca

This is a group of sexual assault centres from across Canada who have united in their common goal to implement the changes necessary to prevent, and ultimately eradicate, sexual assault.

Sexual violence in a major social problem in Canada today. Indeed, the level of violence against women, in whatever form it takes, is one of the strongest indicators of prevailing societal attitudes towards women.

- **Sexual assault** is any form of unwanted sexual activity including fondling, touching, and penetration, that is forced upon another person without that person's consent. It includes a wide range of criminal acts ranging from rape to sexual harassment. All forms of sexual assault are crimes under the *Criminal Code*. Consent is a key component of defining an act as sexual assault. Consent is an active choice and the voluntary agreement of two adults to engage in sexual activity. Someone who is under the influence of medication, drugs, or alcohol is not considered to be in the position to give consent (Status of Women 2002, 19).

- **Sexual harassment** is any unwanted behaviour, comment, gesture or contact of a sexual nature that treats the person receiving it as a sexual object.

In 2001, 24,419 sexual assaults were reported, but only 43 percent of the reported sexual assault cases resulted in a conviction. Women made up the majority of victims of sexual assault (86 percent) and other types of sexual offences. However, most sexual assaults are not reported, because women often feel afraid to report, or don't want to go to court, or know the probability of conviction is low.

Recovering from a sexual assault can often be a long and painful process. Women often feel as though they should have done more to prevent the situation or they are worried that people will not believe them. Many women seek support to help them deal with ongoing nightmares, distrust, fear, anxiety, difficulties with sex, depression, guilt, shame—and social workers are often at the front line.

Date Rape

In addition, most sexual assaults occur when women are on a date, and these assaults are reported far less frequently than assault by a stranger. Forty percent of female victims of sexual assault were assaulted by a friend or casual acquaintance, 23 percent by a stranger, and 23 percent by a family member, including a spouse or ex-spouse (CCJS 2002a).

Acquaintance sexual assault (also called date rape) presents new issues. In addition to the trauma experienced in stranger assaults, self-doubt, self-blame, betrayal of trust, and lack of confidence in her/his own ability to make judgments and good decisions all complicate the recovery process when the assailant is known to the victim. Acquaintance sexual assault is highly under-reported. It is important to be aware that this type of assault is common and can happen to anyone.

Social workers work for rape crisis centres, sexual assault centres and helplines, sexual assault and domestic violence care and treatment centres, sexual assault survivors' centres, and shelters or transition houses. Figure 10.2 illustrates the range of counselling, legal, and medical services that a sexually assaulted woman might need.

Social workers also act to educate the public about sexual violence, advocate for women, and campaign for policy and systemic change. Social workers in this field recognize that sexual violence is not only an individual problem, but reflects wider social and structural dimensions.

TABLE 10.2: Victims of Spousal Violence by Offence Type Reported to Police

Offence	Total		Female		Male	
	No.	%	No.	%	No.	%
Homicide/Attempt	132	0	105	0	27	1
Sexual Assault	521	2	514	2	7	0
Major Assault (Assault Levels 2 & 3)	4,446	13	3,355	12	1,090	21
Common Assault (Assault Level 1)	21,526	63	18,419	64	3,107	60
Criminal Harassment	2,453	7	2,159	7	294	6
Uttering Threats	4,167	12	3,592	12	575	11
Other Violent Offences	862	3	809	3	53	1
Total Offences	34,107	100	28,953	100	5,154	100

Note: Percentages may not add up to 100% due to rounding.

1. Excludes incidents where the sex and/or the age of the victim was unknown.
2. Data are not nationally representative. Based on data from 94 police departments representing 56% of the national volume of crime in 2002.
3. Includes victims aged 15 to 89.
4. Spousal violence refers to violence committed by legally married, common-law, separated and divorced partners.
5. Other violent offences include robbery, unlawfully causing bodily harm, discharge of firearm with intent, assault against peace-public officer, criminal negligence causing bodily harm, other assaults, kidnapping, hostage-taking, explosives causing death/bodily harm, arson, and other violent violations.

Source: Adapted from Statistics Canada publication Family Violence in Canada: A Statistical Profile, Catalogue 85-224, 2004, page 12, www.statcan.gc.ca.

Rape Relief and Women's Shelter

The Vancouver Rape Relief and Women's Shelter provides a typical range of services for both abused and sexually assaulted women. They provide a 24–hour emergency call line. They offer a safe place for women and their children to stay to escape or prevent an attack. They offer support groups to help counter feelings of isolation, including an ex-residents' group. They believe that sharing emotional support and knowledge helps all women to join together to act for change. They offer information for women interacting with the Ministry of Social Services, the police, the court, or the hospital. Finally, they will accompany women to the hospital, to the police, through court proceedings, as well as to appointments with lawyers, financial aid workers, and social workers, providing emotional support and advocacy.

What Is the Role of a Social Worker?

The role of social workers in helping abused women may include crisis intervention, support and empowerment, support group facilitation, and the provision of information. A social worker in a shelter will frequently be the first person a woman meets when she flees a violent situation. At this critical time, it may be necessary to discuss the cycle of violence and point out that the violence is likely to occur again. The social work process will be assisted by conveying the message that the violence is not her fault and that she is not the only woman to experience this kind of violence.

The social worker should ultimately support the woman in whatever decision she makes and provide her with the kind of support and education she needs to make a good decision. While it is very frustrating for a social worker to see a woman go back to an abusive relationship, sometimes several times, the worker must be sure not to take the power of decision away from the woman, as that has been her experience throughout her relationship. The social worker should empower the woman to make this important decision about her life.

In all such situations, the first priority is the safety of the woman. Within this context, the social worker may partake in one or several of the following activities:

- Intervene in a crisis, which may involve the identification and assessment of danger to the woman and her children.
- Facilitate an empowerment approach with the woman.
- Listen to what the woman has to say and empathetically respond, sharing one's personal experience if appropriate.
- Connect the woman to a support group of individuals who have had a common experience.
- Teach the woman how to assess the assault/homicide potential in domestic and other situations.
- Make an appropriate referral, if for example, the woman has immediate financial needs.
- Teach the woman how to recognize abuse, name the problem and its source, and avoid self-blame.
- Advise the abused woman of her legal rights and link her to legal resources, thereby avoiding the traditional practice of "re-victimization."
- Mobilize safety, legal, and community resources effectively (e.g., linking children to a children's protective service, arranging admission to a shelter for abused women, finding a translator for an immigrant woman, linking a rape victim with an advocate).

- Implement agency policy regarding mandated reporting and keep accurate records, including dental and other X-rays, as these can possibly aid later legal action.

- Use the consultative process (know whom to call under what circumstances, and do it) and review one's referrals and interventions with other health care providers.

- Complete the crisis management and follow-up referral or treatment steps while withholding judgment and the imposition of values on the woman and her significant others.

- Provide full follow-up and counselling with the woman and her assailant.

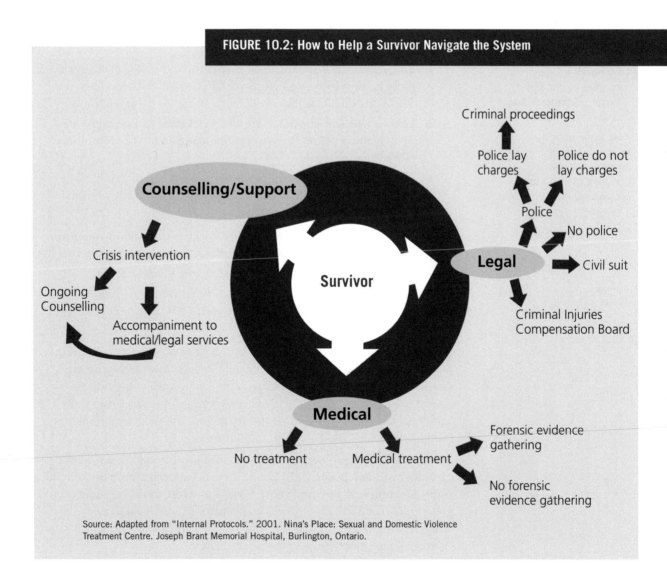

FIGURE 10.2: How to Help a Survivor Navigate the System

Source: Adapted from "Internal Protocols." 2001. Nina's Place: Sexual and Domestic Violence Treatment Centre. Joseph Brant Memorial Hospital, Burlington, Ontario.

Other Areas of Social Work Intervention

Violence is one of the main areas where social workers intervene directly on behalf of women in need. Two other areas are discussed briefly below: women in poverty and women living with HIV/AIDS.

Women and Poverty

Mounting numbers of women, and especially lone-parent mothers, are receiving social services across Canada. So disturbing is the problem that a phrase has been coined to capture it—the **feminization of poverty.**

While the poverty rate undergoes fluctuations, the rate for women is always higher than it is for men. When the economy is weak, as it is now and as it is likely to be in the coming years, the **poverty gap** for women tends to rise even more. Over the past 25 years, the poverty rate for women has fluctuated between 12% and 20%. The most recent statistics available indicate that:

- Single mothers remain the poorest family type in Canada, with a poverty rate (based on before-tax LICOs) of 38.1% compared to 11.9% for single fathers;
- Unattached senior women are also vulnerable to poverty, with 37.2% falling below the poverty line compared to 28.9% of unattached men;
- Of all senior women, 16.6% are poor compared to just 8.3% of senior men;
- The poverty rate of Aboriginal women is 36%;
- 29% of women of colour are poor. African-Canadian women are the poorest racialized group in Canada, with a poverty rate of 57%;
- 26% of women with disabilities fall below the poverty line;
- The overall poverty rate for foreign-born women is 23%, rising to 35% for those who arrived between 1991 and 2000 (Canadian Feminist Alliance for International Action, 2008).

In working with low-income women, social workers need to be aware that women's poverty is caused by different factors than men's poverty. Canadian studies have found that men's poverty is usually more directly related to low-wage employment, whereas women's poverty arises from additional factors such as divorce and separation, and their responsibilities as mothers, homemakers, caregivers, and nurturers.

Issues pertaining to gender inequality need to be addressed in order to tackle women's poverty in Canada. Beyond understanding the unique issues affecting low-income women, social workers should challenge governments at all levels to develop specific strategies to deal with women's employment, child care, old age security, family law, Social Assistance rates, and general income security.

Women and HIV/AIDS

The first recorded AIDS case in Canada was in 1982. HIV/AIDS in Canada has changed from the early epidemic, which primarily affected men who have sex with men, to the current epidemic, which increasingly affects other groups such as injecting drug users and heterosexuals. As a result, the number and percentage of women living with HIV/AIDS is increasing.

The Public Health Agency of Canada estimated that by the end of 2005 there were about 58,000 people in Canada living with HIV/AIDS. Of those, the Agency estimated that 15,000—or just over 25 percent— don't know it. The greatest number of new infections continues to be among men having sex with men (45%). However, women account for 27 percent of new infections and now make up more than 20 percent of those with HIV/AIDS. In 2007, within the 15-19 age group, the proportion of new diagnoses of women with HIV/AIDS was 36 percent.

The HIV/AIDS epidemic among women is of particular concern because of the potential for transmission to their infants. Social work practitioners are increasingly engaged in efforts to secure specific services for women affected by HIV/AIDS. Because they are at the front lines, they are in an ideal position to address the HIV/AIDS problem.

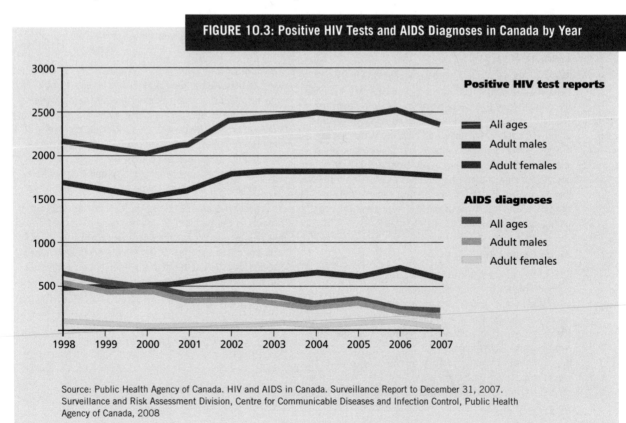

FIGURE 10.3: Positive HIV Tests and AIDS Diagnoses in Canada by Year

Source: Public Health Agency of Canada. HIV and AIDS in Canada. Surveillance Report to December 31, 2007. Surveillance and Risk Assessment Division, Centre for Communicable Diseases and Infection Control, Public Health Agency of Canada, 2008

EXPLAINING VIOLENCE AGAINST WOMEN

Violence against a woman by a man is a social act, a behaviour for which the perpetrator is accountable to the community. A variety of theories have been advanced to explain why this phenomenon occurs in Canadian society. Each of these attempts to conceptualize violence against women contains a great deal of truth, and any social work assessment of a situation of violence by a man against a woman needs to consider the following major theories: power theory, learning theory, anger-control theory, and cycle-of-violence theory.

Power Theory

This theory argues that wife abuse is a societal problem that occurs because of the power imbalance between men and women, specifically, because of the dominance of men and men's roles. Wife abuse continues because there has been historical acceptance of abuse and of men's right to control women, even by force. This theory maintains that society must change its attitudes, values, and responses with respect to women if wife abuse is to be prevented. This theory is consistent with a structural or feminist approach to social work.

Learning Theory

The main idea behind this theory is that violence is a behaviour learned in childhood. Boys learn that it is okay to be violent, and girls learn that is it okay to be on the receiving end of violence—this is what relationships are about. This theory holds that all children in our society are socialized to accept violence and that this, coupled with the different roles into which boys and girls are socialized, supports and perpetuates abuse. Children who witness violence in the home are much more likely to become abusers or be abused. The emphasis here is on changing the behaviour of the perpetrator.

Anger-Control Theory

This theory focuses on the idea that men must be held accountable for their violent behaviour. They must learn to deal with and control their anger and express it in more appropriate ways. This theory does not attempt to explain the root cause of wife abuse, and in that, it is different from the other two theories. Instead, it focuses on poor anger control—if men could control their anger, violence would stop. It is a changed-behaviour model. Within this theory, a criminalization and a punishment-based social work approach would be the most successful.

Cycle-of-Violence Theory

This theory does not explain why violence occurs; rather, it explains what happens in individual relationships in terms of a three-step process. First is the tension-building phase. In this phase, the woman sees that tension is building in the relationship and that there is going to be an explosion. The man is expressing more anger every day. He may be kicking the dog or yelling at the children.

The second phase in the process involves an acute battering incident. The tension has reached a point where the violence erupts against the woman. She is abused, hit, bruised and battered. This is usually a shorter phase than the first, lasting from between two and twenty-four hours.

The third phase is called the honeymoon period. In this phase, the man says he is sorry; he should not have done it; he loves her; he begs her not to leave him; he promises it will never happen again. The man will call relatives to ask them to convince the woman to return to him. If the woman has left during the second phase, she might return to him during this phase. Statistics show that a woman is usually abused and leaves many times before she leaves for the final time.

The honeymoon period is a very powerful phase. Women want to believe that their partner has changed; they may also feel that it will be their fault if the marriage breaks down as they perhaps didn't work hard enough at the relationship. Some women stay for the sake of the children or believe that a bad marriage is better than no marriage at all. Statistics show that single mothers are among the poorest in our society, and this is where income security programs come into play.

These theories are useful in that they look at different aspects of the problem of violence against women. In one's daily practice, a concrete assessment that takes account of the specifics of the situation will always be needed so as to ensure that any intervention addresses the full range of possible solutions.

Conclusion

The women's movement has dramatically changed the status of women in Canadian society. Legislation and policies on employment equity, pay equity, abortion rights, discrimination in employment and education, and specialized health programs have been pursued and important gains have been made—yet equality for women is still far from being achieved. Increasingly, it seems, women who are not attached to a man are poor. Women of colour and Aboriginal women are even poorer, and employed women tend to be sex-segregated in low-wage jobs.

Social workers need to help women at both the personal and political level. In helping women deal with personal problems, social workers need to analyze the social and economic context of women's problems. The feminist approach emphasizes the harmful role of patriarchal relations within the family and within the wider society. The recognition that sex-role stereotypes and social structures perpetuate women's subordination also necessitates a response that addresses the institutions, structures, and policies in Canadian society. Social workers should not minimize the importance of helping women deal with personal changes in their attitudes, behaviours, and relationships, but workers also need to challenge the ways in which sexism supports oppression and inequality.

Since the early 1970s, social workers have been concerned with eliminating sexism from social work education and thereby enabling graduating social workers to work more effectively with women. Facts about the historical roots of patriarchy and gender inequality are now generally woven into the curriculum, and feminist social work practice skills are increasingly taught in both core and specialized courses. To be effective, practitioners need to be continually aware of how sexism pervades social work practice, and understand the social, economic, and cultural context of women's problems.

CHAPTER REVIEW

Key Terms

- Suffragette movement
- Maternal feminists
- Equal-pay policies
- Equal employment
- Employment equity
- Gender
- Gender equality
- Sexism
- Patriarchy
- Consciousness-raising groups
- Sexual assault
- Sexual harassment
- Acquaintance sexual assault
- Feminization of poverty
- Poverty gap
- Power theory
- Learning theory
- Anger-control theory
- Cycle-of-Violence theory

Review Questions

1. What was the general approach of the women who were involved in early social work?

2. List and define five persistent problems that Canadian women confront.

3. What is meant by the *feminization of poverty*?

4. Define and compare the terms gender equity and gender equality.

5. List and define five components of feminist social work practice.

6. Describe two ways in which social workers put feminist principles into practice.

7. What are two theories that explain violence against women?

8. What is the role of social workers when working with women who have been abused?

Exploring Social Work

1. Read through the section entitled "Persistent Problems" on pages 198 and 199, and choose one of the identified issues to explore in greater depth. Write a brief paper that outlines in detail how women tend to be at a disadvantage in terms of programs and legislation related to minimum wage, pensions, or Employment Insurance. Include your thoughts on changes that would increase equality in the area you've chosen to examine, and provide research to support your ideas.

2. According to Health Canada, the health-related costs of violence against women in Canada exceed $1.5 billion a year. Go to the Health Canada website (**www.hc-sc.gc.ca**) and explore this issue further. How does violence directly affect women's health? What can the Canadian government do to combat this social problem? Write a two-page paper in support of your argument.

3. Gender-based analysis (GBA) is a process that assesses the differential impact of proposed and/or existing policies, programs, and legislation on women and men. Go to the Status of Women Canada website (**www.swc-cfc.gc.ca**) and search for gender-based analysis. Write a two-page paper on how GBA can help inform social work practice. While the model was developed to inform policy analysis you might find that it is just as relevant to direct practice. How would the eight steps of GBA be applied in direct practice?

Websites

- - - - - -

Status of Women Canada
www.swc-cfc.gc.ca

Status of Women Canada (SWC) is the federal government agency that promotes gender equality and the full participation of women in the economic, social, cultural, and political life of the country. SWC focuses its work in three areas: improving women's economic autonomy and well-being, eliminating systemic violence against women and children, and advancing women's human rights.

National Clearinghouse on Family Violence
www.phac-aspc.gc.ca/ncfv-cnivf/familyviolence

National Clearinghouse on Family Violence is a national resource centre for those seeking information about violence within the family and new resources being used to address it.

Canadian Health Coalition
www.healthcoalition.ca

The Canadian Health Coalition is dedicated to preserving and enhancing Canada's public health system for the benefit of all Canadians. Founded in 1979, the coalition includes groups representing unions, seniors, women, students, consumers, and health care professionals from across Canada.

International Museum of Women
www.imow.org

Founded in 1985 as the Women's Heritage Centre, the International Museum of Women is based in San Francisco. In addition to exhibits, the museum provides an online community and educational materials that foster the transformation of women's lives.

CHAPTER 11

SOCIAL WORK AND ABORIGINAL PEOPLES

The Canadian Legacy

Aboriginal peoples in Canada comprise 4 to 5 percent of Canada's total population. They include the Métis, the Inuit, and many First Nations. Many endure conditions found only in the poorest countries of the world. Poverty (35 percent below LICO) and unemployment (38.4 percent) are widespread. The situation is not only unjust, it is a national disgrace.

There is much that remains to be done to reverse the damage done to Aboriginal communities across Canada. The causes of the current crisis are deep and can be traced back to the history of colonialism on the part of the European settlers towards the original inhabitants of this land. Social workers, Aboriginal and non-Aboriginal alike, will play an important part in this healing process. But the urgency of addressing this national problem cannot be understated.

Who Are the Aboriginal Peoples?

Aboriginal peoples are the original inhabitants of the portion of the North American landmass known as Canada. Aboriginal is a collective term which includes the First Nations, Inuit, and Métis peoples. The term Indian is widely believed to have originated with the early explorers who thought they had reached India in their search for a passage to the east. Whether this is true or not, today the term is used to define a group of indigenous people registered as such according to the *Indian Act*. Menno Boldt notes that the term Indian "serves the Canadian government as a convenient political, legal, and administrative categorization of the culturally diverse first peoples of Canada" (1993, 192). It is used in much the same way as native, as a means of "outside-naming" those "who are descendants of the first inhabitants of what is now Canada" (Chartrand 1991, 3–4). The term *Aboriginal* "appears to be associated with a general, emerging emancipation of Aboriginal peoples from domination of all sorts by the settler society" (Chartrand 1991, 3–4). Of course, the Aboriginal peoples have their own names in their respective languages, such as Anishinabe, Inuit, Innu, Nuu-chah-nulth, and Métis.

The First Nations include culturally, linguistically, and geographically diverse groups of people—some examples are the Cree, Dene, and Mi'kmaq peoples. Because of the *Indian Act* and the significance of the Indian Register, the term Indian is still used in a legal context and usually defines a person as being either a Status or non-Status Indian. Status Indians are persons of Aboriginal ancestry who are registered as Indians according to the *Indian Act*. Non-Status Indians are not, or have lost the right to be, registered as Indians as defined by the Act, but identify with the Indian community culturally and/or linguistically. Individuals who are "Indians" within this context are also First Nations people.

The Inuit are Aboriginal peoples of Canada "that have traditionally used and occupied, and currently use and occupy, the lands and waters" ranging from the Yukon and Northwest Territories to northern Quebec (Nunavik) and Labrador (Nunatsiavut) (INAC & Tungavik 1993, 4). April 1, 1999, marked the creation of Nunavut, a new territory born from the eastern part of the Northwest Territories. The agreement between the Inuit of Nunavut and the federal government recognizes that the Inuit are best able to define who is an Inuk (or member of the Inuit peoples) according to their own understanding of themselves. Like other Aboriginal peoples, the Inuit have a diversity of cultures and ways of living.

The Métis have often been neglected in the consideration of the Aboriginal peoples of Canada, an injustice that obscures their role in the westward expansion of this country. Unlike other Aboriginal peoples, the Métis cannot assert that they have inhabited this continent *as a distinct people* for thousands of years. The term Métis is most often used to refer to descendants of the historic Métis—those whose origin can be traced back

Aboriginal Peoples

Collective term for original inhabitants of Canada; includes First Nations, Inuit, and Métis.

to the Red River in the early 1800s. Now located mainly in the prairies and the north, they formed a language and culture that was a unique blend of Indian and European cultures (Purich 1988).

When Europeans began to arrive on this continent, Aboriginal peoples numbered between 500,000 and 2 million. They lived a wide variety of lifestyles, depending on the natural resources available to them. The oral traditions of some Aboriginal cultures assert that the pre-contact population was even greater than the estimates of anthropologists and historians. Across Canada, there were approximately fifty Aboriginal languages spoken, which made up eleven main language groups. Within each Aboriginal language there are several dialects. For example, the Algonkian (or Algonquian) language group includes the Ojibwa language, which in turn includes the Saulteaux, Odawa, Potawatomi, and other dialects.

Aboriginal nations were also characterized by richly diverse social organization, including systems of governance, health care practices, and cultural and spiritual rituals. These social aspects were not separated into functionally specialized institutions, but were organized holistically. Such social organization usually included some formal means by which different nations agreed to coexist. Some, such as the Haudenosaunee (Iroquois) or the Mi'kmaq, formed confederacies. Much of Aboriginal history is based on unwritten oral accounts passed down over generations. These accounts often contain spiritual concepts foreign to European experience.

Relationship with Europeans

The relationship between Aboriginal peoples and Europeans was initially friendly. During the sixteenth and seventeenth centuries, Aboriginal peoples served as partners in exploration and trade. Later, as the English and French became locked in a struggle to control North America, the relationship with the Aboriginal peoples evolved into military alliances. As European peoples and their governments exerted dominance over territories that had been inhabited by Aboriginal peoples, they were no longer seen as military allies, but were gradually viewed as irrelevant, or worse, as an obstacle to imperial domination (Miller 1989, 84).

The movement westward in the later eighteenth and nineteenth centuries caused increasing displacement and conflict for the Aboriginal peoples who lived on the land that the newcomers wanted for agriculture and homesteads. The presence of Aboriginal peoples on these lands demanded a response from the European governments. With the colonization of what would become known as Canada, the land's original inhabitants became "the Indian problem," and impediments to "civilization." Colonial representatives (and, later, government officials) devised various schemes to address the problem, including land-cession treaties and assimilation policies. Such schemes came at an exorbitant cost to the original inhabitants, not only financially, but more importantly, in terms of the loss of Aboriginal lives and ways of living.

The Colonial Legacy

The policy subsequently adopted by the settlers, best described as **colonialism**, amounted to nothing less than an attempt to completely subjugate the Aboriginal peoples. As a direct result, to this day living conditions and income levels for the Aboriginal communities and those living off reserves continue to be lower than for the rest of Canada. Aboriginal people are also more reliant on various forms of Social Assistance.

Typical of this colonial legacy, a primary factor contributing to the high rates of poverty among Aboriginal people is unemployment. According to the 2001 Census data, the unemployment rate for the "Aboriginal Identity Population" was 19.1 percent and the percentage of Aboriginal households living below the Low-Income Cut-off (LICO) was 31.2 percent (Statistics Canada 2001a).

Aboriginal peoples are also incarcerated in correctional centres and penitentiaries more than other groups. They are twice as likely to be imprisoned in the first place and are more likely to receive a full prison sentence than non-Aboriginal people. The rate of suicide and suicide attempts is at least three to four times higher among Aboriginal peoples, especially among those 15 to 20 years old, than among the rest of Canadians (RCAP 1996).

These poor social conditions have caused many Aboriginal peoples to leave their own communities for urban centres, particularly within the last thirty years. According to the 2006 census, 53 percent of Aboriginal people lived in metropolitan areas of Canada. Winnipeg had by far the largest Aboriginal population at 68,385 or almost 11 percent of the total urban Aboriginal population. However, poverty doesn't disappear when Aboriginal people reside in cities. According to K. Lee, of the total Aboriginal urban population, over 50 percent lived below LICO as compared to just over 20 percent of the non-Aboriginal population in 1999. Perhaps the most shocking statistic is that 77 percent of Aboriginal lone-parent families live below LICO. The poorest urban Aboriginal people live in Saskatoon (63.7 percent), Regina (62.2 percent), and Winnipeg (60.5 percent) (Lee, K. 1999, 10).

Interestingly, while the mainstream Canadian population ages and its birth rate declines, the Aboriginal population continues to grow. Currently, the median age of Status Indians (recognized as Indians under the *Indian Act)* is 10 years younger than the Canadian median age, and for Inuit it is 12 years younger. While the Canadian population, as a whole, is aging into retirement, Aboriginal populations are moving from youth into working age (CMA 1993, 7). Unless real action is taken soon to address and resolve the serious social problems in Aboriginal communities, social alienation and unrest, especially on the part of the growing numbers of Aboriginal youth, is likely to become even more acute.

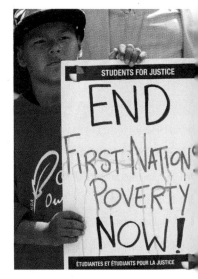

A child protests the poor social conditions of many First Nations peoples during the Aboriginal Day of Action in 2008.

Colonialism

Forced political domination of one nation over another including administrative, economic, and cultural control.

The Indian Act

With the signing of **land-cession treaties**, the government of Canada changed its relationship with the continent's first inhabitants in the later nineteenth century. "The intention of the civil government, now that Indians no longer were militarily useful, was to concentrate Indians in settled areas, or reserves; to subject them to as much proselytization, schooling, and instruction in agriculture as 'circumstances' made necessary" (Miller 1989, 100).

The legal instrument for this was the *Indian Act*. The **Indian Act of 1876** sought strictly to define who would be considered an Indian so as to exert government authority over Aboriginal peoples. The Act fragmented the Aboriginal population into distinct groups with different rights, restrictions, and obligations. As a consequence, Canada today is one of the few countries to still have separate laws for a specific group based on race or ethnicity. The *Indian Act* was, and still is, a piece of social legislation of very broad scope that regulates and controls virtually every aspect of the lives of Aboriginal people.

Historically, an **Indian Agent** administered the Act in Aboriginal communities. These agents were to displace traditional Aboriginal leaders so as to institute a new way of living consistent with the intentions of the Canadian government at the time. The Indian Agents had extraordinary administrative and discretionary powers. In order to ensure this, Clause 25 of the Act established the government's guardianship over Indian lands.

Assimilationist Policies

The social control aspects of the *Indian Act* placed Canada's First Nations firmly in the position of a colonized people. The Act spelled out a process of enfranchisement, whereby Indians could acquire full Canadian citizenship only by relinquishing their ties to their community; that is, by giving up their culture and traditions and any rights to land. Consequently, the cost of Canadian citizenship demanded of an Aboriginal person far surpassed that for an immigrant to Canada.

The Canadian government saw the *Indian Act* as a temporary measure to control Aboriginal peoples until they had been fully assimilated through enfranchisement. Assimilation refers to the absorbing of one cultural group into another. It was not until 1960, however, that the government granted First Nations the right to vote in federal elections. In 1958, the Prime Minister at the time, John Diefenbaker, named a member of Alberta's Blood tribe, as Canada's first Native Senator. In 1960, the government gave non-enfranchised Aboriginals the right to vote in federal elections. For the first time, citizenship for Aboriginal peoples was not conditional upon their assimilation into mainstream Canadian society. Despite these moves, however, the federal government remained opposed to Aboriginal self-government.

The Reserve System

Once land was ceded and Canadian settlements had been established, Aboriginal peoples were shunted aside onto small parcels of land largely devoid of any economic potential. This land could not even be used as collateral to develop business ventures, since that land was held "in trust" by the government. It has been argued that by confining Aboriginal peoples to reserves, Inuit communities, and Métis settlements

> the welfare of Aboriginal societies was systematically neglected. Famines and tuberculosis were allowed to virtually decimate Aboriginal communities, unaided except for relocation of survivors to state institutions. Housing provided was of the poorest quality, and health care and education were until quite recently, left to the Church. (Scott 1994, 7)

The federal government then established the Department of Indian Affairs as the main vehicle to regulate and control Aboriginal movement and ways of living. The modern equivalent of the department is known as Indian and Northern Affairs Canada (INAC), and its stated mission is to support Aboriginal communities in their quest to become healthy, safe, and economically self-sufficient.

TABLE 11.1: Size and Growth of the Population by Aboriginal Identity, Canada, 1996 and 2006

Aboriginal identity	2006	Percentage change from 1996 to 2006[3]
Total population	31,241,030	9%
Aboriginal identity population	1,172,790	45%
First Nations people[1]	698,025	29%
Metis[1]	389,785	91%
Inuit[1]	50,485	26%
Multiple and other Aboriginal responses[2]	34,500	34%
Non-Aboriginal population	30,068,240	8%

Notes: 1. Includes persons who reported a North American Indian, Métis or Inuit identity only.

2. Includes persons who reported more than one Aboriginal identity group (North American Indian, Métis or Inuit) and those who reported being a Registered Indian and/or Band member without reporting an Aboriginal identity.

3. Data have been adjusted to account for incompletely enumerated reserves in 1996 and 2006.

Source: Statistics Canada, censuses of population, 1996 and 2006.

Residential schools took Aboriginal children, like these girls, away from their communities and forced them to assimilate to the dominant European culture. The last residential school closed in 1996.

Racist Legislation

The *Indian Act,* still in force, certainly seems to be wildly out of step with the bulk of Canadian law. It singles out a segment of society—largely on the basis of race—removes much of their land and property from the commercial mainstream, and gives the Minister of Indian and Northern Affairs and other government officials a degree of discretion that is not only intrusive but frequently offensive.

The Act has been roundly criticized. Many want it abolished because it violates normative standards of equality, and these critics tend to be non-Aboriginal; others want First Nations to be able to make their own decisions as self-governing policies and see the Act as inhibiting that freedom. Even within its provisions, others see unfair treatment between, for example, Indians who live on reserves and those who reside elsewhere. In short, this is a statute of which few speak well. However, for fear of losing much needed special status, some Aboriginal groups seek to protect the Act.

It is a controversial issue with no easy answers. It is important to remember that Aboriginal peoples are not all the same and many bands, nations, and individuals disagree and hold varying relationships with the government.

The Métis and Inuit

The situation among the Métis in the late nineteenth and early twentieth centuries was unique. The Métis in western Canada could seek to become status Indians by aligning themselves to certain treaty areas or they could "take scrip." The **scrip system** entitled the bearer of a scrip certificate to either land or money; in exchange, the person who took scrip gave up all further claims to land. Although the scrip system offered to the Métis was different from the treaty-making process for First Nations, the result was the same. Neither Métis nor First Nations have been treated fairly (Purich 1988, 125).

The *Indian Act* also governed the Inuit. No land was formally set aside for their use, nor were any treaties signed with the Inuit peoples. However, because of the extensive mineral and oil exploration on their lands, many Inuit communities have been relocated, forcing a substantial change in their lifestyles.

One example of the nature of state intervention in Inuit lives is the **disk list system**. As bureaucrats could not, or perhaps would not, acknowledge Inuktitut names, the disk list system assigned a numbered disk to each Inuk. Although originating as an administrative measure in the 1920s and not universally employed, the disk list system ultimately came to define a quasi-legal status that affected all aspects of Inuit life. By the 1960s, however, "it was evident that Governments attempts to implement a "disc list" system was largely a failure" (D.G. Smith 1992).

Residential School System

The now-infamous **residential school system** was established in the mid-1800s by Indian Affairs in conjunction with several Christian churches. Aboriginal children were removed from their Aboriginal communities and placed in residential schools. By restricting Aboriginal culture and language, the schools sought to fulfill the **assimilationist policies** of the federal government. The children were denied their language, spiritual rituals, and more importantly, access to their families. Aboriginal children were regularly subjected to emotional and physical abuse, and many were also victims of sexual abuse.

As a result of their having resided within an institution that regulated every aspect of their lives, individuals' decision-making skills were impaired: "residential schools were no preparation for life in any type of community" (Armitage 1993, 142). Some struggled with drug and alcohol addiction and problems with mental health that arose from the psychological trauma they had endured. Many found themselves with a limited ability to parent their own children, as parenting models had been unavailable to them.

While many individuals who emerged from these institutions retained a positive outlook, a true testament to their adaptability and resilience, it must be stressed that the residential school experience systematically crippled many Aboriginal children and families. This legacy will take many generations to heal. In 2007 an out-of-court settlement between the Government of Canada, the Churches, and the Aboriginal peoples of Canada was established. The *Indian Residential Schools Settlement Agreement (IRSSA)* is the largest class action settlement in Canadian history (see page 226). In 2008, the federal government formally apologized to Aboriginal peoples for the residential school system (see photo, page 245).

The Sixties Scoop

In 1951, the *Indian Act* was amended such that provincial laws of application (and therefore child welfare legislation) applied to reserves (Timpson 1990). With this legislative change, the government's approach to Aboriginal assimilation veered from residential schools towards the apprehension and placement of Aboriginal children in non-Aboriginal foster homes. Child welfare agencies also assumed responsibility for services to Aboriginal communities.

One result is what is known as the **Sixties Scoop**. In the 1960s, massive numbers of children were removed from their communities and placed in non-Aboriginal foster and adoptive homes. By the late 1970s and early 1980s, at any given time, one in seven Status Indian children was not in the care of his or her parents, and as many as one in four Status Indian children was spending at least some time away from the parental home (Armitage 1993, 147). Between 1959 and 1970, the percentage of

Residential School System

System—established in the mid-1800s by Indian Affairs in conjunction with several Christian churches—through which Aboriginal children were removed from their communities and placed in residential schools.

Sixties Scoop

Massive removal of Aboriginal children in the 1960s from their families and placement in non-Aboriginal homes.

INDIAN RESIDENTIAL SCHOOLS SETTLEMENT AGREEMENT (IRSSA)

Aboriginal researchers have argued the theory of *historic trauma* to describe the consequences of numerous stressors, such as residential schools, experienced by whole communities over generations. Traumatic events and adaptive or maladaptive responses have become imbedded in the shared memories of Aboriginal communities and are then passed on to successive generations by storytelling, community interaction and communication, and patterns of parenting. The IRSSA is the federal government's latest attempt to address this historic trauma.

The IRSSA follows a four stage process beginning with acknowledgement, naming the harmful acts, and admitting that they were wrong. Next is redress, taking action to compensate for harms inflicted. The third step is healing or restoring physical, mental, social/emotional, and spiritual balance in individuals, families, communities, and nations; and finally reconciliation, which is the accepting of one another following injurious acts or periods of conflict and developing mutual trust. Reconciliation within the IRSSA involves perpetrators asking for and victims offering forgiveness, as they acknowledge and accept the past and recognize the humanity of one another.

The Truth and Reconciliation Commission (TRC) has been established with Thomas R. Berger and Marlene Brant Castellano as co-chairs. The TRC will facilitate reconciliation among former students, their families, their communities, and all Canadians. As this is accomplished, the TRC will present an accurate and public historic record of the past, thereby promoting awareness and public education about the residential schools, and its impacts on the human dignity of former students.

The IRSSA includes the following:

- Common Experience Payment to be paid to all eligible former students who resided at a recognized Indian Residential School. It is based on the number of years of residency ($10,000 for the first school year or portion thereof and $3,000 for each subsequent year);

- Independent Assessment Process for claims of sexual and serious physical abuse;

- Truth and Reconciliation Commission;

- Commemoration Activities;

- Measures to support healing such as the Indian Residential Schools Resolution Health Support Program and an endowment to the Aboriginal Healing Foundation.

The Aboriginal Healing Foundation is undertaking many of the healing programs under the IRSSA. Their main interventions are healing/talking circles, mentoring by elders, ceremonies, one-on-one counselling, legacy education, workshops, and ceremonies. They use a four stages of healing model as shown in the figure to the left.

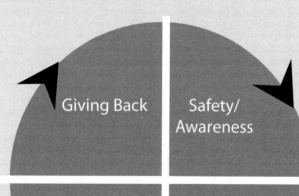

Source: Adapted from "Indian Residential School Settlement Agreement," *IRSSA—Official Website*, www.residentialschoolsettlement.ca, 2007, and "Residential Schools Resources," Aboriginal Healing Foundation, www.ahf.ca/publications/residential-schools-resources, 2008.

Aboriginal children who were made legal wards of the state increased from 1 percent of all children in care to 30–40 percent (Fournier & Crey 1998, 83). Recently, Assembly of First Nations Chief Phil Fontaine reported that there are 27,000 First Nations children in care, and only 8,300 of these children are in the care of Aboriginal agencies, which are significantly underfunded (AFN 2008). As Fontaine argued, these numbers are a sign of poverty, not a lack of parental love. In 2008 the Canadian Human Rights Commission agreed to allow a tribunal to hear a human rights complaint regarding the First Nations child protection system.

The 1998 and 2003 cycles of the Canadian Incidence Study of Reported Child Abuse and Neglect found that First Nations children were hugely overrepresented in the child welfare system at every point of intervention despite the fact that they were not overly represented for reports of sexual abuse, physical abuse, emotional abuse, and exposure to domestic violence. In addition, they found that the higher rates are not due to higher rates of physical and emotional harm, but are within the much less clear-cut category of neglect. This type of child maltreatment is most often fuelled by poverty, poor housing, and caregiver substance misuse.

Aboriginal Child Welfare Agencies

In 1981, the federal government entered into agreements with the provinces, insisting that child and family services for Aboriginal peoples adhere to provincial standards and regulations. Under this legislative mandate, many Aboriginal welfare agencies came to resemble mainstream service providers. While it was recognized that a distinctive Aboriginal approach was required in order to redress the damage done over generations, the provincial welfare system did not foster it.

Canadian child welfare authorities subsequently recognized the damage caused by this approach, and the federal government has made efforts to fund Aboriginal child welfare agencies. In 1990–91, the federal government funded 36 Aboriginal child and family agencies, covering 212 bands; in this same period, a total of $1.5 million over a period of two years was allocated to First Nations for the development of Aboriginal child and family service standards.

Most Aboriginal child care agencies have adopted placement protocols that specify the following placement preferences: first, with the extended family; second, with Aboriginal members of the community with the same cultural and linguistic identification; and third, alternative Aboriginal caregivers. As a last resort, placement is considered with non-Aboriginal caregivers.

However, the Scoop of the 1960s appears to be occurring again today, and recent data shows that it may, in fact, be worse. According to Cindy Blackstock (2003), a member of the Gitksan Nation and Executive

A SURVIVOR REFLECTS ON RESILIENCE—MADELEINE DION STOUT

My father holds the reins in his hands while my mother alights from the horse-drawn wagon. I fix my red-rimmed eyes on my mother's red tam—the splash of colour, the statement, the heartbeat, the moment.

Two hours later I am fighting for dear life. The parlour is stone cold; the benches knocked wood; the windows large and paned. I beg my mother and father not to leave me. I cry until my nose bleeds. Then and there colours fade. There is nothing left to say; hearts break and moments die. I surrender the loose change I'm left with to my superiors. I buy jawbreakers and black licorice pipes for a few weeks running. Strange is how they taste.

Colonization, healing, and resilience reveal themselves to me. As Survivors, we ride waves of vulnerability for a lifetime and for generations. We were subjected to real risk factors including hunger, loneliness, ridicule, physical and sexual abuse, untimely and unseemly death. As we struggle to throw off the shackles of colonization we lean heavily toward healing, and resilience becomes our best friend.

Today, triggers continue to work on my body, mind, and spirit but, ironically, they have given me a shot at life. My mother and father hoped they would; why else would they have loosened my desperate clutch on them in the parlour?

Their resilience became mine. It had come from their mothers and fathers and now must spill over to my grandchildren and their grandchildren. If we truly believe the pain of the residential school legacy has had an intergenerational impact, then it necessarily follows that there will be intergenerational Survivors too.

I firmly believe that a lot of the healing began in residential school. I have asked myself and others, did I, did we, suffer uselessly in residential school? Like any hard question I have ever posed to my mother, her answer might have been *kiýa nitānis,* which roughly translates to "reflect on it, my daughter." The words spoken at this conference have driven me closer to home and have me reflecting on my good fortune. I have been wearing your messages like the blanket we were gifted with here.

I say that our healing began in residential school when I think of the times I lived second-hand love there. My grade four teacher, Miss Walker, spent as much time watching out the window for her RCMP boyfriend as she did watching over us students. I recall vividly her sparkling, flashing blue eyes and her pretty blue nylon blouse—the splash of colour, the statement, the heartbeat, the moment. I also well-remember looking up to a window and catching an unmistakable aura of affection between a Cree woman who worked at the school and her Dene suitor. She was radiant as she beamed down on us from the window, large and paned, while he, strikingly handsome, beamed at her.

While I was deprived of love in residential school, I lived it second-hand to the fullest. Love literally filled my empty heart and soul, even though it was not rightfully mine. Second-hand love does save lives. Because of it, I can honestly say I began my healing journey in the most ungodly place. Healing is the midsection of a continuum with colonization marking one end and resilience the other. Knowing what I know now, a large part of my response to being and becoming in an ungodly place was an act of resilience.

In the name of our best friend resilience, we can look forward to the future because we are very, very good at so many things.

We are very good at wearing splashes of colour: we wear red tams as a tribute to our beloved ancestors, we display our Sundance flags, and we proudly wear our Métis sashes and our Northern prints, making a statement whether we talk "moose, geese, or fish."

We are very, very good at acting in a heartbeat in the most ordinary way at the most everyday level because as Survivors we help one another do the same.

We are very, very good at living the moment while marking time by preserving residential schools as monuments, producing films about them, and working together to keep important healing work going.

In the name of our best friend resilience, we must give fervent thanks to our ancestors, our beloved Elders, and our Brothers and Sisters and for all the work in the service of healing that will surely be transformative when we look back.

Thank you, Merci, Hai,hai!

Source: Madeleine Dion Stout. Excerpt from speech to the Aboriginal Healing Foundation's National Gathering in Edmonton, Alberta, 10 July 2004. Reprinted with permission of Madeleine Dion Stout.

Director of the First Nations Child and Family Caring Society of Canada (FNCFCS), there were over 22,500 First Nations children in the care of child welfare authorities in 2003 and few of these children were placed with Aboriginal families. The rate at which First Nations children on reserve are entering foster care has also increased by 71.5 percent from 1995–2001 based on INAC data (NCW 2007).

Most provinces also have a disproportionate percentage of Aboriginal children in care. For example, in Alberta Aboriginal children comprise 9 percent of all children, but 57 percent of children in care. The same numbers for BC are 7 percent and 50 percent and for Manitoba, 23 and 85 percent (NCW 2007).

Today Aboriginal peoples work to regain a small fraction of what they lost to colonization. Here, members of the Pimicikamak Cree Nation march on the Manitoba Hydro Jenpeg power dam in 2007, demonstrating in response to thirty years of unfulfilled commitments by the Manitoba government and Manitoba Hydro.

Government Policy Objectives

In *Arduous Journey: Canadian Indians and Decolonization*, Roger Gibbins and Rick Ponting outline the goals of national government public policy towards Aboriginal peoples (Gibbins & Ponting 1986). While these goals are historical, many remain with us today.

Protection

Some officials developing policy had "humanitarian" goals and sought to protect Aboriginal people until they could be assimilated into white society. They saw the reservation system as a way to isolate Aboriginal people. It can also be argued that these goals of protection were mostly illusory, glossing over the underlying goal of exploitation. For example, by isolating Aboriginal people on reserves, the government was free to exploit the vast Aboriginal lands.

Assimilation

The central pillar of federal government policy was assimilation—that is, to prepare Aboriginal peoples for complete absorption into Canadian society. Some would argue that the goal appeared to be annihilation rather than simply assimilation. It was desired and expected that eventually all Aboriginal people would give up their customs, culture, and beliefs. The failure of this assimilation process can largely be attributed to barriers posed by systemic and societal discrimination. As Gibbins and Ponting state, "government policy tried to induce Indians into a mainstream that was unwilling to receive them." Another reason was the determination and cultural resilience of Aboriginal peoples in the face of formidable odds.

Christianization

To the colonial government, civilizing the Aboriginal peoples was synonymous with their Christianization. Aboriginal ceremonies and cultural practices were officially discouraged or outlawed. Education through church residential schools was seen as a way to destroy the social, spiritual and cultural systems, and relations of the Aboriginal people. Because the residential schools isolated Aboriginal people from the mainstream, they worked at cross purposes to the goal of assimilation.

Land Surrender

The desire by the government to obtain land held by Aboriginal peoples for the settlement of non-Aboriginal people was a primary goal. Reserves were a way to move them into agriculturally based communities, both to assimilate them and to free vast tracts of land for settlement. As immigration increased, the government moved to make more land available for settlement. To this end, numerous treaties were signed between First Nations peoples and colonial officials between 1670 and 1923.

Land Treaties

While the treaties were quite different in their terms and complexity, they generally served to establish peaceful relations, institute payments, and gain the surrender of land. The major treaties were signed in the West, starting with Treaty No. 1 in 1871 and ending with Treaty No. 10 in 1906. This allowed the vast territories of the West to be settled and the construction of the CP Railway. It is important to note that no treaties were signed between the First Nations of Quebec, the Maritimes and most of British Columbia. In fact, almost half of the population of Registered Indians did not sign land treaties. Treaties and other land claims are now disputed across the country.

Government Authority

As discussed above, a major goal of the *Indian Act* was to give sweeping power and authority to the colonial administrators. The assistant deputy minister of Indian Affairs branch described the *Indian Act* as follows:

> The Indian Act is a lands act. It is a municipal act, an educational act, and a societies act. It is primarily social legislation, but it has a very broad scope: there are provisions about liquor, agricultural and mining as well as Indian lands, band membership and so forth. It has elements that are embodied in perhaps two dozen different acts of any of the provinces and overrides some federal legislation in some respects. . . . It has the force of the criminal Code and the impact of a constitution on those people and communities that come within its purview (Gibbins & Ponting 1986, 19).

This external political control is a fundamental aspect of colonization. In the case of Canada, it was explicitly embodied in the *Indian Act*.

Six Nations protesters stand outside a barricade in Caledonia, Ontario, where a lengthy dispute over who had the right to control land slated for a housing development took place in 2006.

Income Security and Health Care

Although income security and health care in Canada are available to every citizen who meets the conditions of a particular program, a double standard exists for Aboriginal peoples.

Income Security

Until the early 1900s, any kind of relief taken from the trust accounts of Indian bands was granted at the discretion of the local Indian Agent. The decision to grant relief was based on the old practice of distinguishing between the "deserving" and the "undeserving" poor—and Aboriginal people were generally considered undeserving. These rations were grossly inadequate and were used just as much as a means to sanction behaviour as for relief (Moscovitch & Webster 1995, 211). When "the first universal and statutory old age pension was enacted in 1927 it excluded Indians and Inuit, but was available to the Métis" (Scott 1994, 18). The first *Unemployment Insurance Act*, passed in 1940, also excluded most Aboriginal people from eligibility (Scott 1994, 20).

YOUNG INNU OF LABRADOR

Nothing better illustrates the tragedy bestowed on Aboriginal peoples by successive federal and provincial governments than the plight of the Innu of Labrador.

Sheshatshiu

In November 2000, Peter Penashue, president of the Innu Nation, reported that there were at least thirty children sniffing gas in Sheshatshiu, a village of 1,200 people and part of an Innu community of about 1,800 in Labrador. What was unique was the fact that the chief of Labrador's largest Innu community was requesting that the provincial government get involved and take the children out of the community to ensure that they received the treatment that they needed.

This situation sparked debate about the role of non-Aboriginal social workers. The legacy of government policy had left the Innu community without opportunities or prospects and many were rightly skeptical of the help that outsiders could provide. Yet the situation in Sheshatshiu was clearly desperate and the leaders were calling for help. (In the end, these children were taken to centres elsewhere for treatment.)

Davis Inlet

Meanwhile, Davis Inlet, another Innu community in Labrador, had even bigger problems. The town had been established in 1967 after government officials decided the nomadic Innu should settle down. They were promised comfortable homes with indoor plumbing. Instead, the residents found themselves living in squalor and slipping out of touch with their traditional way of life. Violence and addiction were widespread in the community. In 1993, Davis Inlet made headlines in Canada and around the world after a police officer released a videotape showing six Innu children getting high by sniffing gasoline and shouting that they wanted to die. A government response was required.

The federal government finally moved into action and subsequently spent about $200 million carving out the new community of Natuashish, 15 kilometres away on the Labrador mainland, where they built and furnished modern split-level bungalows for the Innu to live in. The move began in December 2002 and was completed within seven months. However, as might have been expected, the new houses in Natuashish became homes to the same old social problems as in Davis Inlet. A recent report by an Ottawa-based consulting company warned that, despite the millions of dollars spent by the federal government on this new town, there was virtually no progress. Moreover, there are only two social workers trying to cope with a staggering caseload. And, according to a report on child, youth, and family services, the social work system is in a crisis and about to tip over into disaster.

Between 1951 and 1966 the Indian relief system collapsed and was replaced by access to the mainstream welfare state (Moscovitch & Webster 1995). This occurred after the development of several federal Acts related to income security, amendments to the *Indian Act* in 1951, and the establishment of the Canada Assistance Plan. Through the development of an administrative structure with huge discretionary powers that minimized community control, the government of Canada effectively came to control the day-to-day lives of Aboriginal peoples across the country.

Health Care

In the 1950s, the responsibility for health care was transferred to the medical services branch of the Department of Health and Welfare. This led to the development of a system of primary care clinics, public health programs, and regional hospitals for Aboriginal peoples. Unfortunately, this change did not mean an end to the denigration of Aboriginal cultures or the isolation of Aboriginal peoples from their own societies. Health care was still provided by non-Aboriginal practitioners who had little or no sensitivity to the differing cultural and social systems among Aboriginal peoples. Well into the twentieth century, for example, the Indian Act outlawed the spiritual ceremonies of Aboriginal peoples, reflecting the assumption that indigenous healing methods were non-existent, ineffective, harmful, or even criminal. As a result, "encounters were often clouded by suspicion, misunderstanding, resentment, and racism" (Scott 1994, 8). These feelings were exacerbated when Aboriginal peoples were removed from their communities to outside medical facilities for treatment.

The Congress of Aboriginal Peoples

www.abo-peoples.org

The Congress of Aboriginal Peoples (CAP) is an organization that represents off-reserve and Métis people. Founded in the 1970s, the organization's mission is to represent the interests of Aboriginal people who are not legally recognized under the *Indian Act*, including non-Status Indians and Métis peoples.

In Vancouver, participants march in a rally to raise public awareness of Native concerns during the Aboriginal Day of Action in 2007.

Royal Commission on Aboriginal Peoples

Royal Commission on Aboriginal Peoples (RCAP)

Commission called by the federal government to examine the status of Aboriginal peoples in Canada. The commission's final report was released in 1996, and included over four hundred recommendations to rebalance the relationship between Aboriginal nations and the Canadian government.

The **Royal Commission on Aboriginal Peoples (RCAP)** of 1996 brought together six years of research and public consultation on Aboriginal issues. It was the most concise and comprehensive distillation of material on Aboriginal issues ever published and provides the factual basis for significant strides forward. Among the many issues discussed, the Report examines the need for Aboriginal people to heal from the consequences of domination, displacement, and assimilation.

The conclusion of the Commission was that the relationship between Aboriginal and non-Aboriginal people for the last 400 years was built upon "false premises"—government policies, which were always presented as beneficial, invariably resulted in harm. The foundation for a renewed relationship, according to the RCAP, involves a recognition of Aboriginal nations as political entities.

Core Recommendations

At the core of the RCAP's 440 recommendations is a rebalancing of political and economic power between Aboriginal nations and other Canadian governments. The *Report* points to five key themes:

- Aboriginal nations have to be reconstituted.
- A process must be established for the assumption of powers by Aboriginal nations.
- There must be a reallocation of lands and resources.
- Aboriginal people need education and crucial skills for governance and economic self-reliance.
- There must be economic development if the poverty and despondency of lives defined by unemployment and welfare are to change.

As part of this, there also has to be a sincere acknowledgement by non-Aboriginal people of the injustices of the past.

Aboriginal Social Services

With respect to social services, the Commission recommended incorporating traditional knowledge and training in the development of Aboriginal health and social work. It also recommended that mainstream social work and social service systems be adapted to complement Aboriginal institutions.

The RCAP final report notes that Aboriginal peoples want to develop and control health and social services for both urban and on-reserve communities. The control of social services by external agencies and bureaucracies continues to frustrate attempts to organize holistic responses to need, and variations in available services reflect systematic inequities rather than adaptations to community diversity. The fact that health and social services are under the authority of provincial legislation while funding obligations are a federal responsibility often creates barriers. Aboriginal groups are asking that federal, provincial, and territorial governments, in consultation with Aboriginal nations and urban communities, cooperate to establish new funding and programs.

Beyond the development of services controlled by Aboriginal people, the Report outlines how the transformation of mainstream social services could make a more positive contribution to the well-being of Aboriginal people. Owing to the small population and remoteness of many Aboriginal communities, some health and social services, particularly specialized services, may be available only from mainstream providers. Initiatives to improve the effectiveness of mainstream health and social service programs will need to take many forms, including:

- employment equity inspired hiring policies
- specialized Aboriginal units staffed by Aboriginal employees within larger mainstream programs
- cross-cultural education programs for non-Aboriginal staff
- Aboriginal input into mainstream programs and decisions
- Aboriginal customary practices included in the services offered by mainstream agencies.

Aboriginal Healing

A prominent theme throughout the RCAP final report is the restoration of Aboriginal health from the wounds of culture loss, paternalistic and racist treatment, and official policies of assimilation. The RCAP detailed how healing is already underway in many communities and how restoring unity and harmony is an extension of healing at the personal level.

The Royal Commission on Aboriginal Peoples acknowledged that the convergence between Aboriginal perspectives and Western science provides a powerful foundation for moving forward. The core of the strategy is to develop a system of healing centres in urban, rural, and reserve settings for front-line services and healing lodges for residential treatment. These would operate under Aboriginal control and deliver integrated health and social services. Sagamok Anishnawbek First Nation, a reserve of just over 1,000 people located in the village of Blind River, along the north shores of Lake Huron, developed such a centre.

The Report acknowledges that Aboriginal people have also developed alternative correction programs that actually work. Although they are still few and far between, they bear little resemblance to conventional correctional services. The Aboriginal approach typically involves a healing lodge, bush camps, and wilderness programs. They also work with traditional skills and spiritual practices. In taking a "justice as healing" approach, they consider the whole of the person's life when dealing with people who commit crimes.

Aboriginal Social Work Practice

Two factors make it difficult to formulate a comprehensive **Aboriginal approach to practice**. First, the Aboriginal peoples of Canada are exceedingly diverse, with many languages, cultures, and traditions, and Aboriginal peoples have a variety of healing and helping philosophies and techniques. Second, a legacy of mistrust and animosity exists towards those in the helping professions, including social work. An Aboriginal approach to social work needs to be flexible enough to incorporate a variety of healing methods and must avoid repeating the mistakes of the past. It is imperative that the approach be based on the wants of Aboriginal peoples and give power to Aboriginal communities.

An Aboriginal approach to social work does not mean that mainstream methods are of no value. The Nechi Institute, founded in 1974 by a group of elders located in Edmonton, is a good example of a training organization that incorporates both traditional Aboriginal and mainstream standards. Their holistic approach is based on the belief that true physical, mental, emotional, and spiritual healing occurs when an individual is in harmony with his or her environment. They also contend that problems must be understood within the context of history, community setting, personal experience, culture, and the social institutions that have had influence on the individual.

The development of an Aboriginal approach to social work practice should be consistent with four key principles. These principles are:

- the recognition of a distinct Aboriginal world view

- the development of Aboriginal consciousness regarding the impact of colonialism

- an emphasis on the importance of cultural knowledge and traditions

- the use of the concept of Aboriginal empowerment

These principles need to be practiced alongside adherence to a holistic approach, a belief in equity, Aboriginal self-control, and a respect for diversity (Morrissette et al. 1993, 91).

Distinct Aboriginal World View

The first principle acknowledges that there is a distinct **Aboriginal world view**. The First Nations (as well as the Inuit and Métis) of Canada have a different approach to healing and helping. While Aboriginal peoples do not have one single philosophy, one can draw upon the fundamental differences between non-Aboriginal and Aboriginal world views. For example, the concept of the circle captured in the Medicine Wheel illustrates the notion of balance prevalent in Aboriginal societies, in contrast to the typically linear models of cause and effect common in Western society.

Impact of Colonialism

The second principle involves an analysis of the impact of colonization, which has greatly contributed to the current situation in Aboriginal communities. Colonizers attempted to subordinate Aboriginal peoples and displace traditional spirituality, governance systems, leadership, and knowledge by using missionaries, residential schools, child welfare, and artificial legal distinctions in the *Indian Act*. Using the reserve system and treaties, the colonizers also sought to subordinate Aboriginal economic systems in order to facilitate the extraction of benefits for themselves. A recognition and analysis of colonialism will assist the social worker in framing problems, in recognizing solutions that emphasize self-determination and in seeing the importance of the reclamation of Aboriginal culture and identity in the social work process.

Residential schools and child welfare work in Aboriginal communities are illustrative of the damage done by colonialism. Even today, social work with Aboriginal families is premised on the Western perception that individuals are members of nuclear families that provide economic support and affection, and that individuals can turn to specialized institutions for problem-specific help. This is not consistent with the Aboriginal view. Aboriginal peoples often perceive themselves to be members of a family network in which everyone is obliged to contribute their resources and support all community members.

These dissimilar conceptions of family, community, and social obligation lead to different ideas about how to carry out social work, as described by an Anishinabe social worker and his colleagues:

> Members of the Aboriginal community potentially (and normally do) play multiple roles in relation to one another—friend, neighbour, relative, and community service volunteer, as well as job-related service giver and receiver roles. All of these roles are reciprocal, each (at least potentially) being played by each person in relation to all others in the community.
>
> The individual or family who is the focus of concern assumes the role of "client" [in the] system—a more dependent and generally stigmatized role. In like manner, the community member functioning in the job of human service worker is cast in the role of "worker"—a more powerful and generally more expert role. The worker is not seen by formal human service agencies as an individual simply fulfilling an expected role in the mutual aid system of the Aboriginal community. In the formal system, the worker-client role relationship becomes single faceted rather than multiple, and uni-directional (helper-helped) rather than reciprocal. Both worker and client become removed and isolated from the interpersonal network that gives their needs and behaviour meaning and that will ultimately provide the support and resources, or obstacles, to satisfaction of those needs.

The discrepancy between Aboriginal ways of helping and conventional social work services are even more pronounced when the worker is an outsider to the community. The conventional methods of social work, in which community members are required to turn to outside agencies for help, weakens internal bonds of mutual aid. People in Aboriginal communities begin to question their ability to help one another as they are unable to contribute to the external social work process that becomes the community's source of help. This situation fosters dependent relationships and weakens the traditional community bonds of mutual aid.

Cultural Knowledge and Traditions

The third principle of *reclaiming Aboriginal culture* emphasizes an awareness of and reflection on common aspects of culture and identity. By examining Aboriginal history, culture, and traditions and dispelling the conventional views of Aboriginal reality flowing from colonialism, Aboriginal people can begin to see the underlying causes of their individual problems.

Of course, there may be differences in how much individuals identify with traditional Aboriginal culture and therefore in how much the reclamation of Aboriginal culture will assist in social work intervention. Some will adhere to the teaching of elders and follow traditional ways, while others may not.

In many cases, traditional healing techniques and teachings will be combined with non-traditional methods. This combining of traditional healing and mainstream techniques is evident at the Strong Earth Woman Lodge in Manitoba, where the power of Aboriginal spirituality and traditional teachings are combined with crisis intervention techniques. Working with the Sagkeeng First Nation, Strong Earth Woman Lodge has a holistic healing centre based on First Nation spirituality and traditional teachings. They see holistic healing as the healing of the mind, body, emotions, and spirit. Traditionally, this is done through sweat lodges, fasts, vision quests, herbal medicines, ceremonial healing with the eagle fan and rattles (in which sacred songs and the drum are key components), traditional teachings at the sacred fire, sharing circles, individualized counselling, and guidance and direction through traditional teachings.

The Strong Earth Woman Lodge uses traditional teaching to create individualized healing programs based on the needs of each client. All clients are instructed in the seven sacred teachings of respect, love, courage, humility, honesty, wisdom, and truth, and are encouraged to seek understanding of the four elements—fire, earth, water, and air—and the four directions.

The Lodge also offers 24-hour care focusing on holistic healing for grieving, loss of identity, and suicide crisis intervention.

Nechi Institute

www.nechi.com

Nechi Training, Research and Health Promotions Institute is an Aboriginal healing movement advocating holistic healing and addiction-free lifestyles, located in St. Albert, Alberta.

Empowerment

In the context of social work practice, the principle of **Aboriginal empowerment** emphasizes the participation of community members in bringing about lasting social change. For example, the National Aboriginal Women's Association (NAWA), a not-for-profit, membership-based organization formed in 2001, stresses empowerment of Aboriginal women as the means to provide for the betterment of the political, economic, and social conditions for Aboriginal peoples, families, communities, and Nations.

In the 1990s, when a substance abuse problem among young people arose (among other long-standing problems) within Innu communities in Labrador leaders asked for help and the federal government spent millions of dollars to try and resolve issues in a Western way; it didn't work. The tragedy of the Innu Nation of Labrador illustrates how important empowerment is to community healing. Chief Tshakapesh stressed the need to involve Innu members in finding long-term solutions to the problems of substance abuse and suicide among their children. He criticized the federal and Newfoundland governments for imposing unsuccessful programs on his community in the past: "We are here today because the solutions didn't work. We will never allow others to control our future."

At its most basic level, the principle of empowerment implies that services must be defined and controlled by those seeking help.

Many colleges and universities offer programs specifically designed for Aboriginal students, taking their needs, traditions, and experiences into account.

Holistic Healing

Holistic Approach to Healing

Examining the whole of a person, addressing the social, cultural, mental, and spiritual aspects of well-being.

Traditionally, many Aboriginal people have used some form of the "healing circle" to underpin their approach to healing. The circle is representative of the fact that we are all one and that the entire universe is connected. The circle approach can also serve to teach social workers to balance or consider all aspects of a presenting problem. Another basic teaching common to many First Nations is the four sacred directions of North, South, East, and West. These directions likewise represent aspects of life that must be considered when looking at a situation.

In many Aboriginal societies, the circle and the four sacred directions are the symbols of holistic healing, embodying the four elements of whole health:

- spiritual health, which can mean many things depending on the individual's approach to spirituality, and may include participating in ceremonies, gaining traditional knowledge, and exploring his or her spiritual heritage
- mental health, which includes education, knowledge of Aboriginal history and cultural contributions, and activities that promote self-confidence
- physical health, including nutrition, sports and recreation, and cultural activities
- emotional health, gained through access to sharing circles, counsellors, and elders

The circle best captures what is often referred to as a **holistic approach to healing**, or looking at the physical, emotional, spiritual, and mental aspects of a problem or situation. For example, an approach that stresses only the psychological aspects of a problem would not be consistent with these teachings. Social workers using the circle to inform their practice would begin with the physical aspect, and then move to the mental, the emotional, and the spiritual. After going around the wheel completely, the practitioner would begin again, only at a deeper level.

The situation of the Innu of Davis Inlet in Labrador illustrates the importance of the healing circle. The community captured national attention in January 1993 when television stations across the country reported youth suicide attempts (see page 232). Seventeen youths were sent to the Poundmaker Lodge in Alberta for substance abuse treatment, yet when the youth returned to the community, many resumed abusing substances. Their bodies had been healed, but there was nothing to nourish their minds, emotions, or spirits. In order to have a lasting effect, healing must address not only individuals, but also the community; not only the physical, but also the spiritual, emotional, and mental aspects of life. The initiative to heal must be holistic and must come from, and be rooted in, the community.

The holistic approach to healing at Matootoo Lake, near the Peguis First Nation in Manitoba, benefits young women and men. The teachings prepare young women for their emotional, physical, and spiritual transition to womanhood. A major goal of the program is to reduce the number of unplanned pregnancies by helping young women acquire confidence in their ability to deal with sexuality. A parallel program for boys enhances self-esteem, develops respect for girls and women, and raises awareness of issues such as violence against women.

Healing Lodges

Community healing centres that incorporate an Aboriginal approach are opening across Canada. They provide a forum for exploring how Aboriginal and mainstream approaches can be brought together to meet Aboriginal community needs. Traditional healers, elders, community health representatives, medical interpreters, nurses, addiction counsellors, midwives, therapists, social workers, doctors, psychologists, and rehabilitation specialists all come together to address common problems.

There has also been a marked increase in the number of **healing lodges** that provide residential treatment for people who are overwhelmed by social, emotional, and spiritual problems. The Nechi Institute and Poundmaker's Lodge in Alberta, for example, provide healing and lodging for people dealing with addictions. First Nations and Inuit groups have identified the need for such lodges, since most Aboriginal people suffering from addictions and substance abuse continue to receive treatment in urban facilities, isolated from their communities and culture.

Visits with elders, cultural and spiritual ceremonies, sharing circles, stints in a sweat lodge, drumming, and arts and crafts are all part of the path to healing at the Stony Mountain Institution in Manitoba.

Aboriginal Peoples and the Corrections System

The over-representation of Aboriginal people within the Canadian criminal justice system is indisputably the most egregious example of the racist legacy of colonization. Aboriginal peoples are nine times more likely to go to prison than the majority of the non-Aboriginal population in Canada. Overall, Aboriginal prisoners were 11 percent of the jail population in 1992, 16 percent in 1999, 20 percent in 2001, and 27 percent in 2003.

While Aboriginal youth form 5 percent of the youth population across Canada, they constitute 27 percent of those on remand, 30 percent of those in open custody, 27 percent of those in secure custody, and 17 percent of those on probation.

Sources: Adapted from Canadian Association of Elizabeth Fry Societies, 2003, *Elizabeth Fry Week—Fact Sheet*, www.elizabethfry.ca, and National Council of Welfare, 2007, *First Nations, Métis and Inuit Children and Youth: Time to Act*, www.ncwcnbes.net.

Integrating an Aboriginal Approach

The integration of an Aboriginal approach to mainstream social work services is not always straightforward. Federal and provincial governments often legislate the work of social workers in state agencies. To secure funding for these needed services, First Nations are obliged to follow rules and procedures.

However, First Nations are developing intervention processes that slot Aboriginal healing practices into the legislated practices. For example, a child welfare worker may apprehend a child who has been abused, as stipulated by legislation and the court system. The next step, however, may be a holistic conflict-resolution sentencing circle based on an Aboriginal approach to healing.

Empowering Communities— the Atikamekw Nation

The Atikamekw are the original inhabitants of the area they refer to as Nitaskinan in the upper St. Maurice valley of Quebec (300 kilometres north of Montreal). Their population is about 4,500. They have a tradition of agriculture as well as fishing and hunting. Atikamekw, a language of the Cree subgroup of Algonquian, is in everyday use, but their land has largely been appropriated by logging companies and little remains of their indigenous way of life.

In their Atikamekw Social Policy regulations, the Atikamekw Nation stipulates an intervention process that is responsive to the social needs of Atikamekw communities and is a part of a self-government process, but also complies with provincial government legislation. They outline fairly typical mainstream "temporary measures for protection of a child or youth," and then proceed to detail Aboriginal processes of healing. These processes include Family Council, the Circle of the Wise Counsel, and a Circle of Helpers. The Family Council process involves numerous family members and community participants. In a case where the family, friends, and community cannot resolve the problem adequately, a Circle of the Wise Counsel replaces the Family Council. The Circle of Helpers, which includes social workers, is responsible for implementing the intervention plan. The social worker is called a Community Protection Delegate, signifying that the worker represents the protection interests of the whole community.

The community healing centres and the child welfare policy of the Atikamekw demonstrate how the incorporation of mainstream social work techniques into an Aboriginal approach to healing can work as effective social work practice models. Once again, at the root of this success is the recognition of a distinct Aboriginal world view, the development of Aboriginal consciousness regarding the impact of colonialism, an emphasis on cultural knowledge and traditions, and the empowerment of communities to control their own futures.

Urban Social Services for Aboriginal Peoples

Many Canadians think of Aboriginal people as living on reserves or in rural areas. This is a misperception, since a great many Aboriginal people in Canada live in cities and towns. Aboriginal people who live off the reserve are often left with no alternative to mainstream conventional social work services, as few urban centres offer distinct Aboriginal social services.

Many Aboriginal people migrating to urban centres are women moving to the city to escape abuse, seek healing, or find employment. This naturally distances Aboriginal women from their community support networks and makes it very difficult for them to maintain a connection to their culture. Access to their teachers, grandmothers, clan mothers, and healers is limited. Off-reserve Aboriginal women have also found mainstream social work services to be less than welcoming. At the Royal Commission on Aboriginal Peoples hearings, women stated that the existing services were not culturally sensitive nor designed with an Aboriginal approach to social work in mind.

> When a non-native woman goes in they don't even bother to take her children away. They are there to comfort her and give her counselling. When people like me or someone else goes in, right away they take their children. You really have to fight to hang on to them. You really have to prove yourself as a mother, and the other non-native women do not have to do so (Ellison 1992).

Aboriginal people have found that mainstream social work services rarely offer traditional spiritual practices, access to elders, healing medicines, or women's teachings that reflect Aboriginal values. They have also found that the social workers in mainstream agencies are not trained to be culturally aware and sensitive nor do they know how to deal with issues critical to Aboriginal women, such as cultural expectations with regard to family roles and the impact of colonization.

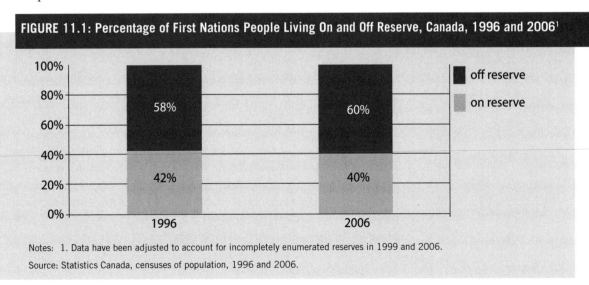

FIGURE 11.1: Percentage of First Nations People Living On and Off Reserve, Canada, 1996 and 2006[1]

Notes: 1. Data have been adjusted to account for incompletely enumerated reserves in 1999 and 2006.

Source: Statistics Canada, censuses of population, 1996 and 2006.

Inuit Tapiriit Kanatami

www.itk.ca

The Inuit Tapiriit Kanatmi is a national Inuit organization that represents the four Inuit regions in Canada: Nunatsiavut (Labrador), Nunavik (Northern Quebec), Nunavut, and the Inuvialuit Settlement Region in the Northwest Territories. Founded in the 1970s from earlier organizations, the ITK advocates for Aboriginal rights, land claims, and resource development, and it fights against global warming and climate change as public heath and human rights issues.

Towards Aboriginal Self-Government

The social service and health problems that have long plagued Aboriginal peoples are well documented, although more change is needed before Aboriginal health and well-being is comparable to that of the general population. Individuals, private organizations, and governments have had much to say about what is needed to address these issues. However, these recommendations still tend to be embedded in attempts to define the role of Aboriginal peoples in Canadian society and to impose that role upon them, attempts that have to this point abjectly failed.

As part of a lasting solution, it is time to acknowledge that non-Aboriginals can no longer presume to institute their will upon the First Nations, Métis and the Inuit. Aboriginal peoples across Canada are finding their own voice and, with that, the hope of establishing political, financial, and moral control over their lives. Eventually, there will be a dialogue and partnership with the rest of Canada in addressing the issues facing their communities, whether those communities are on traditional lands or within urban centres.

Who Will Provide Services to Aboriginal Peoples?

Aboriginal people today are healing from the ravages wreaked upon them by residential schools and the child welfare system and from the results of the systemic racism and discrimination within Canadian society. They are in the process of redefining themselves in the context of their traditional cultural practices.

Perhaps most important in this process is the reaffirmation of Aboriginal rights to land, rights that are inextricably linked to the principle of **Aboriginal self-government**. Such an affirmation is one of the key recommendations of the RCAP and the foremost demand of Aboriginal leaders. Aboriginal peoples are seeking the formal recognition of rights that already exist, rights that existed prior to the European incursions.

An important factor today is the tenacious resistance on the part of Aboriginal people, over a very long period of time, to all efforts to eradicate both them and their distinct ways of living. Also important are the beginnings of Aboriginal economic development, the resurgence of Aboriginal languages, the establishment of Aboriginal education with a culturally based curriculum, the development of working models of Aboriginal justice systems, and Aboriginal control of social services that are no longer based exclusively upon the mainstream social work model but increasingly integrating an Aboriginal approach to social work practice. All these positive developments point a way out of the present predicament toward one that allows Aboriginal people their rightful place in Canadian society.

Aboriginal Organizations

The resurgence of *Aboriginal political activism* that began in the 1970s has helped advance this process of redefinition. It has led to the development of several national organizations representing and uniting distinct constituent groups. Among these organizations are: (1) the Assembly of First Nations, which represents Status Indians who reside on Indian reserves across Canada; (2) the Inuit Tapiriit Kanatami, representing Canada's Inuit population; (3) the Métis National Council; (4) the Congress of Aboriginal Peoples, representing off-reserve Aboriginal peoples; and (5) the Native Women's Association of Canada. These national organizations are generally affiliated with provincial or territorial and local groups that lobby the Canadian government to develop inclusive policies to protect the rights and interests of Aboriginal peoples—rights guaranteed in section 35 of the *Canadian Charter of Rights and Freedoms*. They also seek to educate governments and Canadians about the issues facing Aboriginal peoples.

Phil Fontaine, then national chief of the Assembly of First Nations, receives a standing ovation in the House of Commons in June 2008 as he responds to the government's apology for more than a century of abuse and cultural loss involving Indian residential schools. Shawn Atleo, a 42-year-old educator and businessman from B.C., was chosen as the new AFN chief on July 23, 2009, as Fontaine stepped down.

Grassroots Aboriginal Organizations

In addition to these national organizations, there are grassroots organizations that are taking responsibility for the administration of social programs devolved to them from the federal government.

The Métis have historically advocated for inclusion within mainstream services, but have recently made strides in developing their own services related to education, economic development, and social support, among others. The Nunavut Land Claims Agreement provides for mechanisms to assist the majority of Inuit living in Canada in developing cultural and social services in the new territory of Nunavut. Tripartite agreements between an individual Aboriginal organization and the federal and provincial governments are another means of enabling Aboriginal peoples to deliver services. These include agreements that provide for child welfare services, law enforcement, and elementary and secondary education, as well as Social Assistance and community health prevention and treatment programs.

In some cases, provincially funded organizations are the main service providers, especially in the case of elementary and secondary education or child welfare services. However, since the late 1970s, there has been an overall shift towards community control. For example, in 1969 the YWCA opened a second-stage supportive housing facility (first stage being an emergency shelter) for Status Indian women in downtown Toronto. When it opened, it was called simply "Y Place." Aboriginal women gradually became more involved in the operation of the facility and, in 1973, renamed it *Anduhyaun*, Ojibwa for "our home." Anduhyaun still provides Aboriginal women and their children with a culturally based supportive environment and the resources to work on a variety of problems, including abusive relationships, family and marital breakdown, legal and financial difficulties, and alcohol and drug abuse. Other services help the women find housing, medical services, further education, skills development, and employment. It also operates a food bank.

Within grassroots organizations such as Anduhyaun, it is still a challenge to balance the dictates of provincial or federal legislation and administrative criteria with the determination to provide culturally based and culturally appropriate services. This means that it has been difficult for Aboriginal peoples to secure stable funding for programs and services that supersede the limitations of the funding criteria for mainstream programs and services. For example, Indian Child and Welfare Services for reserves are funded by Indian Affairs, which may not necessarily provide funding for prevention programs such as courses in traditional parenting styles; instead, funding may be based simply upon the number of children taken into care.

In the past, service providers (including social workers) have usually been non-Aboriginal people who lived outside the community or only lived in the community for a short period of time. This too is beginning to change. Communities are increasingly looking within their own ranks to find the human resources to build an infrastructure to heal and foster well-being. This option is becoming more and more viable as more Aboriginal people complete a mainstream professional education, and as the communities themselves create training programs that prepare community members to deliver social services to their own communities. Genuine self-government will create the conditions where Aboriginal peoples take greater control of their own destinies and the provision of social services.

Conclusion

The *Indian Act*, residential schools, and other government policies are the immediate roots of today's problems, which began with attempts by the European settlers to subjugate Aboriginal peoples and take away their rights to the land. Gradually, much of this is being acknowledged, as evidenced by the 1996 Royal Commission on Aboriginal Peoples and the 2008 Indian Residential Schools Settlement Agreement (IRSSA). On a less hopeful note, Canada was one of only four nations worldwide to not adopt the 2007 United Nations Declaration on the Rights of Indigenous Peoples. The remaining three were the United States, Australia, and New Zealand—countries with large indigenous populations and tragic histories.

Social justice and self-determination for the Aboriginal peoples of Canada are principles upon which to build effective social work with Aboriginal populations. The Aboriginal holistic approach to healing provides a useful starting point. It encourages service providers to consider all aspects of problems that arise. Social workers with an understanding of such an approach are already breaking new ground by initiating community healing centres, implementing restorative justice, setting up healing lodges, developing innovative child welfare policies, creating culturally appropriate urban social services, and establishing holistic health care programs.

The Assembly of First Nations

The Assembly of First Nations (AFN) was founded in 1982. It is the national organization representing First Nations communities in Canada. The AFN provides a national voice for Aboriginal peoples, advocating for issues such as treaty rights, economic development, education, languages and literacy, health, housing, social development, justice, taxation, land claims, and the environment.

The Assembly is made up of chiefs who meet annually and they elect a national chief every three years. The AFN also includes regular meetings of the Confederacy of Nations, made up of the Chiefs and regional leaders, whose number is determined by population. The Assembly of First Nations is funded mainly by Indian and Northern Affairs Canada.

CHAPTER REVIEW

Key Terms

- **Aboriginal peoples**
- **Colonialism**
- **Land-cession treaties**
- *Indian Act of 1876*
- **Indian Agent**
- **Scrip system**
- **Disk list system**
- **Residential school system**
- **Assimilationist policies**

- **Sixties Scoop**
- **Royal Commission on Aboriginal Peoples (RCAP)**
- **Aboriginal approach to practice**
- **Aboriginal world view**
- **Aboriginal empowerment**
- **Holistic approach to healing**
- **Healing lodges**
- **Aboriginal self-government**

Review Questions

1. What bearing does the history of the relationship between Aboriginal peoples and the people of Canada have on the social welfare of Aboriginal peoples?

2. Why were the residential schools established?

3. What were the six major goals of public policy in relation to Aboriginal peoples, as identified by Gibbins and Ponting?

4. What are the four principles of an Aboriginal approach to practice?

5. Why should one be careful in describing a uniform Aboriginal approach to social work practice?

6. What is the relevance of the circle for social work? How can it inform our approach to social work practice?

7. Is there a way for non-Aboriginal people to work productively with Aboriginal peoples? Under what circumstances might this take place?

Exploring Social Work

1. Visit the Vote Out Poverty website (**www.voteoutpoverty.ca**) and watch the video "Tammy—An Aboriginal women who can't manage on minimum wage" If Tammy came to you, as a social worker how would you work with Tammy to help her? Discuss this in small groups and write a short paper. Provide rationale for your intervention choice and try to relate it to a theory that was discussed in Chapter 4.

2. The federal government formed the Truth and Reconciliation Commission (TRC) as part of IRSSA. Research the mandate and scope of the TRC and present your results in a three-page paper.

3. On September 13, 2007, the United Nations adopted the Declaration on the Rights of Indigenous Peoples (the Declaration). The Declaration establishes a universal framework of minimum standards, but Canada was one of four nations to reject it. What is the federal government's rationale for this? Do you think that Canada should sign on to the Declaration? Beginning with the Assembly of First Nations website (**www.afn.ca**), research this issue and write a two-page paper summarizing your findings.

Websites

Aboriginal Canada Portal
www.aboriginalcanada.gc.ca

This is a window to Canadian Aboriginal online resources, contacts, information, and government programs and services. The portal offers ease of access and navigation to listings of Aboriginal associations, businesses, organizations, bands, communities, groups, news, and so forth.

Report of the Royal Commission on Aboriginal Peoples (RCAP)
www.ainc-inac.gc.ca/ap/rrc-eng.asp

The Final Report of the Royal Commission on Aboriginal Peoples brings together six years of research and public consultation on Indigenous issues.

Aboriginal Policy Research Conference
www.aprc-crmpa.ca

First held in 2002, the Aboriginal Policy Research Conference, co-sponsored by the University of Western Ontario and Indian and Northern Affairs Canada, was the first international conference of its kind and was recognized in 2003 at the United Nations. The Conference brings together prominent Aboriginal and non-Aboriginal researchers, policy-makers, and Aboriginal leaders from Canada and around the world. Subsequent conferences were held in 2006 and 2009.

First Nations Child and Family Caring Society of Canada
www.fncfcs.com

The purpose of the society is to promote the well-being of all First Nations children, youth, families, and communities, with a focus on preventing and responding to child maltreatment. The website includes fact sheets, newsletters, access to the society's online journal, recommended reading, and child welfare resources and links.

CHAPTER 12

SOCIAL WORK WITH RACIALIZED CANADIANS AND IMMIGRANTS

Resisting Resistance to Change

anada is one of the most culturally diverse nations in the world. According to a 2004 Ipsos World Monitor poll, Canada is also one of the most accepting nations of ethnic diversity—it sees itself as more of a "mosaic" than a "melting-pot." Four out of five Canadians (85 percent) agreed that "multiculturalism" is important to Canadian identity (Statistics Canada 2004a).

However, this widespread acceptance of racial and cultural diversity should be contrasted with the information that many *visible minority* Canadians (36 percent) reported that they had experienced discrimination or unfair treatment in the past five years. The current trend towards increasing numbers of immigrants from Asia, Africa, and Central and South America means that there is a strong likelihood of persistent problems in this area in the future.

History of "Race Relations" in Canada

Canadians take great pride in the ethnic and racial diversity of their country. By comparison with many other countries, there is much to feel good about. However, one need not reach too far back into Canadian history to see that ethnic conflict and racism are not at all foreign to the Canadian experience and that problems in this area continue to the present day. One of the most pervasive and established conflicts is that between Aboriginal peoples and dominant white culture.

Racism persists and even thrives in Canada, according to Lincoln Alexander, chair of the Canadian Race Relations Foundation:

> As Canadians, we are not doing a very good job. We're not making the grade. We get a failing grade when police officers in Saskatoon drive Aboriginal men to the outskirts of town and leave them in sub-zero temperatures without winter coats. We get a failing grade when 600 Chinese arrive by ships off the coast of British Columbia looking for sanctuary in Canada only to be met with fear and even hatred. . . . We get a failing grade when our schoolyards become a war zone for some visible minority youth because they're bullied on a regular basis, some-times with fatal results. We get a failing grade when new immigrants, especially non-white immigrants, . . . subsidize Canada's economy to the tune of 55 billion dollars each year. . . because skills acquired in their homelands are not recognized in this country. (Alexander 2001)

To begin with, then, let us briefly review some of the historical background that contributes to this troubling state of affairs. For an exploration of the conflict between Aboriginal peoples and the dominant white culture see Chapter 11.

Chinese Immigration and the Head Tax

Between 1881 and 1884, 15,700 Chinese workers were brought over from China as contract labourers to work on the Canadian Pacific Railway (Isajiw 1999). Thereafter, a series of laws were put in place to exclude or limit the number of Chinese and South Asian immigrants to Canada: the *Chinese Immigration Act* of 1885; the Head Tax of $50 on Chinese immigrants set in 1885 (raised to $100 in 1901 and to $500 in 1904, an average two-year wage for a Chinese person in Canada); the *Immigration Act* of 1910 (which established "undesirable" classes of immigrants); and the *Chinese Exclusion Act* of 1923 (which admitted to Canada only certain specified classes of Chinese and almost stopped Chinese immigration completely). William Lyon Mackenzie King, then deputy minister of labour, claimed in 1907, that it was "natural that Canada should remain a White man's country." The head tax was eliminated in 1923, but other laws, which made it nearly impossible for Chinese men to bring their families to Canada and forced many to be separated from their wives and children for years at a time, remained in place until 1947. In 2000, the

Racism

The subordination of one group by another using arbitrary physical features such as skin colour. It can occur at individual, institutional, or societal levels in the form of attitudes, beliefs, policies, or procedures.

Anti-Racist Social Work

An approach to practice that aggressively combats racism on the individual, institutional, and societal level.

Canadian government was faced with a lawsuit by Chinese Canadians demanding compensation for the Head Tax and other racially motivated measures aimed at limiting immigration from China in the first half of the twentieth century; however, it was unsuccessful.

In 2005, the federal government signed a $2.5-million deal with the National Congress of Chinese Canadians and fourteen other Chinese Canadian groups to set up education projects to commemorate those who paid the tax. On June 22, 2006, Prime Minister Stephen Harper formally apologized in Parliament for the Head Tax.

Japanese-Canadians and Internment

In World Wars I and II, the Canadian government instituted a policy of internment of members of ethnic minority groups whom it defined as "enemy aliens." Immigrants from the Austro-Hungarian Empire, with whom the Allies were at war, were interned in World War I, and Japanese-Canadians were interned in World War II. In both cases, the basic human rights of the respective minorities were violated. The homes, businesses, and property of Japanese-Canadians were confiscated and their lives were turned on end (Isajiw 1999).

Many claim that the forced eviction of Japanese-Canadians from the Pacific Coast in the early months of 1942 was the greatest mass movement in the history of Canada. It was not until 1949, four years after Japan had surrendered, that the majority of displaced Japanese-Canadians were allowed to return to British Columbia. By then, most had begun new lives elsewhere in Canada. It was not until four decades later, in 1988, that the government announced a comprehensive settlement with surviving members of the Japanese wartime community and formally apologized.

Jewish Refugees

In addition to racial categories, racist ideologies may be focused through policies directed towards specific ethnic groups. During and immediately after World War II, the Canadian government was reluctant to admit European Jews as refugees to Canada. It undertook informal measures to restrict their immigration. When asked how many Jews would be allowed into Canada after the war, a senior immigration official issued his famous reply: "None is too many." During the war, the Canadian government refused entry to a ship called the *St. Louis*, which carried a shipload of Jews desperate to be admitted to Canada. Instead, they were compelled to sail back to Europe on a voyage of the damned. Anti-semitic beliefs and practices are still widespread today.

Blacks in Canada

The first account of the presence of Black people in Canada was in 1605. Mattheu de Costa was with the French explorers who landed in Nova Scotia (formerly Port Royal) in the early seventeenth century. Later, slaves were brought to Canada by the French. Slavery was officially introduced in Canada by the French in 1628 and continued by the British until 1833–1834, when slavery was abolished in the British Empire.

The next significant early migration of Black people into Canada was that of the Black Loyalists, brought by the British in 1784 following the American War of Independence. Hundreds, who had fought for their freedom on the side of the British against the Americans, were brought to Nova Scotia. They were emancipated and promised education, employment, and citizenship, but were instead left to fend for themselves. Many were forced back into slavery through abject poverty. The situation forced them to ask the British government in England to send them to Africa, and in the late 1790s, many were shipped to the British colony of Sierra Leone. In response to the need for cheap labour, the British also deceived and brought Maroons (runaway slaves) from Jamaica to work on the fortifications at Citadel Hill in Halifax. The Maroons were militant and refused to be controlled as slaves by white Nova Scotians, who used them as forced labourers. Many were also shipped to Sierra Leone.

Another group of Black people taken to Nova Scotia were refugees from the War of 1812 between Britain and the U.S. Most Black Nova Scotians are offspring of these refugees. Finally, Black people used what is known as the Underground Railroad to escape slavery in the United States between 1820 and 1860. These Black Americans, as fugitives, slaves, and as freedmen, formed sizable settlements, particularly in southwestern Ontario and the Maritimes. More recently, immigration from the Caribbean and Africa accounts for the majority of Black Canadians.

The history of racism towards Black people in Canada should not be minimized. Canada actively practiced slavery until the early nineteenth century (Sheppard 1997); even the Black Loyalists who entered Canada as free persons were subject to racist policies. Black Canadians were subject to legislation that enforced segregated schools and communities and limitated property rights. In 1939, Canada's highest court found that racial discrimination was legally enforceable (Walker 1997). Not until 1953–54 did Canada delete from its statutes discriminatory laws that denied Black citizens the right to pursue formal education, respectable jobs, welfare assistance, and civil and humanitarian rights. For over four hundred years, white Canadians have discriminated against Black Canadians.

There have been many reports documenting continuing anti-Black racism that suggest that much of it is systemic. According to Frances Henry, relations between police and the Black community are "fraught with tensions." She notes in particular that "stop-and-search procedures and other forms of harassment have exacerbated tensions and contributed to the 'criminalization' of young Black males" (Henry 1994). Similar serious conclusions were reached by the Commission on Systemic Racism in the Ontario Criminal Justice System (1995), which reported that discriminatory practices by police against Black men were widespread.

Remember Africville

Today, Canada is a country that prides itself on its multiculturalism and ethnic diversity. But, in the 1960s, a different approach was evidenced in a small village on the edge of Halifax, named Africville. In the name of urban renewal, this poor African-Canadian community was erased. The government of the day insisted that this action was legal and appropriate and not a matter of racism, but today few people see it this way. Between 1964 and 1969 Africville was plowed under to make way for a park and a new bridge over the narrows to Dartmouth. Former residents were moved to nearby public housing in the depressed north end of Halifax.

The New Immigration

Recent Immigrants and Earnings

During the last twenty-five years, the gap in earned income between recent immigrants and Canadian-born workers has widened considerably. According to Statistics Canada, recent immigrant men and women who had some employment income in 1980 earned 85 cents for each dollar received by Canadian-born individuals. By 2005, the ratio had dropped to 63 cents for men and 56 cents for women. This despite the fact that educational attainment of recent immigrant earners rose much faster than that of their Canadian-born counterparts during this 25-year period. Table 12.1 illustrates the significant earnings gap between recent immigrants and Canadian-born workers, regardless of education.

As might be expected in a country comprised largely of immigrants and their descendants, ethnic and race relations in Canada have been heavily influenced by **immigration policy**. Prior to 1967, when important new immigration legislation came into force, "nationality" was one of the criteria used to qualify for admission to Canada. Canadian immigration policy was undoubtedly Eurocentric; immigration was encouraged from white Europe and discouraged from the rest of the world. In 1967, new legislation introduced a point system, whereby prospective immigrants had to qualify based on such criteria as education, work experience, language fluency, and age. "Country of origin" was no longer an explicit criterion in the selection process. The inevitable consequence of the new legislation was a new wave of skilled immigrants from Asia, Africa, and South and Central America.

The shift was dramatic. Prior to 1961, over 90 percent of all immigrants were from Europe, and over half of these were from Northern and Western Europe and the United Kingdom. Immigrants from Asia constituted only a small percentage (3.1 percent) of all immigrants arriving in the country. By the 1990s, Europeans made up only about one-fifth of all the immigrants, and the largest number, close to 60 percent, came from Asia. The remaining proportion—almost one-fifth (16.6 percent)—came from Central and South America, the Caribbean and Bermuda, and from the United States. The largest proportion of European immigrants came, not from the United Kingdom or Northern and Western continental Europe, but from Eastern Europe.

"Visible Minorities"

With this shift in immigration came a substantial increase in the "visible minority" population in Canada and it is continuing to shift. In the 2001 Census close to four million Canadians (or 13.4 percent of the population) identified themselves as members of "visible minorities." In the 2006 census over 5 million or 16.2 percent were "visible minorities." According to Statistics Canada projections, the number of Canadians in visible minority groups is expected to increase to 7.1 million by 2017 (Bélanger & Malenfant 2005).

It is projected that roughly one-half of all visible minorities in Canada will belong to one of two groups by 2017: South Asian or Chinese. The projections show that the population of each group would be around 1.8 million. In 2001, Chinese and South Asians were already the largest visible minority groups in Canada, but their share of the total population differed. According to the 2006 Census, 1,216,570 individuals identified themselves as Chinese and 1,262,865 as South Asian, 783,795 as Black, and 410,695 as Filipino.

Public Policy Implications

Projections show that the Black population will remain the third largest visible minority, reaching about 1 million in 2017, compared with about 662,000 in the 2001 Census. The visible minority groups that are projected to grow fastest between now and 2017 are the West Asian, Korean and Arab groups. Under most projections, the population of each group will more than double (Bélanger & Malenfant 2005).

The substantial increase in the visible minority population in recent years has already affected public policy (e.g., multiculturalism and anti-racism policy), and will continue to do so. The new period of ethnic and racial diversity has enriched Canada and the lives of each of its citizens, and there is no reason that the demographic changes need result in serious ethnic and racial conflict. However, other factors, such as a serious downturn in the economy, and policies and institutional procedures that intervene and foster ethnic and racial divisions, may affect the social impact of this underlying demographic change.

As a result, social workers and other front line workers face a new set of issues today. They need to continue to be sensitive to religious and cultural differences within the Canadian population they serve. They also need to deal directly with damaging effects of discrimination and racism on the personal well-being of their clients.

TABLE 12.1: Immigrant Wage Gap in Canada, Earners Aged 25 to 54

	Median Income Recent Immigrant Earners*				Median Income Canadian-Born Earners*			
	University Degree		No Degree		University Degree		No Degree	
	Males	Females	Males	Females	Males	Females	Males	Females
1980	48,541	24,317	36,467	18,548	63,040	41,241	43,641	21,463
1990	38,351	25,959	27,301	17,931	61,332	41,245	40,757	23,267
2000	35,816	22,511	25,951	16,794	61,505	43,637	39,902	25,622
2005	30,330	18,969	24,470	14,233	62,566	44,545	40,235	25,590

*Numbers refer to all earners, whether or not they worked on a full-time basis for a full year. Individuals with self-employment income are included, while those living in institutions are excluded.

Source: Adapted from Statistics Canada publication, *Earnings and Incomes of Canadians over the Past Quarter Century, 2006 Census*. Catalogue 97-563-XWE2006001, www.statcan.gc.ca.

Multiculturalism Policy

Multiculturalism

The social preservation, recognition, and celebration of racial, ethnic, cultural, and religious diversity.

In 1971, Canada became the first country to adopt **multiculturalism** as an official policy. The policy was aimed at a greater integration of Canadian society by providing the diverse ethnic minority groups with a sense of belonging to Canada. Its original aim was to give ethnic minority groups a public recognition of their identity. The policy gave them a chance to reinforce their identity, but within the Canadian context, and with the recognition that ethnic diversity is part of Canadian identity (Isajiw 1999). The basic principles of the policy were expressed by Prime Minister Pierre Elliott Trudeau in his introduction of the policy in the Canadian Parliament on October 8, 1971:

> A policy of multiculturalism within a bilingual framework commends itself to the government as the most suitable means of assuring the cultural freedom of Canadians. Such a policy should help to break down discriminatory attitudes and cultural jealousies. National unity if it is to mean anything in the deeply personal sense must be founded on confidence in one's own individual identity; out of this can grow respect for that of others and a willingness to share ideas, attitudes and assumptions. A vigorous policy of multiculturalism will help to create this initial confidence. It can form the base of a society which is based on fair play for all.

In 1988, the *Multiculturalism Act* was passed, restating and reinforcing the 1971 policy and mandating federal departments to ensure equal opportunities in employment for all ethnic and racial groups. In order to implement the policy, the Canadian government created the Multicultural Directorate, which in turn developed a range of programs designed to help it fulfill the policy's objectives. The federal multicultural program stimulated the development of other programs and the establishment of other agencies and institutions. For example, in many Canadian provinces, particularly Alberta, Saskatchewan, and Manitoba, the idea of multiculturalism has been instrumental in the inclusion of a number of "heritage" languages into regular secondary school programs. In 1996, by a special Act of the federal Parliament, the Canadian Race Relations Foundation was established to deal more directly with issues of race.

Canada's multiculturalism policy has set a positive framework within which all issues relating to ethnic and racial equality are now discussed. Nevertheless, while the policy's impact on Canadian society has been significant, and ethnic and racial groups have experienced some improvement in their conditions, they are still relatively disadvantaged. In a 2000 report, for example, the Canadian Race Relations Foundation noted that members of visible minority groups continue to have poorer outcomes with respect to employment and income and still face barriers to socioeconomic equality (CRRF 2000).

Human Rights Legislation

National *human rights legislation* in Canada began with the passage of the Canadian Bill of Rights in 1960. Later in that decade other provinces enacted similar legislation, and by 1975 all provinces in Canada had human rights codes. In general, both federal and provincial human rights law prohibits the dissemination of hate propaganda and discrimination in all aspects of employment, the leasing and sale of property, public accommodation, services and facilities, and membership in labour unions and professional associations. Grounds of discrimination vary slightly depending on the jurisdiction.

In 1982, the Canadian Bill of Rights was superseded by the **Charter of Rights and Freedoms**. The Charter guarantees the fundamental freedoms of conscience and religion, thought, belief, opinion and expression (including freedom of the press and other media of communication), and peaceful assembly and association. It guarantees democratic rights, geographical mobility rights, legal rights (including the right to life, liberty, and security of person), and equality rights that protect against "discrimination based on race, national or ethnic origin, colour, religion, sex, age or mental or physical disability." The Charter also reinforces official bilingualism in Canada by affirming the equality of the English and French languages and by affirming the rights of children to be educated in either language. It also affirmed the multicultural character of Canada and recognized the rights of Canada's Aboriginal peoples. Finally, it emphasized that all the rights and freedoms referred to within it are guaranteed equally to male and female persons (Isajiw 1999).

In 1986, the *Canadian Human Rights Act* and the *Employment Equity Act* were passed with the purpose of redressing some of the past injustices against designated groups in Canada. The designated groups are women, persons with disabilities, Aboriginal peoples, and visible minorities. The purpose of **employment equity** is to ensure equity in the workplace so that no one is denied access to employment for reasons unrelated to merit and skills (see Chapter 10, page 196).

In relation to its own minority groups, Canada is also bound by the international covenants on human rights to which it is a signatory. These include the United Nations Charter of 1945, the Universal Declaration of Human Rights adopted by the United Nations in 1948, the International Convention on the Prevention and Punishment of the Crime of Genocide of 1948, the International Convention Concerning Discrimination in Respect of Employment and Occupation of 1958, the International Convention on All Forms of Racial Discrimination of 1965 (ratified in 1969), the International Covenant on Economic, Social and Cultural Rights of 1966 (ratified in 1976), the International Covenant on Civil and Political Rights (ratified in 1976), and various other resolutions of United Nations assemblies and international conferences (Isajiw 1999).

Canada uses the term visible minority to denote people who are non-white; there is some debate as to whether our use of language should change.

Responding to Hate Online

What do you do if you come across hateful online content or e-mails? Youth are often the targets, and are sometimes left wondering, "What can I do about it?" It's important to remember that such material is not only offensive, it is also illegal.

First, you can contact the website's Internet Service Provider (ISP). Most ISPs now have Acceptable Use Policies that clearly define the guidelines for using their services, as well as the penalties for violating those guidelines.

Second, you can contact the police or Cybertip using an online reporting form or toll-free phone line (1–866–658–9022) to make a complaint.

A number of Canadian sites, such as B'nai Brith Canada's League for Human Rights, also monitor and document illegal material on the Internet.

Visit the Media Awareness Network (www.media-awareness.ca) for more information.

Passing laws is one thing; implementing them is another. The provinces and territories and the federal government have *human rights commissions* charged with dealing with human rights abuses. While these commissions have had some success, they have unfortunately often been hampered by limited resources and case backlogs. Furthermore, since such commissions are by their nature complaints-driven, it is generally felt that many victims of discrimination, perhaps themselves new to the country, do not have the financial resources or even the time to report discrimination and initiate the lengthy complaints process.

Combatting Hate Crime

When people are the targets of violence solely because of who they are, or who they are thought to be, they are the victims of **hate crimes**. The most common targets of hate-motivated crime are Black people, Jews, and gay people. Canada's police agencies report that just after September 11, 2001, there were increased numbers of hate crimes with 15 percent of incidents directly attributed to those events.

More than half (57 percent) of the reported hate crimes in 2001–02 were motivated by racial and ethnic origins, 43 percent involved religious motivations, and issues of sexual orientation motivated 10 percent. Members of visible minorities report fearing becoming victims of a hate crime at a rate more than twice that of Canadians generally, and fears of victimization are also heightened for members of Hindu, Jewish, and Muslim religions (Statistics Canada 2004a). Such crimes create a climate of fear within an entire targeted group.

The promotion of hate based on race, religion, ethnic origin, or sexual orientation is widespread. Catalogued hate sites on the Internet increased from 50 to more than 800 in the period from 1998 to 2001. The Toronto Police Hate Crimes Unit reports that 19 percent more hate crimes, or 110 incidents, were reported in the first six months of 1999 compared with the previous six-month period. There were 584 reported incidents of anti-Semitic harassment and vandalism in Canada in 2003, according to the League for Human Rights of B'nai Brith Canada. This represents a doubling of rates in the late 1990s and early 2000s (League 2003).

Individuals acting out conscious feelings of hate, bias, or prejudice commit most hate crimes in Canada. A survey in 1994 by Canada's Department of Justice to assess the tone of race relations found that people involved in racially motivated hate crimes tend to be young—in their teens or early twenties—and that the perpetrators of such crimes are not, as some have suggested, experiencing bouts of teenage angst and rebellion (Roberts 1995). To the contrary, the study concluded that it is young people who are acting out on long-held views shared by their families and friends about those unlike themselves. Organized hate groups are responsible for about 5 percent of hate-motivated activities in this country.

There is a growing consensus on the need for consistent policy and service delivery responses from the criminal justice system at all levels. The federal government demonstrated strong leadership in this area by amending the *Criminal Code* in 1996 to strengthen sentencing for any offence that is motivated by hate (Bill C-41). The move prompted community discussion, raised overall awareness of the issues, and helped to mobilize communities. It also highlighted the need for stronger responses where hate-motivated incidents occur and may go unreported.

For their part, front-line social workers are using innovative anti-racist approaches that emphasize community empowerment to combat hate crimes. Since hate crimes do not occur in a vacuum, education and community work can prevent hate crimes and act as an important complement to hate crime laws. Social workers are involved in outreach and consultation, education, and awareness activities and fostering the creation of advocacy and support groups. In struggling against overt racism of this kind, social workers also work closely with community organizations to promote an anti-racist perspective through education. This may involve producing brochures on anti-racism, going into schools and engaging students in the issues, or speaking out about community conditions and government inaction.

With their roots firmly in the locality, community workers can also provide feedback on what works and what does not. This kind of collaborative, community-based approach to combatting overt racism can help to minimize the extent of hate crime activity and strengthen the resolve and solidarity of its victims.

Canadian Human Rights Commission

www.chrc-ccdp.ca

This government website of the CHRC offers countless resources as well as updates on court and tribunal decisions regarding human rights.

Hate Crimes

Crimes which target people solely because of who they are or are perceived to be; usually committed against members of marginalized groups.

A poster at the scene of a murder in Toronto in July 2002 after a Jewish father of six was slain outside a pizzeria in a Jewish section of the city.

Concepts and Terms

- - - - - - - - - - - - - -

The terms used to describe and understand complex social issues such as race and racism evolve over time. In the 1970s, for example, racism tended to be seen as the result of individual prejudice. Negative and stereotypical attitudes were deemed to be "the cause" of racist discrimination; if individual attitudes were corrected through education and the sharing of cultures, racism would no longer exist. Much of federal multicultural policy is premised on this understanding.

More recently, we have seen the emergence of a comprehensive "anti-racist" approach. In general, this has involved a shift from seeing the causes of racism only within personal prejudice and individual behaviour to seeing racism as interlinked with the larger structures and social systems in Canadian society.

Some of the key concepts in this area are reviewed below.

- **Stereotype.** When applied to people, *stereotyping* refers to the forming of a fixed picture of a group of people, usually based on false or incomplete information.

- **Prejudice.** *Prejudice* literally means to "prejudge" others based on preconceived ideas. No law can prevent prejudiced attitudes. However, the law can prohibit discriminatory practices and behaviours that flow from prejudice.

- **Ethnicity or ethnic group.** The term *ethnicity* refers to the characteristics of a group of people who share a common heritage, identity, or origin or are descendants of those who have shared a distinct culture and who identify with their ancestors, their culture, or their group. Most commonly, the term *ethnic group* is used to mean minority ethnic groups, for example, Black, Chinese, or Sikh Canadians (as opposed to the majority ethnic group, white Anglo-Saxons). Interestingly, in today's multicultural Canadian society, the term ethnic is used both in a derogatory sense (i.e., as a racist slur) and in a positive sense as describing a group and its food, customs, and so forth as being different and interesting.

- **Culture.** The concept of culture generally refers to behaviours, beliefs, and practices that are meaningful in terms of some shared, even if implicit, cognitive and value assumptions derived from a unique historical community experience (Isajiw 1999).

- **Ethnocentrism.** Ethnocentrism is an attitude by which members of a group tend to consider their group to be in some (or all) ways better or superior to other groups. Such an attitude is especially significant in relation to the majority groups because it is conditioned by the positions of power that members of a group hold.

- **Race.** Race is an arbitrary classification of human beings based on skin colour and other superficial physical characteristics.

Racialized Group vs. Visible Minority

In 2007, the United Nations suggested that Canada reconsider its use of the term visible minority, as it might be in violation of the International Convention on the Elimination of All Forms of Racial Descrimination (1966). Many argue that the term racialized group is preferred because it makes it clear that race is not determined by biology, but is socially constructed. Further, the term reflects the process by which non-white groups are considered almost solely by race while white people are not. Finally, the term visible minority is often used with the intention of negative connotation (Jackson & Smith 2002).

This classification, conceived in Europe in the colonial period, placed the populations of the world in a hierarchical order with white Europeans superior to all others. Modern biologists do not recognize "race" as a meaningful scientific category and recent human genome research is conclusive on this point.

■ **Visible minorities.** Canadian legislation, such as the *Employment Equity Act*, even today refers to "visible minorities"—defined as "persons, other than Aboriginal peoples, who are non-Caucasian in race or non-white in colour." However the term begs the question: visible to whom? It may be time to abandon this term (see sidebar on page 260).

■ **Racism.** Racism is a relationship or attitude based on the subordination of one group by another using arbitrary physical features such as skin colour. One can identify three types of racism: personal racism, cultural racism, and institutional racism. Racism is manifested in overt (obvious and unconcealed) and covert (subtle and hidden) forms.

■ **Discrimination.** Discrimination refers to actions, situations, or policies that have the effect, whether intentional or not, of putting some people at an unnecessary disadvantage on grounds such as race, sex, or religion. Discrimination is usually based on prejudice and stereotypes. Canadian courts have recognized two types of illegal discrimination: (1) direct discrimination; and (2) adverse effects discrimination (also called indirect discrimination or systemic discrimination).

■ **Systemic racism.** Systemic racism (or institutional racism) refers to the existence of policies and structures built into our social institutions that serve to subjugate, oppress, and force the dependence of individuals or groups. The recent finding by a commission of inquiry of systemic racial discrimination within the Ontario criminal justice system is an example. The forced-assimilationist policies underlying the residential schools were of this kind, as were the pre-1968 Canadian immigration laws that explicitly excluded persons based on their country of origin.

■ **Anti-racist social work.** In the past, racism tended to be presented as if it took place only at the individual level (i.e., that there were individuals with racist opinions), and there was a belief that it could be eliminated at this level by education alone. The new anti-racist approach goes beyond this and recognizes that racism is also deeply rooted in the wider institutions of our society—most notably, in employment, education, justice, media, policing, immigration, and government policies. Certainly, there is now ample evidence that deep-rooted racism exists. It is incumbent upon social service workers to be aware of this wider problem and to combat racism wherever and however it manifests itself.

In 2005, a world-wide controversy was sparked when a Danish newspaper published a cartoon depicting the Prophet Muhammad (which is forbidden in Islam), highlighting the challenge of reconciling traditional Western ideals (like freedom of speech) with the new-found ideals of multiculturalism and respecting diversity.

Towards an Anti-Racist Social Work:
The Personal, Institutional, and Societal

What does it mean to practice *anti-racist social work*? The Canadian Association of Social Workers' code of ethics states that "a social worker shall identify, document, and advocate the elimination of discrimination." As part of this, there is an obligation to not only challenge and eradicate racism in others, and in policies and organizations, but also to examine one's own beliefs and behaviours.

Lena Dominelli, one of the pioneers in developing anti-racist social work, summarized anti-racist social work:

> Social work, redefined according to anti-racist criteria, is about realizing significant improvement in the life chances and well-being of individuals regardless of their gender, race, class, age, physical or intellectual abilities, sexual orientation, religious affiliation or linguistic capabilities. Anti-racist social work, therefore, is a bridge between social work in a racist society and social work in a non-racist one (Dominelli 1988, 164).

Institutional or systemic discrimination is still prevalent in the workplace. Even though the *Employment Equity Act* protects people from explicit discrimination in the workplace, it doesn't prevent implicit racism. Anti-racist social work is concerned with the deeply rooted racism of our institutions.

At the same time, many practitioners have emphasized a broad anti-oppressive framework that recognizes the need to continue the fight against racial oppression and to do so alongside combatting oppression based on class, gender, and other factors.

Effective anti-racist social work practice addresses these issues at the personal, institutional, and societal levels. At the personal level, social workers must ensure that their own practices are free of racism and challenge what are considered to be individual racist practices by others. In other words, workers should be "culturally competent" (see page 339) and aware that cultural practices will vary among the different groups of people with whom they work. At the institutional and societal levels, social service agencies must pursue policies and practices that are non-discriminatory, and legislation and government policies must be changed to remove barriers to racial groups. This includes working to eliminate unintentional racism in policy and procedures.

Exemplary Practice

There are many examples of social workers and social service agencies that integrate an anti-racist approach to their practices. Take, for example, the work done by the Nanaimo Youth Services Association in British Columbia, which serves youth and integrates an anti-racism approach within its social services. Social workers at the agency focus on youth with difficulties that affect their physical and emotional well-being and development. Services offered include job-readiness training, employment counselling, wage subsidies, community development, internships, housing, supportive living, student summer programs, a youth drop-in centre, a youth newspaper, work experience, meal programs, a recycling building materials centre, and a teen talkline. The Supportive Living Program within the association helps facilitate the process of the youths' transition from residential care to successful independent living. The program objective is to obtain input from the caseworker, youth, and the caregiver (when appropriate) to develop an individual program plan for the youth. The work done by social workers at the association does not stop with the individual youth. First Nations youth often face racism in finding employment and training opportunities. In this case, social workers relate directly with the community and employers in undertaking awareness training and organizational development activities directed at systemic changes. The workers understand that the youths' difficulties in finding employment cannot be addressed only through education and training of the youth. Barriers and systemic discrimination must also be tackled.

Anti-racist social workers often use an empowerment approach or elicit the direct participation of those affected by racism in developing solutions. The Urban Native Youth Association (UNYA) in Vancouver, for example, was formed to address Aboriginal youth issues when it became apparent that growing numbers of young people were leaving reserves

National Anti-Racism Council of Canada

www.narcc.ca

NARCC is a national, community-based, member-driven network that works to combat racism, racialization, and all other forms of related discrimination in Canada.

for the city of Vancouver. A disproportionate number of First Nations youth end up on the streets with little or no knowledge of where to go for help. UNYA's goal is to serve as a safe place for Aboriginal youth to come and find out about other services in the community and to develop their own solutions. Their involvement in the development of youth services has enabled the youth to raise difficult questions around racism in the community, suggest solutions, and work towards implementing the changes. The youth have taken it upon themselves to work with social workers to challenge the racism they confront in their daily lives.

When faced with mainstream services that are not fully meeting their needs, minority communities have sometimes needed to create separate social service agencies to act on their behalf. The Black Community Resource Centre in Montreal helps Black English-speaking youth and advocates for systemic change. The centre promotes the social, health, education, and economic needs of the youth by collaborating and partnering with Black community organizations, public agencies, and community-wide agencies. The Black Community Centre works with community organizations to monitor and review public policy that affects Black youth. The Centre attempts to improve the cultural and racial appropriateness of other public and government-funded agencies by organizing cultural and racial sensitivity workshops, and it works with other Black organizations in providing operational support and training. The Centre's approach is two-pronged—it has created a separate agency to address unmet needs, while also working to improve the cultural appropriateness and anti-racist perspective of mainstream agencies.

Harry Gairey takes questions from children at Frankland Community School in Toronto after sharing stories of the racism he experienced in the city in the mid-1940s.

Anti-Racism Analysis Tool

An anti-racist approach to social work practice emphasizes placing personal difficulties within the larger social context. Not doing so leads to viewing problems as personal pathologies or problems of interpersonal relations and can result in "blaming the victim," thereby diverting attention away from social structures and thus inhibiting social change. The *anti-racism analysis tool* provides a way to apply this approach by focusing our attention on the personal, institutional, and ideological aspects of a particular problem.

Take, for example, racism inherent in the context of Aboriginal youth caught up in the criminal justice system, with apparently little way out, which continues to be one of the most obvious examples of institutionalized racism. Studies show that, provincially, Aboriginal peoples are incarcerated at rates that are six to seven times higher than the overall provincial rate. The anti-racist analysis tool can be used to broaden our understanding of issues associated with the overrepresentation of Aboriginal people in the criminal justice system.

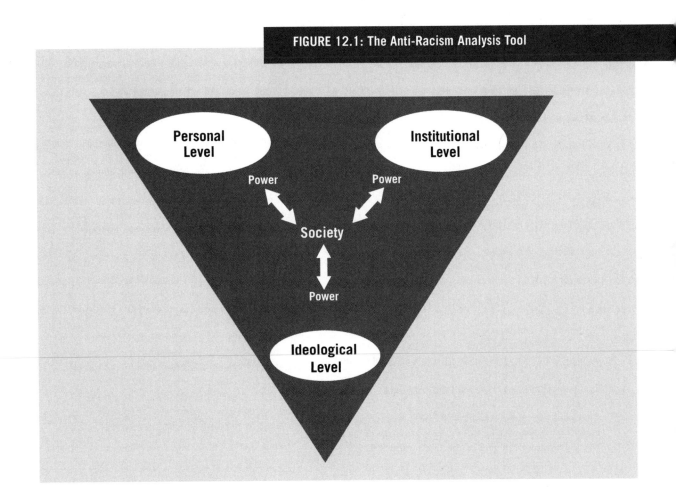

FIGURE 12.1: The Anti-Racism Analysis Tool

In the context of Aboriginal youth, the anti-racist analysis tool redirects us to the personal, institutional, and ideological aspects of the problem:

- Personal racism can be found in policing practices, since Aboriginal people are three times more likely to be charged after arrest than non–Aboriginal people. Instances of overt racism by police officers have also been widely reported.

- At the institutional level, social workers find that few police officers are Aboriginal, almost all judges are white, and less than one percent of lawyers are Aboriginal. This combination often results in lawyers advising Aboriginal people to plead guilty (75 percent do so) to charges even when they are innocent.

- At the ideological level, Aboriginal people are alienated from the mainstream justice system, which emphasizes an adversarial rather than a healing and community approach. Cultural differences and language barriers also compound the problem—for example, in one study almost one-third did not understand the sentencing process.

CASE STUDY: USING THE ANTI-RACISM ANALYSIS TOOL

Tom is an 18-year-old living in a large hostel run by a family as a profit-making business. The hostel mainly houses young single people with mild disabilities. Tom is Aboriginal and has mild brain damage incurred in a car accident four years ago. He currently works in a day program for people with mild disabilities. The manager at the hostel referred Tom to a social worker in a local community health centre because Tom is creating problems at the hostel (refusing to clean his room, arguing with the other residents, and causing damage to the common living areas). It is rumoured that he is an alcoholic (these are rumours, without evidence). For the first four months Tom lived at the hostel, there were no problems; it has been only recently that problems have been reported. Tom will not discuss the reasons for his behaviour, and has not responded to requests to follow hostel rules.

The hostel owner arranges an interview between Tom and the social worker. Tom does not want to see the worker, but the owner threatens to evict him if he does not. He admits to the worker that he has caused some damage, but claims that the other hostel residents are ganging up on him and spreading rumours about him because he is Aboriginal. He has no friends at the hostel, and no family with whom he could live. His mother has thrown him out of her house because he argued with her new boyfriend. He does not know what he will do if he has to leave the hostel, and would continue to stay there if the other residents would only get off his back. However, he would consider going somewhere else if something became available. He agrees that his behaviour has not been without fault, but blames the manager and residents for setting him off.

There are numerous ways to approach this case, but the social worker who is taking an anti-racist approach avoids jumping to conclusions about Tom's rumoured alcohol abuse. The worker explores the issue with Tom and discovers that Tom does not drink at all. He produces a letter from an Elder stating that Tom once had an alcohol problem, but that he has been dry for years. In exploring what "sets Tom off" or makes him angry, the worker discovers that several of the hostel residents taunt him and call him names, such as "drunken Indian."

Working at the personal, institutional, and societal levels, the worker undertakes sensitivity training with the hostel residents and the owner, emphasizing the importance of managing an environment that is non-racist. The worker also investigates the reasons for the lack of other hostel opportunities closer to Tom's community, and connects with Native Friendship Centres or other organizations in advocating for such facilities in First Nations communities. There are a wide variety of options, but the anti-racist social worker addresses the multi-level aspects of the problem and avoids racist stereotyping.

- This cultural racism continues in prison where ceremonial and spiritual practices are often forbidden. And, later, only 18 percent of First Nations inmates are released on parole as compared to 42 percent of the general inmate population (Satzewich 1998).

It is important for social workers addressing the problem of the overrepresentation of Aboriginal people in prisons to work on all levels to achieve a complete and effective solution. Using this tool may enable you, as the social worker, to view an Aboriginal client who is in conflict with the law in a different light. While not ignoring individual problems and individual responsibilities, the anti-racism tool places the person within a broader historical and contemporary context.

Conclusion

Anti-racist social work has an important role to play in creating a non-racist society. It demands that practitioners work to change their own awareness and practices, the practices of those around them, institutional policies and procedures, and social relations and systems that operate, both overtly and covertly, to perpetuate racism. The implementation of an anti-racist approach requires the employment of workers who have an ability to work across racial divides, and who have an empathy based on knowledge of the differences between people. It also means asserting the values of being human—respect and dignity to all.

The anti-racist approach to social work is gaining acceptance in the profession, but challenges remain. Anti-racist social work writers and researchers are few in number, and as a result, it is often necessary to go beyond social work literature. Additionally, social workers who confront racism sometimes face opposition because they are often challenging deeply held beliefs and values. Responding to this will often involve joining with other advocacy and social action groups.

Anti-racist social work practice is a framework for analysis as well as a form of practice pertinent to all aspects of social work, including individual and group counselling, community work, social policy development, and advocacy. It is multifaceted and relevant for practitioners from all backgrounds.

CHAPTER REVIEW

Key Terms

- **Immigration policy**
- **Multiculturalism**
- **Charter of Rights and Freedoms**
- **Employment equity**
- **Hate crimes**
- **Stereotype**
- **Prejudice**
- **Ethnicity**
- **Ethnic group**

- **Culture**
- **Ethnocentrism**
- **Race**
- **Visible minorities**
- **Racism**
- **Discrimination**
- **Systemic racism**
- **Anti-racist social work**

Review Questions

1. Describe three major events in Canadian history that illustrate racial injustice.

2. How has immigration changed in the past twenty years?

3. Describe the origins and basic principles of Canada's multiculturalism policy.

4. What is meant by a "hate crime"? What is the extent of hate crime in Canada? What is the best way to combat such crimes?

5. Explain what is meant by systemic racism and give some examples of systemic racism in Canada.

6. What is anti-racist social work? How has the approach to racism changed in the last few decades?

Exploring Social Work

1. A story in the *Globe and Mail* included an account of a police arrest operation: "Parked directly outside his. . . office was a large, grey, cube-shaped truck and, on the ground nearby, he recognized one of the two brown-skinned young men who had taken possession of the next door rented unit. . ." Critics consider the use of the term "brown-skinned" racist. In 2006, Robert Fisk, a prominent British journalist, published a column in the *Independent* (**www.independent.co.uk**) about the use of this term, called "How Racism Has Invaded Canada." What do you think? Is this an example of racism in the Canadian media?

2. Some researchers have identified systemic barriers in our mental health care system for racial and ethnic minorities. Research systemic racism in the mental health care system and write a two-page report. Get started by reading "A Rationale for an Anti-Racist Entry Point to Anti-Oppressive Social Work in Mental Health Services" in *Critical Social Work* (Vol. 2 No. 1, 2002) at **www.criticalsocialwork.com.**

Websites
- - - - - -

Canadian Race Relations Foundation
www.crr.ca

The Canadian Race Relations Foundation is committed to building a national framework for the fight against racism in Canadian society. They have an excellent online media centre with access to their publications.

World Conference Against Racism, Racial Discrimination, Xenophobia and Related Intolerance
www.un.org/WCAR/coverage.htm

The United Nations Office of the High Commissioner for Human Rights held this conference in Durban, South Africa in 2001. The conference focused on developing practical, action-oriented measures and strategies to combat contemporary forms of racism and intolerance. The Durban Review Conference in 2009 evaluated progress toward the goals set at the 2001 conference.

Anti-Oppressive Social Work Electronic Resource Center
aosw.socialwork.dal.ca

Designed to be of use to social work students, educators, and practitioners, the Center: provides a general introduction to anti-oppressive social work; explores the key theoretical concepts underpinning anti-oppressive social work; discusses pedagogical issues related to teaching anti-oppressive social work; offers a bibliography of selected readings related to anti-oppressive social work; provides links to relevant resources and organization; provides a forum for debate and discussion concerning anti-oppressive social work.

CHAPTER 3

SOCIAL WORK WITH THE ELDERLY

- -

The Implications of an Aging Society

The elderly are the most rapidly increasing age cohort in Canada. Back in 2000, there were an estimated 3.8 million Canadians aged 65 and older, up 62 percent from 2.4 million in 1981. Statistics Canada projects that by 2021 there will be almost 7 million seniors, comprising 19 percent of the total population; by 2041 there will be over 9 million seniors, comprising 25 percent of the population. Twenty-seven percent of seniors are immigrants, which presents special issues for social work practice with the elderly.

In the coming years, this demographic fact will increasingly affect most aspects of our society, particularly health care needs and provision across the country. All of this will mean that the issues affecting older Canadians will become increasingly prominent. And because of the sheer size of this cohort, their concerns will likely be heard loud and clear. Already an important area of activity, social work with the elderly may well become a veritable growth industry.

A Portrait of Canada's Seniors

The aging of the Canadian population can be attributed to three main factors. The main factor contributing to the aging of the Canadian population is the baby boom generation—those born from 1946 to 1966. The eldest of this age group are now approaching retirement. In addition, their consumer patterns are unique: growing up in the prosperity of the post–World War II period, they are relatively well-educated and affluent.

The second factor causing the increase in the elderly age cohort is the fact that many couples are postponing having families, and many are deciding not to have children at all. This trend is due to a number of reasons, among which are the increased participation of women in the labour force, the importance of women establishing their own careers, and the increasing economic demands placed on young families.

In addition, Canadians' life expectancies have increased as a result of healthier lifestyles and universal health care. Many of the baby boomer generation's grandparents, for example, are still alive. Between 1981 and 2005, the number of seniors between the age 75 and 84 more than doubled and their share of the total population rose from 2.8 percent to 4.6 percent (Turcotte & Schellenberg 2007, 13).

A Diverse Group

The senior population in Canada, as elsewhere, is not a homogeneous group. Seniors aged 85 and over are obviously the most likely to have serious medical conditions and disabilities. About one in ten seniors is now 85 or over, up from one in twenty in the early 1920s. Statistics Canada estimates that there will be almost 2 million people aged 85 and over in 2051, almost five times the current figure (2001c). Needless to say, older people in this age range generally have greater needs for social support and health care than younger seniors.

The living arrangements of older Canadians are also varied. Most (93 percent) live in a household and many (68 percent) live in their own household. Ninety percent of senior homeowners have paid off their mortgage. Fifty-seven percent live with a spouse; 7 percent live with members of their extended family; 29 percent live on their own; and 7 percent live in a long-term care institution (Chappell 2001, 3).

Women comprise an ever larger share of the senior population, and in the oldest categories, they are even more numerous. In 2005 women accounted for almost 75 percent of persons aged 90 or older and 52 percent of persons aged 65 to 69. Longer life expectancy among women explains their over-representation in older age groups (Turcotte & Schellenberg 2007, 13).

Each of these sectors has special needs, and unique methods of social work practice need to be applied in each case.

Baby Boom Generation

The large number of individuals born between 1946 and 1966, who are now reaching their senior years. Canada's growing senior population will place increasing pressure on government services, particularly health care and the pension system.

TABLE 13.1: Population Profile and Projections—Percentage Over 65 Years, 1921–2051

Year	Men	Women	Total	% of population
		in thousands		
1921	215.0	205.3	420.2	4.8
1931	294.6	281.5	576.1	5.6
1941	390.9	376.9	767.8	6.7
1951	551.3	535.0	1,086.3	7.8
1961	674.1	717.0	1,391.1	7.6
1971	790.3	972.0	1,762.3	8.0
1981	1,017.2	1,360.1	2,377.3	9.6
1986	1,147.6	1,589.3	2,737.0	10.4
1991	1,349.8	1,867.4	3,217.2	11.4
1996	1,515.3	2,066.7	3,582.0	12.1
1998	1,587.4	2,142.3	3,729.8	12.3
2000	1,645.4	2,204.4	3,849.9	12.5
Projections				
2016	2,521.2	3,181.2	5,702.4	16.6
2021	2,989.6	3,681.1	6,670.6	18.9
2026	3,515.5	4,237.4	7,753,0	21.4
2031	3,950.2	4,705.9	8,656.1	23.6
2036	4,132.7	4,934.0	9,066.7	24.4
2041	4,197.1	5,035.8	9,232.9	24.9
2046	4,231.4	5,087.2	9,618.7	25.2
2051	4,257.5	5,108.9	9,366.4	25.4

Source: Adapted from Statistics Canada publication *Population Projections for Canada, Provinces and Territories, 2000–2026*. Catalogue 91–520–XIB.

Canada's Pension System

Canada's pension system is held in high regard throughout the world for the way it combines basic income security with public and private pension plans that together provide income security to seniors.

The Canada pension system has three tiers:

- **Old Age Security and the Guaranteed Income Supplement.** These plans provide income security for seniors independent of their prior participation in the workforce.
- **Canada Pension Plan (Quebec Pension Plan in Quebec).** The CPP provides pension benefits when the individual retires or becomes disabled and benefits for dependants of disabled or deceased contributors. The amount of the benefit depends on the level of contributions during the contributory period.
- **Private pension plans.** These consist of (1) workplace plans and (2) Registered Retirement Savings Plans (RRSPs), both of which receive tax breaks on contributions..

Until recently, this three-tiered system served seniors well. Canadian seniors' financial status improved significantly over the last 25 years. The median after-tax income of elderly married couples in 2005 dollars rose from $29,000 in 1980 to $38,900 in 2005, an increase of 34 percent (Statistics Canada, 2006a). By any measure, this was a major success story.

The Erosion of Seniors' Incomes

More recently, however, the stock market crash and the financial crisis of 2008 has placed the income of seniors under considerable stress and has brought the call for pension reform to the foreground. Individuals and families have recently seen the value of their RRSP investments drop considerably. Many have been forced to postpone their retirement.

Likewise, many business pension funds are now underfunded and some may not be able to meet their legal obligations to pay out to retirees. Many businesses are also cutting back on company benefits and pensions or getting out of the pension business altogether.

There is also a concern that the OAS and the GIS are no longer adequate to cover the most vulnerable citizens. The maximum amount an individual can currently receive from OAS and GIS is $14,033, whereas the poverty line for someone in a large metropolitan area is $18,373. Indeed, more than 14 percent of senior women living on their own are in poverty, according to this measure.

Canada's pension system now faces serious challenges as it tries to accommodate the aging baby boomers in the context of a major economic downturn. If the incomes of seniors are to be protected, and previous gains secured, these issues will need to be addressed at the highest policy levels.

Pension Reform

Canada's pension system needs urgent attention, according to a detailed report released by the Canadian Centre for Policy Alternatives (CCPA) in October 2009.

The report outlines some of the problems with Canada's pension system and examines the options that have been proposed to deal with them.

- Public pension programs such as Old Age Security and the Canada Pension Plan provide only a modest income for people when they retire.

- Only 38% of paid workers have workplace pensions. Everyone else must rely on public pension programs supplemented by their own savings.

- Only a small minority of Canadians (31% of those eligible to contribute) take advantage of tax-assisted private savings through RRSPs.

- Almost $500 billion in unused RRSP contribution room is being carried forward.

Source: "What Can We Do About Pensions?" by CCPA Research Associate and pension expert Monica Townson. October 8, 2009. Canadian Centre for Policy Alternatives. www.policyalternatives.ca.

Theories of Aging

Two early micro-level theories that have held considerable sway over social work practice with the elderly are activity theory and disengagement theory. **Activity theory** holds that as people age they have a decrease in life satisfaction and that this can be relieved by engaging in various activities such as joining clubs, doing volunteer work, or participating in sports. **Disengagement theory**, by contrast, asserts that individual adjustment to aging is accomplished by withdrawing from social life and that this is a natural and inevitable process.

These theories or approaches focus almost exclusively on individuals and how seniors adjust to aging. There are other more contemporary theories that are beginning to inform social work practice with the elderly. For example, **continuity theory** suggests that to age successfully, one must maintain a consistent lifestyle. According to this view, older Canadians will be most satisfied if they continue the roles and activities of their middle years. This theory is based on the notion that old age is a continuation of a person's past, rather than a break with it.

Role theory, an expansion on the above approaches, seeks to understand the "adjustment" of aging people to the new roles entailed in getting older. In the context of disengagement, for example, role theory looks at how "normal aging" involves a functional and voluntary process in which the elderly withdraw from social life, letting go of social roles and activities. In the context of seniors' activity, role theory focuses on how successful aging involves "slowing down but keeping active"—that is, as people age, they may need to replace old roles with new and equally fulfilling ones.

Life Course Theory

An alternative to the theories described above is the **life course theory**, which focuses more on how individuals take various distinct pathways through life as they move through different periods. This approach does not view old age as any less satisfying than other periods of life, such as early parenthood. Rather, it views each period as having particular benefits, limitations, and characteristics. The approach is also unique in that it discusses issues in terms of life events rather than age.

The life course theory likely has the largest potential with respect to informing effective social work practice. Glen Elder (Elder & Johnson 2002), the originator of the life course theory, posits four main principles for the approach:

- The life course of a person is shaped by his or her historical and geographic placement.
- The impact of a transition or event depends on when it occurs in a person's life.

- Lives are lived interdependently—the actions and relationships of one person can affect the lives of others.
- Individuals construct their own life course through choices and action, but these are contingent upon the constraints and opportunities presented.

The life course theoretical approach has the advantage of addressing both the individual and broader contextual issues surrounding aging. Being broader in scope, it also allows for the incorporation of ideas from feminist theory, critical theory, and political economy theory.

Ageism: Negative Images of the Elderly

Common phrases such as "over the hill" and "don't be an old fuddy-duddy" symbolize society's negative image of old age and elderly people in general. **Ageism**, as this kind of discrimination is called, can be defined as any attitude, action, or institutional structure that subordinates or oppresses a person or group on the basis of age. Of course, ageism is different from other "isms," such as discrimination on the basis of race or gender, in that at some point everyone will be old (unless, of course, he or she dies young) and will therefore likely experience ageism.

Researchers have found that different cultures regard their elderly in a variety of ways. Lena Dominelli, a professor of Social and Community Development at Southampton University in England, believes that the decline in the economic status of older people in the West is part of the explanation for ageism (Dominelli 2004, 135). Ageism, according to Dominelli, is oppression of people on the basis of age, where seniors are presented as a homogeneous group that are a burden to society. According to Dominelli, Western countries tend to regard people in materialist terms—people's worth or value to society is often based on how much they make, the size of their house, or the kind of car they drive. In retirement, the income of seniors usually drops, and this may have the effect of lower self-esteem on the part of the seniors themselves and negative views from other Canadians. Furthermore, with urbanization, and especially with the breakdown of the extended family, the elderly have tended to lose their status in the family and in society as a whole.

Indeed, North Americans and Western societies generally may fear aging more (and be more ageist) than others. This is perhaps best exemplified by the sales of beauty products and the use of painful plastic surgery to restore a youthful look. However, not all societies and cultures view the elderly this way. Many Aboriginal, Asian, and African societies (and many cultures within Western societies) place a higher value on the wisdom and traditions of the elderly. In many societies the elderly are traditionally viewed as sources of guidance and knowledge. Perhaps, as our population as a whole continues to age, some of these negative attitudes and perceptions will gradually begin to change.

While there are many theories of aging, most agree that to stay healthy and happy, seniors must be active and engaged; social workers can help both individuals and communities achieve this.

Ageism

Any attitude, action, or institutional structure that subordinates or oppresses a person or group on the basis of age.

How Healthy Are Seniors?

Life expectancy has doubled over the past one hundred years, and seniors in Canada seem to be enjoying their improving health in most instances (see Table 13.2), and life expectancies are increasing. Moreover, the majority of seniors do not engage in behaviours harmful to their health (NACA 2001b, 5). Many analysts believe that our public health care system plays a particularly important part in preventing seniors' health problems, promoting and restoring health, and preventing further health deterioration.

Nevertheless, as is the case with other age groups, there is a health gap between seniors with low income and those with higher income. Seniors with low income are more likely to have chronic conditions or long-term activity limitations. The 2005 Canadian Community Health Survey (Statistics Canada 2005a) found that one in four seniors rated their own health status as being either fair or poor, while 40 percent rated their health as being either very good or excellent. Over the past decades, we have learned that health is determined by many factors that go beyond access to health care.

IN THE EYE OF THE BEHOLDER: THE FEAR OF AGING

The "fear of aging" is largely based on a series of myths about old age and the elderly. Some such views depict aging negatively, while others portray an unrealistic picture of the joys of later life—travel, golf, dinner, and dancing. The following are a few of these myths.

Myth: "To be old is to be sick."

Reality: Most seniors are relatively healthy and active. Three-quarters of Canadian seniors report that their health is good, very good, or excellent. In addition, according to the National Advisory Council's Seniors in Canada Report Card 2006, an even greater number—95 percent— of seniors also considered their mental health to be good, very good, or excellent.

Myth: "Seniors and technology don't mix."

Reality: Seniors are the fastest growing group online, and they are capable of using the new technology for more than just e-mail. For example, seniors in the Seniors' Education program at Ryerson University developed, produced, and moderate an interactive website. The webmaster and all those working on the site came to computers with no background in the field.

Myth: "Most seniors live in nursing homes."

Reality: Just 5 percent of men and 9 percent of women over age 65 live in health care institutions; most are 85 or older. And the percentages have declined.

Myth: "Seniors don't pull their own weight."

Reality: Up to a third of seniors provide help to friends and family, including caregiving for spouses and grandchildren and financial assistance to children. Senior volunteers (about 18 percent of all seniors) spend an average of five hours a week on their activities. And seniors pay taxes—just as they've done all their lives.

Myth: "Seniors are too set in their ways to undertake new things."

Reality: Evidence suggests that the opposite can be true. For example, Dorothy Rungeling of Fonthill, Ontario, published her first book, *The Road to Home*, at the age of 91 in 2001. She has since published three more books, including one about her experiences as a pilot in the 1950s and 1960s, One might say that during the senior years, more time and greater security can lead to opportunities that were not available earlier in life.

As mentioned in Chapter 9, the Canadian Institute for Health Information (2006c) report showed a link between low income and poorer health outcomes. It found that residents of higher-than-average median income neighbourhoods were more likely to report excellent or very good health status and to be physically active compared to those in lower-than-average median income neighbourhoods. They also found that poor housing leads to increased health problems. Seniors are affected by both of these dynamics.

Acute and Chronic Pain

A major concern for older Canadians is pain. Pain not only causes physical suffering, but also affects emotional and mental well-being. Seniors are more likely to have conditions that cause pain, such as arthritis, osteo-porosis, or diabetes. Regrettably, seniors are also more likely to suffer untreated pain. Over one-third report some level of pain or discomfort, and the figure is higher for those over age 75.

To an extent, some pain is subjective—each person feels and reports pain differently, and identical injuries can cause widely different percep-tions of pain. However, most of it is real and it is crucial for social workers to understand the nature of pain and the terminology used by medical professionals.

Pain can be of two types: *acute* and *chronic*.

- **Acute pain** is temporary. It may be severe at the beginning but decline over time, lasting from a few seconds to several days or weeks.
- **Chronic pain** lingers, lasting from a few months to many years. It can be mild or excruciating, episodic or continuous, merely incon-venient or totally incapacitating.

Sometimes chronic pain begins as acute pain. It can also stem from disease, such as arthritis, diabetes, or shingles, but often an immediate cause cannot be found. Both types of pain need to be addressed before interven-tion around other issues can be undertaken.

Because they often work closely with individuals over an extended period of time, social work practitioners may be in a better position than other health care professionals to listen to the reports of pain from seniors and communicate these concerns to the medical team. Social workers also need to be aware of the reasons for undertreatment of pain with seniors. First, seniors may be reluctant to report pain, believing that they are supposed to just bear it. Second, medical professionals may lack training and experience in managing pain and may hold myths about seniors— these myths might include the belief that seniors are less sensitive to pain or can tolerate it better than younger people, that pain is a natural part of aging, or that older patients cannot tolerate strong painkillers.

Acute Pain

Temporary pain that is often severe and can last from a few seconds to several days or weeks.

Chronic Pain

Ongoing, lingering pain that can last from a few months to many years and can be mild or severe, episodic or continuous, inconvenient or incapacitating.

Issues of Increasing Concern
- - - - - - - - - - - - - - - - - - - -

While they are all different in many respects, seniors also face a number of issues in common:

- **Inactivity.** Physical activity may not appear to be a social work issue, but many emotional, spiritual, and mental health issues—perhaps especially among seniors—are directly related to it. Inactivity can lead to preventable health problems, such as heart

TABLE 13.2: Percentage of Persons at Different Levels of Activity, by Province—2006

	Age 25 to 64			Age 65 and Over		
	Active	Moderate	Inactive	Active	Moderate	Inactive
Newfoundland and Labrador	18.6	24.9	56.5	13.5	15.4	71.1
Prince Edward Island	18.1	22.0	59.9	12.5	20.0	67.5
Nova Scotia	20.9	24.0	55.1	12.6	21.7	65.8
New Brunswick	18.8	25.3	55.9	12.5	16.1	71.4
Quebec	19.9	25.2	55.0	17.1	22.7	60.2
Ontario	22.9	25.4	51.7	18.9	23.0	58.1
Manitoba	24.3	25.4	50.3	16.1	18.6	65.3
Saskatchewan	23.7	25.0	51.3	14.2	21.5	64.4
Alberta	27.3	25.9	46.9	18.4	23.8	57.8
British Columbia	31.3	27.6	41.4	24.9	26.3	48.7

Source: Adapted from Statistics Canada publication, *A Portrait of Seniors in Canada, 2006*. (M. Turcotte & G. Shellenberg) Catalogue 89-519-XIE, www.statcan.gc.ca.

disease and stroke. According to the Fitness and Lifestyle Research Institute, physical inactivity can also lead to depression, lack of energy, chronic disease, weight problems, disability, and premature death. The Canadian government estimates that billions of dollars per year could be saved if physical activity rates increased. For many seniors, walks, gardening, or light sports could lead to a better emotional state. Unfortunately, the majority of seniors are inactive, with 55 percent of men and 67 percent of women reporting being physically inactive in 1998–99. There is recent evidence that this trend may be reversing in the younger elderly age categories. Seniors aged 65 to 74 had an improvement in their physical activity levels, with 51.1 percent reporting being physically inactive in 2000–01 compared with 54.7 percent in 1998–99. Seniors 75 and older reported inactivity levels of 63.3 percent in 2000–01, a little worse than the 62.5 percent in 1998–99 (Statistics Canada 2003).

- **Accidents.** Canadian seniors also face significant risks due to common accidents such as falling. Hospital admissions for unintentional injuries occur most often among seniors. The situation has not improved—36 percent of all injury admissions in 1997–98 involved seniors, up by 3 percent from 1995–96 (CIHI 1999).

- **Victims of Fraud.** Often isolated in their homes, seniors are also the leading targets of fraudulent crimes, such as fake investment opportunities, phony contests, and false fundraising campaigns. People over the age of 60 comprised three-quarters of those defrauded of more than $5,000 in 1997 and the vast majority were victimized more than once (NACA 2001a). In some cases, seniors have lost their life savings. Criminals are using more and more sophisticated techniques, often misrepresenting themselves as employees of a person's bank or other financial institution.

- **Mandatory Retirement.** Finally, retirement is often presented to Canadians as something that enables hard-working seniors to take a break from the grind of work and to relax, travel, and enjoy life. Unfortunately, the reality is often quite different, since retirement usually means a substantial drop in income as well as greater social isolation. Forced or unexpected retirement can be bad enough, but when combined with other misfortunes (illness or illness of a spouse) it can be particularly stressful. Forced retirement, whether it is early or not, can create financial and emotional troubles that seniors are left to face alone. This can affect women even more negatively, since many women enter the labour force later, after they have raised their children. Mandatory retirement in such cases dramatically reduces the pension income of senior women. On the other hand, unions are hesitant to abolish mandatory retirement as it may be a precursor to the elimination of government income security benefits.

Abuse and Neglect of Seniors

Elder abuse is the mistreatment of older people by those in a position of trust, power, or responsibility for their care. Neglect is frequently associated with abuse. Abuse may take place in the home or in an institutional care setting.

Like other forms of violence within families, senior abuse is largely hidden from view. Isolated and often frail, seniors are highly vulnerable to mistreatment, and often by those closest to them and responsible for caring for them.

According to 2005 police victimization data, overall rates of violence within family relationships were higher for senior women at 47 per 100,000 compared to 36 per 100,000 for males over 65. Rates of family violence against seniors were highest when the accused was an adult child (15 per 100,000) or a current or former spouse (13 per 100,000) (CCJS 2007). Senior females were most likely to experience family violence at the hands of their current or ex-spouse (17 per 100,000) or their adult children (16 per 100,000); while senior males were more likely to be victimized by their adult children (13 per 100,000).

Researchers have found that older seniors are more likely to be victimized by family than younger seniors, but due to their increased dependence on family, they are unlikely to report the abuse for fear of losing support (Wolf 1997). Another study found that those over 85 years of age are most likely to suffer from dementia or other chronic illnesses and that this can render an individual physically or mentally incapable of reporting violence to the police (Welfel et al. 2000).

COMPASSIONATE CARE BENEFITS AND CAREGIVER TAX CREDIT

As of 2004, there is a new type of special benefit administered by Human Resources and Skills Development Canada (HRSDC) through Employment Insurance (EI), called compassionate care benefits.

The federal government expanded the Employment Insurance (EI) program to extend compassionate care benefits to a person who must be absent from work to provide care or support to a gravely ill family member. Benefits may be paid up to a maximum of six weeks to an employee looking after a loved one who is at risk of dying within twenty-six weeks. Unemployed persons on EI can also ask for this type of benefit. Benefits can be shared with other members of the applicant's family, but they also must be eligible and must apply for them.

Providing care to a family member means providing psychological or emotional support, arranging for care or directly providing or participating in the care. More information is available on the Social Development Canada website at www.sdc.gc.ca.

The Canada Revenue Agency (CRA) also allows Canadians to claim deductions and credits for individuals supporting people with disabilities. For example, care could have been provided to parents, parents-in-law, and grandparents. The caregiver amount is a non-refundable tax credit which reduces the amount of federal income tax paid. For more information, consult the CRA website, at www.ccra-adrc.gc.ca

The above statistics deal with physical violence, but as we know, family violence can take other forms as well. Perhaps the most reliable source of data is the 1999 General Social Survey (GSS), which shows that about 7 percent of seniors report experiencing some form of emotional or financial abuse by an adult child, caregiver, or spouse (in the five-year period preceding this survey) (Dauvergne 2003). The breakdown by types of abuse is as follows: emotional abuse (7 percent), financial abuse (1 percent), and physical or sexual violence (1 percent). In addition, almost 2 percent of older Canadians said they had experienced more than one type of such abuse.

Occasional Relief from Caregiving

One step in preventing elder abuse within families is to understand the possible causes. Mia Dauvergne (2003) discusses several lines of reasoning that have been advanced: the stressfulness of a family situation, the fact that some of this violence may have been learned earlier and is simply a way of responding to stressful situations, the fact that the lives of the senior and family caregiver are so intricately intertwined, and the possible effects of discriminatory attitudes towards the aging family members. Doubtless all of these are contributing factors, but a major factor must be the seemingly relentless strain put on family members who have the responsibility of caring for seniors.

Women make up the majority of seniors, and represent 70 percent of seniors over the age of 85.

The extent of informal caregiving is often understated. Over 1.7 million adults in Canada aged 45 to 64 are providing informal care to almost 2.3 million seniors with a long-term disability or physical limitation. According to Stobert and Cranswick (2003), "most are looking after their own parents (67 percent) and their spouse's parents (24 percent). Many (24 percent) are providing help to close friends and neighbours." Women dedicate almost twice as much time to the task. Working outside the home does not appear to reduce the amount of time middle-aged women spend providing care—26.4 hours a month for women and 14.5 for men. "In other words," Stobert and Cranswick note, "the caregiving labour is divided along traditional gender lines, which may reflect the provider's level of comfort performing tasks that mirror their areas of competence in their own homes."

Equally troubling is the fact that less than one in five of the care providers reported that they received help if they needed a break. Yet, when asked to identify the most useful thing to allow them to continue providing help, the most common answer (51 percent of those aged 45 to 64) was "occasional relief or sharing of responsibilities." Flexible work arrangements and financial compensation were also on the list.

There is the additional complication of seniors looking after seniors. Stobert and Cranswick report that over one in twelve seniors (321,000) is also looking after at least one other senior: a spouse (25 percent), a close friend (33 percent), or a neighbour (19 percent). The gap between men and women with respect to giving care in this age group is higher than for younger caregivers. Moreover, only 18 percent of the senior caregivers indicated that someone else could take over should they need, or want, time off—pointing to an even greater need for support.

The physical and psychological effects of violence against seniors are traumatic, if not completely devastating, for the senior and perhaps even the abuser. In the face of all these concerns, and the growing senior population, it is a primary concern that governments at all levels (as well as family members and friends) find more ways to provide those who are giving care to seniors the relief they need when they need it.

SIGNS AND SYMPTOMS OF ABUSE AND NEGLECT IN INSTITUTIONS

Neglect

- Dehydration, malnourishment
- Missing dentures, glasses, hearing aids
- Poor hygiene, lack of appropriate clothing
- Untreated medical problems
- Poor condition of skin
- Being left unattended or tied to a bed or chair
- Failure to monitor restraints
- Failure to allow outside services or medical appointments

Medical Abuse

- Reduced/absent therapeutic response
- Poor documentation of medical records
- Improper administration of drugs
- No reason for treatment given

Physical Abuse

- Unexplained injuries—fractures, bruises
- Unexplained falls
- Unauthorized or inappropriate restraints
- Delay in seeking and receiving medical treatment

Sexual Abuse

- Pain, swelling, bleeding in the genital area
- Fear of specific persons or of being alone with them
- Sexually transmitted diseases
- Drawing back from touching

Psychological/Emotional Abuse

- Feelings of fear, passivity, shame, or guilt
- Extreme passivity and withdrawal
- Symptoms of depression
- Exclusion from activity and family
- The use or threat of punishment
- Decisions made for resident

Financial Abuse

- Lack of necessities or comforts
- Unauthorized use of resident's money or property
- Disappearance of resident's property
- Unexplained changes in a deed or will
- Inadequate facilities to protect resident's property
- Resident constantly lacking money to buy small personal comforts
- Lack of accounting for the way finances have been spent

Violation of Rights

- Difficulty visiting, calling, or contacting resident
- Resident not permitted to manage their own financial affairs
- Lack of choices in life
- Lack of privacy
- Resident not permitted to participate in decision making about his or her own affairs
- Lack of confidentiality in use of health care records

Source: L. McDonald & A. Collins. 2000. *Abuse and Neglect of Older Canadians: A Discussion Paper.* Ottawa: Health Canada.

Abuse in Institutional Settings

Another issue of concern to social workers is abuse in facilities providing care to older people, including acute care hospitals, nursing homes, and retirement homes. In this context, **institutional abuse** is any act or omission directed at a resident that causes the person harm, or that wrongfully deprives that person of her or his independence.

This definition focuses on the consequences of acts on residents and less on the intent. The abuse could be of an individual nature, whereby a staff member at the institution directly abuses the resident. But often the abuse is systemic, whereby situations are allowed to develop that facilitate or permit abuse and neglect. It could also involve the failure to provide adequate safeguards for residents and staff. Guarding against such forms of abuse and neglect, both intentional and unintentional, is important not only for family members and relatives but for social workers associated with these seniors and the institutions in which they find themselves.

Combatting the Abuse of Seniors in Institutions

Systemic abuse in institutional settings often results from policies, procedures, and processes that appear to be designed to maximize care. For example, a facility may have a policy that permits staff members to search residents' rooms at any time for alcohol or medication. The intent of the policy may be protecting cognitively impaired residents from harm, but the outcome is an invasion of privacy. Institutions typically have numerous policies regarding eating, wake-up, and sleep times. Often, these conflict with residents' lifelong eating and sleeping patterns. Residents also might find it difficult to question these policies as they are framed in terms of protection. One important way that social workers can assist with preventing abuse of seniors is by using various advocacy strategies, resident councils, and family councils. Ongoing staff training and policy reviews are also important.

The "home" or "residence" model for long-term care can help overcome some of the problems of abuse in institutional settings. Some facilities have found that developing a charter of rights works well in addressing abuse. An example is the Yvon-Brunet seniors' residence in Montreal. Their charter includes five basic rights: information and freedom of expression, privacy, dignity and respect, continuity, and responsibility and participation. These rights translate into a variety of procedures that ensure that residents' needs are being met, such as a residents' council, flexible schedules, and consultation about medications and menu choices (NACA 2004).

Awareness of the widespread abuse of older adults is growing and social service agencies are responding with community-based initiatives that are more effective in reducing the incidence of abuse and eliminating some of the causes.

Immigrant Seniors

According to Turcotte and Schellenberg's 2007 report, the immigrant population is older than the non-immigrant population. One million or 19 percent of all immigrants were over age 65 (compared to 11 percent of non-immigrants) in 2001. In 2001, 29 percent of individuals aged 65 to 74 and 28 percent of those aged 75 to 84 were immigrants.

Immigrant seniors, and in particular recent immigrants, may have different life experience and needs. For example, many immigrants who are now seniors entered the labour market in Canada at a later age and often have had less time to save for retirement. As well, fewer are likely to be eligible for Canadian public pension plans.

Immigrant seniors face health care challenges because fewer have insurance coverage. Recent immigrant seniors are much less likely to have health insurance. Immigrant seniors who live alone also have high rates of low income. This is particularly true for women. The situation is worse for the most recent immigrants.

Social Work in Long-Term Care Settings

Social workers play an important role in the provision of long-term care. The percentage of seniors living in institutions declined from 8.1 percent in 1991 to 7.3 percent in 1996 (Lindsay 1999), but it remains a key area of social work practice. Projections for 2031 estimate that the number of long-term care beds will triple or even quadruple. The percentage of the population aged 85 and over is growing at the fastest rate, and it is this group that is most likely to require long-term care.

Long-term care commonly means nursing home or rehabilitation centre care, primarily for the elderly. Often, this care involves specialty programs for persons with developmental, physical, mental, or emotional impairments. In some provinces the term has a wider meaning and may refer to ongoing care within day programs or even within home-based programs. The 1995 Canadian National Population Health Survey established that 75 percent of long-term care residents required help with one or more activities of daily living (i.e., personal care, moving about the institution, getting in and out of bed, getting in and out of a chair) and 39 percent needed help with all these activities (Tully & Mohl 1995, 27–30).

Work in this field is multidisciplinary, thereby providing an opportunity for social workers to practice collaboratively with health professionals. The principal components of long-term care are health care and social services designed to provide assessment, treatment, rehabilitation, and supportive care, as well as to prevent the increased disability of individuals of all age groups who have chronic physical, developmental, or emotional impairments.

Phases of Long-Term Care

Social workers in long-term care settings are involved during all the phases of care, from pre-admission through residency to the termination of residency at the time of discharge or death. The four phases in long-term care are briefly described below.

- **Pre-admission phase.** As the first contact with the resident and family, the social worker deals with feelings about placement and provides information about the facility and its services. This is an important phase, as potential future issues with the resident and the family can be identified here.

- **Admission phase.** Social workers are generally responsible for the admission process. During admission, the social worker helps the resident and his or her family become familiar with the facility and its services. The social worker is often the first liaison between the resident and family and any other community agency that was previously involved. Often social workers engage in counselling during this phase as the resident and family members adjust to their new reality.

- **Residency phase.** A variety of interventions may occur that involve the social worker. Social workers regularly work at the individual, family, community, and policy levels. Work at the individual level focuses on the social and emotional impacts of physical and mental illness or impairment and the prevention of further physical and mental health problems. Social workers work with families in discussing palliative care and end-of-life issues, dealing with the resident's family members who are feeling guilt related to placement or providing information regarding care and prevention issues. Commonly, social workers are involved in locating and arranging resources and in developing or implementing innovative programs and policy.

- **Discharge, transfer, or death phase.** Discharge and transfer planning is a key aspect of social work in long-term care. In the case of the death of the resident, social workers may provide grief counselling for the family.

Hospice Palliative Care

Palliative care is a special kind of health care for individuals and families who are living with a life-threatening illness, usually at an advanced stage. The goal is to provide the best quality of life for the critically or terminally ill by ensuring their comfort and dignity.

Hospice palliative care focuses on holistic care by offering a wide range of health, emotional, and spiritual support services. Palliative care expert Madeleine Saint-Michel emphasizes that a terminally ill person requires much more than physical comfort—they need help in mindfully addressing the deep-seated emotions and feelings related to dying. In Canada, we tend to use the terms hospice and palliative care interchangeably. When the distinction is drawn, people use the term hospice to refer to care in the home or community and palliative care to refer to care in the hospital.

Palliative care is provided in a variety of places—at home, in long-term facilities, in hospitals, and occasionally in hospices. Hospitals either admit patients into a general ward or, if available, a special palliative care unit. The Sunnybrook Health Sciences Centre in Toronto, for example, has a palliative care unit that serves cancer patients. Other centres, such as the Maison Michel Sarrazin facility in Quebec (the first opened in Canada in 1985), offer a network of care, providing care at the facility and support in the home.

Social workers offer hands-on support and assistance in such situations. They provide instruction on how to care for the person, for example, or how to give medication, recognize signs of pending problems, or how and where to call for assistance in an emergency. They may also help family members work through emotions and grief regarding the illness and death of a loved one.

Aboriginal Seniors are Respected Elders

In contrast to mainstream Canadian culture, Aboriginal cultures tend to respect and even revere their seniors for their knowledge and experiences. Elders play an integral role in the well-being of their families, communities, and nations, acting as key sources of traditional knowledge, wisdom, and cultural continuity. Aboriginal seniors only comprise 1 percent of the overall senior population in Canada (compared with 3 percent in the total population). Manitoba and Saskatchewan have the largest proportion of Aboriginal seniors in their senior populations (Turcotte & Schellenberg 2007).

Social Work and Home Care

In the past two decades, there has been a devolution from institutional-based services to community- or home-based services. Recent data shows that more and more seniors are healthy and living on their own—composed of what some are now calling the "wellderly." Recent studies have estimated that between 85 and 90 percent of care for the elderly is provided in the home by relatives. This has resulted in an increasing need for support for those providing home care.

ALZHEIMER'S DISEASE AND DEMENTIA

First described by Alois Alzheimer, a German physician, Alzheimer's disease is the most common form of dementia—a condition that results in progressive loss of mental functions.

Dementia involves mental impairment caused by chronic, irreversible brain damage, whether that damage is caused by multiple strokes or by a deterioration of the brain cells of the Alzheimer's type. About 60 percent of persons with dementia (cognitive impairment) are believed to have a cerebral degeneration of the Alzheimer's type (Lyons 1995).

Prevalence and Effects

Approximately 250,000 Canadians, representing 8 percent of the population aged 65 and over, met the criteria for dementia. Among those aged 85 and over, the prevalence of dementia rose to 34.5 percent. The vast majority of people with dementia are elderly. The impact of losing one's cognitive abilities is momentous and is generally accompanied by feelings of fear, loss of self-esteem, resentment, and even anger.

People with Alzheimer's gradually lose their independence, becoming incapable by degrees of performing simple tasks, remembering recent events, controlling thoughts or moods, or relating to others. The most common form of dementia, Alzheimer's slowly destroys nerve cells in the brain. It affects primarily those over the age of 65, but it is considered to be an illness and not a normal part of aging.

There is no cure for Alzheimer's, but there are medications that can help relieve some of the symptoms. According to Health Canada (2001), Canadians spend about $3.9 billion each year for the treatment of persons with Alzheimer's disease and other dementias.

Family Crisis

The onset of Alzheimer's has distressing reverberations. It can cause emotional and financial stresses. Often, spouses or children are left in a precarious position, attempting to care for their loved ones and earn a living at the same time. It is not only the victims of the disease who become increasingly dependent, but also the families and primary caregivers. Family caregivers become dependent upon physicians, other family members, friends, household help, a variety of health and social services, and institutional services.

Family members have mixed feelings about entrusting the care of a helpless relative to strangers over whom they have little control. Dealing with these feelings and reactions is often the job of the social worker.

Role of the Social Worker

The first activity of the social worker is to help the family examine different possible courses of action. Family members close to the illness may not see all the options available. And, in other cases, family members may think that they can do it all and may not be open to a stranger's suggestions. The social worker needs to assess the family's feelings and desires before making recommendations.

It is imperative that the social worker has a basic clarity about his or her task: It is to help the families of people with dementia to develop an understanding among themselves about the situation that enables them to act. This helps the family to gain a sense of direction in what seems to be an impossible situation.

The Alzheimer Society of Canada's website (www.alzheimer.ca) is an excellent resource for information about Alzheimer's and working with those who suffer from it.

Home care involves a range of services, including health promotion, curative medicine, end-of-life care, rehabilitation, support and maintenance, social adaptation and integration, and support for the informal (family) caregiver. Home care programs also link formalized health care delivery services in the home setting with community-based services (e.g., Meals on Wheels, respite care, and volunteer services). While the recipients of home care are often elderly Canadians, these services are also provided for infants, children, and adults.

Home care services include the:

- assessment of client needs (medical and social) and determination of the best care setting based on a client's health and social situation and support network.

- development of an in-home care plan, which includes family involvement, teaching, interventions, and community support.

- provision of nursing services, therapy services, and home support services.

- coordination of medical supplies, equipment, pharmaceuticals, and assistive devices.

- ongoing monitoring and evaluation of the client, family, and caregiver's status and needs.

- respite care to assist informal caregivers and support families in their role as caregivers.

- discharge planning and coordination of placement services to long-term care facilities (if required).

Additional services, such as long-term care placement, ambulatory care clinics, home adaptation and home maintenance, are coordinated and provided through or in conjunction with home care programs. Home care services generally include the provision of health services by two tiers of workers: professionals, such as social workers, physicians, nurses, physiotherapists, occupational therapists, speech therapists, and dieticians; and unregulated workers, such as homemakers, personal support workers, and personal care attendants.

A Provincial Responsibility

Home care falls within provincial jurisdiction. In Canada, there are at least 663 agencies providing home care services, with 93 percent of delivery agencies receiving some government funding and just over 50 percent receiving all of their funding from government sources. Under the *Canada Health Act,* home care is an extended health service, which is not insured and to which the principles of the Act do not apply. The home care workforce is largely unregulated and largely composed of women. Many work part-time and must hold multiple jobs to make an adequate income. They receive few fringe benefits and face limited career options.

The type of services, the amount of service, and the criteria for accessing services vary from province to province. The responsibility for home care has been delegated to a regional or local health authority in ten of thirteen jurisdictions. Six provinces require an income test to obtain public funding for home care.

Veterans Affairs Canada provides home care services to clients with wartime or special-duty area service when the service is not available to them through provincial and territorial programs. Home care services are also offered jointly by Indian and Northern Affairs Canada and Health Canada, which together have joint responsibility for on-reserve First Nations home care.

Many Canadian social workers are convinced that nothing short of a universal and comprehensive national home care system is necessary. While health care spending increased by 43 percent from 1997 to 2002, with 2003 spending (both public and private) totalling $121 billion, home care is still a marginal part of the health care system.

The slow pace and the piecemeal development of these services has left many without programs that properly meet their physical, emotional, and social needs.

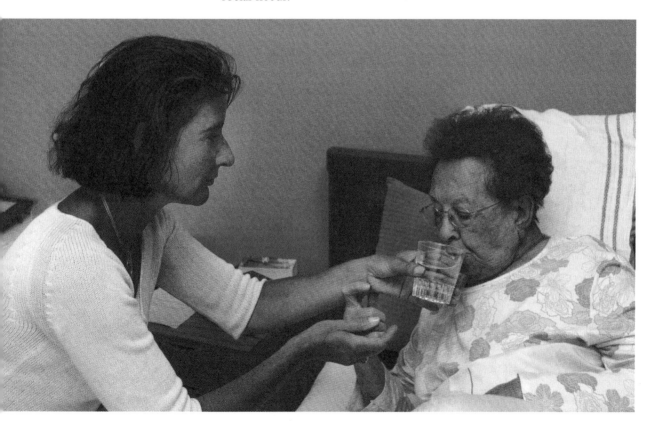

Later in life, seniors may move into situations that involve interacting with social workers, such as living in an institution or receiving home care.

Conclusion

Of course, becoming a senior does not automatically mean that you will need the services of a social worker. People age differently. Some will remain physically and mentally fit; others will face a number of problems such as isolation, health problems, loss of mobility, inadequate income and housing, discrimination, crime victimization, and abuse. It is in these more difficult situations that the social worker and other social service professionals get involved.

With the rapidly aging population, issues around home care for the elderly are increasingly important. Caring for the elderly at home puts enormous strains on their family members, not to mention the seniors themselves. However, the availability of publicly supported home care is uneven across Canada. In some provinces, such as Ontario, home care is increasingly being provided by large American health care corporations. There is a strong case that home care provision needs more public support if it is to reach all citizens and not just those who can pay for it.

As knowledge of the aging process increases, social service providers are looking at innovative ways to meet the needs of older citizens. One model or approach that appears to have wide usefulness is life course theory. Using this approach, social workers relate to seniors in different ways as they move through the different periods of their lives. Every senior's life experience is unique, but it may also have certain similarities with the experiences of others. As a way of approaching social work with the elderly, the *life course model* seems to have wide applicability.

Social work with the elderly is a growing field of social work practice. It offers not only abundant employment opportunities but also the satisfaction of helping those who are, in some cases, less able to help themselves. It is challenging, yet it is also a rewarding and highly important field of social work today and will continue to be so in the decades to come.

The Rise of the "Wellderly"

Growing old at home could be the wave of the future, if home support services are available. The Ontario government has piloted a program called Aging in Place which aims to support seniors in their homes as long as possible. Although not a panacea for those with complex medical needs, the program addresses what experts say can be a premature decision by older people to give up their homes in response to a fairly minor problem.

CHAPTER REVIEW

Key Terms

- Activity theory
- Disengagement theory
- Continuity theory
- Role theory
- Life course theory
- Ageism

- Acute pain
- Chronic pain
- Elder abuse
- Institutional abuse
- Palliative care
- Home care

Review Questions

1. What are the primary issues facing Canada's aging population with which social workers will increasingly be involved?

2. Should the mandatory age of retirement be extended? Why or why not?

3. What are the advantages of using the life course theory as a lens for effective social work practice?

4. How does the contemporary Western view of aging differ from that of other societies?

5. What are some of the issues of increasing concern regarding the elderly in Canada?

6. Define and explore the causes of the abuse and neglect of seniors in institutional settings.

7. How are seniors affected by social isolation and loneliness?

8. What are the three types of care provided by social workers who work with the elderly?

9. Discuss the role of home care in social work with the elderly.

Exploring Social Work

1. Seniors in mainstream Canadian society are often not treated with the respect and dignity afforded to elders in other communities or countries. This was touched upon in the section on Aboriginal seniors. After reflecting on why you think that this is the case, write a short two-page paper on the topic. To get started, you may want to consider the nature of our economic system, and how this has changed family relationships and living arrangements.

2. According to the Census, the vast majority of seniors (93 percent) aged 65 and over live in private households, while the remaining 7 percent reside in collective dwellings (primarily health care institutions such as nursing homes and hospitals). What kind of social work services do you believe will be necessary for seniors to continue to live on their own? What are the roles of social workers in this?

3. A major part of social work practice with the elderly is helping dying seniors deal with end-of-life difficulties including pain and despair, but also spiritual and emotional questions. Discuss this topic in small groups and do a group presentation that depicts how social workers might assist in seniors hospice care. Include reflections on the kind of training that might help social workers in this type of work.

Websites

Seniors Canada Online
www.seniors.gc.ca

This site provides access to information and services that are relevant to those 55 and older, their families, caregivers, and supporting service organizations. The publications section is great, and the listing of services available for seniors is a good resource for social workers.

Canadian Association on Gerontology (CAG)
www.cagacg.ca

Founded in 1971, the Canadian Association on Gerontology is a national, multidisciplinary scientific and educational association established to provide leadership in matters related to the aging population.

CARP: Canada's Association for the Fifty-Plus
www.carp.ca

Originally know as the Canadian Association for Retired Persons, CARP is an advocacy group dedicated to improving the quality of life for Canadians as they age. With an expansive membership and strong financial support, CARP is a powerful voice for seniors in Canada, promoting active lifestyles, financial security, access to health care, and an end to age discrimination.

CHAPTER 14

SOCIAL WORK AND SEXUAL AND GENDER DIVERSITY

- -

Celebrating Human Diversity

With the rise of **LGBTTQ** (lesbian, gay, bisexual, transgendered, transsexual, and queer) activism and the 1973 removal of homo-sexuality from the *Diagnostic and Statistical Manual of Mental Disorders* (DSM), social workers are increasingly celebrating what sexual and gender diversity contributes to the profession and to society in general. While many of the gay, lesbian, bisexual, transgendered, and trans-sexual people with whom social workers work have the same needs as their non-LGBTTQ counterparts, sexual orientation and gender identity may shape how members of LGBTTQ communities experience their problems, what resources are available to them, and the ways in which their problems are shaped by the broader society.

Historical Context

Two major developments have shaped our thinking about gender and sexuality. The first is *sexology*, which is the field of study that invented the identities of heterosexual and homosexual, and struggled with gender identity. The second is *community activism*, a movement that subsequently evolved to signify a shared history of oppression and marginalization.

Sexology

In the late nineteenth century, scientists and philosophers in Europe and North America increasingly applied notions of science and formal reason to explain and categorize the world around them. Part of that process of categorization involved documenting what was considered to be proper sexual attraction (Katz 1995, 51). It is through this process that the science of sex—**sexology**—was invented, and the "heterosexual" emerged.

It is not that same-sex and different-sex desire did not exist before this point in time, but the turn of the century marked a shift in how we made sense of these desires and behaviours. So, for example, while there are historical records throughout time of men having sex with men, such behaviour was not considered to reflect a "homosexual" or "gay" identity. In other words, before the late 1800s, the concept of "a homosexual"— that is, a person whose identity was defined by their sexual practice—did not exist.

Another aspect of the invention of sexual identities that occurred at the turn of the century is often termed *medical colonization*. The end of the nineteenth and beginning of the twentieth century was a time when medical authority increasingly began to replace pre-existing religious and judicial authority. Before this transition, gender and sexual non-conventionality were most often understood as sinful or illegal. With the rise of professional "scientific medicine," sexologists were called into courtrooms to provide evidence that such transgressions were caused by biological or neurological abnormalities that required treatment, rather than punishment.

At the turn of the century, much of the concern around sexual normality and abnormality was focused on whether people were engaging in sex primarily for reproduction (normal) or pleasure (deviant). One of the pioneers in creating categories of normal and abnormal was Richard von Krafft-Ebing (1840–1902). Krafft-Ebing's most famous piece of writing is a categorization of abnormal sexual behaviour entitled *Psychopathia Sexualis*. It is in Krafft-Ebing's work that the heterosexual begins to represent normality—he implicitly defined heterosexuality as reproductive sex between a man and a woman, and homosexuality as same-sex desire.

Heterosexism

Discriminatory laws and practices are changing to ensure that people of all sexual orientations and gender identities have equal rights and protection in our society.

Such changes challenge what is sometimes referred to as heterosexual privilege—the comfort and power accorded to people who are in, or are expected to be in, a relationship with a person of a different sex and who conform to dominant gender norms.

While some researchers were inventing the heterosexual, others were developing scientific theories of homosexuality. Karl Heinrich Ulrichs (1825–1895), a German lawyer, was one of the first to do so and was vocal in the fight to decriminalize sodomy (anal sex). Ulrichs created categories of the *Urning* (a female caught in a male body) and *Urningin* (a male caught in a female body) to make sense of same-sex attraction. He saw homosexuality as inborn and natural. Ulrichs was also one of the pioneers of gay and lesbian movements. In 1885, as a result of activists such as Ulrichs, Berlin police were convinced to stop closing down gay bars. By 1897 the first gay rights organization, the Scientific Humanitarian Committee, had been founded by German psychiatrist Magnus Hirschfeld (1868–1935). The creation of spaces for "homosexual" congregation and interaction was an important step in the development of homosexuality as an identity and homosexuals as a type of person.

Hirschfeld was one of the strongest advocates for the progressive liberalization of laws against "deviant" sexual behaviour. He fought tirelessly against paragraph 175 of the German criminal code that made male

SEX AND GENDER TERMINOLOGY

Sex and gender are often seen as the same when, in fact, they refer to quite different aspects of our identities. *Sex* (usually man or woman) is what doctors attribute to babies based largely on the size of their genitalia. In fact, sex is determined by genetics, chromosomes, and hormones, which can combine to create an indeterminate number of sexes. *Gender* has two components, first gender identity, which is the sense we have of ourselves as male, female, or transgendered, and secondly our gender role, which is our adherence to cultural norms of femininity and masculinity.

Homophobia, biphobia, and transphobia describe an individual's and/or society's fear and hatred of gay men, lesbians, bisexuals, and transgendered persons.

Sexual orientation is an emotional, romantic, sexual, or affectional attraction to another person. It is not dependent upon a person's gender identity (our sense of ourselves as being male, female or transgendered) or our ability or willingness to adhere to cultural norms of masculine or feminine (i.e., gender roles).

Transgender includes those who identify as bigender, gender benders, gender outlaws, cross-dressers, drag queens, drag kings, transvestites, and transsexuals. Some intersexuals also identify as transgender. Some transgendered persons understand their experience in dimorphic absolutes (i.e., a man trapped in a female body), while others inhabit an ambiguous zone "between" the sexes.

Transsexuals are individuals whose gender identity is at odds with their physical sex. Transsexualism is classified in the *Diagnostic and Statistical Manual* under Gender Identity Disorders. Some transsexuals undergo gender re-assignment surgery to have their anatomy coincide with their gender. Others use hormones to shape their body. Not everyone who identifies as transsexual uses medical interventions to change their physical appearance.

Intersexuals are individuals whose external sex or genitalia are indeterminate. That is, people who appear to be males but are biologically females, people with female physical attributes who are biologically males, as well as those having the external appearance of both sexes and the DNA chromosome karyotypes of both sexes.

Heterosexism is the system of oppression that assumes that heterosexuality is normal and superior.

Cissexual/Cisgender are terms used in recent academic literature to define persons who are not transsexual and who have only ever experienced their subconscious and physical as being aligned. Cissexism refers to the belief that transsexuals' identified genders are inferior to, or less authentic than, those of cissexuals. Cisgender is used by transgender activists to de-privilege those who consider themselves of normal gender expression and to allow for the understanding of transgender identities as simply variants of gender expression, not deviant statuses.

homosexuality a crime. He was the first person to systematically describe and work with transsexuals—people whose gender identity is inconsistent with their biological sex. Most importantly, he challenged the notions of sexual polarity that existed at the time, in favour of sexual pluralism. Hirschfeld suggested that gender and sex were not limited to the opposites of male and female, but were spread across a spectrum of sexual diversity.

In their efforts to provide ever-finer classifications of sexual difference, researchers sought physical markers. It was argued that one could determine a homosexual by the way that he walked, the size of his hips, the shape of his penis, or his "womanly" behaviour. Female homosexuality was seldom explored scientifically until the end of the nineteenth century. This was to some extent a result of prevailing beliefs that women lacked sexual desire and did not enjoy sex. Sexologists largely considered female homosexuality in relation to "abnormal" or enlarged clitorises, hermaphroditism, and gender-reversed body types. By the 1920s, lesbianism was linked with "inappropriate female behaviour," such as avoiding motherhood, or political activism. Many of the beliefs of early sexologists remain part of our common thinking about sexuality.

Second Generation Theorists

In the years following this early exploration, a second generation of sexologists emerged. One of the most well-known scientists of this generation was Alfred Kinsey (1894–1956). The **Kinsey Report**, published in 1948 under the title *Sexual Behavior in the Human Male*, surveyed a variety of people about their sexual habits and surprised the American public by revealing that 37 percent of men in his survey reported some homosexual experiences to the point of orgasm. He also reported that most Americans masturbated. Most significantly, he showed that people's sexual behaviours combined so-called perverse behaviours with those considered normal. In 1953, he published *Sexual Behavior in the Human Female*.

This research was groundbreaking because it suggested that everyday sexual behaviour often transgressed laws, public opinion, and social norms. However, with the rise of Cold War anti-communism in the 1950s, Kinsey's work was viewed with suspicion. Rumours spread that he was a communist, working to destroy American values. He lost his research funding and died of a heart attack two years later. Kinsey's research provided much of the basis for the political analysis that was developed by members of the gay liberation movement in the early 1970s.

The second generation of sexologists suggested that our social world plays a significant role in shaping our sexual desires and behaviours. This change in the understanding of sexuality was, in itself, a result of social and political changes. Second-generation sexologists were, for instance, influenced by the feminist movement, which challenged the notion of a woman's "natural" place in society, suggesting that the "female" gender role is as much about social expectations as any innate characteristics.

Diverse Communities and Sexuality

People's experiences of sexual or gender diversity are different depending upon their ethnicity, age, and physical abilities.

Ethnicity. Members of LGBTTQ communities are ethnically diverse. Communities of colour are no more bi/trans/homophobic than white communities.

Age. In North American, sex is largely seen as the terrain of the young. Seniors who identify as gay, bisexual, or lesbian often face discrimination.

Disability. People with disabilities are typically perceived as asexual (devoid of or without sexuality). Stereotypes make it difficult for people with disabilities to feel confident enough to seek out a partner.

The Rise of Community Activism

In spite of these new understandings, the psychiatric profession in the 1950s officially labelled homosexuality as a mental disorder. Their response to such deviance included administering drugs, giving people lobotomies, and having gay men and lesbians undergo electroshock treatment. Some lesbians endured hysterectomies and estrogen injections (Warner 2002, 24). Early gay and lesbian organizing challenged this medical authority, and homosexuality was removed from the Diagnostic and Statistical Manual (DSM-V) of the American Psychiatric Association in 1973.

World War II was an important period in the emergence of gay communities. During this period of time, the traditional patriarchal family structure was to some extent disrupted. There were increasing opportunities for people to socialize in predominantly same-sex groups. Men were in the army and at war, while many women were working together in large factories. Many people moved to cities where anonymity and lack of parental supervision also allowed more opportunities for sexual exploration. However, this freedom was quickly circumscribed by the hunt for subversives that characterized the Cold War in the 1950s. Any kind of deviance became suspect, because the logic of the day was that if someone had anything to hide (and same-sex attraction was considered something to hide) then the individual had a greater likelihood of being blackmailed into working for a foreign government (Girard 1987).

Thus, the 1950s were a terrible time for gay men and lesbians in the Canadian civil service. The RCMP collected close to 9,000 names of people within the civil service who were suspected of being lesbians or gay men (Kinsman 2003). Many of these people were subjected to police interrogation and surveillance. It was within this climate that in 1952, homosexuals were prohibited from entering Canada under the *Immigration Act*. While the next few decades were a period of easing anxieties over communism, it would not be until 1976, after significant activism, that the provision denying entrance to homosexuals was removed from the Act.

Throughout the late 1950s and 1960s there was a growing gay and lesbian political movement that began to shape public discourse and scientific understandings about sexuality. This movement symbolically coalesced on June 27 and 28, 1969, when a series of riots erupted in response to a police raid on a New York City gay bar, the Stonewall Inn. The riots, which were later called the **Stonewall Rebellion**, marked the beginning of a more public, large-scale movement for gay and lesbian rights. A new national organization, the Gay Liberation Front (GLF), was formed with the mandate of creating freedom for all oppressed people, not just members of LGBTTQ communities. Prominent transgender activists at the time, such as Sylvia Rivera and Marsha P. Johnson, who subsequently co-founded Street Transvestite Action Revolutionaries (S.T.A.R.), also were involved in clashes with the police during the Stonewall Riots.

The Heterosexual is Invented

In 1892, American doctor James Kiernan was the first to use the term heterosexual. He used the term to describe people who were seen as deviant because they had sex primarily for pleasure, not procreation, and were erotically attracted to people of both sexes. In other words "heterosexuality" was initially a perversion.

Kiernan's 1892 article was also the first North American publication to use the term homosexual, which described persons whom we would now think of as transgendered—people who bend or cross conventional gender roles (Katz 1995).

Egale Canada

www.egale.ca

This organization is a LGBTTQ rights group focused on equity and justice issues across Canada.

In the 1970s gay and lesbian organizations were able to work systematically to begin challenging laws that limited the civil and social rights of members of LGBTTQ communities. An important year for the recognition of the civil rights of gays, lesbians, and bisexual persons in Canada was 1969. With the passing of Bill C-150 and then-Justice Minister Pierre Trudeau's statement that "there is no place for the State in the bedrooms of the nation," gross indecency and buggery—the legal terms used to describe gay sex—were decriminalized if committed in private between two consenting adults over the age of 21.

Since that time, there have been a number of changes to the Criminal Code. The age of consent for anal sex is now 18, two years more than the age for other forms of sexual activity, despite court decisions that this difference is unconstitutional. While same-sex sexual activity was decriminalized in 1969, it was not until decades later that it became illegal to discriminate against gay men, lesbians, and bisexual persons in the areas of immigration, employment, military service, housing, pensions and other benefits, marriage, and custody of children. The removal of prohibitions against same-sex relations had little effect on the lives of transsexual people. Discrimination against transgendered and transsexual people is, even today, not explicitly illegal under the same human rights laws that formally recognize the human rights of gay, lesbian, and bisexual persons.

Queer Activism

Queer—a disparaging term often directed at gay men and lesbians—was reclaimed by LGBTTQ communities to represent an inclusive celebration of all persons whose sexual and gender expression differs from heterosexual norms. The founders of the first queer activist group, Queer Nation, were from ACT UP, a radical AIDS activist group that was instrumental in having pharmaceutical companies and governments finally respond to the AIDS pandemic.

As gay and lesbian activism became more powerful, institutionalized, and less radical in the 1990s, a space opened up for grassroots **queer activism** that demanded dramatic changes to the ways we understand difference and diversity. Activists popularized the use of the term "queer" to be "more inclusive of sexual minorities and other marginalized people...By adopting queer they reclaimed and politicized a derogatory term commonly used before gay and lesbian liberation. It represented the belief in an identity that is more ambiguous and more fluid than gay, lesbian, or homosexual" (Warner 2002, 262).

Queer activists distanced themselves from gay and lesbian organizing by critiquing identity-based movements. Queer activists are skeptical of viewing identities as coherent, stable, and with clear boundaries. They suggest that such identities mask a significant amount of diversity among the members within categories, and also ignore similarities between different categories.

Freud and Sexuality

Sigmund Freud (see Chapter 4, page 67) critiqued many of the biological explanations for homosexuality, coming close to arguing that masculinity and femininity are socially constructed. However, Freud also suggested that homosexuality is an immature stage of development, less developed than heterosexuality. Freud's theories about sexuality marked an important move away from biology to psychology, but his approach, as adopted by psychologists, was not necessarily liberating for gay men and lesbians. More often, Freud's theories were mobilized to further pathologize homosexuality as a mental illness that needed to be cured.

Theoretical Perspectives

This short account of modern Western responses to sexual diversity highlights the shifting theoretical understandings of sexuality. These theories each provide a piece of the very complex puzzle of sexuality, but none have been able completely to explain the complex and multiple ways we constitute our gender identity, sexual desire, and sexual practices and how this varies through history and cultural context.

AIDS AND SEXUALITY

Over the past three decades, AIDS has had a significant impact on our thinking about sexuality. It ushered in an era of safer sex practices that has broadened our discussion about sexual practices. Today at least 40 million people worldwide are HIV positive. The epidemic has hit low-income countries the hardest, affecting men and women equally. In sub-Saharan Africa alone, there are more than 13 million orphans whose parents have died from AIDS.

In North America and much of Europe, AIDS has taken an enormous toll on gay communities. In the beginning of the epidemic in North America in the 1980s, AIDS was perceived as a gay disease. This resulted in an increase in homophobia and gay bashing. Gay men often found it hard to find doctors and dentists who would offer care. They lost their jobs as a result of HIV/AIDS and received substandard care in hospitals. Gay and lesbian communities responded to this hostility and a lack of response by mobilizing their own creativity and resources. While governments, health care systems, and pharmaceutical companies were very slow in responding to the pandemic, the LGBTTQ community organized ways to take care of itself. This history of volunteerism and activism is strong within LGBTTQ communities. They established educational campaigns, hospices, and their own support networks. Community activists continue to be very involved in the struggle to ensure that medicine to treat HIV/AIDS is accessible to everyone.

Over the past three decades many gay men have experienced successive losses of partners, friends, and colleagues. After decades of loss and trauma, many older gay men now experience survivor guilt, which can affect their well-being. Other gay men continue to live with HIV/AIDS and the uncertainty of how long new treatments will ensure they can live reasonably healthy lives. Many people who are taking AIDS medications are also living with the side effects of these drugs, which can be severe and disabling. Moreover, decades of using condoms and being continually concerned about the possibility of becoming infected has left some gay men longing for the intimacy of skin to skin sex; so there has been a rise in what is called barebacking—penetrative sex without a condom.

The desire for the intimacy of intercourse without condoms is not just an experience of gay men, but has been one of many reasons why people of all sexual orientations and genders continue to practice unsafe sex. For others, sex is too uncomfortable to talk about or their partners are clear that they do not want to use condoms. If people live in abusive relationships, negotiating condom use can be an impossibility. As a result, in addition to condom use, international activists have increasingly focused attention on microbicides, which are a range of products that have the ability to prevent the sexual transmission of HIV and other sexually transmitted diseases. Microbicides can be produced as gels, creams, suppositories, films, or as a sponge or ring that releases the active ingredient over time.

Microbicides are increasingly important as we realize that it is the people in our society with the least economic and social power who are at the greatest risk of HIV. For these persons, negotiating condom use or abstaining from sex is made more difficult by the structural oppression they experience in their daily lives. For example, many women around the world cannot risk angering their male partners because to do so would threaten their shelter and their access to the money and resources necessary for survival. Despite the hopefulness of microbicides, they too have limits. For women without a place to hide a microbicide, it may not be possible for them to keep the substance in their home without risking violence from their partner.

Biological Determinism

Early sexologists attempted to explain sexuality in terms of biology. These explanations are understood as **biological determinism**, which has traditionally focused on the organic causes of non-conventional gender and sexual identities and behaviours. This continues today. Recently, Simon LeVay, former Harvard University researcher and founder of the Institute of Gay and Lesbian Education, argued that the brain structures of gay men differ from those of heterosexual men. We have also witnessed the hunt for the "gay gene." Such theories have been used to demand rights for queer communities on the grounds that queer persons are *born* queer.

While it has a certain potential for liberation, biological determinism also has serious limitations. Firstly, the argument that sexual diversity and gender identity are rooted in biology has not ended homophobia, heterosexism, and cissexualism. In fact, it has often been used to entrench inequality. Secondly, scientific "truths" have consistently been shown to reflect current socio-political norms and values. The search for a clear identifiable difference also raises ethical concerns; what if parents want to test their fetus for the "gay gene" and choose abortion based on the results? This line of reasoning also accentuates the differences that heterosexual privilege relies upon, rather than exploring the similarities shared by people who desire those of a different sex and those of the same sex.

Social Constructionism

Another group of theories fall under the heading of **social constructionism**. These are predominantly the theories of the second generation of sexologists. Using this perspective, theorists argue that sexualities are constructed by our social and cultural context and by our cultural histories. It is as a result of such theories that gender reassignment surgery at birth was introduced for babies who were determined to be intersexuals—persons whose sexual organs are not clearly male or female. It is also why psycho-therapeutic approaches to "curing" sexual orientation (if an individual is attracted to people of the same sex) or gender identity (if inconsistent with an individual's sex) evolved.

While it is clear that society plays a large role in our sexual and gender expression, this theory has a number of shortcomings. First, research has found that people cannot change their sexual orientation: while some individuals can decide not to act on their desires, the desires themselves do not disappear. Equally, babies who have been reassigned a gender at birth, either as a result of a botched circumcision or because of having ambiguous genitalia, have not easily reinvented themselves as the gendered subjects that doctors have chosen for them. Many face challenges once they enter puberty and find that their gender identity is incompatible with their sex. It seems clear that our sex, gender expression, and sexual orientation rely upon at least some biological potentials.

Biological Determinism

Theory that an individual's personality, behaviour, and attitude is determined by genes, minimizing the role of the environment.

Social Constructionism

Theory that sexualities and gender identities are constructed by our social and cultural context and experience.

Queer Theory

Queer Theory

Maintains that sexual and gender behaviours, identities, and categories are social constructs.

One significant theory that has recently emerged to explain sexuality and gender falls largely within the social constructionism school of thought—**Queer theory**. This body of thought raises doubts about the possibility that legislative changes within a capitalist democracy will result in liberation. Indeed, these theorists argue for radical transformation.

By the late 1980s, people began to see the ways in which people of colour, women, and members of LGBTTQ communities were still marginalized, discriminated against, and oppressed, despite hard-won legislative protections. Such observations led some activists to conclude that the existing social structures of Western society, while having many benefits, also have some fundamental problems that limit the possibility for freedom, equality, and justice.

Queer activists and theorists argue for a rethinking of the entire terrain upon which we create categories of people and distribute power among them. In part, Queer theory responds to the realization that many people do not fit easily or neatly into the binary oppositions of man–woman, heterosexual–homosexual, and so on. Queer theorists suggest that identifying as gay or straight does not provide an unquestionable or complete description of who people are sexually attracted to, whom they have sex with, or with whom they share loving relationships.

Queer theory is informed by the work of Michel Foucault (1926–1984), who wrote persuasively that the entire social structure through which we make sense of sexuality is a modern invention. He insisted that there is nothing "natural" about sexual expression—our behaviours and understandings are a product of the particular era (and the social regulations therein) in which we live. Foucault highlighted the social mechanisms that were at work in societies where particular sexual desires and practices were promoted, denied, or punished, and how these resulted in people resisting social regulations by organizing themselves around their sexuality.

Many Queer theorists and others who theorize about sexuality have attempted to challenge the polarization that exists between biological determinism and social constructionism. This theory lets us attend to the ways in which our biological makeup intersects with cultural norms to produce our particular gender, sex, and sexual orientation.

Queer theory has much to say about transgendered people—those whose gender identities blend or reject the "gender binary." Transsexual people, however, see their foundation within their innate knowledge of their embodied sex, though counter both to their anatomy and what is assigned at birth. While the expression of their affirmed sex may well be influenced by their environment, it is built upon an understanding of their sexual identity that remains beyond the knowledge of those whose

RECENT DEVELOPMENTS IN LGBTTQ RIGHTS IN CANADA

In February 2001, the *Immigration and Refugee Protection Act* was reformed so that same-sex partners are recognized as members of the family class of immigrants. Now a common-law partner is recognized as someone who has been in a conjugal relationship for at least one year. If the applicant lives within Canada, then there is a cohabitation requirement in place. Refugee processes have also begun to recognize that people might have legitimate refugee claims because of fears that they will be persecuted for their sexual orientation in their country of origin.

Until 1992, gays, lesbians, and bisexuals were not allowed to serve in the Canadian military. Similarly, it was not until 1996 that federal employees could claim benefits for their same-sex partners. In 1999, the Act regulating survivor benefits, the *Public Service Superannuation Act*, was amended to extend such benefits to same-sex couples. Also in 1996, the *Canadian Human Rights Act* was finally amended to explicitly prohibit discrimination based on sexual orientation. However, human rights protection at a national level has yet to be extended to transgendered persons.

The most comprehensive package of changes for people living in same-sex relationships came with Bill C-23, the *Act to Modernize Benefits and Obligations*. This bill amended 68 federal statutes to provide everyone within any common-law relationship with nearly all the rights and responsibilities of heterosexual married couples under federal law.

Legal battles were also fought to challenge Canada's "obscenity" laws which allowed Canada Customs to confiscate gay literature, including safer sex material that depicted anal sex. In December 2000, the Supreme Court of Canada confirmed that Canada Customs discriminated against lesbian, gay, bisexual, and transgendered materials, and placed the burden on the Crown to prove obscenity as opposed to requiring community bookstores or other importers to defend against the charge.

It was not until 2001 that the Canadian Census asked whether people "were living with a common-law partner," which was defined to include both opposite and same-sex partners. For many gay men, lesbians, and bisexual persons, this term still does not represent their relationships. "Common-law" is generally used to describe a heterosexual relationship. No questions were asked about Canadians' sexual orientation, nor was the opportunity provided for respondents to identify as transgendered. Such silences make the experience of people with diverse sexual identities and gender expression invisible, and thus conveys, at best, insignificance, and at worst, shame and disdain.

In 2005, Canada enacted federal legislation providing for marriage for same-sex partners. Prior to this, Ontario, Saskatchewan, British Columbia, and the Northwest Territories allowed same-sex couples the right to be legally married.

life questions do not touch upon what it is to be a man, what it is to be a woman, to be both or neither. Only after such questions are answered is it possible to begin to consider who one is attracted to. Many transsexual people seek only to live their lives in their affirmed sex—not to challenge the "gender binary."

This has often led to friction with those who adopt "queer identities" and may well explain why the human rights status of transsexual people lags far behind that of gay, lesbian, and bisexual people.

PFLAG

Families and friends of queer people also sometimes need support, and support each other. It is important to not just consider the needs of people's biological families, but also the needs of people's chosen families.

The largest family organization is PFLAG, which includes parents and friends of gay, lesbian, bisexual, and transgendered persons (see Chapter 7, page 118).

Social Work Counselling

In 1999, Carol-Anne O'Brien highlighted the ways in which social work may be implicated in the pathologization of gay, lesbian, and bisexual identities. She found that social workers often promote the belief that homosexuality is a phase that some people pass through. She concluded that the most common way social workers reinforce heteronormativity—the "normalcy" of heterosexuality—is through silence about non-heterosexual identities. This is exacerbated by the lack of openly gay, lesbian, bisexual, transgendered, or transsexual role models in the profession.

There are two extremes in social work counselling with lesbians, bisexuals, transgendered or transsexual persons, and gay men. The first is when social workers exaggerate the difficulties of living in a heterosexist society. In this context, counsellors tend to obscure that LGBTTQ persons are often happy and have positive relationships with family members, straight colleagues, and friends. The second extreme occurs when workers assume that sexual orientation and gender identity make no difference to a person's experience. The challenge is to find a way of working between these extremes and providing balanced support to members of queer communities (van Wormer et al. 2001).

There has been a long history of people in social work who challenge the heterosexist norms of society. Gay men, lesbians, bisexuals, transgendered and transsexual persons have enriched society as a whole and our profession specifically. Their contributions have helped to develop queer-positive practice, AIDS services, responses to women's health and activism for social justice, and have contributed to social work knowledge and practice.

The homophobia, transphobia, and heterosexism institutionalized within schools, the health care system and social services have led many gay, lesbian, bisexual, transgendered, and transsexual people to feel reluctant to ask for help. As a result, LGBTTQ communities are developing queer-positive social services. These organizations are involved in policy change, community organizing, and individual advocacy and service provision. Most medium and large cities have social services specifically organized to meet the needs of LGBTTQ persons.

The personal experience of heterosexism and oppression is felt through stigma, stress, guilt, and shame. It is often difficult to accept one's sexual and romantic attractions to people of the same sex because we live in a society that is generally hostile to such desires. It is equally difficult to accept one's sexual identities as different to what one is assigned at birth. As a result, many members of LGBTTQ communities experience internalized homophobia. External cultural messages that suggest that lesbians, transgendered and transsexual people, and gay men are somehow failing to meet social standards become internalized as guilt, shame, and stress.

This can, though does not necessarily, result in members of LGBTTQ communities struggling with self-acceptance. On average, gay adolescents and young men are six to sixteen times more at risk for attempting suicide (Dorais 2004). Studies have shown that it is not gay sexuality that causes suicide, but rather having a homosexual or bisexual orientation in highly homophobic environments. Young gay men, lesbians, and transgendered youth are known to experience both ostracism and harassment in their everyday lives. They are sometimes rejected by their families and end up on the streets, where they are vulnerable to sexual and physical violence.

Coming Out of the Closet

Young gay men and lesbians often feel as though they are a tiny minority and that no one in their immediate environment will be like them. Teachers and administrators often turn a blind eye to sexist and homophobic comments. Gay teachers often have to keep their sexual orientation a secret for fear of being exposed and possibly losing their jobs. In turn, queer youth are more likely to drop out of school, especially since they have few role models.

Coming out is a process through which gay and lesbian people disclose their sexual orientation to themselves and others. Those who keep their LGBTTQ identity secret are referred to as living "inside the closet" (because the closet is used in our culture as a metaphor for keeping secrets). Therefore when one reveals one's identity, it is said that he or she is "coming out of the closet." Because many people assume that everyone, or at least the people closest to them, are straight, and because homosexuality and bisexuality and transgendered and transsexual persons are stigmatized, LGBTTQ persons have a particular set of challenges when it comes to openly claiming their identity. It is also a process through which transgendered persons can experiment with gender identities until they find one that fits. In such situations, it is often important for people to be open with their family members and friends.

Coming out can be a difficult and terrifying process, as families and friends can and sometimes do react badly. This said, many gay men, transgendered persons and lesbians report feeling relief once they have come out and no longer have to hide their feelings. People who live lives "out of the closet" tend to have fewer experiences of isolation and depression.

Some people are only out to themselves and their partners. Others are out to family and friends, but remain closeted at work. There are many variations in how "out" someone is. Social workers can help support people through the coming out process, but they need to be careful to also respect what people are saying. If people are not ready to come out, or assess the risks to be too high, it is important to trust that they are the experts in their own experience and to support them.

Coming Out

Katherine van Wormer and her colleagues (2000) identify a number of stages of coming out.

Not everyone goes through these stages, or necessarily goes through them in this order. Also, people can be content without moving through all the stages:

- The first stage occurs before a person comes out. People may feel discomfort, but do not consciously recognize themselves as being attracted to people of the same sex or as not fitting within their assigned gender.

- The second stage takes place when people begin to become aware of their same-sex attraction or their gender discomfort.

- In the third stage, "exploration," people develop gay, lesbian, or transgender friendships and participate in the LGBTTQ community.

- The final stage is marked by integration— people accept their identities and incorporate their identities into their lives.

Counselling Issues

For social workers who are gay, lesbian, bisexual, transgendered, or transsexual, there are issues to consider when working with clients and colleagues:

Jan Buterman speaks to protestors at the Alberta Legislature in September 2009. A transgendered teacher from the Edmonton area, Buterman was dropped by the Roman Catholic school board after being told his gender change from woman to man is not aligned with the teachings of the Catholic church.

- Social workers who are gay, lesbian, bisexual, transgendered, or transsexual can be excellent role models for people who are dealing with their own same-sex desire or transgendered identity. Hiding one's sexual orientation can send a message that gay, lesbian, or bisexual persons are ashamed. Hiding one's gender identity or history can also send the message that transgendered and transsexual people are ashamed. However, LGTTBQ social workers also have to assess the risks that might accompany coming out in your workplaces, particularly as clients are not bound to confidentiality.

- It may also be challenging for sexual or gender diverse social workers to deal with clients who are hostile to LGBTTQ communities. It may be appropriate for these clients to be referred to a heterosexual counsellor, particularly if you feel threatened.

- As members of a marginalized community, often the risks of making mistakes are higher as they may be attributed to your identity or community. This may add pressure to your work if you are not practising in a queer-positive workplace. It is important to try to find allies and people who can offer support.

- Gay, lesbian, transgendered, and bisexual service providers can also be uncomfortable with some forms of sexual and gender diversity. You can also have stereotypes and beliefs that you have to think through when working with members of LGBTTQ communities.

Working in a small community can present particular challenges. You are more likely to meet clients outside of the counsellor-client relationship. It is important to be aware of the possibility of roles overlapping and to get support from colleagues to help with maintaining professional boundaries.

Social Work with Members of Intersexual Communities

Social workers can play a key role as society struggles with long-held misconceptions that sex is a binary category (which has only two possibilities, male or female). At the individual level, social workers can support parents whose newborns transgress the sex binary most of us take for granted, reassuring that their child is normal and can have a fulfilling life.

Parents also need information, and sometimes advocacy, so that they can negotiate with doctors regarding what medical interventions they want taken or whether they would rather wait until their child reaches puberty to see what biological potentials become visible. The Intersex Society of North America argues that intersexuality is mainly a problem of stigma and trauma and not gender, and that intersex children (whose external sex or genitalia is indeterminate) should not undergo surgery, but should be assigned a gender based on their genetic and hormonal test results.

Social Work with Transgendered and Transsexual Persons

While transgendered and transsexual persons deal with the same life issues that affect people who are not negotiating their gender identity, there are some counselling issues that may arise that are specific to members of transgendered and transsexual communities. Particularly, many transgendered and transsexual persons experience harassment, physical violence, and estrangement from family and friends.

In addition to brokering appropriate services, social work practitioners may also help to advocate for the needs of transgendered and transsexual persons. The following are useful points to consider in this context:

- Just because someone presents outwardly as a particular gender, it does not mean that person sees themselves as always, or even often, fitting within that gender norm.

- People make sense of gender discomfort in many ways. Attempting to be supportive of how people understand their gender, however complicated or counterintuitive, is important.

- There are no "cures" for transsexualism. In fact, the profession of social work has largely discredited practices of conversion therapy that are sometimes used to "treat" homosexuality and gender identity disorders such as transsexualism. To the contrary, the problems experienced by persons who are transsexual or transgendered are often a result of society's hostility towards people who do not fit within dominant gender norms.

- Gender transitioning, hormonal therapy, or sex reassignment surgery are some of the options for people who are transsexual.

- Gender transitions can cause a great deal of anxiety and uncertainty in a family, so support for family members is also important. Couples and families do sometimes stay together during and after a gender transition.

- Employers/workplaces may need education and sensitivity training to respond respectfully to someone making a gender transition.

The social and regulatory issues that surround sex reassignment are highly specialized areas of practice. In most large cities there are practitioners who specialize in gender counselling. It is important, when possible, to provide support and refer people to counsellors with expertise in this area.

Social workers might also play an important role in challenging how we organize washrooms, personal identification, and demographic forms that exclude, marginalize, and silence people who do not fit within the binaries of male and female or seek transition from one to the other (e.g., washrooms can be dangerous spaces for someone who does not fit within gender binaries. If someone cannot pass as the "appropriate" gender, transgendered persons often face verbal harassment, and sometimes physical violence).

Transitions for Transsexual People

While the stages of coming out describe those who become aware of their same-sex attraction and those whose gender discomfort falls short of full identification with the opposite sex, only transition through the several aspects of their lives allows the integration of transsexual people into society.

This process—"transition is a process, not an event" is often heard among transsexual people—is governed by an international document formerly called the Benjamin Standards of Care, which is revised periodically by an international association.

This document recognizes the only path for the integration of those who identify with the opposite sex is the triadic therapy of hormones, gender transition, and genital surgery.

CREATING A QUEER-POSITIVE SPACE

For social workers who are not members of LGBTTQ communities, the following are some preliminary guidelines for creating the space for diverse sexual and gender identities in your practice:

- Never assume people are heterosexual. Use words like "partner" and other gender-inclusive language. When asking a person about their life, explicitly articulate the possibility that a person may be attracted to people of the same sex. For instance, you can ask if a person is dating a man, woman, or a transgendered person—in other words, leave open the possibility of non-heterosexual relationships.

- If someone discloses that they are transgendered, gay, lesbian, or bisexual, it is important for social workers to affirm and validate their identity. Queer-positive counsellors view same-sex desire and transgender identities as normal human diversity. Similarly, they recognize same-sex relationships as having the same value as heterosexual partnerships.

- It is important to remain aware of your feelings about gender and sexual diversity. You cannot expect to grow up in a culture that is hostile to gender and sexual diversity and not internalize some of those feelings and stereotypes. If you cannot provide affirming counselling, or if someone would prefer to work with a counsellor who is a member of a LGBTTQ community, then you are obliged, whenever possible, to make the appropriate referrals.

- Sometimes heterosexual counsellors avoid their own discomfort with same-sex desire by letting gay, lesbian, and bisexual clients talk only about their positive experiences of sexual diversity, but not their struggles with feelings of shame or ambivalence.

- When working in areas of sexuality or gender that are uncomfortable, heterosexual counsellors may say supportive things, but their body language may convey discomfort. Body language may do more to alienate clients with diverse sexual and gender identities.

- When working with clients to explore the problems that people bring to counselling, it is important to explore homophobia and heterosexism as problems rather than perceiving sexual or gender diversity, in themselves, as being the problem.

- It is important to see a client's decision to accept a transgendered, bisexual, gay, or lesbian identity as one of many positive outcomes of counselling.

- Gay men, lesbians, bisexuals, and transgendered persons often seek social work support for issues similar to their non-queer counterparts. These problems may also be shaped by their experience of oppression. LGBTTQ persons may also struggle with issues of depression, suicide, alcoholism, and drug abuse, all of which can be prevalent among persons who live in a society that is hostile to their identity, desires, and relationships.

- Support colleagues who are gay, lesbian, bisexual, or transgendered. Do not rely on them to teach you about sexual or gender diversity.

- Increase your own self awareness. This begins by exploring the heterosexist attitudes that we have all developed as a result of living in a heterosexist culture. In particular, it can be helpful to unpack our binary assumptions about gender and sexual orientation.

Many of us also need to move from positions of pity, tolerance, and acceptance to explore ways we can celebrate diversity and to encourage others to do the same. If you are heterosexual, it is important to challenge the ways you take your heterosexual privilege for granted. If you identify as LGBTTQ, it is important to be aware of over-identifying with clients who are queer identified. Particularly in small, tight-knit queer communities, it is important to be careful about boundaries and dual relationships.

However we identify, we need to ensure we have the emotional and intellectual competency to provide queer-positive services. We need to think through what we communicate about the worth of LGBTTQ persons. If straight, what feelings are aroused if you imagine having a same-sex partner? Ask yourself: What homoerotic fantasies, feelings, or behaviours have I had or do I have and can I celebrate these parts of myself? In terms of intellectual competency, we need to attain sound information and training in issues of concern for LGBTTQ persons.

Despite the range of sexual and gender variety, many people assume that everyone is heterosexual and **cissexual** (having a gender identity or gender role that society considers appropriate for the sex one was assigned at birth—the prefix "cis" is pronounced like "sis"). For example, how many heterosexuals and cissexuals have to think twice before putting a photograph of their partner up in their office? Without thinking through the ways in which heterosexuals and cissexuals move through the world, without an awareness of or support for gender and sexual diversity, heterosexual and cissexual social workers may consciously and unconsciously maintain heterosexual and cissexual privilege.

Social Work with Persons who are Homophobic

Often in practice social workers encounter people who are hostile to persons who identify as lesbian, gay, or bisexual. Generally, individual feelings of homophobia are rooted in three different areas:

- **Religion.** For some people, religious beliefs result in a hostility towards people who are attracted to persons of the same sex. In this situation, it can help to refer to other religious teachings that promote acceptance and understanding. In addition, some authors have argued that religious texts have been interpreted in homophobic terms, but that the original text does not have homophobic references. For example, Daniel Helminiak's book, *What the Bible Really Says About Homosexuality*, may be helpful.

- **Insecurity in gender roles.** Sometimes homophobic feelings are about one's own insecurity in one's gender identity. In this situation, exploring childhood messages about sexuality and gender and encouraging increased self-reflection can help to reframe the situation and make encounters with persons of diverse gender and sexual identities less threatening.

- **Negative past experience with someone who identified as lesbian, gay, or bisexual.** At times, people develop homophobic responses because of a negative experience with someone who identifies as LGBTTQ. In this situation, it can often be helpful to increase someone's exposure to more positive experiences, first through film or books, and, when possible and safe for others, with people who are members of LGBTTQ communities.

In all of these situations, the challenge is to develop compassion for people who show so little compassion for others and to see how such attitudes are often a survival skill for people who feel powerless and insecure. In these situations, it can be important to help people refocus their anger in a more appropriate and positive way that encourages healthy living.

Intersex Society of North America

www.isna.org

This organization advocates for intersex children and adults and works to end the shame and stigma that lead to forced genital surgery; this website provides extensive information on causes and types of conditions that lead to a person being intersex.

Implications for LGBTTQ-Positive Practice

It is a mistake to make assumptions about a person's sexual behaviour based upon the way in which he or she identifies. As a society, we learned this lesson well during the AIDS crisis. Initially, it was assumed that the virus only affected gay men, and we paid no attention to the fact that straight men sleep with other men and gay men have sex with women. Social workers need to be careful not to assume that people's identities signify a set of consistent sexual practices at one time, or over their lifespans.

CASE STUDY: GLBTTQ COMMITTEE AT SOMERSET WEST CHC

In 2004–2005 a cultural competency project was completed to help guide Ottawa's Community Health Centres and Community Resource Centres to become safe places for gay, lesbian, bisexual, transgendered, two-spirited, and queer-identified persons. The goals of this project were to respond to anecdotal and survey data that has consistently found that many members of LGBTTQ communities are reluctant to seek health and social services as a result of negative past experiences or fears that they will be stigmatized and silenced by service providers. The project outlined indicators that could help providers assess and then improve upon how welcoming health centres and resource centres were to members of LGBTTQ communities.

The problems that LGBTTQ persons face when seeking health and social services are seldom the result of people feeling explicitly hateful or hostile to persons who are queer identified. Instead, most negative experiences unfold because service providers assume patients and clients are heterosexual, lack knowledge of LGBTTQ experiences and/or are uncomfortable when a client or patient discloses a gender identity or sexual orientation that does not fit within the heterosexual and gender norms of our society. These are often well-meaning, well educated, talented professionals, but the results of their lack of knowledge and discomfort can be hurtful and isolating. They can present a significant barrier to service for members of LGBTTQ communities.

As a result of the heterosexist culture in which we live and work, it is important for health and social services to make explicit their commitment to LGBTTQ persons. Otherwise people may assume the organization reflects broader heterosexist norms and expectations. The cultural competency project initiated a process through which health centres and resources centres could challenge heterosexism. In response, key staff and board members at Somerset West Community Health Centre (SWCHC) organized the GLBTTQ Committee to look at how their health centre could create a welcoming space for queer identified persons from a wide range of cultural and ethnic groups who are served through the centre.

Over the past few years, the committee has worked closely with the SWCHC Board and senior leadership to increase the welcoming nature of the health centre. This has included ensuring that the mission statement makes explicit reference to the needs of people who may face additional challenges as a result of their gender identity and/or sexual orientation. They have also worked to have the rainbow stripes visible on the health centre's website, posters, and publications. For many members of LGBTTQ communities the rainbow stripes quickly communicate an organization's commitment to celebrate gay, lesbian, bisexual, transgendered, transsexual, and queer persons and their contributions to society.

Most recently, the committee developed a survey that explored the knowledge that health centre staff have regarding LGBTTQ issues. The purpose of this survey was to provide the centre with some baseline data from which they could understand staff knowledge about LGBTTQ persons and experiences, gaps in service and any barriers to providing services to members of queer communities. From this, the committee is making suggestions about staff training and support that might help to increase knowledge and decrease discomfort with LGBTTQ issues while providing services to multiple and diverse marginalized communities.

Thanks to the Somerset West Community Health Centre GLBTTQ Committee for their help in crafting this case study.

The range of gender identities and sexual behaviours and attractions that humans experience can at times be confusing. Social workers need to remain supportive, and be open-minded to new situation and to the possibility that the people they are working with may experience confusion.

Social work as a field now maintains that people cannot change their sexual orientation. Sexual orientation usually emerges in early adolescence without any prior sexual experience—choice is not a factor. We now understand that gender identities may not fit within a male/female binary and that some people experience incongruity between their sex and gender identity. While social workers actively support people who are questioning their sexual orientation or struggling with homophobia and heterosexism, it is generally considered unethical to work with someone to change their sexual orientation.

Gay, lesbian, bisexual, transgendered, transsexual, or queer people often prefer working with counsellors who are members of LGBTTQ communities. We need to learn not to take these preferences as an attack on our abilities as social workers. Counsellors who identify as gay, lesbian, bisexual, or queer likely know more about issues of concern to people who are negotiating their sexual orientation or gender identity. LGBTTQ counsellors can act as role models, and appropriate self-disclosure can decrease a client's sense of isolation.

Thousands of people watch the annual Pride Parade in Toronto in June 2009. Toronto will be the host city for WorldPride 2014, a festival that promotes acceptance and diversity on an international level.

THE SEX TRADE
What Social Workers Should Know

The exchange of sex for money is often referred to as the "oldest profession," as it can be traced far back in human history. The sex trade has a particular shape in our modern, globalized society. In Canada it is illegal to engage in activities that facilitate prostitution. However, in some Canadian cities, municipal governments have tried to regulate the sex trade by licensing escort services.

By trying to legalize the sex trade, many people argue that we move to make it safer for sex trade workers. Many sex trade workers who are victims of crimes do not go to the police because they are afraid that they will be charged with prostitution. The fear of going to jail also leads workers to isolated, dark spaces that only increase the dangers of their work. Because of the dangers involved in prostitution, many sex trade workers rely on a pimp, usually a man, who manages their work for a fee. Pimps often provide sex trade workers with protection from violence, bail in the event of an arrest, and sometimes a place to live. For these services the pimp will take a percentage (or all) of the sex trade worker's income. Pimps are also often violent and abusive towards the women they manage.

Many, but not all, sex trade workers are poor, and in the sex trade, there is a class hierarchy. Some women work as expensive escorts and earn a great deal of money for their services (as do some men). At the other end of the spectrum are people who walk the streets and receive money to help pay the rent, pay for food, or to help finance their drug or alcohol addiction.

There are also teenagers (many of whom are gay, lesbian, bisexual, or transgendered) who work in the sex trade so that they can earn money to live. Many of these teenagers have left or been kicked out of their homes and must earn a living to survive on the streets. Prostitution is often referred to as survival sex—the only means by which people can support themselves.

At the same time, it is important to note that not everyone who works in the sex trade feels coerced into doing so. Some women, men, and teenagers say that they are making a living and that sex trade work should be considered to be a job like any other type of work. Increasingly, sex trade workers have challenged social workers to not always see them as victims. Some people say that they are making good, sound choices and that sex work is only stigmatized because of the way people who are not in the sex trade perceive it.

Most people who pay for sex services are male and they do so for a number of reasons. Some want sex without a commitment, or because they want sex that is novel or kinky. Other times, men do not feel comfortable asking for certain types of sexual activities with their partners, so they seek out the services of sex trade workers. Oftentimes, men are away from home and want to purchase sex. Some men hire sex trade workers because they are lonely and are not able to have sexual intimacy in their personal relationships.

There is increasing concern about prostitution on a global scale, particularly about the global trafficking in women. In these situations, women are promised citizenship in a country such as Canada, but when they arrive are forced to live in inhumane conditions and work as prostitutes. Also, legislatures in many income-poor countries are starting to address the problem of wealthy Westerners travelling to income-poor countries to pay for sex with children. Both of these issues present particular challenges as those who are providing services often have little, if any, choice as to whether they participate in the sex trade.

Social workers often work with sex trade workers who are in trouble with the law or who are dealing with the challenges of poverty. People who work in the sex trade are human beings who have private lives. Many of them have families, children, and partners. In addition, for many people leaving the sex trade is very difficult because they have few other economic choices; without sufficient education or job experience, many people feel that the sex trade is the only way for them to support their families and pay the rent.

If you are straight and cissexual and working with a gay, lesbian, or bisexual person, or a person who is questioning their gender identity, it is often helpful to ask the individual if they would prefer to work with a member of an LGBTTQ community and facilitate that referral. If such a connection is not possible, it is important not to rely on the client to educate you about issues of sexual orientation or gender identity. You need to seek out literature and training opportunities. Heterosexual and cissexual counsellors can also model respect and acceptance of a person who is lesbian, gay, bisexual, transgendered, or transsexual.

Conclusion

Across the world and throughout history there has been a broad spectrum of social responses to sexual and gender diversity. At one end of this spectrum, many indigenous cultures have traditionally been accepting of sexual and gender diversity. At the other end, non-conventional gender and sexual expression has been considered a sign of immorality that may be, even today, punishable by death in some countries.

In Canada, many social workers are part of the movement to challenge heterosexual privilege and to celebrate people, including colleagues, who are lesbian, gay, bisexual, transgendered, transsexual, and/or queer. Gay and lesbian social workers and their allies have been leaders in initiating a community response to AIDS. Social workers have been active in the movement to change laws that discriminate against members of LGBTTQ communities, and have worked with queer persons to celebrate their diversity and the contributions they make to our communities.

To be sure, the struggle for sexual and gender equality is far from over, and it is important that social workers continue to be participants in this long struggle. Among other things, social workers need to reflect on their own practice to ensure that they do not reproduce heterosexism or cissexualism (see sidebar on page 307) in their silence, or replicate myths and stereotypes about sexuality or gender diversity. In addition, gay-positive and queer-positive values must not be sidelined or ignored but rather brought to the forefront as required.

Possibly more than in other areas, the complex issues surrounding sexual and gender diversity present challenges both to social work theory and to social work practice. To be effective in addressing these issues requires not only a deeper understanding of the theoretical foundations and traditions of social work, but also an openness to new ways of doing things. In their training to become social work practitioners, it is therefore especially important that students acquire a firm grasp of sexual and gender diversity principles and, drawing on the best practices in the area, develop a good understanding of the range of responses that may be effective in particular situations.

Finding Allies

Transsexual people are homosexual, bisexual, asexual, and transgender—adopting non-normative or queer identities—in about the same proportions as cissexual people. Many transsexual people seek not to be part of LGBTTQ communities, but to live quite ordinary lives in their affirmed sex and gender.

This difference in life path makes for challenges in finding allies not only within LGBTTQ communities but between queer and non-queer transsexual people.

To date this has not allowed transsexual people to speak with a single voice. This has made any struggle on the model of the gay rights movement difficult.

CHAPTER REVIEW

Key Terms

- **LGBTTQ**
- **Heterosexual privilege**
- **Sex**
- **Gender**
- **Homophobia, biphobia, and transphobia**
- **Heterosexism**
- **Sexual orientation**
- **Transgendered**
- **Transsexuals**

- **Intersexuals**
- **Sexology**
- **Kinsey Report**
- **Stonewall Rebellion**
- **Queer activism**
- **Biological determinism**
- **Social constructionism**
- **Queer theory**
- **Coming out**
- **Cissexual**

Review Questions

1. What are the main theories that are helpful in understanding sexuality? Briefly explain each.

2. What is "internalized homophobia," and why is it important for social workers (and others) to understand it?

3. What is the social work profession's perspective on gender and sexual diversity, and how has it changed in the last few decades?

4. What is "coming out," and what are some of the factors involved of which social workers should be aware?

5. How serious is the problem of suicide among gay, lesbian, and bisexual persons, and what are its underlying causes?

6. What are important considerations when supporting parents of a newborn child who is intersexual?

7. How might social work practitioners ensure that their workplaces are supportive to those who do not fit within the expected gender binaries?

Exploring Social Work

1. The Trans Ally Quiz helps the general public and service providers understand how to effectively support members of trans communities. Download the quiz at **www.trans–academics.org/TransAllyQuiz. doc** and test your ability to provide trans-positive service. Once you have completed the quiz consider the implications your answers have for your practice.

2. In 1995 Kimberly Nixon filed a human rights complaint against the Vancouver Rape Crisis centre for expelling her from their volunteer training program because she was not born a woman. Read the press release and backgrounder from the Disabled Women's Network **http://dawn.thot.net/nixon_v_vrr.html** and, in small groups, discuss the implications this case has for social service providers and how it challenges your own understandings of gender.

3. Consider how you might approach a client who asks you about your sexual orientation. How might you respond to this question and why? Whether you identify as lesbian, gay, bisexual, or straight, this question has implications for a client and for you in your workplace. Some social workers consider their sexual orientation to be a private issue, but for someone who is exploring their sexuality it can be important to know the sexual orientation of the social worker with whom they are working. In small groups, strategize different responses you could make to this question.

Websites

- - - - - -

Equality for Gays and Lesbians Everywhere (EGALE)
www.egale.ca

This national organization is committed to advancing, at the federal level, equality and justice for lesbians, gays, bisexuals, and trans-identified people. The website has a vast collection of news, articles, and resources. Included is a summary of lesbian and gay rights in each jurisdiction in Canada.

Gender Education and Advocacy
www.gender.org

Gender Education and Advocacy (GEA) is a national organization focused on the needs, issues, and concerns of gender variant people. It seeks to educate and advocate for all persons who experience gender-based oppression in all of its many forms.

PFLAG
www.pflag.ca

Information and resources for gay men, lesbians, and bisexuals and their families and friends. Most chapters have scheduled meetings that provide support and information.

International Gay and Lesbian Human Rights Commission
www.iglhrc.org

IGLHRC's mission is to protect and advance the human rights of all people and communities subject to discrimination or abuse on the basis of sexual orientation, gender identity, or HIV status. Their website contains excellent resources, news, and urgent action items.

CHAPTER 15

SOCIAL WORK WITH PERSONS WITH DISABILITIES

Helping Individuals and Their Families

by Roy Hanes

It is estimated that 4.4 million Canadians or approximately one out of
every seven people in Canada have a disability. This number represents
approximately 14.3 percent of the total population. It is estimated that
there are approximately 600 million people worldwide with disabilities.
In other words, disability and impairment affect large numbers of people
and their families; most if not all social workers will at some point in
their careers work with someone who has a disability or has a family
member who has a disability. This includes social work practice with
individuals, families, groups, and communities, as well as in international
development.

Who Are People with Disabilities?

The federal government carried out a detailed investigation into the nature and extent of disability in Canada in 2006: the **Participation and Activity Limitation Survey (PALS)**. Changes in research criteria and data collection in the 2006 investigation make comparisons to an earlier PALS survey in 2001 difficult. The most recent survey does, however, show that the number of Canadians reporting a disability in 2006 went up when compared to the 2001 study (Statistics Canada 2001b, 2006b).

Children with Disabilities

Determining and diagnosing disabilities in children, particularly young children, can be difficult. Over 200,000 children under 14 reported having a disability of some kind, a 3.3 percent increase from the 2001 survey.

Chronic health condition. Among children 0–14 years, the most widespread disability is that related to a chronic health condition. For children with disabilities, almost 70 percent of children under 4 years and just over 66 percent of children 5 to 14 years old are reported to have a disability related to chronic health problems, the most common being asthma, severe allergies, attention deficit disorder, and autism.

Developmental delay. Developmental delay is the most common disability in children aged 0–4, and just over 30 percent of school-aged children with disabilities are reported to have developmental disabilities.

Learning disabilities. Among children between the ages of 5–14, learning disabilities represent a high number of disabling conditions. The number of children reported as having learning disabilities is over 120,000, or 3.2 percent of all children in this age group.

Profile of Adults with Disabilities

Since the 2001 PALS report, the rate of disability among adults rose from 14.6 to 16.5 percent. The most marked increase was for learning disabilities, which rose by almost 40 percent to approximately 631,000 in 2006.

Problems relating to pain, mobility, and agility were the most commonly reported disability among adults, accounting for almost 3 million people over the age of 15. Five percent of the adult population report a hearing disability, just over 3 percent report a vision disability, and almost 2 percent report speech disabilities.

The overall increase in disability is attributed partly to the aging population, but this is not the only factor. There is also evidence to suggest that the social acceptance of disability has increased—the respondents report the disabilities to the interviewers and may be more likely to make a complete report. The PALS 2006 report also shows that the largest increase occurred in the number of people reporting mild disabilities.

Defining Disability

The Participation and Activity Limitation Survey (PALS) uses the World Health Organization's framework of disability, which defines disability as the relationship between body structures and functions, daily activities, and social participation, while recognizing the role of environmental factors. For the purpose of PALS, persons with disabilities are those who reported difficulties with daily living activities, or who indicated that a physical or mental condition or health problem reduced the kind or amount of activities they could do.

TYPES OF DISABILITY

ADULTS

The PALS survey questions allow the identification of the following types of disabilities among adults aged 15 and over:

Hearing: Difficulty hearing what is being said in a conversation with one other person, in a conversation with three or more persons, or in a telephone conversation.

Seeing: Difficulty seeing ordinary newsprint or clearly seeing the face of someone from 4 metres (12 feet).

Speech: Difficulty speaking and/or being understood.

Mobility: Difficulty walking half a kilometre or up and down a flight of stairs, about 12 steps without resting, moving from one room to another, carrying an object of 5 kg (10 pounds) for 10 metres (30 feet), or standing for long periods.

Agility: Difficulty bending, dressing, or undressing oneself, getting into and out of bed, cutting own toenails, using fingers to grasp or to handle objects, reaching in any direction (for example, above one's head) or cutting own food.

Pain: Limitations in the amount or kind of activities that one can do because of a long-term pain that is constant or recurs from time to time, for example, recurrent back pain.

Learning: Difficulty learning because of a condition, such as attention problems, hyperactivity, or dyslexia, whether or not the condition was diagnosed by a teacher, doctor, or other health professional.

Memory: Limitations in the amount or kind of activities that one can do, due to frequent periods of confusion or difficulty remembering things. These difficulties may be associated with Alzheimer's disease, brain injuries, or other similar conditions.

Developmental: Cognitive limitations due to the presence of a developmental disability or disorder, such as Down's syndrome, autism, or mental impairment caused by a lack of oxygen at birth.

Psychological: Limitations in the amount or kind of activities that one can do, due to the presence of an emotional, psychological, or psychiatric condition, such as phobias, depression, schizophrenia, drinking or drug problems.

CHILDREN

The PALS survey questions allow the identification of the following types of disabilities among children under 15:

Hearing*: Difficulty hearing.

Seeing*: Difficulty seeing.

Speech**: Difficulty speaking and/or being understood.

Mobility**: Difficulty walking. This means walking on a flat firm surface, such as a sidewalk or floor.

Dexterity**: Difficulty using hands or fingers to grasp or hold small objects, such as a pencil or scissors.

Learning**: Difficulty learning due to the presence of a condition, such as attention problems, hyperactivity, or dyslexia, whether or not the condition was diagnosed by a teacher, doctor, or other health professional.

Developmental delay***: Child has a delay in his/her development, either a physical, intellectual, or another type of delay.

Developmental disability or disorder**: Cognitive limitations due to the presence of a developmental disability or disorder, such as Down's syndrome, autism, or mental impairment caused by a lack of oxygen at birth.

Psychological**: Limitations in the amount or kind of activities that one can do due to the presence of an emotional, psychological, or behavioural condition.

Chronic condition*: Limitations in the amount or kind of activities that one can do, due to the presence of one or more chronic health conditions that have lasted or are expected to last six months or more and that have been diagnosed by a health professional. Examples of chronic conditions are asthma or severe allergies, heart condition or disease, kidney condition or disease, cancer, epilepsy, cerebral palsy, spina bifida, cystic fibrosis, muscular dystrophy, fetal alcohol syndrome, etc.

* Applicable to all children under 15.
** Applicable to children aged 5 to 14.
*** Applicable to children under 5.

Source: Adapted from Statistics Canada publication *Participation and Activity Limitation Survey* 2001. Cat. no. 89-577-XIE.

TABLE 15.1: Prevalence of Disability by Age for Canada, 2006

Age Group	Number			Percent
	Total Population	Population with Disabilities	Population without Disabilities	Total Disability Rate
Total—All Ages	30,893,640	4,417,870	26,475,77	14.3
Total—Aged less than 15	5,471,360	202,350	5,269,010	3.7
0 to 4	1,656,040	27,540	1,628,500	1.7
5 to 14	3,815,310	174,810	3,640,500	4.6
Total—Aged 15 and over	25,422,280	4,215,530	21,206,760	16.6
15 to 64	21,373,150	2,457,940	18,915,210	11.5
15 to 19	2,102,370	96,060	2,006,310	4.6
20 to 24	2,044,710	99,440	1,945,270	4.9
25 to 34	3,942,260	239,600	3,702,660	6.1
35 to 44	4,747,62	456,930	4,290,690	9.6
45 to 54	4,912,800	740,990	4,171,810	15.1
55 to 64	3,623,390	824,920	2,798,470	22.8
65 and over	4,049,140	1,757,590	2,291,550	43.4
65 to 74	2,239,630	739,500	1,500,130	33.0
75 and over	1,809,500	1,018,090	791,420	56.3

Note: The sum of the values for each category may differ from the total due to rounding.

Source: Adapted from Statistics Canada publication *Participation and Activity Limitation Survey (PALS)*. 2006b Cat. no. 89–577–XIE. http://www.statcan.gc.ca/pub/89-628-x/2007002/t/4125010-eng.htm

History of Services for People with Disabilities

As a social category, disability is very complex because the onset varies considerably from one person to the next.

For example, a **disability** can be the result of sensory impairments, such as blindness and/or deafness. People can also have psychiatric disabilities, developmental disabilities, learning disabilities, or neurological disabilities. Many people have mobility as well as agility impairments and many people with disabilities live with chronic and persistent pain.

People can be born with disabilities or people can become disabled at any age through a variety of means from illness to injury, war to famine, disease to the aging process.

The purpose of this chapter is simply to provide some basic information and guidelines for prospective social workers who may eventually find themselves working with persons with disabilities.

At the time of Confederation, most provinces established their own methods of charitable support or *social welfare* for populations in need, including people with disabilities. When Canada became a country, the federal government was primarily concerned with what the *British North America Act* identified as "peace, order and good government." The federal government was not interested in issues such as health, education, and social relief—these were assigned to the provinces. As a result, provinces developed their own unique charitable relief programs (as well as schools and institutions) and because of these provincial differences, no universal support care programs were established for people with disabilities and no national support care programs exist in Canada to the present day (Hanes & Moscovitch 2002).

Outdoor relief was a common form of assistance provided to persons with disabilities when their families could not take care of them. An early form of outdoor relief established in England, and later transported to British North America, was begging. Through the Poor Laws, the deserving poor, such as persons with disabilities, were given license to beg.

As time passed, other forms of outdoor relief supplemented begging. When families could not provide for a family member (usually an elderly person or a person with a disability), these persons were housed in private homes, and funds to cover expenses for food, clothing, shelter, and medical care were often provided through municipal taxes, charitable organizations, and religious organizations. In essence, outdoor relief meant that persons with disabilities were cared for through non-institutional methods of relief and were more or less part of the community.

Institutionalization

By the mid-nineteenth century, outdoor relief came to be seen as a mechanism that *created* rather than *relieved* dependency, and institutions such as asylums, poor houses, and houses of industry replaced the former methods of outdoor relief (Splane 1965). The replacement of outdoor relief measures by indoor relief measures represents a significant shift in the philosophy regarding charitable relief.

Persons with disabilities, who were once considered part of the social order, were now viewed as nuisance populations. They were to be removed from society, isolated, and placed in segregated institutions. During this time, disability was often considered a source of shame and many persons with disabilities who were not sent to institutions were often hidden away in their homes by their family members. There are numerous examples of people with various forms of disabilities being hidden or kept at home in Canada, the U.S., and the U.K. throughout the nineteenth and twentieth centuries (Hanes 1995).

By the mid-nineteenth century there was a major shift in the public attitude towards social dependency and social relief, and the public's attitude towards the provision of relief changed as well. The social rejection of "defective" populations was so severe that many persons with disabilities were treated as common criminals and banned from the streets of many cities in Canada. Many were charged under vagrancy laws and sent to jail. Many of those who were not sent to jail were sent to a local poor house, a house of industry, or an asylum. Provincial governments were reluctant to fund support programs for dependent populations, including people with disabilities, and very coercive means were used to provide for the relief of dependent populations (Hanes 1995).

By the mid-twentieth century, many provinces had "special" residential schools for blind and deaf children and adolescents. Provincial institutions were established for people with psychiatric disabilities and in many provinces there were institutions for people with developmental disabilities. Specialized hospitals were established for many different disabled populations including tuberculosis hospitals, orthopaedic hospitals and rehabilitation hospitals. The institutionalization of people with disabilities was so widespread that it became the common belief that this was the natural order of things, and that people with disabilities had always been separated from their communities (Bowe 1978).

With the advancement of scientific medicine following World War I, the disability category fell under the domain of the medical profession and since that time it has been medical professionals who determine the need for specialized care, income supports, pensions, educational supports, transportation supports, home care supports, and other benefits.

Learning disabilities are one of the most common disabilities among children and pose a serious challenge to school systems in Canada.

Rehabilitation Services

Another important era in the history of disability in Canada emerged following World War II. In the post–World War II era, Canada witnessed the establishment of the "welfare state," wherein social security programs such as pensions and disability benefits were established for a wide spectrum of people with disabilities. In addition to the rise of the welfare state, the post–World War II era witnessed the onset of the multidisciplinary rehabilitation team, which included the physiatrist (rehabilitation physician), nurse, occupational therapist, physiotherapist, and later, the social worker, psychologist, vocational counsellor, and recreologist.

The establishment of rehabilitation services following World War II thus laid the foundation for the modern era of medical and social services for people with disabilities. During this era, medical and social services were expanded to people with disabilities, including the establishment of special schools, training programs, sheltered workshops, summer camps, recreational programs, as well as the establishment of special trades and industries, and special hospitals and after-care facilities.

Approaches to Disability: The Medical and Social Models

The post-WWII dominance of medical professionals over the lives of people with disabilities remained unchallenged until the 1970s, when the disability rights movement developed in Canada. The rise of disability rights organizations is linked to the rise of the consumer movement, the civil rights movement, the peace movement, the gay rights movement, and the women's movement of the late 1960s and the early 1970s.

Rather than be labelled "defective" or "handicapped," disability rights advocates argued that persons with disabilities also should be seen as members of a minority group. "Many persons with disabilities," Lex Frieden suggests, "considered themselves members of a minority group related not by colour or nationality but by functional limitation and similar need" (Frieden 1983, 55).

Charter of Rights and Freedoms 1982

The *American Vocational Rehabilitation Act* of 1973 represents a pivotal point in the history of persons with disabilities, because this legislation prohibited discrimination against people with disabilities. "No otherwise qualified handicapped individual in the United States as defined by Section 7 shall, solely by reason of his handicap, be excluded from participation in, be denied the benefits of, or be subject to discrimination under any program or activity receiving federal financial assistance" (Zola 1986, 1). Similar legislation followed in Canada at both the provincial and federal levels, and in 1982 the rights of people with disabilities were enshrined in the *Charter of Rights and Freedoms*.

Currently, two broad approaches characterize the discussions of disability. The **medical model** of disability has its roots in rehabilitation medicine, where the focus of the intervention is on the individual. It focuses on disability as an "impairment" and a "personal tragedy" and the need of the individual to adapt or otherwise to fit within mainstream society as much as possible. The **political rights model**, on the other hand, is concerned with the broader social and political context and the need for society as a whole to adapt and to address the needs of those persons with a disability.

The shift to defining disability in terms of rights, instead of medical need, was influenced not only by the disability rights movement but also by the development of disability theories that challenged the dominant medical model view of disability. The pre-eminent British disability advocate and theorist Michael Oliver has coined the terms "personal tragedy theory" and "social oppression theory" of disability to describe the differences between a medical model of disability and a socio-political model of disability (Oliver 1990).

Medical Model

Views disability as an unfortunate life event where some form of professional or medical assistance is required.

Political Rights Model

Primarily concerned with broader social and political change, contending that a comprehensive understanding of disability can only occur through examination of the social and political inequality that exists between disabled people and people without disabilities.

Medical Model: Personal Tragedy Theory

From the perspective of the personal tragedy theory of disability, a disabling condition is viewed as an unfortunate life event where some form of professional and medical assistance is required (Oliver 1990). This theory holds that disability is primarily a medical problem. The various forms of interventions are therefore introduced as a means of "curing" or "fixing" the individual.

According to the personal tragedy theory, persons who become disabled, as well as their loved ones, go through various stages of psychological and emotional adjustment before they can accept themselves or their loved one as disabled. Much of the literature pertaining to the impact of disability on the individual and on the family focuses primarily on the stages of adjustment to the disability. Oliver (1996) argues that many of these explanations of adjustment to disability are based on psychological theories pertaining to or coping with death and dying—stages of shock, denial, grief, loss, reconciliation, and acceptance. Such an approach is usually based on an interpretation of coping that involves the following assumptions:

- An individual or family must move sequentially through the coping stages to become fully adjusted.
- There is but one path through the sequence.
- An individual can be placed clearly in one stage or another by analyzing their behaviour.
- There is an optional length of time for staying in each stage.

Political Rights Model: Social Oppression Theory

In contrast to the medical model, the social oppression theory of disability suggests that the problems faced by people with disabilities are not the result of physical impairments alone, but are also the result of the social and political inequality that exists between people with disabilities on the one hand and people without disabilities on the other (Oliver 1990). This model thus challenges the widely prevalent view that disability is essentially an individual problem requiring individual treatment and individual solutions to problems.

The social oppression model tends to see people with disabilities as members of an oppressed minority population and that environmental factors—such as the lack of employment opportunities, lack of affordable housing, lack of accessible transportation, as well as the presence of negative stereotypes and prejudicial attitudes—are a primary cause of problems for people with disabilities. This, in turn, has implications with respect to resolving problems. Because many problems stem from structural and attitudinal barriers, systemic change, both social and political, is required if these obstacles are to be overcome. Among other things, this requires the incorporation of a *human rights* focus for addressing the needs of people with disabilities.

The Independent Living Movement

The Independent Living Movement (ILM) has been a key player in the struggle to achieve human rights legislation for people with disabilities. Originating in the United States during the early 1970s and introduced to Canada in 1979, the Independent Living Movement has become a dominant force in disability rights activity in Canada. .

The origins of the Independent Living Movement can be traced to the Cowell Residence Program at the University of California, Berkeley. In the early 1960s, students with severe disabilities who were wheelchair users were housed in Cowell Hospital on campus. Within the 1960s context of student protests and civil rights, a group of students with disabilities began to recognize that medical and rehabilitation professionals largely controlled their lives. Their efforts to gain control inspired the ILM and disability rights movement of the 1970s to today.

The Independent Living Movement

The philosophy underlying the **Independent Living Movement (ILM)** is to encourage and help persons with disabilities achieve self-direction over the personal and community services needed to attain their own independent living.

Three major events in 1981 were central to the full development of the ILM in Canada: (1) the United Nations declaration of the International Year of Disabled Persons, (2) the Canadian government's release of its *Obstacles* report concerning disability, and (3) the personal contribution of one of its founding members, Henry Enns, to the independent living (IL) philosophy. These helped provide legitimacy to the social oppression approach to disability and promoted the philosophy of IL to the various levels of government, academics, and other disability organizations.

Canadian Association of Independent Living Centres

www.cailc.ca

CAILC is an organization of independent living centres across Canada; the website offers extensive resources on the movement.

By 1985, Independent Living Resource Centres (ILRCs) were operating in Waterloo, Winnipeg, Thunder Bay, Calgary, and Toronto. In 1986, at the first IL conference in Ottawa, the Canadian Association of Independent Living Centres (CAILC) was formed to act as a national coordinating body for the ILM, and the definition of a Canadian ILRC was developed. In 2008, a total of twenty-six ILRCs were operating across Canada.

The IL philosophy empowers consumers to make choices necessary to control their community and personal resources. Consumer control means that ILRCs are governed and controlled by persons with disabilities. At least 51 percent of the members of each board of directors must have a disability, and each board must have a mix of people with and without a disability. ILRCs are non-profit and responsive to persons with all types of disabilities, including mobility, sensory, cognitive, emotional, psychiatric, and so forth. The IL philosophy believes that persons with disabilities are citizens with the right to participate in community life and advocates an alternative model of program delivery.

In 1997 the CAILC undertook a study of the effects of the ILRCs and found that they succeed, in large part, not simply because they provide an opportunity to learn skills, access information, or receive support, but because they do so in a way that is consistent with the independent living philosophy. The Association concluded that improvement in the quality of life for people with disabilities requires skill development as well as the removal of environmental, social, and economic barriers. Individual empowerment was found to be a key benefit. It was particularly important in fostering competency in a variety of community living skills, as well as resulting in increased confidence and self-esteem. The Association found that individuals involved with some of the programs of the ILRC have knowledge of other IL programs as well and highly value the programs with which they are directly involved.

TABLE 15.2: Theories of Disability—Contrasting Approaches

	Rehabilitation Paradigm (Medical Model)	Independent Living Paradigm (Political Rights Model)
Definition of Problem	Physical impairment/lack of employment skills	Dependent on professionals, relatives, etc.
Locus of Problem	In the individual	In the environment and rehabilitation process
Solution to Problem	Professional intervention by physician, therapist, occupational therapist, vocational rehabilitation counsellor, etc.	Peer counselling, advocacy, self-help, consumer control, removal of barriers
Social Role	Patient/client	Citizen/consumer
Who Controls	Professional	Citizen/consumer
Desired Outcome	Maximize activities, living skills	Independent living

Source: Adapted from G. DeJong. 1978. *The Movement for Independent Living: Origins, Ideology, and Implications for Disability Research.* Boston: Tufts–New England Medical Center, Medical Rehabilitation Institute.

PEOPLE FIRST—"PERSONS WITH DISABILITIES"

In recent years, many debates have taken place in the fields of sociology, social work, political science, and disability studies with respect to the most appropriate term to be used when writing about or speaking about people who are disabled. While still commonly used in everyday conversation, terms such as "defective," "crippled," "lame," or "gimp" are now generally considered to be derogatory and certainly inappropriate.

Since the early 1980s, the terms "person with disabilities" and "people with disabilities" have come to be accepted as the most appropriate terms to be used when referring to individuals who have disabilities. This new terminology was promoted by "people first" initiatives and the terms indicate that disability is one of many characteristics of the individual.

In recent years, however, many disability rights advocates and disability theorists have challenged the "person first" conceptualizations of disability. Those who do so advocate for the replacement of the terms "people with disabilities" and "person with a disability" with the term "disabled person." The argument is that "person first" language tends to minimize and de-politicize disability.

Both terms—"disabled person" and "people with disabilities"—are acceptable, providing the disadvantages of each term are properly acknowledged. But for the purposes of this book, the terms "people with disabilities" or "persons with disabilities" will mainly be used throughout.

The Stigma of Disability

In Unison Report

In Unison: A Canadian Approach to Disability Issues (2000) marked the first time that Canada's federal, provincial, and territorial governments came together to express a common vision on disability issues (Social Union 2000). This report provides Canadians with a broad view of how adults with disabilities have been faring in comparison with those without disabilities, using both statistical indicators and examples of personal experiences.

Examples of effective practices that have been implemented across Canada are also woven into the report. The situation of Aboriginal persons with disabilities is specifically highlighted.

Today, in most social work courses, students learn about discrimination and prejudice towards people because of their race, religious beliefs, ethnic background, gender, and sexual orientation. It is less common that social work students are informed about discrimination and prejudice towards people with disabilities. Yet, disability is a human constant—since disablement has always existed, there is nothing inherent in disability that should lead to the stigmatization of people with disabilities, nor is there anything inherent in disability that should lead to the development of belief systems wherein biological difference is linked to biological inferiority. But unfortunately in many countries, including Canada, disability is viewed as undesirable and people with disabilities are often stigmatized. They are discriminated against, and they often have low social status.

It is possible to identify and describe, in general, various types of stigma towards persons with disabilities as well as the possible motives that may underlie them (Livneh 1982).

In most Western industrialized societies there is a growing cultural emphasis on the "body beautiful." Physical attractiveness, sexuality, and desirability have become a valued cultural norm. People with disabilities often do not meet cultural standards of physical attractiveness and this contributes to a stigma of disability: that to have a disability is to be undesirable and unlovable. For the person with a disability, this has implications for many aspects of life—developing friendships and intimate relationships, socializing, or being involved in recreational activities.

It is commonly believed that when people become disabled, or a loved one becomes disabled, individuals and family members go through a long period of grieving. When people with disabilities do not show signs of long-term grieving and mourning, they are considered to be in a state of denial. There is a common expectation that people with disabilities should be in a continuous state of emotional distress and psychological suffering.

A common stereotype is that people with disabilities are often psychologically damaged. This stems from the long-held belief that there is an interconnection between the physical, mental, and emotional aspects of the human body. Therefore, it is theorized that if there is damage to one aspect of the system (physical disability) then there would be damage to the emotional and mental aspects as well.

Sometimes the person with the disability is portrayed as deserving the disability. For example, a young person who may have become disabled as a result of driving while intoxicated may be viewed as someone who received what he or she deserved. Another example might be a person who became disabled as a consequence of a particular lifestyle—there tends to be little public sympathy for adults who have disabling conditions because of drug use, prostitution, or through unprotected sex.

Because of the influence of religious and cultural beliefs, some people believe that a disability is a consequence of sinful activities on the part of an individual or parent. Also, congenital disorders are often attributed to the risky or immoral actions or behaviours of mothers during pregnancy. There is also a stereotype of the individual with a disability as an "evil person." There are many examples that portray persons with disabilities as evil people in folklore, literature, TV programs, and movies.

Many people without disabilities feel physically and psychologically uncomfortable when they are in the company of people with disabilities. Such fearful and negative reactions are often more common when there is a lack of exposure and a lack of contact between those without disabilities and people with disabilities.

Most people greatly fear becoming disabled themselves. The presence of people with disabilities reminds some people that they too can, and likely will, become disabled. Such a fear may lead to avoidance of people with disabilities by people without disabilities and this contributes to the social isolation of people with disabilities. Disability may also remind people of their own mortality and much of the literature pertaining to the psychological adjustment to the onset of disability comes from literature based on the study of death and dying.

Ableism

Many students of social work are familiar with terms such as racism, sexism, heterosexism, and ageism, but they may be unfamiliar with the term ableism or the stigmatization of disability and the existence of prejudicial attitudes held by people without disabilities towards people with disabilities. **Ableism** denotes the consequences of the belief in the superiority of people without disabilities over people with disabilities. The PCS model can be used to characterize ableism:

- *Prejudice* towards disabled people at a personal level, which refers to revulsion, avoidance, infantilization, condescension, and other forms of prejudice.
- *Cultural norms*, which reflect a positive image of being without disability and a negative image of being disabled (people without disabilities are valued more than people with disabilities). Society's cultural norms stigmatize people with disabilities and emphasize the horror of being disabled. People with disabilities are often the target of jokes and derogatory statements.
- *Social stratification and social division*, which focus on the manner in which people with disabilities are kept out of the mainstream. Social stratification and social division also explore ways in which people with disabilities are marginalized because of structural and attitudinal barriers.

UN Report on Disabilities

In 1998, the UN's Report of the Committee on Economic, Social and Cultural Rights questioned Canada's actions on disability, citing cuts to services such as home care, attendant care, and transportation as well as the tightening of eligibility rules for people with disabilities. The committee also questioned the issue of homelessness and lack of adequate support services among discharged psychiatric patients, as the Canadian government did not provide data on this matter.

Ableism

Discrimination and prejudice based on physical and mental ability towards people with disabilities, supporting the belief that people without disabilities are superior to people with disabilities.

Income Security Programs

Canada's disability income support system is based on a loosely knit set of programs. These programs have different eligibility criteria, guidelines, and procedures. Social and income security programs for disabled people are derived from private and public sources in the form of contributory or non-contributory benefits.

- **Publicly funded disability programs** are covered by federal, provincial, and municipal legislation. These programs include the Canada Pension Plan Disability Pension (a federal program), the Family Benefits plan (a provincial program), and the General Welfare Assistance plan (a municipal program in Ontario). These types of programs are funded through government taxation, and except for the Canada Pension Plan, do not require the financial contribution of recipients.

- **Privately funded disability programs** include programs that are provided through private insurance plans or through long-term disability plans as part of job benefits. These private income security programs are based on the amount of funding that the recipient has contributed directly to the plan, or funding that has been contributed to a plan on behalf of the recipient.

TABLE 15.3: Percentage of Working-Age Adults with Disabilities by Income Source

Year	Wages and Salaries	Self-Employment Income	Government Sources	Investment Income; Private Insurance Pensions	Other Income
1999	49.7	5.3	31.7	7.8	2.0
2000	51.1	5.6	31.3	6.7	1.5
2001	51.2	5.6	30.6	7.0	2.1
2002	53.0	6.2	28.2	7.0	2.6
2003	54.2	6.1	26.8	7.3	2.6

Source: HRSDC. 2006. *Advancing the Inclusion of People with Disabilities 2006*. Ottawa: Human Resources and Social Development Canada. Reproduced with permission of Her Majesty the Queen in Right of Canada 2006.

In 1988, in an analysis of disability benefits provided through Canada's income security programs, the G. Allen Roeher Institute (a research group associated with the Canadian Association for Community Living) noted the "insecurity" of income security programs for persons with disabilities. Between 1996 and 2004, income security was radically altered—many would say, for the worse—with the introduction of the Canada Health and Social Transfer (CHST). The CHST was a per-capita grant to the provinces, without regard to provincial circumstances or needs. The CAILC maintains that this policy shift significantly jeopardized the livelihood of people with disabilities, making them even more insecure than in the mid-1980s. Since 2004, the CHST has been divided into the Canada Social Transfer and the Canada Health Transfer (see Chapter 2 page 28).

While Canadians have a universal health care system, the benefits do not extend to providing full support for all people with disabilities. The primary similarity across the provinces is the range and types of supports and services provided. For example, provincial programs, whether in Newfoundland or British Columbia, will cover the cost of wheelchairs, canes, eyeglasses, walkers, attendant care services, home care, transportation, and so forth. The differences among the provinces are found in two areas. One is eligibility requirements, which may be different from one province to the next; the other is the amount of funding for supports and services, which may vary from one province to the next. Each province has its own legislation and mechanisms for providing services to people with disabilities. As a consequence of this lack of universality, the care and treatment of persons with disabilities varies across the country. For example, some provinces, such as Newfoundland and Labrador, Prince Edward Island, Saskatchewan, and New Brunswick, have a single-tier program wherein supports and services are directly funded by the province to the individual in need. Other provinces, such as Nova Scotia and Manitoba, have a two-tier system of support for people with disabilities—basically, the programs are funded though a system of General Welfare Assistance at the municipal and/or county level. The province provides the funding, and the money for supports and services is then transferred to the local government, which, in turn, funds the individual.

The types of programs indicated above (one-tier and two-tier systems) are directly related to provincial social welfare spending, but there are also provincial programs based on specific legislation aimed at people with disabilities. In Ontario, people with disabilities are covered under the *Ontario Disability Supports Program Act*; in British Columbia, they are covered under the *Disability Benefits Program Act*; and in Alberta, they receive benefits through the Assured Income for the Severely Handicapped program. These provincial programs are based on distinct legislation covering people with disabilities and are not directly connected to any provincial welfare legislation.

Council of Canadians with Disabilities

www.ccdonline.ca

The CCD is a national cross-disability advocacy group representing provincial organizations such as the DisAbled Women's Network (DAWN) of Canada, the Canadian Association of the Deaf and the Alliance for Equality of Blind Canadians.

Canada's immigration laws
make it difficult for people
with disabilities to immigrate
to Canada.

If it is determined that an
individual is disabled he
or she may not be granted
permission to immigrate
here. And, if a landed
immigrant or his or her family
member is determined to
be disabled, the individual
as well as family could be
deported.

Canada's immigration laws
do not specifically state
that people with disabilities
are not welcomed but the
excessive demand clause,
section 38(1)c, of the
*Immigration and Refugee
Protection Act* makes it
very difficult for people with
disabilities.

The regulations define
"excessive demand" as (a) a
demand on health services or
social services for which the
anticipated costs would likely
exceed average Canadian per
capita health services and
social services costs or (b) a
demand on health services
or social services that would
add to existing waiting lists
and would increase the rate
of mortality and morbidity
in Canada (*Immigration and
Refugee Protection Act*,
Regulations 1(1)).

As noted above, provincial supports and services vary from one province to the next and so does legislation concerning human rights coverage for people with disabilities. In many provinces, discrimination against people with disabilities is covered under provincial as well as federal human rights legislation. Some provinces have additional legislation such as the *Ontarians with Disabilities Act*, which specifically addresses the concerns of people with disabilities. Unlike the United States, which has federal legislation (*Americans with Disabilities Act*) aimed at securing and maintaining the rights of people with disabilities, Canada does not have such legislation at the present time.

Gaining Access to Services

For people with a disability, the first step in gaining access to municipal or provincial programs, such as General Welfare Assistance or Family Benefits, is an eligibility determination carried out by a physician. The physician determines whether or not the applicant has a disability that seriously impedes his or her potential for employment. Once a person is deemed to be disabled, a Social Assistance review takes place.

First, there is an investigation of assets, which means that a person with a disability cannot have assets beyond a specific limit. For example, people with disabilities living in Ontario who receive Family Benefits are not allowed to accumulate savings beyond the amount of $3,500. Only in special circumstances can this asset exemption be waived. Each province has its own types and levels of exemption. For example, in Quebec, benefits are reduced if the value of the applicant's house exceeds $50,000, and automobiles are exempt only to a certain amount.

The next step in a Social Assistance review is a needs test. A needs test consists of three basic steps:

1. The applicant's basic requirements for living are identified (food, clothing, shelter, utilities, other household expenses, and personal allowances). Each requirement is designated with a maximum dollar allotment, and the requirements are then totalled to determine the funds needed to meet basic needs.

2. The applicant's available financial resources are determined, that is, income from resources such as other pensions, including public or private funds, savings, money received through paid employment or training programs.

3. The difference between total resources and total basic needs is calculated. A negative remainder indicates a "budget defect" upon which eligibility for assistance is determined.

The amount of assistance will then be assessed according to a variety of factors, including size of family, degree of employability of the family's main decision maker, size and type of accommodation and so on.

In addition to basic financial assistance, people with disabilities who receive either General Welfare Assistance, Family Benefits, or who are covered by the Canada Pension Plan are also entitled to other forms of assistance. These may include dental services, prescriptions, eyeglasses, technical aids and devices, prosthetic and orthotic equipment, wheelchairs, child care subsidies and so forth (referred to as "in kind"). Recipients who work must notify authorities and are allowed to keep only a percentage of their income, with the remainder being deducted from benefits.

Canada Pension Plan

With work-related or contributory income security programs, contributions are made through an individual's employment, and the amount of financial benefits received is based on the amount paid into the plan. The CPP is an example of an income security program based on contributory payments. Eligibility for CPP benefits is based on the following criteria:

- A physician must first determine eligibility for benefits.
- Benefits are granted only to individuals who have either contributed during two of the last three years or five of the last ten years.
- Pension benefits consist of a flat rate plus earnings equal to 75 percent of the normal retirement pension entitlement.

The Canada Pension Plan does not consider the day-to-day financial needs of the disabled individual, however. Low-income workers therefore receive lower benefits and may require additional assistance through programs such as Family Benefits or General Welfare Assistance.

Protesters and members of activist organization, the Raging Grannies, demonstrate against low welfare and disability rates in Peterborough, Ontario, as part of the nationwide "Raise the Rates Campaign."

Disability and Social Work Practice

What skills should social workers have in order to work effectively with people with disabilities? Social workers should obviously have generic practice skills, which include an understanding of individual and family counselling, as well as an understanding of group work and community organization. In addition, they should have a working knowledge of mediation and advocacy and be able to connect clients to available resources.

But, to be effective, whether working with persons with disabilities or with other groups, the social worker must be able to help an individual and family cope, while at the same time recognize that many of the difficulties may stem from the social context in which the individual and family find themselves. At times this may require that the social worker become a direct advocate for social and political change with, and on behalf of, their clients. In the case of working with persons with disabilities, this may involve petitioning for more or better services, organizing clients to protest a lack of accessible housing, or leading or supporting boycotts against businesses that are not accessible to people with disabilities.

While barriers such as these are the visible challenges of disability, the greatest limitation for people living with disabilities is social stigma and prejudice. It is espcially important for social workers to help challenge these stereotypes.

Families and Disability

Until the 1970s, the medical care and treatment of people with disabilities for both children and adults was predominantly directed at the physical needs of the individual who was disabled. Less attention was paid to the emotional needs of the individual and the family. During the past twenty-five years there has been a greater recognition of the importance of the family and family members.

This new focus was influenced by the introduction of **family systems theory** to social work. This theory argues that the family is an interrelated network and an impact on one component has significant consequences for all others in the system. In other words:

- all parts of the family unit are interrelated

- each member affects and is affected by other members of the unit

- no one part of the family system can be understood in isolation from the other parts

Obviously, the onset of disability, whether at birth or later in life, will have a great effect on the entire family unit. Family members (especially parents of a child with a disability) therefore have a critical role to play in the care, treatment, and emotional adjustment of the person who is disabled. Much of the work of the social work practitioner must therefore focus on those persons on whom the person with the disability will increasingly depend upon.

There are some basic guidelines that can be kept in mind to help social workers deal with family members' adjustment to the onset of the disability of a loved one.

- **Emotional coping and functioning skills.** The intensity and impact of disability on the family may be influenced by the family's ability to cope in previous life crises. Families that have dealt with previous crises, and done so effectively, may have acquired problem-solving and coping skills that can be used again to help them deal with the disablement of a family member. If the social worker is aware of this, he or she can build on these abilities and help the family or family member apply these skills in the new situation.

- **The family's post-trauma functioning.** It is important for the social worker to help individuals and family members recognize their strengths and find, maintain, and develop resources and supports. These would include "internal supports"—such as strong, effective relationships between family members, marital stability/partners' stability, strong parent-child bonds, as well as the effective decision-making and problem-solving skills of the family members. They would also include "external supports"—such as extended family members, friends, peer support, self-help groups, community resources, and supportive outside environments such as the school or workplace.

Family Systems Theory

Families operate as social systems or interrelated networks in which an impact on one component has significant consequences for all others in the system.

Some disabilities are easy for the public to understand; but as the Participation and Activity Limitation Survey (PALS) demonstrates, the term disability covers a wide range of issues that interfere with an individual's participation in society.

- **The person's status within the family.** The impact of disability on the family is influenced by who in the family has come to be disabled. For example, is the person a newborn, an infant, the spouse or partner, the primary wage earner, the primary decision maker, or the individual who provides most of the emotional support for other family members? Each circumstance will be different and each will call for a particular type of response with respect to how family members may or may not cope with the onset of disability.

- **The stage in the life cycle of the family.** The life cycle stage of the family will influence how people cope with the onset of disability. For example, if the onset of disability comes late in life, family members may have had an opportunity to plan for the onset of chronic illness or impairment. However, if the onset of the disability comes earlier as a consequence of birth impairment or injury, the family may well be affected quite differently. For example, a young couple may have significant financial difficulties resulting from loss of income and, depending on the type of disability, there may be consequences for intimacy and sexuality. For others, the onset of disability may be with the birth of a child who has significant impairments and the hopes, plans, and dreams of the parents may be dramatically altered. Again, each situation is unique and will require a unique solution.

- **Understanding the nature and extent of the disability.** This relates to the relationship of the family members with professionals who may be involved (especially medical professionals). Uncertainty, use of medical jargon, and lack of information can create tension and frustration for the family members. To be able to cope effectively, family members must be treated with dignity and respect and need to be involved in all aspects of treatment. In many situations, the social worker is a member of a multidisciplinary team and part of his or her role will be to serve as advocate for the individual and the family in relation to the professional support services being provided.

- **Facilitating access to resources is important.** The impact of disability on the family unit is often influenced by the availability of community resources. Such services include support networks, daycare, schools, jobs, attendant care, retraining, respite care, hospice care, transportation, or recreational facilities. Other important community resources include access to financial resources, including private pension plans, insurance plans, or government-sponsored financial programs, such as the federal government's Canada Pension Plan or the various provincial financial assistance programs. Helping families access financial, community, social, recreational and/or medical resources is often central to the social work practitioner's role.

Conclusion

Rehabilitation services are a primary area of social work with persons with disabilities. These services include hospitals, rehabilitation centres, group homes, chronic care facilities, as well as educational institutions. Social workers are also employed by provincial and federal governments and by a variety of charitable organizations, both in the provision of direct services and in the development of social policies. For those involved in direct practice, work focuses on counselling and helping with support services, including assisting with access to resources. This may include, for example, working with individuals with FASD and learning and developmental disabilities.

Since the 1970s, there has been a shift away from a narrow medical approach to disability to more of a socio-political model in which persons with disabilities are accepted as equal citizens. In line with the newer approach to disability, increasingly social workers are involved in campaigning on behalf of persons with disabilities, as advocates for social and political change. The Independent Living Movement has been a key development in the promotion of human rights for persons with disabilities. Their successful philosophy is one that promotes self-direction, self-determination, and full participation in the life of communities. This shift is to be welcomed and points the way towards significant advances in services and programs and a better life for persons with disabilities across Canada.

CHAPTER REVIEW

Key Terms

- Participation and Activity Limitation Survey (PALS)
- Disability
- Persons with disabilities
- Medical model
- Political rights model
- Independent Living Movement (ILM)

- Ableism
- Publicly funded disability programs
- Privately funded disability programs
- Family systems theory

Review Questions

1. Give some of the basic statistics that capture the extent of disability within the Canadian population.

2. What are important highlights in the history of disability in Canada?

3. What are the differences between a medical model and a social model of disability?

4. Define and outline some causes of *ableism* in our society.

5. What are six important issues that a social worker should consider when working with the family of a person with a disability?

6. Briefly trace the origins of the Independent Living Movement and describe its main objectives.

Exploring Social Work

1. Persons with disabilities face barriers to becoming fully participating citizens. Pick a type of disability (see page 316), and spend a few days considering how this disability might interfere with your daily life. Where do you live? How do you get to class? Do you have a job? Keep a log of your activities. Think too of your social interactions: What do you do for fun? How do you communicate with your friends or your partner? How would casual interactions with store clerks, neighbours, or strangers on the bus be affected? Write a report on your findings to share with your class.

2. Write a four-page paper outlining the difference between the two major models of disability: the medical model or personal tragedy theory and the political rights model or social oppression theory of disability.

Websites
- - - - - -

Human Resources and Social Development Canada
www.hrsdc.gc.ca

HRSDC offers information on federal programs for persons with disabilities. Select People with Disabilities from the A–Z Index.

Council of Canadians with Disabilities
www.ccdonline.ca

The Council of Canadians with Disabilities advocates at the federal level to improve the lives of men and women with disabilities in Canada by eliminating inequality and discrimination. Members include national, regional, and local advocacy organizations that are controlled by persons with disabilities.

Disabled Women's Network Ontario
dawn.thot.net

DAWN Ontario is a progressive, volunteer-driven, feminist organization dedicated to the advancement of equality of rights of women with disabilities.

Canadian Association for Community Living
www.cacl.ca

CACL is an organization that strives for the full inclusion of people with intellectual disabilities by providing leadership, promoting awareness, and using research and knowledge to inform efforts to advance rights and opportunities.

MOUTH magazine
www.mouthmag.com

First published in 1990, *MOUTH* magazine is a bi-monthly, disability rights-oriented publication.

CHAPTER 16

INTERNATIONAL SOCIAL WORK PRACTICE

Helping People Help Themselves

The history of international social work is a distinguished one. Since the early days of Jane Addams, the profession's first Nobel Prize winner, social workers have been actively involved within various national and international forums. Social workers have also been and remain involved with the resettling of refugees and other persons displaced by war, operating emergency relief services for victims of natural and human-made disasters, advocating on behalf of disadvantaged and vulnerable populations, organizing groups of oppressed people into effective political entities, and otherwise extending various programs of assistance to populations in need.

In all these areas, social workers play an indispensable and often unacknowledged role, sometimes working in very difficult and dangerous conditions.

What is International Social Work?

The term "international social work" has a variety of meanings. It can refer to the examination and comparison of the social welfare systems in different countries (comparative social welfare). It can also denote work within international organizations, such as governmental or voluntary organizations, that carry out social planning, social development, and welfare programs abroad, particularly in underdeveloped regions.

Finally, of course, it can simply refer to the day-to-day social work that social workers do with individuals, groups, and communities in a country other than their own.

The North-South Divide

In the context of underdeveloped regions, any discussion of international social work must begin by acknowledging the severe economic disadvantages faced by countries in the so-called "developing world." Nearly 11 million children under 5 die each year in these countries, mainly from preventable causes. Malnutrition contributes to 60 percent of all childhood deaths. Combined with preventable diseases, it is a "deadly duo." Poverty, of course, is one of the main causes of malnutrition and early death.

The economic world divides, broadly speaking, along the lines of the Northern and Southern hemispheres, the so-called **North-South divide**, with the countries of the First World awash in relative affluence and many of those in the **Third World** in abject poverty. The countries of the global south have 75 percent of the world's people, but only:

- 15 percent of the world's energy consumption.
- 17 percent of the world's GNP.
- 30 percent of the world's food grains.
- 18 percent of the world's export earnings.
- 11 percent of the world's education spending.
- 9 percent of the world's health expenditure.
- 5 percent of the world's science and technology.
- 8 percent of the world's industry.

Given this desperate state of affairs, dedicated social workers quickly realize that opportunities for bringing about effective social change, even change on a local scale, are limited. For this reason, social work activists are increasingly advocating a new approach to development based on adherence to two complementary guiding principles. These principles are:

- the promotion and protection of human rights, and
- ensuring sustainable development.

A great deal of useful international social work has taken place in pursuit of these two key objectives, which are discussed below.

North-South Divide

Economic division of the world along the lines of wealthy nations in the North and poor or developing nations in the South.

Third World

Developing countries of Central and South America, Africa, and Asia; also referred to as the global south or developing world.

International Social Work Practice Models

Within international social work practice, three broad approaches or models can be identified. They are not mutually exclusive; one might pursue more than one approach.

Social Welfare Model

The more conventional **social welfare model** of international social work is largely based on Keynesian economics (see Chapter 2, page 31) and American economist W.W. Rostow's "stages of industrialization" theory. Rostow's theory postulates that all societies go through five stages on the road to becoming a developed country: (1) traditional society, (2) long-growth preconditions, (3) short period "take-off," (4) a rapid drive to maturity, and (5) the era of mass consumption (Rostow 1960). Using this approach, the primary goal is to create the basic welfare conditions required to help move countries through the necessary stages of development. The main concern is with the satisfaction of basic social and material needs of people (e.g., minimal standards of living and access to at least basic health, education, and other essential social services).

New World Order Model

The **new world order model** has its origins in the idea that the current world order is not a democratic one, but rather one controlled by a relatively small number of wealthy countries and powerful corporations. Rather than being concerned with incremental change, those who follow this approach are concerned with bringing about widespread change in institutional arrangements that govern relationships between nations and, within nations, between groups of people. They focus on: (1) the active participation of all relevant sectors in the transformation process, (2) world peace and war prevention, (3) the alleviation of human suffering in the world, (4) the creation of effective systems of social protection and social service provision, (5) increased social and political justice, and (6) the protection and enhancement of the natural environment.

Social Development Model

A third approach, which is known as the **social development model**, falls somewhere between the two approaches introduced above and has its origins in the community development field. Social workers who use this approach to international work seek primarily to address the immediate causes of human degradation, powerlessness, and social inequality, and to guide collective action towards the elimination of all forms of oppression, injustice, and violence. Social development social workers are concerned with the fuller participation of people at all levels of the political and economic system and with fostering social, political, and economic systems that are more humane, inclusive, and participatory.

Respect for Cultural Diversity

Working in another country obviously involves being a practitioner in another cultural context. How does one prepare for such work? How does one ensure that one is "culturally competent"?

In social work literature, the term **cultural competence** emphasizes the need for social workers to gain an understanding of the world view or cultural frame of reference of the client. Thus, workers must make an effort to understand the history, language, and background characteristics of the cultural groups with which they are working. However, practitioners working abroad also need to be careful to avoid what may amount to stereotypes based on a limited knowledge of another culture. A sound understanding of cultural contexts will help the international social worker to be more effective in bringing about positive change.

For example, it would be inappropriate to work in China without considering the cultural differences among the various ethnic groups within the Chinese population. In addition, social workers must take their knowledge of the "other" culture and combine it with an analysis of how their own cultural outlook may influence their interventions. In other words, social workers need deep respect for the unique social conditions and cultural contexts within which they are working. Without such an appreciation of cultural differences, they will be less effective at assessing the problems at hand.

Cultural competence is clearly important for social workers actively engaged in working in other countries. As Canada continues to evolve as a modern, ethnically diverse nation, it is also becoming an increasingly necessary skill set in our work, home, and community lives.

Cultural Competence

An understanding of the world view or frame of reference held by a client, including his or her history, language, and background, while avoiding stereotypes and assumptions based on generalizations.

DID YOU KNOW?

- Among the seventy-three countries for which there is data (representing about 80 percent of the world's people), forty-eight have seen inequality increase since the 1950s, sixteen have experienced no change and only nine—with just 4 percent of the world's people—have seen a fall.

- Every year about 11 million children die of preventable causes, often for want of simple and easily provided improvements in nutrition, sanitation, maternal health, and education. That is twenty-one children per minute.

- At the end of 2000, more than 12 million people were refugees, 6 million were internally displaced and nearly 4 million were returning refugees and asylum seekers—in all, this represented an increase of 50 percent from 1990.

- Seven rich countries hold 48 percent of the voting power at the International Monetary Fund and 46 percent at the World Bank.

- The worst plague in human history is AIDS: its death toll surpasses that of the bubonic plague in Europe during the Middle Ages. By the end of 2000, almost 22 million people had died from AIDS, 13 million children has lost their mother or both parents and more than 40 million were living with HIV/AIDS—90 percent of them in developing countries, 75 percent of them in sub-Saharan Africa.

- International development aid from rich countries is only $65 per person living in those countries.

Source: Adapted from UNDP. *Human Development Report 2004: Cultural Liberty in Today's Diverse World*. United Nations Development Programme. 2004. www.hdr.undp.org.

The Promotion and Protection of Human Rights

The basic legal instruments

- Charter of the United Nations (1945)

- Universal Declaration of Human Rights (1948)

- The Covenants on Human Rights (1966)

- (a) International Covenant on Civil and Political Rights

- (b) International Covenant on Economic, Social and Cultural Rights

- International Convention on the Elimination of All Forms of Racial Discrimination (1965)

- Convention on the Elimination of All Forms of Discrimination Against Women (1979)

- Convention Against Torture and Other Cruel, Inhuman and Degrading Treatment or Punishment (1984)

- Convention on the Rights of the Child (1989)

- International Convention on the Protection of the Rights of All Migrant Workers and Members of Their Families (1990)

The idea of **human rights** is based on an acknowledgment that individuals possess certain inalienable political and civil rights. The notion that there is a duty to protect the rights of all people has become a recognized part of our human heritage.

The recognition of universal human rights was finally consolidated in the *Universal Declaration of Human Rights* which was adopted by the General Assembly of the United Nations in 1948. All the major countries of the world are now signatories to the UN *Declaration*. While the Universal Declaration of Human Rights is a non-binding document, it is a foundation document and is often invoked by national and other judiciaries around the world.

Three Types of Rights

When thinking about rights, it may be useful to distinguish between three types (or "generations") of human rights. This broad division was initially set out by the Czech legal scholar Karel Vasak in 1979. Vasak's divisions closely align with the famous watchwords of the French Revolution: Liberty, Equality, Fraternity.

- **Negative rights.** The first type represents civil and political rights as set forth in Articles 2 to 21 of the *Universal Declaration of Human Rights*. They pertain to liberty and political participation. These rights ensure protection of basic rights such as freedom from torture, false imprisonment, or summary execution.

- **Positive rights.** The second type represents economic, social, and cultural rights as detailed in Articles 22 to 27 of the Declaration. These rights are aimed at ensuring justice, freedom from want, and participation in society. These rights would include employment rights, housing and health care rights, as well as the right to social security.

- **Collective rights.** The third type encompasses the collective rights contained in Article 28, which states that "everyone is entitled to a social and international order in which the rights and freedoms set forth in this Declaration can be fully realized." This category goes beyond formal civil and social rights usually enshrined in national and international law. They would include such things as self-determination, economic and social development, healthy environment, communication, cultural heritage, and sustainability.

Historically, the social work profession has tended to focus on meeting basic needs rather than affirming human rights, but social workers have increasingly moved in the direction of affirming and fostering all three levels of rights.

TABLE 16.1: The Three Generations of Human Rights

	First Generation	Second Generation	Third Generation
Type	Civil and Political Rights	Economic, Social, and Cultural Rights	Collective Rights
Origin	Liberalism	Socialism, Social Democracy	Collectivism, Communitarianism
Examples	Right to vote Right to run for office Equality before the law Freedom of expression Freedom of assembly Right to a fair and prompt trial Freedom from torture and abuse Freedom from arbitrary arrest Freedom from discrimination Right to legal representation Freedom of association Freedom of movement Freedom from slavery	Right to education Right to housing Right to employment Right to health Right to income security Right to earn an income Freedom to spend money as one chooses Choice of partner Right to raise a family Right to safe working conditions Freedom of cultural expression Right to land Right to property Children's rights	Environmental rights: right to clean air, water Right to enjoy nature Right to benefit from development Right to belong to a strong, cohesive society

International Policy on Human Rights

The *International Policy on Human Rights* adopted by the International Federation of Social Work (IFSW) affirms that all social workers have a special responsibility to advance the cause of human rights throughout the world. In its preamble, it states:

> The history of human rights is that of the struggle against exploitation of one person by another. It is based on the recognition of basic rights founded on the concept of the inherent dignity and worth of every individual.

The policy asserts that human rights are a common standard and guide for the work of all professional social workers. It points out that social workers not only need to respect human rights, but also to work to oppose and eliminate all violations of human rights.

Human Rights

Rights inherent in our nature and without which we cannot live as human beings: include individual political, civil, collective cultural, social, and economic rights.

Ensuring Sustainable Development

Sustainable Development

Development that meets the needs of the present without compromising the ability of future generations to meet their own needs.

An important principle of international social work is that of **sustainable development**. The most frequently quoted definition of sustainable development is from the report Our Common Future (also known as the Brundtland Report): "Sustainable development is development that meets the needs of the present without compromising the ability of future generations to meet their own needs" (World Commission 1987, 43).

Sustainable development is not a new idea, of course—indigenous cultures have emphasized the need for a holistic approach or harmony between the environment, society, and economy. What is new is the reaffirmation of these ideas within the context of global capitalism and an information-based society.

Sustainable Social Progress

As an important extension to this concept of sustainable development, the International Council on Social Welfare (ICSW) advocates what it calls **sustainable social progress**, which goes beyond ecological and environmental concerns. The members of ICSW believe that, in order to promote sustainable social progress, social workers should support cooperation to strengthen governance and social standards internationally. International sustainable development, in this broader sense, includes all of the activities that international social workers carry out to enhance the participation of people in making decisions for themselves, combatting poverty, promoting women's health, and advancing the cause of peace.

Sustainable development (or sustainable social progress) is a central organizing principle for international social workers. Its application involves three basic operating premises:

- **Equity and justice for all**—upholding the rights of the poor and disadvantaged within and between nations, and the rights of future generations.

- **Long-term view**—advancing the view that all claims on the earth's resources today have implications for future generations.

- **Structural understanding of the broader society**—taking into account the many interconnections between individuals, communities, the economy, and the environment.

The concept is an important one for international social work practitioners and others involved in international development work. The idea challenges us to think beyond the here-and-now and look to the wider implications of our actions. In essence, it is a call to action—a call to do things differently and to realize that our actions have ripple effects throughout our interdependent world.

CLIMATE CHANGE

Over the last twenty years scientists, governments, environmentalists, and corporations have debated the existence and effects of global warming, greenhouse gases, and climate change. However, in recent years even carbon emission–producing industries such as oil companies and car manufacturers have recognized the need to reduce our impact on the environment (thanks, in part, to market forces) and most scientists agree that climate change is a fact and a major global threat.

The exact impact of greenhouse gas emission is uncertain. But we now know that there are large risks, potentially catastrophic ones, including the melting of the polar ice caps (which would place many countries under water) and changes in the course of the Gulf Stream that could bring about drastic climatic changes.

How we deal with climate change today will have a huge impact on the prospects of a large section of humanity. Failure to deal with this issue will dramatically affect the poorest 40 percent of the world's population—some 2.6 billion people. It will exacerbate deep inequalities within and between countries. Rich nations produce the overwhelming bulk of the greenhouse gases, but poor countries and their citizens will pay the highest price.

Mahatma Gandhi once reflected on how many planets might be needed to support the world's population if India were to follow Britain's course of industrialization. The impact of climate change on the poorest members of society is, and will continue to be, an issue that social workers must face.

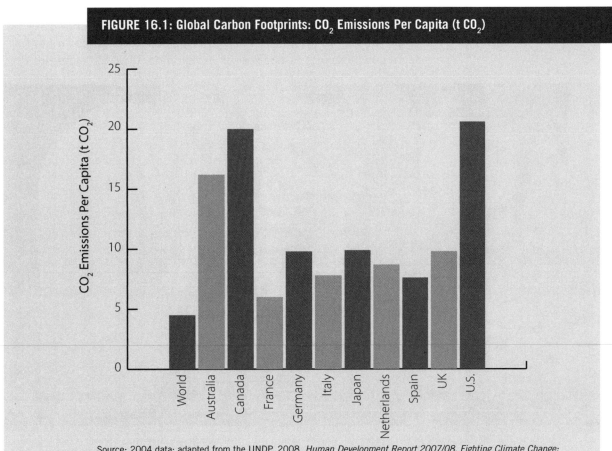

FIGURE 16.1: Global Carbon Footprints: CO_2 Emissions Per Capita (t CO_2)

Source: 2004 data; adapted from the UNDP. 2008. *Human Development Report 2007/08. Fighting Climate Change: Human Solidarity in a Divided World*. United Nations Development Programme. page 48. www.hdr.undp.org.

The Human Development Report

Human Development Report

hdr.undp.org

An annual report prepared by the UN's Human Development Programme examining the welfare of the global population; the reports often explore a specific theme each year.

The *Human Development Report* (HDR) is an independent report that is released each year. It is commissioned by the United Nations Development Programme (UNDP) and is the product of a team of leading scholars, practitioners, and members of the Human Development Report Office. The HDR was first launched in 1990 with the goal of putting people back at the centre of the development process in terms of economic debate, policy, and advocacy. It goes beyond income to assess the level of people's long-term well-being, emphasizing that the goals of development are choices and freedoms.

Since the first report in 1990, four composite indices for human development have been developed by the HDR team—the Human Development Index, the Gender-related Development Index, the Gender Empowerment Measure, and the Human Poverty Index. In addition to releasing new indicators for the previous year, each HDR also focuses on a highly topical theme, providing path-breaking analysis and policy recommendations. The Human Development Report Office also issues global, national, and regional reports on topics of the day. The Reports' messages—and the tools to implement them—have been embraced by people around the world, evidenced by the publication of similar human development reports at the national level in more than 120 countries.

Three-quarters of the people living in the world's 50 least developed countries survive on an income of less than a dollar a day. This woman collects garbage in Calcutta, India, where 34% of the population falls into this category.

The Human Development Index

While the concept of human development is much broader than any single index can measure, the HDR's principal human development indicator, the **Human Development Index (HDI)**, offers a powerful alternative to using income alone as a measure of human well-being. The HDI focuses on three basic dimensions of development: (1) a long and healthy life, as measured by life expectancy at birth; (2) knowledge, as measured by the adult literacy rate and the combined gross enrolment ratio for primary, secondary, and tertiary schools; and (3) a decent standard of living, as measured by GDP per capita in purchasing power parity (PPP) with U.S. dollars. The HDI was created to re-emphasize that people and their capabilities should be the ultimate criteria for assessing the development of a country, not economic growth. The index is constructed using indicators that are currently available and is based on a methodology that is simple and transparent.

The HDI itself does not claim to be comprehensive—for example, it does not include important aspects of human development, notably the ability to participate in political decisions. Likewise, it does not capture gender disparity and human deprivation, which are measured in other HDR indices (Gender-Related Development Index, and the Human Poverty Index). Nevertheless, the HDI is a powerful starting point for understanding and advocating for human development.

Human Development Index

Indicator used by UNDP to measure human well-being and assess the development of a country.

High Human Development
Med Human Development
Low Human Development
Not Ranked

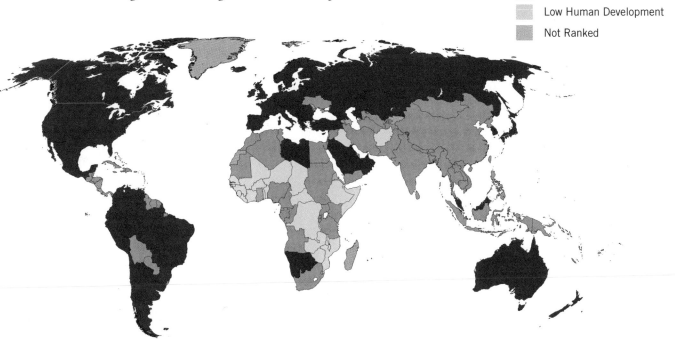

The Human Development Index takes into account life expectancy at birth, adult literacy, and gross domestic product per capita. It is a useful indicator of the overall well-being of countries and regions.

Source: Adapted from UN Human Development Index—Trends. 2007. UN Development Programme. http://hdr.undp.org/en/statistics/data/hd_map.

What Do International Social Workers Do?

Social work, as a helping profession, is especially concerned with the problems and rights of the disadvantaged. In working towards these ends, international social workers can be found undertaking a wide range of activities in a variety of national, international, and overseas organizations. These organizations include:

1. international intergovernmental organizations,
2. non-governmental organizations,
3. churches and other humanitarian organizations, and
4. community organizations.

International Intergovernmental Organizations

Many social workers are active in various international *intergovernmental organizations* (IGOs), of which the United Nations (UN) is best known. Formed at the end of World War II, the UN seeks to develop a framework of international law that will be followed by all nation states around the world. Social workers function in a variety of roles in its twelve specialized agencies, which include the UN Development Programme, UNICEF, World Health Organization, International Labour Office, and the UN High Commissioner for Refugees.

Within this arena, social workers participate as analysts and as direct practitioners in applying and monitoring the assistance and protection provided by UN declarations and conventions. Social workers also frequently work in a front-line capacity, providing refugee resettlement services, counselling children traumatized by war, distributing humanitarian assistance during disasters or war, or monitoring human rights abuses.

In Kosovo in the 1990s, for example, UNICEF provided life-saving assistance for children and women, and social workers were involved in distributing hygiene kits, blankets, water purification tablets, and basic medical supplies. They were also a part of trauma teams, along with medical professionals and psychologists, and participated in the long-term relief plans that emphasized support for educational systems and community organizations.

Non-Governmental Organizations

Social workers also work for the multitude of *non-governmental organizations* (NGOs) around the world. NGOs are international organizations, but they are not directly linked to governments. This allows such organizations more freedom to take up important issues and bring about effective change. NGOs tend to be small, dynamic groups that work on a variety of issues related to their particular political or philosophical stances.

Economic Development and Globalization

Clearly, the most pressing concern in poor countries is economic development. Economic development is a prerequisite if the people of these countries are to overcome the crushing poverty that many face daily.

Unfortunately, for the economies of many rich countries, the developing nations serve mainly as a source of raw materials and cheap labour. Indeed, many would argue that, in relation to the industrialized nations, many countries in the Third World are not so much "developing" as "underdeveloping."

In general, the development plans of the International Monetary Fund (IMF) and World Bank have not led to economic prosperity. What has transpired under the banners of "globalization" and "development" appears to be more a continuing enslavement than economic liberation. (For more on globalization, see Chapter 2, page 32.)

Students of social work may find it helpful to do volunteer work for NGOs to build experience and make contacts for future work. Many NGOs have entry-level positions for new social workers without extensive experience. Non-governmental organizations such as Canadian Crossroads International, Canada World Youth, and World University Service of Canada provide excellent opportunities for social workers to gain international experience.

Social workers working with NGOs frequently find themselves directly participating in peace building and conflict resolution. For example, in the central Caucasus region—Georgia, Armenia, and Azerbaijan—social workers are using art therapy to help children heal from the trauma of war and to build peace between the various groups torn by inter-ethnic conflict since the late 1980s. The projects encourage the children to express their thoughts and feelings through coloured pictures and paintings. Children from all ethnic groups attend the projects, and it is hoped that links will be established between communities.

Churches and Other Organizations

Churches and other religious groups and organizations have an extensive variety of *overseas humanitarian programs*, and they frequently employ the services of social workers. These groups tend to operate in the poorer countries of Africa, Asia, and Latin America. Nowadays, few churches use their programs primarily as a way to get new recruits (although some still do). For example, the United Church has excellent preparation and support throughout the world and does not send workers overseas unless requested by partner organizations.

As well as church and religious organizations, there are large international grant foundations that employ social workers as consultants, field representatives and country directors for programs that the foundation supports. The Canadian government also maintains offices in many countries that provide services to visiting Canadians and to local people. These services frequently involve social workers. Other federal government departments, such as the Department of Foreign Affairs and International Trade, the Canadian International Development Agency (CIDA) and the International Development Research Centre (IDRC), hire social workers to help with their work. CIDA is the federal agency charged with planning and implementing most of Canada's development cooperation program in order to reduce poverty and to contribute to a more secure, equitable, and prosperous world.

Working directly for government agencies of other countries is another option for social workers seeking international experience. These agencies are not necessarily international in focus, but certainly can be considered as part of an international social work career. Generally, however, one must have extensive language skills and direct contacts within the country in order to obtain such a position.

One important aspect of a community's well-being is access to clean water. Simple systems such as this one in a village in Africa's Ivory Coast are the first step to raising people's quality of life.

International Community Work

Canadian Government Opportunities

www.dfait-maeci.gc.ca

www.acdi-cida.gc.ca

www.idrc.ca

The federal departments listed above hire social workers to help with Canadian international aid programs.

International community work is a common type of social work activity in developing countries. Social workers work with communities by assisting with problem solving and with planning effective social services. They use community work to organize people to bring about major social change between nations, within nations, and between groups of people. They work with communities to achieve the fullest participation of community members in transforming various aspects of their lives.

The ultimate goal of community work is the empowerment or fostering of the "sense in people that they have the ability and right to influence their environment" (Lee, B. 1999, 43). Empowering people means that they can create and take action on their own behalf to meet their physical, spiritual, and psychological needs and participate directly in the change process.

One aspect of international social work is with IGOs, such as the UN, which assist with disaster relief, refugee resettlement, monitoring human rights abuses, and humanitarian assistance during war.

To be able to act on their own behalf, however, people must see themselves as citizens, with the right and ability to express their opinions and to acquire resources. Reaching these objectives requires a genuine sense of community (Lee, B. 1999). On the basis of community, new organizations can be built or improved upon and change can be effected.

The Canadian International Development Agency (CIDA)

The **Canadian International Development Agency (CIDA)** is Canada's lead agency for development assistance. Its mandate is to support sustainable development in developing countries in order to reduce poverty and to contribute to a more secure, equitable, and prosperous world. CIDA was established in 1968 to administer the bulk of Canada's official development assistance (ODA) program. CIDA's priorities are poverty reduction, democratic governance, private sector development, health, basic education, equality between women and men, and environmental sustainability.

CIDA, for example, sponsors a community-organizing project in Pakistan in which social workers play a key role. The goals of the $4.96–million project are to encourage more of Pakistan's rural poor to become involved in the process of developing their community, as well as to motivate and strengthen community-based organizations and women's development organizations, and to encourage other groups to help get their community members involved in addressing development needs. Through this project, about 360 community organizations are being helped to undertake community development.

Canadian International Development Agency (CIDA)

Supports sustainable development in developing countries to reduce poverty and contribute to a more secure, equitable, and prosperous world.

AH-HAH! Method
Working with Communities

The **AH-HAH! method,** presented in *AH-HAH! A New Approach to Popular Education* (GATT-Fly 1983), was developed in Canada and is frequently used by Canadian social workers in overseas settings. The name refers to the exclamation of "Ah-hah!" emitted by a person at the moment clarity or understanding dawns.

The aim is to enable participants to piece together their individual experiences in a way that clarifies their understanding of political and socioeconomic systems. It closely follows the principles of Paulo Freire (1971), the Brazilian educator whose work has had a profound impact on education and the struggle for rational development (see Chapter 7, page 125). People know the world as they see it, and through this knowledge they are able to intervene to transform their situations. The AH-HAH! method involves, in part, the idea of drawing a picture that represents the experiences of the group. In the process, an image of the economic and social system begins to emerge, leading to a discussion of government, legal systems, ownership of businesses, the military, and so forth.

Problem-posing education of this kind regards dialogue and critical thinking as indispensable to learning. This contrasts with a "banking" perspective towards education, in which participants are treated as empty vessels that must be filled with knowledge and information. The method is highly participatory and transformative, and involves concrete action as its objective.

The Internet and International Social Work

The Internet is not only enabling economic globalization, it is also enabling the connection of people and communities for the promotion of social justice and peace. It is being used for electronic advocacy, human rights protection, and community building.

Electronic Advocacy

Electronic advocacy might be the best way to conceptualize the importance of information technology to social work. **Electronic advocacy** refers to the process of using communication and information technologies to disseminate information and to mobilize support from a large constituency to influence decision-making processes or to support efforts at policy change. It may include the use of telephone, fax, television, radio, e-mail, websites, online discussion groups, network newsgroups, and other modes of communication. These kinds of tools will become increasingly important to social workers in the years to come.

The Internet is also providing new and different ways for people in dispersed communities to connect and advocate for their own rights or the rights of others. In these new virtual communities, people meet, discuss, and share information. This technology allows social workers to connect with people who would have been unreachable in the pre-Internet era, and familiarity with online communication is becoming part of the skill set of international social workers.

The Internet has also become a tool for the promotion and protection of human rights. Human rights abuses often necessitate urgent action, and the Internet provides the obvious tool for disseminating information.

E-WASTED BY THE WEST

Lagos, a city whose population is rapidly approaching 20 million, has a huge waste disposal problem. And, thanks to the monthly arrival of up to 500 shipping containers of waste from the U.S. and Europe, the problem is getting worse. According to U.S. environment group Basel Action Network, up to 75 percent of the loads contain so-called e-waste—obsolete electronic items such as computers and TVs, often in the guise of "charitable donations."

Although there is great demand for second-hand imported electronic goods in the city, the vast majority is discarded on arrival and ends up in dumpsites, where it is burnt. With some of the components containing hazardous substances, environmentalists are extremely concerned.

"It is a very worrisome situation," says Leslie Adogame of the Nigerian Environmental Society. "People around the areas where the waste is burnt are suffering from chest-related diseases because they inhale a lot of noxious substances."

Laws on safe disposal of electronic goods have been introduced in the U.S. and Europe but continue to be flouted, despite campaigners' efforts to ensure companies comply. The U.S. Government recently proposed a new e-waste law which would allow U.S. shippers legally to send waste anywhere in the world as long as it is labelled "recycling."

Source: "Electronic Waste From the U.S. and Europe Disguised as 'Charitable Donations' to Lagos." *New Internationalist Magazine.* Issue 410. April 2008. www.newint.org/columns/currents/2008/04/01/nigeria/. Used with permission.

The Digital Divide

It is important to bear in mind that most of the world's peoples do not have access to information technology—a problem sometimes referred to as the **digital divide**. This is an important social justice issue in its own right. As information and scientific knowledge become increasingly important for economic and social development, addressing the problems associated with unequal access to information technology becomes especially important in the context of international social work.

As the capabilities and capacity of the Internet increase, new uses and applications for social work will emerge. Intranets will enable organizations to streamline work procedures, virtual office environments will allow international NGOs to work together more effectively, and video conferencing will emerge as a key tool for communication. During the Kosovo crisis of the 1990s, for example, the Internet was used to facilitate collaboration within and between social workers in various NGOs.

According to the International Telecommunications Union, a UN agency, in 2009 more than a quarter of the world's population were using the Internet; however, a dramatic divide still exists between the developed and developing worlds. In Africa, there is only 1 subscriber to fixed broadband in 1,000, while in Europe that rate is 200 per 1,000. The cost of broadband remains prohibitively high in Africa, where the relative cost is highest and the income levels are lowest.

Small, low-cost laptops are providing children in developing countries— such as this girl in Peru—with access to technology.

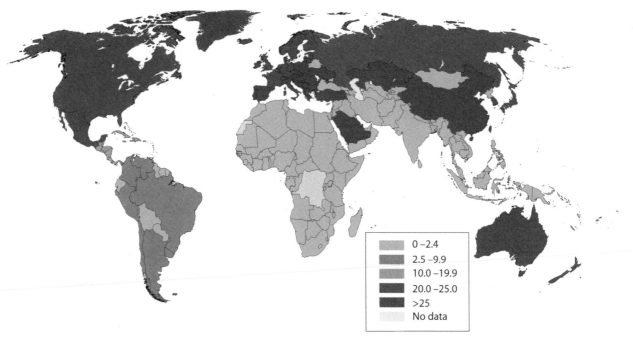

	0 –2.4
	2.5 –9.9
	10.0 –19.9
	20.0 –25.0
	>25
	No data

This map shows the number of fixed broadband Internet subscribers per 100 inhabitants in 2008. In Canada, the number of users is more than 25 per 100; in Africa, it is less than 2.5.

Source: Adapted from "The Global Broadband Divide—2008" in "The World in 2009: ICT Facts and Figures." 2009. International Telecommunications Union. www.itu.int/ITU-D/ict/material/Telecom09_flyer.pdf.

AIDS has ravaged countries throughout Africa; many social workers work with AIDS-related programs, such as orphanages like this one in Addis Ababa, Ethiopia.

Participatory Action Research

Social workers overseas have widely and successfully employed a technique known as participatory research or **participatory action research (PAR)**. Participatory action research has provided social workers with a useful set of techniques with which to bring about social change.

PAR is an approach to knowledge generation that views research as the means by which collective actions against the causes of injustice, exploitation, violence, and environmental degradation can occur. Participatory action research is now promoted by many international development agencies around the world as an important tool for bringing about change within communities and groups.

By the People, For the People

Social workers using PAR in their overseas community work usually combine three types of activity: investigation, education, and action. The objectives are attained through collective processes involving the participation of people who are directly affected by a program or service. People in the community play a large part in all activities, since those involved in a program on a day-to-day basis, or those who are affected by a particular policy, usually know a great deal about it and should become the centre or beginning point of the social work process.

Compared to more traditional forms of research, PAR is ideally carried out by the local people, for the local people. Research is aimed at specific issues that are identified by local people and the results of the research are applied to solving the problems at hand. Often the process is continuous in that the community starts with a particular problem or concern, initiates research, determines a course of action, learns about this action, and then proceeds to a new round of research and action.

The notion of power equalization is important to social workers using PAR. Collective inquiry transfers control of knowledge as people move from being mere objects to acting as subjects in their own development process. Empowerment in the context of overseas community work involves giving control over the decision-making process to the members of the community.

In CIDA's Southern Africa AIDS Training Program, for example, local organizations are given support in their efforts to serve those most vulnerable to HIV/AIDS. This includes setting up anti-AIDS clubs in schools, visiting orphans, working to keep families together, and assisting families with food, counselling, and education. To be successful, local people must have decision-making power in the conception of the program and in its operations.

To take another example, in Ethiopia, War Child, in conjunction with Street Symphony and The Dandelion Trust, is working on projects aimed at providing practical aid, as well as some fun, and greater self-respect to street children. Street Symphony runs drama and dance projects that allow the street children to participate in performances for officials and dignitaries as well as the general public. While being trained as dancers, the children are fed, clothed, and provided with a safe home. They learn to express themselves through drama and dance while also raising awareness of their plight through the performances.

Conclusion

This chapter focuses on the work of social workers in *developing* or *Third World* countries. In particular, it examines the core problems of social and economic development in these countries in the modern context of economic globalization. Since those involved in social work at the international level tend to be heavily involved in local community development and human rights work, much of the chapter focuses on these areas.

International social work is increasingly being recognized as an important area of social work practice. This is due, in part, to the identification of economic globalization as a factor in world poverty and a recognition that our local concerns are connected to global ones. This "internationalization" of social problems implies that social workers increasingly need to be knowledgeable and skilled in international social work theory and practice. Accordingly, social workers need to acquire new technology skills to enhance their ability to work and think both locally and globally.

Social workers who do international work do so through an entire network of government and non-governmental agencies. The most prominent of these agencies are those associated with the United Nations and its various bodies, and those agencies associated with voluntary international aid agencies, such as the ones organized by various religious organizations. A great deal of useful work is being done through these organizations around the world to alleviate suffering and promote economic growth. However, the scope of the problems facing the poor nations of the world is enormous and the potential risks are often great.

It is important to remember that the work that social workers do abroad can be very dangerous at times. Not infrequently, their lives are at risk and their devotion goes well beyond the call of duty. This is a further testimony of the dedication of those individuals who are drawn into the social work profession today, and especially those involved in social work in developing or war-torn countries of the Third World.

CHAPTER REVIEW

Key Terms

- North–South divide
- Third World
- Social welfare model
- New world order model
- Social development model
- Cultural competence
- Human rights
- Negative rights
- Positive rights
- Collective rights

- Sustainable development
- Sustainable social progress
- *Human Development Report* (HDR)
- Human Development Index (HDI)
- Canadian International Development Agency (CIDA)
- Electronic advocacy
- Digital divide
- Participatory action research (PAR)

Review Questions

1. What are some indicators of global economic and social inequality?

2. Define the two key principles that underlie international social work.

3. Define and distinguish the three levels of human rights. Why is it important for social workers to affirm and work towards all three levels?

4. What are three key approaches to international social work practice?

5. Identify and describe the various types of agencies that employ social workers abroad.

6. How is the Internet changing the way that social workers advocate for human rights?

7. What makes the AH-HAH! method (page 349) of working in communities so successful in international social work?

Exploring Social Work

1. Climate change affects people in all countries, but it seems that the poorer countries are more vulnerable. Do you believe that climate change is a real threat to the future of humanity? If so, what do you think that we in Canada should do? Break into small groups and discuss these issues. The 2008 Human Development Report of the United Nations (available online) provides ample background reading on these issues and more.

2. There are many social workers working in poor countries trying to do their best to serve where needed. What role do you see for social workers in poor countries? Is it all one way (us helping them) or do you see it as more of a two-way sharing? What can we learn about community and family from other countries? Record your reflections in a two-page paper.

3. Read the "E-Wasted by the West" feature (page 350) and research the topic online. Explore your thoughts regarding this article in small groups. It seems that this kind of "aid" is growing as rich countries aim to dump their garbage. What do you think should be done about this kind of abuse?

Websites

- - - - - -

New Internationalist
www.newint.org

This monthly print magazine is available online. It provides a clearly written and concise overview of the important global issues of concern to social workers. It is an excellent resource to kick-start an essay on international issues.

United Nations Development Programme (UNDP)
www.undp.org

At the UN Millennium Summit, world leaders pledged to cut poverty in half by 2015. UNDP is charged with helping to make this happen. Their website contains comprehensive links, publications, and various UNDP speeches and reports. Their publications section has numerous complete books online, including their annual Overcoming Human Poverty Report.

Heritage Canada Human Rights Program
www.pch.gc.ca/ddp-hrd

This comprehensive website has basic information about human rights in Canada and internationally. It contains most of the official UN human rights covenants and an excellent overview of how the international human rights system works.

CODE OF ETHICS, 2005

Acknowledgements

The Canadian Association of Social Workers (CASW) acknowledges with thanks the National Association of Social Workers (NASW) for permission to use sections of the copyrighted NASW 1999 *Code of Ethics* in the development of the CASW 2005 *Code of Ethics* and CASW 2005 *Guidelines for Ethical Practice*.

The CASW also acknowledges that other codes of ethics and resources were used in the development of this *Code* and the *Guidelines for Ethical Practice*, in particular the *Code of Ethics* of the Australian Association of Social Workers (AASW). These resources can be found in the Reference section of each document.

Purpose of the CASW Code of Ethics

Ethical behaviour lies at the core of every profession. The Canadian Association of Social Workers (CASW) *Code of Ethics* sets forth values and principles to guide social workers' professional conduct. A code of ethics cannot guarantee ethical behaviour. Ethical behaviour comes from a social worker's individual commitment to engage in ethical practice. Both the spirit and the letter of this *Code of Ethics* will guide social workers as they act in good faith and with a genuine desire to make sound judgements.

This *Code of Ethics* is consistent with the International Federation of Social Workers (IFSW) *International Declaration of Ethical Principles of Social Work* (1994, 2004), which requires members of the CASW to uphold the values and principles established by both the CASW and the IFSW. Other individuals, organizations and bodies (such as regulatory boards, professional liability insurance providers, courts of law, boards of directors of organizations employing social workers and government agencies) may also choose to adopt this *Code of Ethics* or use it as a basis for evaluating professional conduct. In Canada, each province and territory is responsible for regulating the professional conduct of social workers to ensure the protection of the public. Social workers are advised to contact the regulatory body in their province or territory to determine whether it has adopted this *Code of Ethics*.[1]

---

[1] To find the IFSW declarations or information about your relevant regulatory body, visit the CASW web site: http://www.casw-acts.ca

Recognition of Individual and Professional Diversity

The CASW *Code of Ethics* does not provide a set of rules that prescribe how social workers should act in all situations. Further, the *Code of Ethics* does not specify which values and principles are most important and which outweigh others in instances of conflict. Reasonable differences of opinion exist among social workers with respect to which values and principles should be given priority in a particular situation. Further, a social worker's personal values, culture, religious beliefs, practices and/or other important distinctions, such as age, ability, gender or sexual orientation can affect his/her ethical choices. Thus, social workers need to be aware of any conflicts between personal and professional values and deal with them responsibly.

Ethical Behaviour Requires Due Consideration of Issues and Judgement

Social work is a multifaceted profession. As professionals, social workers are educated to exercise judgement in the face of complex and competing interests and claims. Ethical decision-making in a given situation will involve the informed judgement of the individual social worker. Instances may arise when social workers' ethical obligations conflict with agency policies, or relevant laws or regulations. When such conflicts occur, social workers shall make a responsible effort to resolve the conflicts in a manner that is consistent with the values and principles expressed in this *Code of Ethics*. If a reasonable resolution of the conflict does not appear possible, social workers shall seek appropriate consultation before making a decision. This may involve consultation with an ethics committee, a regulatory body, a knowledgeable colleague, supervisor or legal counsel.

Preamble

The social work profession is dedicated to the welfare and self-realization of all people; the development and disciplined use of scientific and professional knowledge; the development of resources and skills to meet individual, group, national and international changing needs and aspirations; and the achievement of social justice for all. The profession has a particular interest in the needs and empowerment of people who are vulnerable, oppressed, and/or living in poverty. Social workers are committed to human rights as enshrined in Canadian law, as well as in international conventions on human rights created or supported by the United Nations.

As professionals in a country that upholds respect for diversity, and in keeping with democratic rights and freedoms, social workers respect the distinct systems of beliefs and lifestyles of individuals, families, groups, communities and nations without prejudice (United Nations Centre for Human Rights, 1992). Specifically, social workers do not tolerate discrimination[2] based on age, abilities, ethnic background, gender, language, marital status, national ancestry, political affiliation, race, religion, sexual orientation or socio-economic status.

Core Social Work Values and Principles

Social workers uphold the following core social work values:

> Value 1: Respect for Inherent Dignity and Worth of Persons

> Value 2: Pursuit of Social Justice

---

[2] Throughout this document the term "discrimination" refers to treating people unfavourably or holding negative or prejudicial attitudes based on discernible differences or stereotypes. It does **not refer** to the positive intent behind programs, such as affirmative action, where one group may be given preferential treatment to address inequities created by discrimination.

Value 3: Service to Humanity

Value 4: Integrity of Professional Practice

Value 5: Confidentiality in Professional Practice

Value 6: Competence in Professional Practice

The following section describes each of these values and discusses their underlying principles.

Value 1: Respect for the Inherent Dignity and Worth of Persons

Social work is founded on a long-standing commitment to respect the inherent dignity and individual worth of all persons. When required by law to override a client's wishes, social workers take care to use the minimum coercion required. Social workers recognize and respect the diversity of Canadian society, taking into account the breadth of differences that exist among individuals, families, groups and communities. Social workers uphold the human rights of individuals and groups as expressed in the *Canadian Charter of Rights and Freedoms* (1982) and the United Nations *Universal Declaration of Human Rights* (1948).

Principles:

- Social workers respect the unique worth and inherent dignity of all people and uphold human rights.

- Social workers uphold each person's right to self-determination, consistent with that person's capacity and with the rights of others.

- Social workers respect the diversity among individuals in Canadian society and the right of individuals to their unique beliefs consistent with the rights of others.

- Social workers respect the client's right to make choices based on voluntary, informed consent.

- Social workers who have children as clients determine the child's ability to consent and where appropriate, explain to the child and to the child's parents/guardians, the nature of the social worker's relationship to the child.

- Social workers uphold the right of society to impose limitations on the self-determination of individuals, when such limitations protect individuals from self-harm and from harming others.

- Social workers uphold the right of every person to be free from violence and threat of violence.

Value 2: Pursuit of Social Justice

Social workers believe in the obligation of people, individually and collectively, to provide resources, services and opportunities for the overall benefit of humanity and to afford them protection from harm. Social workers promote social fairness and the equitable distribution of resources, and act to reduce barriers and expand choice for all persons, with special regard for those who are marginalized, disadvantaged, vulnerable, and/or have exceptional needs. Social workers oppose prejudice and discrimination against any person or group of persons, on any grounds, and specifically challenge views and actions that stereotype particular persons or groups.

Principles:

- Social workers uphold the right of people to have access to resources to meet basic human needs.

- Social workers advocate for fair and equitable access to public services and benefits.
- Social workers advocate for equal treatment and protection under the law and challenge injustices, especially injustices that affect the vulnerable and disadvantaged.
- Social workers promote social development and environmental management in the interests of all people.

Value 3: Service to Humanity

The social work profession upholds service in the interests of others, consistent with social justice, as a core professional objective. In professional practice, social workers balance individual needs, and rights and freedoms with collective interests in the service of humanity. When acting in a professional capacity, social workers place professional service before personal goals or advantage, and use their power and authority in disciplined and responsible ways that serve society. The social work profession contributes to knowledge and skills that assist in the management of conflicts and the wide-ranging consequences of conflict.

Principles:

- Social workers place the needs of others above self-interest when acting in a professional capacity.
- Social workers strive to use the power and authority vested in them as professionals in responsible ways that serve the needs of clients and the promotion of social justice.
- Social workers promote individual development and pursuit of individual goals, as well as the development of a just society.
- Social workers use their knowledge and skills in bringing about fair resolutions to conflict and in assisting those affected by conflict.

Value 4: Integrity in Professional Practice

Social workers demonstrate respect for the profession's purpose, values and ethical principles relevant to their field of practice. Social workers maintain a high level of professional conduct by acting honestly and responsibly, and promoting the values of the profession. Social workers strive for impartiality in their professional practice, and refrain from imposing their personal values, views and preferences on clients. It is the responsibility of social workers to establish the tenor of their professional relationship with clients, and others to whom they have a professional duty, and to maintain professional boundaries. As individuals, social workers take care in their actions to not bring the reputation of the profession into disrepute. An essential element of integrity in professional practice is ethical accountability based on this *Code of Ethics*, the IFSW *International Declaration of Ethical Principles of Social Work*, and other relevant provincial/territorial standards and guidelines. Where conflicts exist with respect to these sources of ethical guidance, social workers are encouraged to seek advice, including consultation with their regulatory body.

Principles:

- Social workers demonstrate and promote the qualities of honesty, reliability, impartiality and diligence in their professional practice.
- Social workers demonstrate adherence to the values and ethical principles of the profession and promote respect for the profession's values and principles in organizations where they work or with which they have a professional affiliation.

- Social workers establish appropriate boundaries in relationships with clients and ensure that the relationship serves the needs of clients.
- Social workers value openness and transparency in professional practice and avoid relationships where their integrity or impartiality may be compromised, ensuring that should a conflict of interest be unavoidable, the nature of the conflict is fully disclosed.

Value 5: Confidentiality in Professional Practice

A cornerstone of professional social work relationships is confidentiality with respect to all matters associated with professional services to clients. Social workers demonstrate respect for the trust and confidence placed in them by clients, communities and other professionals by protecting the privacy of client information and respecting the client's right to control when or whether this information will be shared with third parties. Social workers only disclose confidential information to other parties (including family members) with the informed consent of clients, clients' legally authorized representatives or when required by law or court order. The general expectation that social workers will keep information confidential does not apply when disclosure is necessary to prevent serious, foreseeable and imminent harm to a client or others. In all instances, social workers disclose the least amount of confidential information necessary to achieve the desired purpose.

Principles:

- Social workers respect the importance of the trust and confidence placed in the professional relationship by clients and members of the public.
- Social workers respect the client's right to confidentiality of information shared in a professional context.
- Social workers only disclose confidential information with the informed consent of the client or permission of client's legal representative.
- Social workers may break confidentiality and communicate client information without permission when required or permitted by relevant laws, court order or this *Code*.
- Social workers demonstrate transparency with respect to limits to confidentiality that apply to their professional practice by clearly communicating these limitations to clients early in their relationship.

Value 6: Competence in Professional Practice

Social workers respect a client's right to competent social worker services. Social workers analyze the nature of social needs and problems, and encourage innovative, effective strategies and techniques to meet both new and existing needs and, where possible, contribute to the knowledge base of the profession. Social workers have a responsibility to maintain professional proficiency, to continually strive to increase their professional knowledge and skills, and to apply new knowledge in practice commensurate with their level of professional education, skill and competency, seeking consultation and supervision as appropriate.

Principles:

- Social workers uphold the right of clients to be offered the highest quality service possible.
- Social workers strive to maintain and increase their professional knowledge and skill.

- Social workers demonstrate due care for client's interests and safety by limiting professional practice to areas of demonstrated competence.

- Social workers contribute to the ongoing development of the profession and its ability to serve humanity, where possible, by participating in the development of current and future social workers and the development of new professional knowledge.

- Social workers who engage in research minimize risks to participants, ensure informed consent, maintain confidentiality and accurately report the results of their studies.

Glossary

Capacity

The ability to understand information relevant to a decision and to appreciate the reasonably foreseeable consequences of choosing to act or not to act. Capacity is specific to each decision and thus a person may be capable of deciding about a place of residence, for example, but not capable with respect to deciding about a treatment. Capacity can change over time (Etchells, Sharpe, Elliot and Singer, 1996).

Recent references in law point to the concept of "a mature minor," which Rozovsky and Rozovsky (1990) define as "…one with capacity to understand the nature and consequences of medical treatment. Such a person has the power to consent to medical treatment and parental consent is not necessary" (p. 55). They quote the comments by The Honorable Justice Lambert in *Van Mol v. Ashmore*, which help clarify common law with respect to a minor's capacity to consent. He states:

> At common law, without reference to statute law, a young person, still a minor, may give, on his or her own behalf, a fully informed consent to medical treatment if he or she has sufficient maturity, intelligence and capacity of understanding what is involved in making informed choices about the proposed medical treatment…once the capacity to consent has been achieved by the young person reaching sufficient maturity, intelligence and capability of understanding, the discussions about the nature of the treatment, its gravity, the material risks and any special and unusual risks, and the decisions about undergoing treatment, and about the form of the treatment, must all take place with and be made by the young person whose bodily integrity is to be invaded and whose life and health will be affected by the outcome.

Child

The *Convention on the Rights of the Child* passed by the United Nations in 1959 and ratified by Canada in 1990, define a child as a person under the age of 18 years unless national law recognizes an earlier age of majority (Alberta Law Reform Institute, 1991). The age of majority differs in provinces and territories in Canada. Under the *Criminal Code of Canada*, the age of consent is held to be over the age of 14 years; age in the context of the criminal code frequently refers to capacity to consent to sexual relations. All jurisdictions in Canada have legislation regarding child protection, which defines the age of a child for the purposes of protection. In Canada, in the absence of provincial or territorial legislation, courts are governed by common law. Social workers are encouraged to maintain current knowledge with respect to legislation on the age of a child, as well as capacity and consent in their jurisdiction.

Client

A person, family, group of persons, incorporated body, association or community on whose behalf a social worker provides or agrees to provide a service or to whom the social worker is legally obligated to provide a service. Examples of legal obligation to provide service include a legislated responsibility (such as in child welfare) or a valid court order. In the case of a valid court order, the judge/court is the client and the person(s) who is ordered by the court to participate in assessment is recognized as an involuntary client.

Conduct Unbecoming

Behaviour or conduct that does not meet social work standard of care requirements and is, therefore, subject to discipline. In reaching a decision in Matthews and Board of Directors of Physiotherapy (1986) 54 O.R. (2d) 375, Saunders J. makes three important statements regarding standards of practice, and by implication, professional codes of ethics:

1. Standards of practice are inherent characteristics of any profession.
2. Standards of practice may be written or unwritten.
3. Some conduct is clearly regarded as misconduct and need not be written down, whereas other conduct may be the subject of dispute within a profession.
   (See "Standard of Practice.")

Confidentiality

A professional value that demands that professionally acquired information be kept private and not shared with third parties unless the client provides informed consent or a professional or legal obligation exists to share such information without client informed consent.

Discrimination

Treating people unfavourably or holding negative or prejudicial attitudes based on discernible differences or stereotypes (AASW, 1999).

Informed Consent

Voluntary agreement reached by a capable client based on information about foreseeable risks and benefits associated with the agreement (e.g., participation in counselling or agreement to disclose social work report to a third party).

Human Rights

The rights of an individual that are considered the basis for freedom and justice, and serve to protect people from discrimination and harassment. Social workers may refer to the *Canadian Charter of Rights and Freedoms* enacted as Schedule B to the *Canada Act* 1982 (U.K.) 1982, c. 11, which came into force on April 17, 1982, as well as the *Universal Declaration of Human Rights* (1948) proclaimed by the United Nations General Assembly December 10, 1948.

Malpractice and Negligence

Behaviour that is included in "conduct unbecoming" and relates to social work practice behaviour within the parameters of the professional relationship that falls below the standard of practice and results in, or aggravation of, injury to a client. It includes behaviour that results in assault, deceit, fraudulent misrepresentations, defamation of character, breach of contract, violation of human rights, malicious prosecution, false imprisonment or criminal conviction.

Self-Determination

A core social work value that refers to the right to self-direction and freedom of choice without interference from others. Self-determination is codified in practice through mechanisms of informed consent. Social workers may be obligated to limit self-determination when a client lacks capacity or in order to prevent harm (Regehr and Antle, 1997).

Social Worker

A person who is duly registered to practice social work in a province or territory; or where mandatory registration does not exist, a person with social work education from an institution recognized by the Canadian Association of Schools of Social Work (CASSW) or an institution from outside of Canada that has been approved by the CASW, who is practising social work and who voluntarily agrees to be subject to this *Code of Ethics*. **Note:** Social workers living in Quebec and British Columbia, whose social work education was obtained outside of Canada, follow a separate approval process within their respective provinces.

Standard of Practice

The standard of care ordinarily expected of a competent social worker. It means that the public is assured that a social worker has the training, the skill and the diligence to provide them with social work services. Social workers are urged to refer to standards of practice that have been set by their provincial or territorial regulatory body or relevant professional association (see "Conduct Unbecoming").

Voluntary

"In the context of consent, 'voluntariness' refers to a patient's right to make treatment decisions free of any undue influence, such as ability of others to exert control over a patient by force, coercion or manipulation. ...The requirement for voluntariness does not imply that clinicians should refrain from persuading patients to accept advice. Persuasion involves appealing to the patient's reason in an attempt to convince him or her of the merits of a recommendation. In attempting to persuade the patient to follow a particular course of action, theclinician still leaves the patient free to accept or reject this advice." (Etchells, Sharpe, Dykeman, Meslin and Singer, 1996, p. 1083).

References

AASW. (1999). *AASW code of ethics*. Kingston: Australian Association of Social Workers (AASW).

Alberta Law Reform Institute. (1991). *Status of the child: Revised report* (Report No. 60). Edmonton, Alberta: Law Reform Institute.

BASW. (2002). *BASW: A code of ethics for social workers*. British Association of Social Workers (BASW).

Canadian Charter of Rights and Freedoms. Enacted as Schedule B to the Canada Act 1982, c.11 (1982). [http://laws.justice.gc.ca/en/charter/]

CASW. (1994). *Social Work Code of Ethics*. Ottawa: Canadian Association of Social Workers (CASW).

Criminal Code, R.S., c. C-34, s.1. (1985). [http://laws.justice.gc.ca/en/C-46/40670.html]

Etchells, E.; G. Sharpe; C. Elliott and P. Singer. (1996). Bioethics for clinicians: 3: Capacity. *Canadian Medical Association Journal*, 155, 657-661.

Etchells, E.; G. Sharpe; M.J. Dykeman and P. Singer. (1996). Bioethics for clinicians: 4: Voluntariness. *Canadian Medical Association Journal*, 155, 1083-1086.

IFSW. (1994). *The ethics of social work: Principles and standards*. Geneva, Switzerland: International Federation of Social Workers (IFSW).

_____.(2004). *Ethics in social work: Statement of principles*. Geneva, Switzerland: International Federation of Social Workers (IFSW).

Lens, V. (2000). Protecting the confidentiality of the therapeutic relationship: Jaffe v. Redmond. *Social Work*, 45(3), 273-276.

Matthews and Board of Directors of Physiotherapy (1986) 54 O.R. (2d) 375.

NASW. (1999). *Code of Ethics*. Washington: National Association of Social Workers (NASW).

Regehr, C. and B.J. Antle. (1997). Coercive influences: Informed consent and court-mandated social work practice. *Social Work*, 42(3), 300-306.

Rozovsky, L.E. and F.A. Rozovsky. (1990). *The Canadian law of consent to treatment*. Toronto: Butterworths.

United Nations. (1948). *Universal Declaration of Human Rights*. New York: United Nations. [http://www.unhchr.ch/udhr/]

United Nations Centre for Human Rights. (1992). Teaching and learning about human rights: A manual for schools of social work and the social work profession (Developed in co-operation with International Federation of Social Workers and International Association of Schools of Social Workers). New York: United Nations.

Canadian Association of Social Workers (CASW) Code of Ethics © 2005
383 Parkdale Avenue, Suite 402, Ottawa, Ontario, Canada K1Y 4R4
Telephone: (613) 729-6668 / Fax: (613) 729-9608
Email: casw@casw-acts.ca Web Site: www.casw-acts.ca

CREDITS

REFERENCES

ACPH. 1999. *Toward a Healthy Future: Second Report on the Health of Canadians*. Ottawa: Federal, Provincial, and Territorial Advisory Committee on Population Health.

ACPH. 1996. *Report on the Health of Canadians*. Ottawa: Federal, Provincial, and Territorial Advisory Committee on Population Health.

Adamson, N. et al. 1988. *Feminist Organizing for Change*. Toronto: Oxford UP.

Addams, J. 1961. *Twenty Years at Hull House*. New York: Signet Books.

Adema, W. 1999. *Net Social Expenditure*. Labour Market and Social Policy Occasional Papers No. 39 (August). Paris: Organisation for Economic Co-operation and Development.

AFN. 2008. "National Chief Praises decision regarding Human Rights Complaint on Child Welfare." Press release. Ottawa: Assembly of First Nations.

AFN. 2000. *First Nations Health Priorities 2001–2002*. Ottawa: Assembly of First Nations.

AFN. 1999. *First Nations Health Priorities 2001–2002*. Ottawa: Assembly of First Nations.

AHF. 2008. "Residential Schools Resources." Aboriginal Healing Foundation. www.ahf.ca/publications/residential-schools-resources.

Alexander, L. 2001. *Speech to the Canadian Race Relations Foundation's Award of Excellence Symposium*, Vancouver. March 2. www.crr.ca.

Alinsky, S. 1971. *Rules for Radicals: A Pragmatic Primer for Realistic Radicals*. New York: Vintage Books.

Allen, R. 1971. *The Social Passion: Religion and Social Reform in Canada, 1914–1928*. Toronto: U Toronto P.

AMCS. 2000. *Annual Report, 1999–2000*. Edmonton: Alberta Ministry of Children's Services.

Armitage, A. 1993. "Family and Child Welfare in First Nation Communities." In Brian Wharf, ed., *Rethinking Child Welfare in Canada*. Toronto: McClelland & Stewart Ltd.

Armitage, A. 1970. *The First University Degree in Social Work*. Ottawa: Canadian Association for Education in Social Service.

Armstrong, H. & Armstrong, P. 2008. *About Canada: Health Care*. Halifax: Fernwood.

Auditor General. 2008. *May 2008 Report of the Auditor General of Canada*. Ottawa: Office of the Auditor General of Canada. www.oag-bvg.gc.ca.

Baines, D. 2007. "Anti-Oppressive Practice: Fighting for Space, Fighting for Change." In Donna Baines, ed., *Doing Anti-Oppressive Practice: Building Transformative Politicized Social Work*. Black Point, NS: Fernwood.

BCMCF. 1999. *Annual Report, 1998–99*. Victoria: British Columbia Ministry for Children and Families.

Bélanger, A. & Malenfant, E.C. 2005. "Ethnocultural Diversity in Canada: Prospects for 2017." *Canadian Social Trends*. Cat. no. 11-008. Ottawa: Statistics Canada.

Belcourt, Christi. n.d. *Christi Belcourt: Based on Tradition, Inspired by Nature*. www.belcourt.net.

Blackstock, C. 2003. "Pre-Conference Interview, Social Inclusion Research Conference." Ottawa: Canadian Council on Social Development. www.ccsd.ca/events/inclusion/papers/interview-blackstock.htm. Accessed 10 April 2005.

Blyth, J.A. 1972. *The Canadian Social Inheritance*. Toronto: Copp Clark Publishing Co.

Boldt, M. 1993. *Surviving as Indians: The Challenge of Self-Government*. Toronto: U Toronto P.

Bowe, F. 1978. *Handicapping America: Barriers to Disabled People*. New York: Harper & Row.

CAFB. 2005. *HungerCount 2005*. Toronto: Canadian Association of Food Banks. www.cafb.ca.

CAFB. 2004. *HungerCount 2004*. Toronto: Canadian Association of Food Banks. www.cafb.ca.

Campaign 2000. 2007. *It Takes a Nation to Raise a Generation: Time for a National Poverty Reduction Strategy. Report Card on Child and Family Poverty 2007*. Toronto: Campaign 2000. www.campaign2000.ca.

Campaign 2000. 2006. *Oh Canada! Too Many Children in Poverty for Too Long: 2006 National Report Card on Child and Family Poverty*. Toronto: Campaign 2000. www.campaign2000.ca.

Campaign 2000. 2004. *One Million Too Many: Implementing Solutions to Child Poverty in Canada. 2004 Report Card on Child Poverty in Canada*. Toronto: Campaign 2000. www.campaign2000.ca.

Campaign 2000. 2001. *Child Poverty in Canada: Report Card 2000*. Toronto: Campaign 2000. www.campaign2000.ca.

Canadian Association of Elizabeth Fry Societies. 2003. *Elizabeth Fry Week—Fact Sheet*. www.elizabethfry.ca.

Canadian Feminist Alliance for International Action. 2008. *Women's Inequality in Canada*, Submission to the United Nations Committee on the Elimination of Discrimination against Women on the Occasion of the Committee's Review of Canada's 6th & 7th Reports. http://www.fafia-afai.org/files/ag_report_gb_2009.pdf.

Carniol, B. 2000. *Case Critical: Challenging Social Services in Canada*. Toronto: Between the Lines.

Carrigan, Owen. 1998. *Juvenile Delinquency in Canada: A History*. Concord: Irwin Publishing.

CASSW. 2001. *In Critical Demand: Social Work in Canada, Final Report*. Ottawa: Canadian Association of Schools of Social Work.

CASW. 2005a. *Code of Ethics*. Ottawa: Canadian Association of Social Workers. www.casw-acts.ca.

CASW. 2005b. *Guidelines for Ethical Practice*. Ottawa: Canadian Association of Social Workers. www.casw-acts.ca.

CASW. 1994. *Code of Ethics*. Ottawa: Canadian Association of Social Workers. www.casw-acts.ca.

CCJS. 2007. *Family Violence in Canada: A Statistical Profile, 2007*. Canadian Centre for Justice Statistics. Ottawa: Statistics Canada.

CCJS. 2004. *Family Violence in Canada: A Statistical Profile, 2004*. Canadian Centre for Justice Statistics. Ottawa: Statistics Canada.

CCJS. 2002a. *Canadian Crime Statistics 2000*. Canadian Centre for Justice Statistics. Cat. no. 85–205. Ottawa: Statistics Canada.

CCJS. 2002b. *Incident-Based Uniform Crime Reporting Survey*. Canadian Centre for Justice Statistics. Ottawa: Statistics Canada.

CCJS. 2000. *Incident-Based Uniform Crime Reporting Survey*. Canadian Centre for Justice Statistics. Ottawa: Statistics Canada.

CCPA. 2009. *Women's Poverty and the Recession*. Ottawa: Canadian Centre for Policy Alternatives. www.policyalternatives.ca.

CFS Information. 2002. *Child Welfare in Canada 2000: The Role of Provincial and Territorial Authorities in the Provision of Child Protection Services.* Ottawa: Secretariat to the Federal/Provincial/Territorial Working Group on Child and Family Services Information.

Chappell, N. 2001. "Canadian Social Policy and Ageing." Canada–Japan Social Policy Research Project. Asia Pacific Foundation of Canada, Vancouver. Presented in Osaka, Japan.

Chartrand, P. 1991. "Terms of Division: The Problems of Outside-Naming for Aboriginal People in Canada." *Journal of Indigenous Studies.* 2(2):1–22.

Children and Family Services Act. 1990. Amended 2002. Halifax: Government of Nova Scotia. www.gov.ns.ca/legislature/legc/statutes/childfam.htm.

CIDPC. 2004. *HIV and AIDS in Canada: Surveillance Report to June 30, 2004.* Centre for Infectious Disease Prevention and Control. Ottawa: Health Canada.

CIDPC. 2003. *HIV and AIDS in Canada: Surveillance Report to June 30, 2003.* Centre for Infectious Disease Prevention and Control. Ottawa: Health Canada.

CIHI. 2006a. *Health Care in Canada 2006.* Ottawa: Canadian Institute for Health Information.

CIHI. 2006b. *Health Personnel Trends in Canada 1995-2004.* Ottawa: Canadian Institute for Health Information.

CIHI. 2006c. *Improving the Health of Canadians: An Introduction to Health in Urban Places.* Ottawa: Canadian Institute for Health Information.

CIHI. 2006d. *National Health Expenditure Trends, 1975–2006.* Ottawa: Canadian Institute for Health Information.

CIHI. 2000. *Mental Health and Addiction Services: A Review of Health Information Standards.* Ottawa: Canadian Institute for Health Information.

CIHI. 1999. *National Trauma Registry 1999 Report on Hospital Injury Admissions 1997/98.* Ottawa: Canadian Institute for Health Information.

Clarke, J. 1990. *Health, Illness and Medicine in Canada.* Toronto: McClelland & Stewart Ltd.

CMA. 1993. *Submission to the Royal Commission on Aboriginal Peoples.* Ottawa: Canadian Medical Association.

Coll, B.D. 1973. *Perspectives in Public Welfare: A History.* Washington: U.S. Government Printing Office.

Commission on Systemic Racism in the Ontario Criminal Justice System. 1995. *Report of the Commission on Systemic Racism in the Ontario Criminal Justice System.* Toronto: Queen's Printer for Ontario.

Cook, R. 1985. *The Regenerators: Social Criticism in Late Victorian English Canada.* Toronto: U Toronto P.

Copp, T. 1974. *The Anatomy of Poverty: The Condition of the Working Class in Montreal, 1897–1929.* Toronto: McClelland & Stewart Ltd.

CPA. 1996. *Mental Illness and Work.* Ottawa: Canadian Psychiatric Association.

CRRF. 2000. *Unequal Access: A Canadian Profile of Racial Differences in Education, Employment and Income.* Toronto: Canadian Race Relations Foundation.

Cumming, M.M. 1985. *An Historical Review of Medical Insurance Legislation in Canada and the Effects of Dominant Ideology.* Unpublished master's thesis. Ottawa: School of Social Work, Carleton University.

CWLC. 2003. *A Summary of Current Issues and Trends with Recommendations for Future Research.* Ottawa: Child Welfare League of Canada.

CWLC. 1995. *The Young Offenders Act, Its Implementation and Related Services: A Child Welfare Perspective.* Ottawa: Child Welfare League of Canada.

Dauvergne, M. 2003. "Family Violence Against Seniors." *Canadian Social Trends.* Spring. Cat. no. 11–008. Ottawa: Statistics Canada.

Davis, A. F. 1967. *Spearheads for Reform: The Social Settlements and the Progressive Movement, 1890–1914.* New York: Oxford UP.

DeJong, C. 1978. *The Movement for Independent Living: Origins, Ideology, and Implication for Disability Research.* Boston: Tufts–New England Medical Center, Medical Rehabilitation Institute.

Dominelli, L. 2004. *Social Work: Theory and Practice for a Changing Profession.* Cambridge: Polity Press.

Dominelli, L. 1988. *Anti-Racist Social Work: A Challenge for White Practitioners and Educators.* London: Macmillan.

Dorais, M. 2004. *Dead Boys Can't Dance: Sexual Orientation, Masculinity and Suicide.* Montreal: McGill-Queens UP.

Elder, G.H., Jr. & Johnson, M.K. 2002. "The Life Course and Aging Challenges: Lessons and New Directions." In Richard A. Settersten, Jr., ed., *Invitation to the Life Course: Towards New Understandings of Later Life.* Amityville, NY: Baywood. 49–81.

Ellis, A. & Dryden, W. 1987. *The Practice of Rational-Emotive Therapy (RET).* New York: Springer Publishing Company.

Ellison, K. 1992. *Presentation to RCAP (28 October).* Saskatoon: Aboriginal Women's Council of Saskatchewan.

England, H. 1986. *Social Work as Art.* London: Allen & Unwin.

FBC. 2008. "HungerCount 2008: A Comprehensive Report on Hunger and Food Bank Use in Canada." Toronto: Food Banks Canada.

Ferns, H., & B. Ostry. 1976. *The Age of Mackenzie King.* Toronto: Lorimer Books.

Fook, J. 1993. *Radical Casework: A Theory of Practice.* St. Leonards, NSW: Allen & Unwin.

Foucault, M. 1978. *The History of Sexuality, Volume One: An Introduction.* New York: Vintage.

Fournier, S., & Crey, E. 1998. *Stolen from Our Embrace.* Vancouver: Douglas & McIntyre Ltd.

Freiden, L. 1983. "Independent Living in the United States and Other Countries." *Handicaps Monthly,* 54B61.

Freire, P. 1971. *Pedagogy of the Oppressed.* New York: Continuum.

Friendly, M. et al. 2007. "Early Childhood Education and Care in Canada." 7th ed. Toronto: Childcare and Resource Research Unit.

GATT-Fly. 1983. *Ah-Hah! A New Approach to Popular Education.* Toronto: Between the Lines.

Germain, C. & Gitterman, A. 1996. *The Life Model of Social Work Practice: Advances in Theory and Practice.* New York: Columbia UP.

Gibbins R., & Ponting, J.R. 1986. "Historical Overview and Background." In J. Rick Ponting, ed., *Arduous Journey: Canadian Indians and Decolonialization.* Toronto: McClelland & Stewart Ltd.

Girard, P. 1987. "From Subversion to Liberation: Homosexual and the Immigration Act 1952–1977." *Canadian Journal of Law and Society.* 24(2): 1–27.

Goldstein, H. 1973. *Social Work Practice: A Unitary Approach.* Columbia: U South Carolina P.

Gunderson, M. 1998. *Women and the Canadian Labour Market: Transitions Towards the Future.* Ottawa/Toronto: Statistics Canada/ITP Nelson.

Halwell, B. & Mastny, L. 2004. *State of the World 2004—Special Focus: The Consumer Society. WorldWatch Institute.* New York: W.W. Norton.

Hanes, R. & Moscovitch, A. 2002. "Disability Supports and Services for People with Disabilities in the Social Union." In Allen Puttee, *Federalism, Democracy and Disability Policy in Canada.* Institute of Intergovernmental Affairs, School of Policy Studies, Queen's University. Montreal: McGill-Queen's UP.

Hanes, R. 1995. "Linking Mental Defect to Physical Disability: The Case of Crippled Children in Ontario, 1890–1940." *Journal of Developmental Disability.* 4(1).

Health Canada. 2001. *Hope to Cope with Alzheimer's.* Ottawa: Health Canada. http://www.hc-gc.ca/english/feature/magazine/2001_01/alzheimer.htm.

Health Canada. 1997. *National Health Expenditures in Canada, 1975–1996: Fact Sheets*. Ottawa: Health Canada.

Henry, F. & Tator, C. 2006. *The Colour of Democracy: Racism in Canadian Society,* 3rd Ed. Toronto: Nelson.

Henry, F. 1994. *The Caribbean Diaspora in Toronto: Learning to Live with Racism*. Toronto: U Toronto P.

Hope, A. & Timmel, S. 1984. *Training for Transformation: A Handbook for Community Workers*. Rugby, UK: ITDG Publishing.

HRDC. 2003. *Understanding the 2000 Low Income Statistics Based on the Market Basket Measure*. Applied Research Branch Strategic Policy. Ottawa: Human Resources Development Canada.

Ife, Jim. 2004. "Human Rights Beyond the 'Three Generations.'" Presented at the Activating Human Rights and Diversity Conference. Centre for Human Rights Education. Curtin University of Technology. Byron Bay, NSW.

IFSW. 2000. "Definition of Social Work." International Federation of Social Workers. www.ifsw.org/en/p38000208.html.

Immigration and Refugee Protection Act. 2001. Ottawa: Public Works and Government Services Canada. laws.justice.gc.ca/en/I-2.5/index.html.

INAC & Tungavik. 1993. *Agreement Between the Inuit of the Nunavut Settlement Area and Her Majesty the Queen in Right of Canada*. Ottawa: Indian and Northern Affairs Canada.

INAC. 2001. *Basic Departmental Data 2001*. Cat. no. R12–7/2000E. Ottawa: Indian and Northern Affairs Canada.

"Internal Protocols." 2001. Nina's Place: Sexual and Domestic Violence Treatment Centre. Joseph Brant Memorial Hospital, Burlington, ON.

IRSSA. 2007. Indian Residential School Settlement Agreement. IRSSA—Official Court Website. www.residentialschoolsettlement.ca.

Isajiw, W.W. 1999. *Understanding Diversity: Ethnicity and Race in the Canadian Context*. Toronto: Thompson Educational Publishing.

Jackson, A. & Smith, E. 2002. *Does a Rising Tide Lift All Boats? Labour Market Experiences and Incomes of Recent Immigrants*. Ottawa: Canadian Council on Social Development.

Jacobs, P. et al. 2008. "Expenditures on Mental Health and Addictions for Canadian Provinces in 2003 and 2004." *Canadian Journal of Psychiatry*. May 1.

John Howard Society of Alberta. 1999. "The Harsh Reality of the *Young Offenders Act*." Alberta. www.johnhoward.ab.ca/PUB/C9.htm.

Katz, J.N. 1995. *The Invention of Heterosexuality*. New York: Penguin Group.

Kerstetter, Steve. 2009. "The Affordability Gap: Spending Differences Between Canada's Rich and Poor." Canadian Centre For Policy Alternatives. Ottawa.

Kinsman, G. 2003. "National Security as Moral Regulation: Making the Normal" and "Queerness is Not in Our Genes: Biological Determinism Versus Social Liberation." In Deborah Brock, ed., *Making Normal: Social Regulation in Canada*. Toronto: Nelson.

Lambert, M.J., & Barley, D.E. (2001). "Research Summary on the Therapeutic Relationship and Psychotherapy Outcome." *Psychotherapy*. 38(4): 357-361.

Land, H. 1995. "Feminist Clinical Social Work in the Twenty-First Century." In Nan Van Den Bergh, ed., *Feminist Practice in the 21st Century*. New York: NASW Press.

League for Human Rights of B'nai Brith. 2003. *Annual Audit of Anti-Semitic Incidents*. Toronto: B'nai Brith Canada.

Lee, B. 1999. *Pragmatics of Community Organization*. Mississauga: CommonAct Press.

Lee, K. 1999. "Measuring Poverty among Canada's Aboriginal People." *Insight*. 23(2). Ottawa: Canadian Council on Social Development.

Leiby, J. 1978. *A History of Social Welfare and Social Work in the United States*. New York: Columbia UP.

Leitch, K. 2007. *Reach for the Top: A Report by the Advisor on Healthy Children & Youth*. Ottawa: Health Canada.

Levy, C.S. 1993. *Social Work Ethics on the Line*. New York: Haworth Press.

Lindsay, C. 1999. *A Portrait of Seniors in Canada*, 3rd Ed. Ottawa: Statistics Canada.

Livneh, H. 1982. "On the Origins of Negative Attitudes Toward People with Disabilities." *Rehabilitation Literature*. 43(11/12): 338-347.

Luborsky, L. 1976. "Helping Alliances in Psychotherapy." In J.L. Cleghorn, ed., *Successful Psychotherapy*. New York: Brunner/Mazel. 92–116.

Lyons, W. 1995. *Coping and Helping with Alzheimer's Disease*. Ottawa: National Advisory Council on Aging.

McDonald, L. & Collins, A. 2000. *Abuse and Neglect of Older Canadians: A Discussion Paper*. Ottawa: Health Canada.

McGrath, S., Moffatt, K., George, U., & Lee, B. 1999. "Community Capacity: The Emperor's New Clothes." *Canadian Review of Social Policy*. 44:9–23.

McKnight, J. & Kretzman, J. 1993. "Introduction" and "Asset Based Community Development: Mobilizing an Entire Community." In *Building Communities from the Inside Out*. Chicago: ACTA Publications. 1–11, 345–354.

McLeod, J. 2006. "Narrative Approaches to Therapy." In C. Feltham & I. Horton, eds., *The SAGE Handbook of Counseling and Psychotherapy*, 2nd Ed. Thousand Oaks, CA: Sage Publications. 289–292.

Mesbur, E. 2002. "Social Group Work Practice: The Canadian Experience." In F.J. Turner, ed., *Social Work Practice: A Canadian Perspective*. Toronto: Pearson Education Canada.

Miller, J.R. 1989. *Skyscrapers Hide the Heavens: A History of Indian–White Relations in Canada*. Rev. Ed. Toronto: U Toronto P.

Morrissette V., McKenzie, B. & Morrissette, L. 1993. "Towards an Aboriginal Model of Social Work Practice: Cultural Knowledge and Traditional Practices." *Canadian Social Work Review*. 10(1): 91–108.

Moscovitch, A. & Webster, A. 1995. "Aboriginal Social Assistance Expenditures." In Susan Philips, ed., *How Ottawa Spends 1995–96: Mid-Life Crisis*. Ottawa: Carleton UP.

Mullaly, B. 2002. *Challenging Oppression*. Toronto: Oxford UP.

NACA. 2006. *Seniors in Canada 2006: Report Card*. Ottawa: National Advisory Council on Aging.

NACA. 2004. *Hidden Harm: The Abuse of Seniors*. Ottawa: National Advisory Council on Aging.

NACA. 2003. *Seniors in Canada: Interim Report Card*. Ottawa: National Advisory Council on Aging.

NACA. 2001a. "Beware of Fraud." *Expression*. National Advisory Council on Aging. 14(2): 3.

NACA. 2001b. *Seniors in Canada: A Report Card*. Ottawa: National Advisory Council on Aging.

National Clearinghouse on Family Violence. 2007. *Family Violence in Canada: A Statistical Profile 2007*. Ottawa: Health Canada.

National Clearinghouse on Family Violence. 2001. *Family Violence in Canada: Facts*. Ottawa: Health Canada.

NCW. 2007. *First Nations, Métis and Inuit Children and Youth: Time to Act*. Ottawa: National Council of Welfare.

NCW. 1999. *Poverty Profile 1997*. Ottawa: National Council of Welfare.

Norcross, J.C. 2002. *Psychotherapy Relationships that Work: Therapist Contributions and Responsiveness to Clients*. New York: Oxford UP.

NSDCS. 1993. *Advisory Committee Report on Children and Family Services Act*. December 9. Halifax: Nova Scotia Department of Community Services.

OACAS. 2008. *OACAS Publications: Statistics*. Toronto: Ontario Association of Children's Aid Societies. www.oacas.org.

OACAS. 2006. *OACAS Pre-Budget Consultation Submission.* Toronto: Ontario Association of Children's Aid Societies. www.oacas.org.

OACAS. 2000. *OACAS Facts.* Toronto: Ontario Association of Children's Aid Societies. www.oacas.org.

OAFB. 2009. *In the Midst of the Storm: The Impact of the Economic Downturn for Ontario's Food Banks in 2009.* Toronto: Ontario Association of Food Banks. www.oafb.ca.

OECD. 2006. *OECD Health Data 2006: Statistics and Indicators for 30 Countries.* Organisation for Economic Co-Operation and Development. www.oecd.org/health/healthdata.

OECD. 2004. *International Report on Early Childhood Education and Care Policy: Country Note Canada.* Organisation for Economic Co-Operation and Development.

Oliver, M. 1996. "The Social Model of Disability." In *Understanding Disability: From Theory to Practice.* London: St. Martin's Press.

Oliver, M. 1990. "Disability Definitions: The Politics of Meaning." In *The Politics of Disablement.* London: Macmillan.

Orbach, S. 1990. "Gender and Dependency in Psychotherapy." *Journal of Social Work Practice.* 4(3-4): 1–15.

Pepler, D. & Craig, W. 2007. "Binoculars on Bullying: A New Solution to Protect and Connect Children." *Voices for Children.* February. www.voicesforchildren.ca/report-Feb2007-1.htm.

PHAC. 2006. *The Human Face of Mental Health and Mental Illness in Canada 2006.* Public Health Agency of Canada. Ottawa: Minister of Public Works and Government Services Canada.

PHAC. 2005. *Canadian Incidence Study of Reported Child Abuse and Neglect—2003: Major Findings.* Ottawa: Public Health Agency of Canada.

Philip, M. 2001. "Children's Aid Staff Face Burnout." *Globe and Mail.* Feb. 20.

Pitsula, J. 1979. "The Emergence of Social Work in Toronto." *Journal of Canadian Studies.* 14(1).

Purich, D. 1988. *The Métis.* Toronto: James Lorimer & Co.

RCAP. 1996. *Report of the Royal Commission on Aboriginal Peoples.* Ottawa: Indian and Northern Affairs Canada.

Reid, W. & Epstein, L. 1977. *Task-Centred Practice.* NY: Columbia UP.

Rice, J. & Prince, M. 2000. *Changing Politics of Canadian Social Policy.* Toronto: U Toronto P.

Roberts, J.V. 1995. *Disproportionate Harm: Hate Crime in Canada.* Ottawa: Department of Justice Canada.

Robinson, P. 2004. "Youth Court Statistics, 2002/03." *Juristat.* 24(2). Cat. no. 85–002–XPE. Canadian Centre for Justice Statistics. Ottawa: Statistics Canada.

Rodgers, K. 1994. "Wife Assault: The Findings of a National Survey." *Juristat.* 14(9). Cat. no. 85–002–XPE. Canadian Centre for Justice Statistics. Ottawa: Statistics Canada.

Rogers, C. 1951. *Client-Centred Therapy.* Boston: Houghton.

Romanow, R. 2002. *Building Values: The Future of Health Care in Canada.* Ottawa: Commission on the Future of Health Care in Canada.

Rooke, P. & Schnell, R.L. 1983. *Discarding the Asylum: From Child Welfare to the Welfare State in English Canada, 1800–1950.* Boston: UP of America.

Ross, D.P., Scott, K. & Smith, P. 2000. *The Canadian Fact Book on Poverty.* Ottawa: Canadian Centre for Social Development.

Ross, D.P., Shillington, E.R. & Lochhead, C. 1994. *The Canadian Fact Book on Poverty.* Ottawa: Canadian Centre for Social Development.

Rostow, W.W. 1960. *The Stages of Economic Growth: A Non-Communist Manifesto.* Cambridge: Cambridge UP.

Rothman, J. 1979. "Three Models of Community Organization Practice." In F. Cox et al., eds., *Strategies of Community Organization.* Itasca, IL: Peacock Publishers. 22–39.

Saleebey, D. 2005. *The Strengths Perspective in Social Work Practice,* 4th Ed. Boston: Allyn & Bacon.

Satzewich, V., ed. 1998. *Racism and Social Inequality in Canada: Concepts, Controversies and Strategies of Resistance.* Toronto: Thompson Educational Publishing.

Savoie, J. 1999. "Violent Youth Crime." *Juristat.* 19(13). Cat. no. 85–002–XPE. Canadian Centre for Justice Statistics. Ottawa: Statistics Canada.

Scott, K.A. 1994. *Aboriginal Health and Social History: A Brief Canadian History.* Unpublished.

Service Canada. 2008. *Job Futures National Edition.* www.jobfutures.ca.

Shannon, M. & Kidd, M. 2001. "Projecting the Trend in Canada: Gender Wage Gap 2001–2031." *Canadian Public Policy.* XXVII(4).

Shebib, B. 2007. *Choices: Interviewing and Counselling Skills for Canadians.* 3rd Ed. Toronto: Pearson Education Canada.

Sheppard, B. 1997. *Deemed Unsuitable.* Toronto: Umbrella Press.

Shulman, L. 1992. *The Skills of Helping Individuals, Families and Groups.* 3rd Ed. Itasca, IL: Peacock Publishers.

Siporin, M. 1975. *Introduction to Social Work Practice.* NY: Macmillan.

Smith, D.G. 1993. "The Emergence of Eskimo Status: An Examination of the Eskimo Disk List System and the Social Consequences, 1925–1970." In Noel Dyck and James B. Waldram, eds., *Anthropology, Public Policy and Native Peoples in Canada.* Montreal: McGill-Queen's UP.

Social Union. 2000. *In Unison: A Canadian Approach to Disability Issues.* Ottawa: Federal–Provincial–Territorial Ministers Responsible for Social Services. www.socialunion-gc.ca/pwd/unison/unison_e.html.

Splane, R. 1965. "Review: The Role of Public Welfare in a Century of Social Welfare Development" (originally published in 1965). In Carl A. Meilicke and Janet A. Storch, eds., *Perspectives on Canadian Health and Social Services Policy: History and Emerging Trends.* 1980. Ann Arbour, MI: Health Administration Press. 38–49.

Stall, S. & Stoecker, R. 1998. "Community Organizing or Organizing Community?: Gender and the Crafts of Empowerment." *Gender and Society.* 12(6): 729–756.

Statistics Canada. 2008. "Study: Life Expectancy in the Inuit-Inhabited Areas of Canada 1989–2003." *The Daily.* 23 January 2008. Ottawa: Statistics Canada.

Statistics Canada. 2007. *Income Trends in Canada 1980-2004.* Cat. no. 13F0022XCB. Ottawa: Statistics Canada.

Statistics Canada. 2006a. *Income in Canada.* Cat. no. 75-202-X. Ottawa: Statistics Canada.

Statistics Canada. 2006b. *Participation and Activity Limitation Survey (PALS).* Cat. no. 89–577–XIE. Ottawa: Statistics Canada.

Statistics Canada. 2006c. *Women in Canada: A Gender-Based Statistical Report,* 5th Ed. Ottawa: Statistics Canada.

Statistics Canada. 2005a. *Canadian Community Health Survey Mental Health and Well-Being.* Cat. no. 82-617-XIE. Ottawa: Statistics Canada.

Statistics Canada. 2005b. "Notes and Definitions: Low Income Definitions." *Survey of Labour and Income Dynamics: A Survey Overview.* Cat. no. 75F0011XIE. Ottawa: Statistics Canada.

Statistics Canada. 2004a. "Hate Crime in Canada." *Juristat.* 24(44). Cat. no. 85–002–XPE. Canadian Centre for Justice Statistics. Ottawa: Statistics Canada.

Statistics Canada. 2004b. *The People: Health Services.* Statistics Canada e-Book. Accessed November 25, 2008. www43.statcan.ca/02/02b/02b_008_e.htm.

Statistics Canada. 2003a. *Canadian Community Health Survey Mental Health and Well-Being.* Cat. no. 82-617-XIE. Ottawa: Statistics Canada.

Statistics Canada. 2003b. "Leisure-Time Physical Activity, by Age Group and Sex, Household Population Aged 12 and Over, Canada 2000/01." *Health Indicators.* 2003(2). Ottawa: Statistics Canada.

Statistics Canada. 2001a. *2001 Census of Canada.* Ottawa.

Statistics Canada. 2001b. *Participation and Activity Limitation Survey (PALS)*. Cat. no. 89–577–XIE. Ottawa: Statistics Canada.

Statistics Canada. 2001c. *Population Projections for Canada, Provinces and Territories, 2000–2026*. Cat. no. 91-520-XIB. Ottawa: Statistics Canada.

Statistics Canada. 2001d. "Shelters for Abused Women." *The Daily*. 28 March 2001. Ottawa: Statistics Canada. www.statcan.gc.ca/daily-quoti-dien/010328/dq010328b-eng.htm

Status of Women Canada. 2002. *Assessing Violence Against Women: A Statistical Profile*. Ottawa: Federal, Provincial, Territorial Ministers Responsible for the Status of Women.

Stebner, E. 1997. *The Women of Hull House: A Study in Spirituality, Vocation and Friendship*. New York: SUNY UP.

Stobert, S. & Cranswick, K. 2003. "Looking After Seniors: Who Does What for Whom?" *Canadian Social Trends*. Spring. Cat. no. 11–008. Ottawa: Statistics Canada.

Stone, D. 1984. *The Disabled State*. Philadelphia: Temple UP.

Stout, Madeleine Dion. 2004. "Speech to the Aboriginal Healing Foundation's National Gathering." Edmonton, Alberta. July 10.

Struthers, J. 1991. "How Much is Enough? Creating a Social Minimum in Ontario, 1930–44." *The Canadian Historical Review*. 72(1): 39.

Taft, J. 1948. *Family Casework and Counseling: A Functional Approach*. Philadelphia: University of Pennsylvania Publishing.

Timpson, J.B. 1990. "Indian and Native Special Status in Ontario's Child Welfare Legislation: An Overview of the Social, Legal and Political Context." *Canadian Social Work Review*. 7(1): 49–68.

Toseland, R. & Rivas, R. 2005. *Introduction to Group Work Practice*, 5th Ed. Boston: Allyn & Bacon.

Townson, M. 2000. *A Report Card on Women and Poverty*. Ottawa: Canadian Centre for Policy Alternatives.

Trocmé, N. 1991. "Child Welfare Services." In *The State of the Child in Ontario (Child, Youth and Family Policy Research Centre)*. Toronto: Oxford UP.

Trocmé, N., et al. 2001. *Canadian Incidence Study of Reported Child Abuse and Neglect: Final Report*. Ottawa: Minister of Public Works and Government Services Canada.

Trudeau, P.E., et al. 1971. *Announcement of Implementation of Policy of Multiculturalism Within Bilingual Framework*. House of Commons Debates, October 8, pp. 8545-8.

Tuckman, B.W. 1965. "Developing Sequence in Small Groups." *Psychological Bulletin*. 63(6): 384–399.

Tuckman, B.W. & Jensen, M.A. 1977. "Stages of Small-Group Development Revisited." *Group & Organization Studies*. 2(4): 419–427.

Tully, P. & Mohl, C. 1995. "Older Residents of Health Care Institutions." *Health Reports*. 7(3): 27–30. Cat. no. 82–003. Ottawa: Statistics Canada.

Turcotte, M. & Schellenberg, G. 2007. *A Portrait of Seniors in Canada 2006*. Cat. no. 89-519-XIE. Ottawa: Statistics Canada.

UNAIDS/WHO. 2004. *Report on the Global HIV/AIDS Epidemic 2004*. The Joint United Nations Programme on HIV/AIDS. www.unaids.org.

UNAIDS/WHO. 1998. *Report on the Global HIV/AIDS Epidemic 1998*. The Joint United Nations Programme on HIV/AIDS. www.unaids.org.

UNDP. 2008. *Human Development Report 2007/08. Fighting Climate Change: Human Solidarity in a Divided World*. United Nations Development Programme. hdr.undp.org.

UNDP. 2007. *Millenium Development Goals 2007*. United Nations Development Programme. www.undp.org/mdg.

UNDP. 2006. *Human Development Report 2006. Beyond scarcity: Power, Poverty and the Global Water Crisis*. United Nations Development Programme. hdr.undp.org.

UNDP. 2004. *Human Development Report 2004: Cultural Liberty in Today's Diverse World*. United Nations Development Programme. hdr.undp.org.

UNFPA. 2004. *State of the World Population 2004*. United Nations Population Fund. www.unfpa.org.

UNICEF. 2007. *Child Poverty in Perspective: Report Card on Child Well-Being in Rich Countries*. UNICEF Innocenti Research Centre. www.unicef-irc.org.

UNICEF. 2000a. *Report Card on Child Poverty in Rich Nations*. UNICEF Innocenti Research Centre. www.unicef-irc.org.

UNICEF. 2000b. *The Progress of Nations 2000*. United Nations Children's Fund. www.unicef.org.

United Nations. 2007. *Report of the Committee on the Elimination of Racial Discrimination: Canada. Concluding Observations*. Office of the High Commissioner for Human Rights. www.ohchr.org.

United Nations. 1998. *Report of the Committee on Economic , Social and Cultural Rights: Canada. Concluding Observations, Section 36*. Office of the High Commissioner for Human Rights. www.ohchr.org.

United Nations. 1948. *Universal Declaration of Human Rights*. www.un.org/Overview/rights.html.

Van Wormer, K., Wells, J. & Boes, M. 2000. *Social Work with Lesbians, Gays and Bisexuals: A Strengths Perspective*. Boston: Allyn & Bacon.

Vayda, E. & Deber, R.B. 1995. "The Canadian Health Care System: A Developmental Overview." In R.B. Blake and J. Keshen, eds., *Social Welfare Policy in Canada: Historical Readings*. Toronto: Copp Clark Ltd. 311–325.

Walker, J. 1997. *Race, Rights and the Law in the Supreme Court of Canada*. Waterloo: Wilfred Laurier UP.

Waller, I. 1989. *Current Trends in European Crime Prevention: Implications for Canada*. Ottawa: Supply and Services Canada.

Warner, T. 2002. *Never Going Back: A History of Queer Activism in Canada*. Toronto: U Toronto P.

Welfel, E.R., Danzinger, P.R. & Santoro, S. 2000. "Mandated Reporting of Abuse/Maltreatment of Older Adults: a Primer for Counselors." *Journal of Counseling and Development*. 78(3): 284–292.

White, M. & Epston, D. 1990. *Narrative Means to Therapeutic Ends*. New York: W. W. Norton & Co.

Whitton, C. 1943. *The Dawn of Ampler Life*. Toronto: Macmillan.

WHO. 2002. "Unfinished Business: Global Push to Save 11 Million Children." World Health Organization News Release. www.who.int/mediacentre/news/releases/2002/pr18/en/index.htm. Accessed 25 Nov. 2008.

WHO. 1948. "Preamble." *Constitution of the World Health Organization*. World Health Organization. www.who.org.

Wilkins, R., Berthelot, J.M. & Ng, E. 2002. "Trends in Mortality by Neighbourhood Income in Urban Canada from 1971 to 1996." *Supplement to Health Reports, Vol. 13*. Cat. no. 82-003. Ottawa: Statistics Canada.

Wolf, R. S. 1997. "Elder Abuse and Neglect: an Update." *Research in Clinical Gerontology*. 7: 177–182.

Woodroofe, K. 1962. *From Charity to Social Work in England and the United States*. Toronto: U Toronto P.

Woolhandler, S. & Himmelstein, D.U. 2004. "The High Costs of For-Profit Care." *Canadian Medication Association Journal*. 170(12): 1814–1815.

World Bank. 2004. *World Development Indicators 2004*. www.worldbank.org.

World Commission on Environment and Development. 1987. *Our Common Future*. New York: Oxford UP.

Youth Criminal Justice Act. 2003. Ottawa: Public Works and Government Services Canada. laws.justice.gc.ca/en/showtdm/cs/Y-1.5.

Zola, I.K. 1986. *The Independent Living Movement*. San Francisco: Jossey-Bass Publishers.

GLOSSARY

Ableism Discrimination and prejudice based on physical and mental ability, towards people with disabilities supporting the belief that people without disabilities are superior to people with disabilities.

Aboriginal approach to practice A practice approach that is consistent with four key principles: (1) the recognition of a distinct Aboriginal world view; (2) the development of Aboriginal consciousness regarding the impact of colonialism; (3) an emphasis on the importance of cultural knowledge and traditions; and (4) the use of the concept of Aboriginal empowerment.

Aboriginal empowerment In the context of social work, emphasizes the participation of community members in promoting self-determination and social change.

Aboriginal peoples Used in Canada to refer collectively to First Nations, Inuit, and Métis peoples. A synonym of Native, Aboriginal is a general term; it is preferable to refer to specific bands and nations. Aboriginal people or persons are individuals who have Native origins.

Aboriginal self-government This concept expresses the desire of Aboriginal peoples to control their destiny. It can refer to local government such as on-reserve, as well as sovereignty in relation to the Canadian state within it or outside it, depending on one's view. It precludes accountability to the provincial and federal governments in favour of accountability and responsibility to the Aboriginal peoples by their own Aboriginal leaders.

Aboriginal world view While Aboriginal peoples do not have one common philosophy or world view, there is a distinct difference when compared to the world view in Western culture. For example, the circle captured in the Medicine Wheel illustrates the notion of balance prevalent in Aboriginal societies, in contrast to the typically linear models of cause and effect common in some Western societies.

Accessibility One of five principles of medicare in Canada. Each province is required to provide health care with reasonable access, both financially and geographically. This applies to ward care in a hospital, free choice of a physician, reasonable compensation to physicians, and adequate payments to hospitals.

Acquaintance sexual assault Also called date rape, acquaintance sexual assault involves an assailant who is known to the victim. Forty percent of victims of sexual assault were assaulted by a friend or casual acquaintance. This type of assault is highly under-reported.

Activity theory An early theory of social work practice with the elderly which maintains that a presumed decrease in the life satisfaction of seniors can be mitigated through increased personal and social activities.

Acute pain Pain that is temporary and begins as severe, declining over time. It can progress into chronic pain.

Addiction A compulsive need for, or persistent use of, a substance known to be harmful; also refers to behaviours that can be harmful, such as gambling.

Adjourning stage Fifth stage of group development, when the group moves towards terminating; group members may start disengaging from each other. Some members may express increased anxiety about the group ending, while others might deal with the ending by participating less actively or attending more sporadically.

Affective theories In the group context, theories that argue a change in feelings is fundamental to other changes; being affirming to the person will result in improved self-esteem, more positive thinking, and a change in behaviours.

Ageism Prejudice and discrimination that is based on age, usually applied to older people. Ageism is any attitude, action, or institutional structure that subordinates or oppresses a person or group on the basis of age. Ageism is a universal experience as dominant culture in North America celebrates youth and devalues the worth of individuals as they age.

Alternative dispute resolution (ADR) A streamlining approach to the court process that seeks alternatives to court.

Ambiguity of social work The dilemmas faced by social workers within the social work relationship. While social workers are helpers, they are also expected to enforce rules and regulations in the helping relationship with the client.

Anger-control theory This theory argues that men who are abusive must be held accountable for their violent behaviour. The goal is to have clients learn to deal with and control their tempers, and learn to express their feelings in more appropriate ways.

Anti-oppressive practice (AOP) An approach to practice which argues that a person's environment shapes his or her individual experience and can be the source of significant problems. The goal of anti-oppressive practice is to acknowledge the existence of oppression in all forms and the complex nature of our identities. This knowledge can be used to overcome oppressive relationships at the individual and institutional or societal level, and broadly contribute to social justice.

Anti-racist social work An approach to practice which focuses specifically on how racism affects the lives of people of colour at the individual, institutional, or societal levels in the form of attitudes, beliefs, policies, or procedures; understands racism using an economic and social analysis of relations between members of different groups.

Assessment Part of the second stage of the social work process, assessment involves developing an understanding of the presented problem. It will include different elements and emphasis depending on the perspective or approach of the social worker.

Assimilationist policies Policies of the federal government towards Aboriginal people that attempted to deny and destroy Aboriginal life, culture, and society in favour of integrating Canada's First Nations into the mainstream. These policies were pursued vigorously and viciously in the residential schools.

Behaviour theories In the group context, theories that pursue an objective to change group members' behaviours with the understanding that changed behaviour will lead to a change in feelings and thinking.

Best interests approach An approach to child protection that emphasizes the protection and well-being of the child, no matter what the situation. This approach is in contrast to the least restrictive approach.

Biological determinism The belief that every aspect of an individual's personality, behaviour, and attitude is determined by genes.

This theory minimizes and discounts the role of environmental factors within human development. In regards to sexuality, this theory explains sexual behaviours and preferences in terms of biology and thereby focuses on the organic causes of non-conventional sexual identities and behaviours.

Canada Assistance Plan Federal legislation, passed in 1966 and considered by many as a keystone of the Canadian welfare state. The legislation required the federal government to fund half the cost of social programs undertaken by the provinces.

Canada Health and Social Transfer (CHST) Federal legislation that combined federal funding for health, post-secondary education, and welfare, and transferred a designated amount of money based on population size to each province rather than transferring a percentage of actual costs. It replaced both the Canada Assistance Plan (CAP) and Established Program Financing (EPF).

Canada Health Transfer (CHT) A federal block transfer payment that is made to each province and territory in order to assist in paying for health care. The CHT comprises both a cash transfer and a tax transfer that are allocated on a per capita basis in order to equalize support provided to provinces and territories independent of population size. It is the responsibility of the provinces and territories to allocate this health care funding to their provincial/territorial health care priorities. The CHT replaced the CHST.

Canada Social Transfer (CST) A federal block transfer payment made to each Canadian province and territory to assist them in paying for education, social assistance, and social services. The CST comprises both a cash transfer and a tax transfer that are allocated on a per capita basis to equalize support provided to provinces and territories independent of population size. The CST replaced the CHST.

Casework Refers to using systematic methods of investigation, assessment, and decision making in social work practice.

Caseworker Traditional notion of the social worker with the sole function of applying the practice of casework.

Charity Organization Society Social welfare agencies established in the latter part of the 1800s that used a *scientific charity* approach to studying the needs of individuals and families. It differentiated between the deserving and undeserving poor, believing that indiscriminate material relief would cause pauperism.

Charter of Rights and Freedoms The first section of the *Constitution Act*, the *Charter of Rights and Freedoms*, describes the fundamental individual and group rights of citizens, including freedom of religion, voting rights, and equality rights. The Canadian Constitution was patriated (or brought under Canadian control) in 1982. The government of Quebec did not endorse the act on the grounds that it failed to recognize Quebec's distinctness.

Child abuse The physical, psychological, social, emotional, or sexual maltreatment of a child whereby the survival, safety, self-esteem, growth, and development of the person are endangered. Child abuse is usually divided into the following categories: emotional abuse, which includes both emotional attacks and omissions; physical abuse, which includes any physical attack or omission that could cause injury; sexual abuse, which includes any sexual exploitation whether consented to or not; and neglect, the sustained deprivation of necessary care.

Chronic pain Pain that lasts longer than the normal recovery period for acute pain. Chronic pain varies in intensity and can exist for a few months or can last for many years.

Cissexual/cisgender This term has been used in recent academic literature to define persons who are not transexual and who have only ever experienced their subconscious and physical as being aligned. Cissexism refers to the belief that transsexuals' identified genders are inferior to, or less authentic than, those of cissexuals. In the same way, transgender activists have begun to use the term cisgender to describe those who consider themselves of normal gender expression—that is, not transgender—to de-privilege this position to allow for the understanding of transgender identities as simply variants of gender expression, not deviant statuses.

Client- or person-centred perspective An approach based on the idea that clients are the experts of their problems; clients are viewed as "wholes," and not simply in terms of their diagnoses.

Clinical social work Initially equated with casework and psychotherapy, clinical social work encompasses a varied range of approaches and is not wedded to one theoretical perspective. Critical, feminist, and structural social workers all engage the term to describe their work with individuals.

Code of Ethics The CASW *Code of Ethics* lays out a set of six guiding principles that form the basis of ethical practice. It does not prescribe how social workers should act, but provides guidance that can be used to formulate specific standards.

Cognitive behavioural approaches Approaches which provide practitioners with more practical, time-limited approaches with clear practice guidelines; these approaches are used to modify behaviours by changing the way we understand the world.

Cognitive-behaviour therapy (CBT) A short-term approach that views behaviours as learned and shaped by our interpretations of the world (our cognitions). When flawed or inaccurate, these interpretations can lead to irrational or maladaptive behaviours. Therapists using this approach work with clients to understand the thought patterns that bring about certain behaviours, as well as what sustains these patterns.

Cognitive theories In the group context, theories that argue when people change their thinking or their ideas, other changes will follow.

Collective rights Rights ensuring equitable participation by everyone in a society in the production and distribution of wealth and resources; set forth in Articles 22–27 of the *Universal Declaration of Human Rights*.

Colonialism Forced political domination of one nation over another that is institutionalized in political administration, control of all economic relationships, and a systematic attempt to transform the culture of the subject nation.

Coming out Making one's LGBTTQ identity public to family, friends, etc.; from the phrase "coming out of the closet," where being "in the closet" is keeping one's identity secret. The decision to openly identify as gay or lesbian is up to the individual, and is regarded as an important psychosocial developmental process for many people.

Community A group of people who share either a geographic space, an identity, or an interest and are conscious of themselves as a community.

Community access centre A centralized location where citizens can access a variety of services that are delivered by a service delivery team following a service plan.

Community capacity building An approach to community work which builds upon the strengths and assets of a community rather than focusing on the community's needs; this approach also advocates use of community-based resources rather than relying heavily on state programs, which can be stigmatizing and create a destructive dependency.

Community health centres (CHCs) Centres that provide primary care, health promotion, and prevention services using salaried primary health care professionals. Studies have found that CHCs provide better primary care, decrease the costs of patient care, and decrease hospitalization rates.

Compassion fatigue The anxiety resulting from dealing with emotionally difficult cases under increased workplace pressure and increased workloads.

Comprehensiveness One of five principles of medicare in Canada. Each province's plan must cover all medically necessary services provided by hospitals, medical practitioners, or dentists, and, where permitted, cover services rendered by other health care practitioners.

Consciousness-raising groups Groups that employ the concept of consciousness-raising, or the process by which people become aware of and understand shared experiences of restriction or damage by certain practices, patterns of relations, beliefs, stereotypes, myths, expectations, and social structures. In consciousness-raising groups people begin to understand the relationships between their own biographies, other people's biographies, history, and the social infrastructure.

Continuity theory A contemporary theory that maintains that the continuity of a person's lifestyle should be preserved as he or she progresses through the life cycle. This theory argues that old age is a continuation of a person's past and that seniors should continue the roles and activities of their middle years in order to maintain life satisfaction.

Contracting out The practice of hiring private for-profit companies to implement specified public social welfare activities and deliver certain services in return for payment from public funds.

Critical social work An approach to social work that focuses on the impact of wider social structures on personal problems; critical social work practice must contribute to a transformation of everyday lives, working toward changes in economic, social, and political structures, relations, or organization.

Cueing A skill specific to group work, in which a facilitator invites silent, non-participating, or dominated members to engage. This might be done non-verbally through body language (e.g., by making eye contact with the person you are inviting into the conversation). Other times it is done verbally by specifically inviting someone to comment.

Cultural competence The ability to acknowledge different perceptions and experiences and incorporate these into practice applications. In other words, the worker must take this knowledge of the "other" culture and combine it with an analysis of how his or her own culture affects social work interventions.

Culture The generally shared knowledge, beliefs, and values of members of society. Culture is conveyed from generation to generation through the process of socialization.

Cycle-of-violence theory This theory identifies what happens in a relationship when domestic violence occurs: tension-building, acute battering, and the honeymoon period.

Demogrants These are universal flat-rate payments made to individuals or households solely on the basis of demographic characteristics, such as number of children or age, rather than on the basis of proven need, as in the case of minimum income programs, or as in contributions in the case of social insurance.

Deserving poor This refers to those who are deemed to be deserving of relief. This is a concept that historically underpinned charity relief and continues to influence income security provision today.

Diagnostic and Statistical Manual of Mental Disorders Also known as the DSM, this guide published by the American Psychiatric Association lists all mental health disorders for both children and adults, as well as known causes of these disorders, statistics related to gender, age, and prognosis, and research pertinent to treatment options.

Diagnostic approach An emphasis on understanding the condition of the individual by reference to causal events in his or her early life. This approach requires a skilled worker who can diagnose the problem and establish and carry out a plan for treatment, and was prevalent during the post-WWII period.

Dialectical approach An approach to practice that involves the synthesis or combination of opposing assertions within theories thereby taking a balanced or middle road.

Differential response (DR) An approach to child protection that enables a new flexible intake and assessment model that assesses eligibility for service, safety, and risk, while allowing for greater engagement with families.

Digital divide A divide between "have" and "have not" populations based on a lack of access to computers, the Internet, and advanced communications technology.

Direct social work Involves working directly with people as individuals, in families or households and communities in a direct face-to-face way (e.g., in a counselling role).

Disability Any restriction or lack of ability (resulting from an impairment) to perform an activity within the range considered normal for a human being.

Discrimination The unequal treatment of individuals on the basis of their personal characteristics, which may include age, sex, sexual orientation, ethnic, or physical identity.

Disengagement theory An early, prominent theory within social practice with the elderly maintaining that withdrawing from activities and social life is a natural part of the aging process and that this withdrawal acts to assist seniors to adjust to aging. This theory is in opposition to activity theory.

Disk list system A government-sponsored identity program for Inuit—as bureaucrats would not formally acknowledge the Inuktitut names for individuals, the disk list system assigned a numbered disk to each Inuk in order to identify them.

Duty to report Every member of society has a responsibility to report child abuse or neglect when there are reasonable grounds for believing a child may be in need of protection. People in professions that bring them into contact with children have a particular responsibility or duty to ensure that young people are safe.

Early childhood education This refers to federal, publicly-funded programs for children. Each country regulates its own system of early education and development and countries vary widely in their provision of these services for families.

Eclectic approach An approach to practice that involves the selection of concepts and methods as deemed appropriate, but does not attempt to unify or integrate the pieces.

Economic globalization The growing integration and expansion of global markets for goods, services, and finances. Economic globalization is the latest stage in the development of advanced capitalist economies and includes free trade and investment, international trade expansion, and the development of powerful transnational corporations. Because of a lack of restraining national legislation, economic globalization enables multinational corporations to pursue their agendas of successful markets and inexpensive labour.

Educational groups Groups with a primary focus on education that may also have a strong support aspect. Examples are groups for heart and stroke victims, parenting groups, and groups for families where there has been a recent diagnosis of diabetes. These groups have as a leader someone with expertise on the topic.

Elder abuse The abuse and neglect of seniors by those in a position of trust, power, or responsibility for their care. Elder abuse and neglect may occur within homes or institutional care settings and in either case, is often hidden and silenced.

Electronic advocacy The process of using communication and information technologies to disseminate information and mobilize support from a large constituency to help influence decision-making processes.

Employment equity The use of hiring policies, procedures, and programs to increase employment opportunities for groups previously denied advancement. Designed to help employment and promotion opportunities for women and other marginalized groups, employment equity was not introduced in Canada until the 1980s.

Empowerment The sense that people can create and take action on their own behalf to meet their physical, spiritual, and psychological needs; usually applied to the act of empowering marginalized groups, but can also be an issue in direct practice with individuals. Also a strategy used to address the power imbalance between worker and client.

Equal employment This legislation prohibits discrimination on the basis of race, age, religion, nationality, and sex. Canadian provinces and the federal government have equal employment opportunity legislation in place, usually as part of their human rights codes. The prohibition of discrimination on the basis of sex was generally added during the 1960s and 1970s.

Equal-pay policies Policies that ensure equal pay for equal work. During the 1950s and 1960s, every Canadian province enacted legislation requiring that women receive equal pay for similar or substantially similar work. During the 1970s both Quebec and the federal government introduced pay equity legislation that required equal pay for work of equal value (allowing comparisons between occupations). In the 1980s, most other jurisdictions followed suit, at least with respect to public sector employment.

Ethnic group A group of persons who share a common heritage, identity, or origin.

Ethnicity From a Greek word meaning "people," refers to a category of people who share a common heritage, identity, or origin.

Ethnocentrism An attitude that one's own culture, society, or group is inherently superior to all others. Ethnocentrism means an inability to appreciate others whose culture may include a different racial group, ethnic group, religion, morality, language, political system, economic system, and so on. It also means an inability to see a common humanity and human condition facing all women and men in all cultures and societies beneath the surface variations in social and cultural traditions.

Evaluation Part of the final stage of the social work process, evaluation is aimed at determining whether the goals and needs of the client are being met by identifying the rationale for the actions chosen, whether or not needs were met, the expected and unexpected effects and alternative courses of action that may need to be taken.

Evidence-based practice (EBP) An approach which asks social workers to locate empirical studies to determine how to best relate to a situation presented by a client.

Existential therapies Therapies based on the nineteenth century philosophy of existentialism or the search for meaning in life, which employ the notion that human beings must create meaning and purpose in our lives to guide our existence.

Family systems theory The theory that all families operate as social systems or interrelated networks in which an impact on one component has significant consequences for all others in the system. As such, family members influence the actions of other members and a change in one family member will affect other members.

Feeding programs Programs that provide meals to individuals in many contexts. Some programs are designed for homeless people living in shelters, others are for working people and families who cannot make ends meet. Schools in disadvantaged neighbourhoods sometimes offer breakfast programs to all students as well as lunch programs to students who qualify.

Feminist social work practice Practice which assumes that since social categories (like gender) shape the way we understand and interact with others, particular approaches need to be developed to address the unique needs of women. This approach to practice seeks to understand a client's situation by acquiring knowledge of the client's history, family and social relations, and cultural context, giving greater emphasis to the harmful role of patriarchal relations within the family and within wider society.

Feminist theory There are different definitions of feminism and numerous formulations and debates in feminist theory. There is, however, a common core theory asserting that sex-role stereotypes and social structures perpetuate women's subordination.

Feminization of poverty A concept that captures the overall demographic trend that the number of women in poverty is increasing faster than that of men.

Food banks Programs and centres that provide groceries to individuals and families that cannot make ends meet. Often, clients are permitted only one visit to a food bank per month, and depending on supplies, may receive only a few days worth of food. Food banks are non-profits, often run by charities or churches, which collect donations through public drives and corporate giving and through arrangements with grocery suppliers.

Forming stage First stage of group development, consisting of two tasks: planning the group and getting the group started.

Freudian thought A body of thought based on the theories of Sigmund Freud, father of psychology, which considers a person's psychological make-up as the source of his or her problems. Freudian thought played an increasingly important role in social work in the 1920s.

Functional approach An approach to social work practice developed following World War II which holds that individuals have the potential to determine their own direction. Based on functional theory.

Functional theory Based on personality psychology, functional theory seeks to enhance social functioning in individuals, families, groups, and communities by diagnosing the problem and using one's personal power to effect change in a structured way.

Gender Gender has two components, first gender identity, which is the sense we have of ourselves as male, female, or transgendered; and secondly our gender role, which is our adherence to cultural norms of femininity and masculinity. This is in contrast to sex, which is biological and determined by genetics.

Gender equality The belief that women and men should live in an environment that affords them equal opportunities to realize full human rights; to contribute to national, political, economic, social, and cultural development; and to benefit from the results of that development. To achieve this goal, equity programs provide measures to compensate women for previous historical and social disadvantages.

Gestalt therapy An existentialist approach to social work practice which argues that a unified whole is more significant than the sum of its parts and often focuses on relationships. Gestalt was first used as a concept in psychology to understand the mind as a whole entity, not just the sum of its individual parts.

Global social welfare In this era of globalization, the traditional concerns of social welfare practitioners in addressing the immediate needs of their clients are broadened to include a concern for global human rights. Global social welfare refers to concern for justice, social regulation, social provision, and redistribution between nations.

Great Depression A worldwide economic downturn that originated in the United States with the stock market crash of October 29, 1929 (known as "Black Tuesday"). The Great Depression lasted until the late 1930s or early 1940s and the onset of the Second World War.

Group dynamics The communication and interaction between group members, members' sense of belonging, and the degree to which a group influences its members.

Group work A social work method that involves assisting a collection of people who are dealing with a similar problem or issue.

Hall Report A report completed by the Royal Commission on Health Care, chaired by Justice Emmett Hall in 1964, that highlighted the fact that millions of Canadians did not have medical coverage. This report recommended that a comprehensive, publicly administered universal health service plan be implemented and in 1968, the *Medical Care Act* was passed.

Harm-reduction approach An approach to addictions treatment that seeks to minimize or reduce the adverse consequences of drug use.

Hate crimes Crimes that target people solely because of who they are, or who they are thought to be; usually perpetrated against members of marginalized groups.

Healing lodges Lodges that provide residential treatment or both treatment and lodging for people who become overwhelmed by social, emotional, and spiritual problems. Based upon an Aboriginal approach to healing and spirituality. The Nechi Institute and Poundmaker's Lodge in Alberta are examples, providing healing and lodging for people dealing with addictions.

Health gap The growing difference between the rich and poor in terms of health and well-being. Despite the availability of public health care, the rich are healthier than the middle class, who are, in turn, healthier than the poor. The well-educated are healthier than the less-educated, the employed are healthier than the unemployed, and so on.

Helping Relationship The relationship between a client and a professional social worker, in which the worker should exhibit warmth, empathy, and genuineness toward the client.

Heterosexism Heterosexism describes beliefs and actions that denigrate and stigmatize any non-heterosexual forms of behaviour, identity, relationship, or community.

Heterosexual privilege The comfort and power accorded to people who are in, or are expected to be in, a relationship with a person of a different sex and who conform to dominant gender norms. Heterosexual privilege allows someone to escape the social risks, dangers, and costs associated with not conforming to conventional gender norms.

HIV/AIDS HIV (human immunodeficiency virus) is a sexually transmitted and blood-borne retrovirus that undermines a person's immune system. AIDS (acquired immune deficiency syndrome) is the stage of HIV in which the immune system is destroyed.

Holistic approach to healing The holistic approach involves examining the whole of the person and their situation before acting or pursuing treatment. A common concept in Aboriginal cultures, the holistic approach is now being applied to Western-based health care, addressing the social, cultural, mental, and spiritual aspects of the person.

Home care Health care service delivery provided in one's home rather than in hospitals and other health care settings. Home care includes services such as curative medicine, end-of-life care, rehabilitation, support and maintenance, social adaptation, integration, and caregiver support. Home care programs are often complemented by community-based services that provide additional care and supports.

Hospice care Health care that is provided to individuals who are living with a terminal illness. Also known as palliative care, it is typically provided when the illness is at an advanced stage; its purpose is to provide relief and comfort and to maintain the highest possible quality of life for as long as the person is still alive.

Homophobia, biphobia, and transphobia The fear and hatred of gay men, lesbians, bisexuals, and transgendered persons; can be exhibited by an individual or society as a whole.

Human Development Index (HDI) The indicator of human development used by the United Nations Development Programme in the *Human Development Report* (HDR). This index involves other dimensions besides income in measuring human well-being, emphasiz-

ing that people and their capabilities should be the ultimate criteria for assessing the development of a country.

Human Development Report (HDR) An independent report commissioned by the United Nations Development Programme that assesses the level of long-term well-being of people by nations, specifically those in the developing world.

Human rights Those rights that are inherent in our nature and without which we cannot live as human beings; based on the recognition of individual political, civil, and collective cultural, social, and economic rights.

Immigration policy Legislation and supporting policies that dictate who may enter, live, and work in Canada. Ethnic and race relations in Canada have been heavily influenced by immigration policy. Prior to 1967, "Nationality" was one of the criteria used to qualify for admission to Canada, and Canadian immigration policy was undoubtedly Eurocentric. In 1967, new legislation introduced a point system, whereby prospective immigrants had to qualify based on such criteria as education, work experience, language fluency, and age.

Income security Income support in the form of demogrants, social insurance, social assistance, and income supplementation that can be unconditional or based on an income or needs tests; it can also be provided through the tax system.

Income supplementation Programs that supplement income that is obtained elsewhere whether through paid employment or through other income security programs. These programs are not intended to be the primary source of income. Family Allowance (which was also a universal demogrant) and the National Child Benefit are examples of income supplementation programs.

Independent Living Movement (ILM) Originating in the United States during the early 1970s and introduced to Canada in 1979, this movement argues that persons with disabilities should be in control of their lives and how they chose to live. The ILM has become a dominant force in disability rights activity in Canada. In addition to promoting disability rights, the ILM promotes the social oppression theory of disability.

Indian Act of 1876 Legislation that provides the Government of Canada with the legal framework of authority over Indians and lands reserved for Indians. The main purpose of the Act was to control and regulate Indian lives. An "Indian" is a person who is registered or entitled to be registered in the Indian Register (a centralized record), also referred to as a "status Indian."

Indian Agent A government agent who administered the *Indian Act*, interfering in virtually every aspect of Native life. Indian Agents had extraordinary administrative and discretionary powers, and were meant to displace traditional Aboriginal leaders so as to institute a new way of living consistent with the assimilationist intentions of the government.

Indirect social work Social work of benefit to those in need, but with organizations that advocate, research, plan, and implement social service and income security programs. Most often those who do indirect social work will be working with government, social service agencies, or what are called advocacy or research groups, and organizations whose purpose is to advocate for and with people in need.

Individual-level theories Varied and complex theories that focus on individuals and their interactions. This body of theory concentrates on aspects such as interactions between people or the effect of negative attitudes on people; in contrast to structural-level theories.

In-home services In-home services are provided to help a household or family members live together harmoniously in a secure and safe environment. The main categories of in-home services include family counselling services, parenting supports, child protection, in-home child care, homemaker services, and family educational services.

Institutional abuse Abuse that occurs in health and extended care facilities for seniors and other vulnerable populations. Institutional abuse is defined as any act or omission directed at a resident that causes the person harm, or wrongfully deprives that person of his or her independence.

Institutional view This view of social welfare calls for a publicly funded and organized system of programs and institutions, because the market will not, and cannot, meet the needs and aspirations of all people, the optimal distribution of welfare can only be achieved by such an organized system.

Intake Intake is the first step taken by a worker when a client seeks help. Intake is a process whereby a request for service is made by or for a person, and it is then determined whether and what kind of service is to be provided. The social worker attempts to gather initial information from the client in order to determine what assistance is needed, and whether the agency or worker is the appropriate provider.

Integrated service delivery (ISD) A comprehensive model of service delivery in which social and health services are coordinated to meet the diverse needs of individuals or families. This model is client-focused and team-based and enables people to access different services from a variety of service-providers within one centralized location.

Integrative approach An approach to practice that involves selecting concepts and methods from various sources and theories and building a unified system that is appropriate for the particular worker and setting.

Interdisciplinary teams Teams of health care professionals (that may include doctors, nurses, occupational therapists, social workers, etc.) that work to holistically address health care and ensure that each patient's physical, psychological, social, and cultural needs are met.

Intersexuals Individuals whose external sex (genitalia) are indeterminate, people who appear to be males but are medically/biologically females, people with female physical attributes who are medically/biologically males, as well as individuals having the external appearance of both sexes and the DNA chromosome karyotypes of both sexes.

Intervention The third step of the social work process, intervention is when the social worker or the client enact the plan developed during the assessment and planning stage. This term is also used to describe a social worker's actions on behalf of clients in a direct practice context.

Involuntary clients Those who accept social work services because of a legal mandate, such as prisoners on parole or children in care.

Keynesians Advocates of an economic theory, named after British economist John Maynard Keynes, which holds that economic social spending helps economic recovery, enhances productivity, and keeps the labour market flexible. Also called demand-side economics—if people are employed, they will spend money, the demand for products will increase, and the economy will improve.

Kinsey Report A 1948 report entitled *Sexual Behavior in the Human Male*, published by scientist Alfred Kinsey that documented men's sexual habits and behaviours, demonstrating that people's sexual behaviours combined both normal and so-called perverse behaviours.

Kinship care An approach to child protection that aims to keep children with immediate and extended family members; kinship care refers to placement of children who are in the care of child services agencies with other family members. Kinship care families go through the same process of assessment and preparation as non-kinship families.

Kinship service An approach to child protection that aims to keep children with immediate and extended family members; kinship service refers to placement of children who are not in the care of child services with other family members.

Land-cession treaties Treaties enacted between 1670 and 1923 between various Aboriginal peoples and the British colonial (and later the Canadian) government. The treaties gave control of land occupied by Aboriginals to the government and formed the reserve system, which attempted to move Aboriginal people into agriculturally based communities, both to assimilate them and to free up vast tracks of land for non-Aboriginal settlement. It is these land treaties (in many cases, the lack of them) that are currently in dispute across the country today.

Learning theory Theory of domestic violence that argues that violence is a behaviour learned in childhood. Boys learn that it is okay to be violent, and girls learn that it is okay to be on the receiving end of violence—that is what relationships are about. This theory holds that all children are socialized to accept violence in our society and that this, coupled with the different roles that boys and girls are socialized into, supports and perpetuates abuse. Children who witness violence in the home are much more likely to become abusers or be abused than children who don't.

Least restrictive approach An approach to child protection that emphasizes the least disruptive course of action, usually with the goal of leaving a child with his or her family, if at all possible. This approach is in contrast to the best interests approach.

LGBTTQ The acronym used to identify the diverse community which includes lesbians, gay men, bisexuals, transgendered and transsexual persons, and people who identify as queer.

Life course theory This theory of aging suggests that individuals progress through a variety of distinct stages over the course of their lives. Each stage has particular benefits, limitations, and characteristics. No stage is perceived as more or less satisfactory than another. Further, this theory maintains that within each life stage, various distinct pathways are selected by individuals as they progress through life.

Locality development Approach to community development that organizes around issues that are relevant to a particular neighbourhood or geographic space. Its focus is on community building by engaging a wide number of community participants in the organizing process.

Low Income Cut-offs (LICOs) Level at which individuals and families are considered to be living in poverty; level changes based on region and family size and is determined by Statistics Canada. Those who spend more than 55 percent of their earnings on basic needs are living under the LICO. Although not an official poverty line, many analysts, including the United Nations, treat it as such.

Low Income Measure (LIM) A relative measure of poverty that measures low-income rates as one-half of the median income of a particular country. The LIM is often used around the world to compare international rates of child poverty and is calculated based on information obtained by Statistics Canada.

Market Basket Measure (MBM) A relative measure of poverty calculated by taking the income needed by a particular household to meet its basic needs as determined by pre-existing community norms. By defining income needs, as opposed to terms of bare subsistence, it progresses beyond an absolute measure of poverty to reflect changes in the cost of consumption rather than changes in income.

Maternal feminists Feminists who argue that because of a woman's special roles as mother and homemaker, she has an obligation and a right to participate in the public sphere. Although they brought women into public life and social work, the early maternal feminists now tend to be viewed as conservative, insofar as they supported more traditional conceptions of the family in which women were expected to stay in the home.

Medical model Based on the "personal tragedy" theory of disability, this model views disability as an unfortunate life event that requires professional or medical assistance. Under this model, medical practitioners often dictate how persons with disabilities should live their lives.

Medicare Government-funded health insurance within Canada's health care system. Delivered by hospitals and physicians, the funding for medicare is available to all Canadian provinces and territories as long as they meet the five principles of medicare: public administration, comprehensiveness, universality, portability, and accessibility.

Mental illness A general term referring to psychological, emotional, or behavioural disorders, as well to the view that these disorders are diseases of the mind.

Mindfulness-based interventions Mindfulness is a way of paying attention, on purpose, to the present moment in a non-judgmental way. It can be cultivated using various exercises and with meditation.

Minimum income The provision of monetary assistance to those with no other source of income; primarily geared towards those deemed to be living in poverty, and the quantity of assistance tends to be determined by the minimum amount necessary to meet basic needs. Social Assistance is a minimum income program.

Monetarists Advocates of an economic theory that asserts that governments should keep inflation in check by controlling the supply of money through interest rates. Generally, monetarists argue that social spending stimulates inflation, undermines labour market flexibility and productivity, and distorts the work–leisure trade-off.

Multiculturalism The social preservation, recognition, and celebration of racial, ethnic, cultural, and religious diversity. In 1971, Canada became the first country to adopt multiculturalism as an official policy. The policy was aimed at a greater integration of Canadian society by providing diverse ethnic minority groups with a sense of belonging to Canada.

Narrative therapy Therapy that uses the power of storytelling to make sense of experiences and problems. Proponents of this therapy believe the way people tell stories reveals how they understand the world and their relationships within it and provides insights into their values, morals, and beliefs.

Negative rights Civil and political rights that ensure the protection of basic human rights, as set forth in Articles 2–21 of the *Universal Declaration of Human Rights.*

New world order model This approach to international social work argues that the present world order is not democratic, but controlled by a relatively small number of wealthy countries that manipulate the international system to their own advantage. Those who practice with this approach in mind are oriented more towards a fundamental rebuilding of the global cultural, social, political, and economic structures.

Norming stage Third stage of group development, when group norms (or expectations, standards, common practices) and roles become more clearly defined and members establish a beginning trust with each other; group cohesion increases and the group moves toward working on the agreed upon objectives.

North-South divide The separation of the economic world, broadly speaking, along North-South lines, with the countries of the mostly northern First World awash in relative affluence and those of the mostly Third World, in abject poverty.

Out-of-home services Out-of-home services are implemented when the home situation becomes unsuitable for the upbringing of a child, such as foster care, adoption, daycare centres, community supports, group homes, institutional care, parenting self-help and empowerment groups, and family housing assistance.

Palliative care Health care that is provided to individuals who are living with a terminal illness. Also known as hospice care, palliative care is typically provided when the illness is at an advanced stage; its purpose is to provide relief and comfort and to maintain the highest possible quality of life for as long as the person is still alive.

Participation and Activity Limitation Survey (PALS) A report conducted by the Canadian federal government first in 2001 and again in 2006 that detailed the prevalence of disabilities, the various supports that exist for persons with disabilities, the employment profile of persons with disabilities, as well as their incomes and the extent of their participation within society.

Participatory action research (PAR) A type of community work that involves members in a research process comprised of education, investigation, and action directed at changing the structures that promote inequality and the structures that produce knowledge that perpetuates the current power structures.

Patriarchy Literally meaning "rule by the father," in a broader sense, patriarchy has come to mean the domination of society by men. Men are still the major stakeholders in society, men continue to be represented in higher numbers in positions of authority, and men's interests continue to take precedence over those of women.

Performing stage Fourth stage of group development, when group members work toward achieving the outlined goals; group cohesion is strong and group participation is good, with attendance at sessions generally high.

Person-in-the-environment An approach that goes beyond internal or psychological factors to examine the relationship between individuals and their environment. This is partly what distinguishes social work practice from other helping professions. The environment in question extends beyond the immediate family and includes interactions with friends, neighbourhoods, schools, religious groups, laws and legislation, other agencies or organizations, places of employment, and the economic system.

Persons with disabilities The term used describes a persons whose physical or mental condition limits their ability to perform certain functions. This term is widely endorsed as the most appropriate, since it puts the person first and not the disability: *people with disabilities, person with disability, person with intellectual disability* and so on. *Disabled person* is now also generally acceptable usage, and some advocate this term because it does not minimize or de-politicize disability.

Planning Part of the second stage of the social work process, planning refers to the development of a plan of action. It will include different elements and emphasis depending on the perspective or approach of the social worker.

Political rights model Based on the "social oppression" theory of disability, this model is primarily concerned with broader social and political change, contending that a comprehensive understanding of disability can only occur through examination of the social and political inequality that exists between disabled people and people without disabilities.

Poor relief Assistance to the deserving poor dictated by early English Poor Law. Local parishes provided relief to those who were elderly, ill, or disabled. Parishes were administrative districts organized by the Church of England. Each had a local council that was responsible for poor relief.

Portability One of five principles of medicare in Canada. Allows residents moving to another province to be covered for insured health services by the home province during any minimum waiting period imposed by the new province.

Positive rights Economic, social, and cultural rights that ensure justice, freedom, and social participation, as set forth in Articles 22–27 of the *Universal Declaration of Human Rights.*

Poverty gap The amount of additional income that would be required to raise an individual or household above the LICO; poverty rates alone do not show whether poor people are living in abject poverty or merely a few dollars below the poverty line.

Power theory A feminist-based theory explaining that wife abuse is a societal problem that occurs because of the power imbalance between men and women, specifically because of the dominance of men and men's roles. This theory argues that wife abuse continues because there has been historical acceptance of abuse and of men's right to control women, even by force.

Praxis A process of reflection and action integral to a Freirian approach to community work; Freire believed that a successful action for social change must be reflected upon in advance and afterwards, thereby creating new and more effective actions, which are also then reflected upon.

Prejudice An adverse opinion that "pre-judges" entire groups based on incomplete and inaccurate information.

Pre-payment health plans Voluntary insurance plans did not cover all medical services, and they were available only to those who could afford to pay the premiums. From 1880 to the 1950s there were a variety of pre-payment health plans in place across Canada, sponsored by local governments, industries, and volunteer agencies.

Private charities Organizations that developed during the pre-industrial phase of social work, which includes the period from the formation of Canada up to the 1890s. Private charities offered material relief and lessons in moral ethics. Many were explicitly associated with religious organizations, and it was religiously motivated individuals working through these organizations who became the early social workers.

Private welfare Social welfare programs funded by voluntary charitable contributions of individuals and private organizations, by fees people pay for the services they receive, or which are provided by funds spent by corporations to provide social welfare services for their employees.

Privately funded disability programs Privately funded disability programs include programs that are provided through private insurance plans or through long-term disability plans as part of job benefits. These private income security programs are based on the amount of funding that the recipient has contributed directly to the plan, or funding which has been contributed to the plan on behalf of the recipient.

Privatization The use of the private sector to provide social welfare services, often in addition to or instead of existing public services.

Psychodynamic perspectives Based on the work of Sigmund Freud, these are diagnostic approaches to social work that focus on internal sources for individuals' problems.

Public administration One of five principles of medicare in Canada. Each province must provide a health insurance plan that is administered and operated on a non-profit basis by a public authority, responsible to the provincial government, and be subject to audit of its accounts and financial transactions.

Public sector unions Unions that represent government employees; these differ from trade unions which represent individuals doing a similar type of work. Public sector unions, such as the Canadian Union of Public Employees (CUPE) represent a wide variety of professions and membership is contingent on a person's place of employment. Today most Canadian social workers are members of public sector unions because they are employed by government or government-sponsored agencies and institutions (such as schools or hospitals).

Public welfare The provision of welfare services at the three levels of government: the federal or national government, the provincial and territorial governments, and the regional and municipal governments.

Publicly funded disability programs Programs covered by federal, provincial, and municipal legislation. These programs include the Canada Pension Plan–Disability Pension (a federal program), and various provincial disability support programs.

Queer activism Efforts and actions towards social change by LGBTTQ communities. Queer activism is significantly more confrontational than the gay and lesbian rights movement and demands dramatic changes to ways sexual diversity is perceived within society.

Queer theory A theory which maintains that all sexual behaviours, sexual identities, and sexual categories are social constructs with social meaning and as such, legislative changes within the current capitalist democracy will not result in fundamental social change and liberation for LGBTTQ people.

Race An arbitrary classification of human beings based on skin colour and other superficial physical characteristics. Modern biologists do not recognize "race" as a meaningful scientific category and recent human genome research is conclusive on this point. Rather, race is considered a social construct used to create hierarchies among groups of people; for example, in North America a person with features attributed to "African" heritage will be called black, even if the majority of his or her ancestors are European in origin—a sibling who does not have such features would be considered white, despite having the same genetic background.

Racism Individual and institutionalized beliefs and practices that advocate that some "races" are inferior to others. The belief that one's racial group is somehow superior to other groups leads, with the aid of stereotypes, to discrimination and prejudice.

Rational-emotive psychotherapy The earliest form of a cognitive-behaviour approach to social work practice, in which personal problems are understood to be the result of irrational patterns of thinking and the dysfunctional behaviours that happen as a result. The goal of the therapist is to help a client to see that the negative emotions experienced are due to a flawed perception of reality.

Reflection-action-reflection Process by which a social worker continually thinks things through while acting on the problem at hand, and always acts in consultation with the client.

Residential school system A system of boarding schools that was used to remove Aboriginal children from their homes and communities and to restrict their culture and language. The purpose was to fulfill the assimilation policies of the federal government. Large numbers of children in residential schools experienced emotional, physical, and sexual abuse.

Residual view This view of social welfare asserts that governments should play only a limited role in the distribution of social welfare. The state should step in only when normal sources of support fail and the individual is unable to help himself or herself. This is in contrast to the institutional view.

Risk assessment In the area of child protection, risk assessment refers to an educated prediction regarding the likelihood that a child will be maltreated based on a careful examination of pertinent data.

Role theory This theory maintains that people define and adopt roles. As applied to seniors, this theory attempts to understand the adjustment of aging people to new roles that they adopt throughout the aging process.

Royal Commission on Aboriginal Peoples A commission called by the federal government in 1991 to examine the status of Aboriginal peoples in Canada. The final report of 1996 brought together six years of research and public consultation on Aboriginal issues. This is the most extensive research to date and provides the basis for significant strides forward. Among the many issues discussed, the Report examines the need for Aboriginal people to heal from the consequences of domination, displacement, and assimilation and calls for recognition of Aboriginal nations as political entities.

Scientific philanthropy An historical approach that contributed to the rise of social work with the idea that charities should become organized in order to deal more systematically with the problem of poverty. It emerged from ideals of social reform and social progress, which were increasingly influenced by scientific methods and approaches and employed a medical diagnosis/treatment model of social work.

Scrip system In the early twentieth century, the Métis in western Canada could seek to become status Indians by aligning themselves to certain treaty areas, or they could "take scrip." The scrip system entitled the bearer of a scrip certificate to either land or money; in exchange, the person who took scrip gave up all further claims to land.

Selective programs Target benefits aimed at those determined to be in need or eligible based on a means test (sometimes called an income test) or a needs test.

Self-help groups Groups that do not have a professional facilitator and may be either leaderless, have a rotating leader, or designate a leader from within the group. Alcoholics Anonymous is one of the most well-known and longest running self-help groups.

Settlement house movement A movement that began in the late 1800s, in which the middle and upper classes lived with the poor and advocated for better social and working conditions. The purpose was to bring the educated middle class and even the charitable upper class to live among the urban poor in working class neighbourhoods.

Sex Sex (usually male or female) is what doctors attribute to babies based largely on the size of their genitalia. It is determined by genetics, chromosomes, and hormones, which can combine to create an indeterminate number of sexes. Often conflated with gender.

Sexism Similar to the dynamics of racism, the individual and institutional belief that men are superior to women. When this belief is put into action, women are considered to be less worthy or capable because they do not think and act as men in a society that privileges male behaviours and characteristics

Sexology The systematic study of human sexual behaviour. Sexology developed out of the efforts of early scientists to understand, categorize, and document sexual relations and sexual attraction.

Sexual assault Any form of unwanted sexual activity that is forced upon another person without obtaining that person's consent. Sexual assault includes a wide range of physical and non-physical sexual acts that are all defined as criminal under the *Criminal Code*.

Sexual harassment Any behaviour, comment, gesture, or contact of a sexual nature in which someone is treated as a sexual object. Unlike sexual assault, which is criminal, sexual harassment falls under civil law.

Sexual orientation Sexual activity is not the sole deciding factor for sexual orientation as relatively few people are exclusively homosexual or heterosexual. Instead, orientation is a dominant emotional, romantic, sexual, or affectional attraction to another person. Orientation is not dependent upon a person's gender identity, which is our sense of ourselves as being male, female, or transgendered, or our ability or willingness to adhere to cultural norms of masculine or feminine (gender roles).

Sixties Scoop The massive removal of Aboriginal children from their families and communities and their placement in non-Aboriginal foster and adoptive homes, which took place primarily in the 1960s.

Social action An activist approach to community work which often uses public confrontation and social protest to challenge what are seen as injustices. A social action approach to community work aims to redistribute power, resources, and decision making.

Social action groups Groups that focus on broad social issues and are often inspired by personal experience; these groups are part of community organizing.

Social change/social justice mandate Calls for social workers to work in solidarity with those who are disadvantaged or excluded from society so as to eliminate the barriers, inequities, and injustices that exist in society.

Social constructionism In relation to sexual attraction, this approach considers socio-cultural experience as the source for construction of a homosexual identity and role. Social constructionism gave rise to perspectives of "choice" and "lifestyles," challenging the innate deterministic understanding of sexual orientation as advanced by essentialist perspective.

Social development model In the international context, social workers who hold to this approach seek primarily to address the immediate causes of human degradation, powerlessness, and social inequality and to guide collective action towards the elimination of all forms of oppression, injustice, and violence. They are concerned with the fuller participation of people at all levels of the political and economic systems of their countries and with fostering social, political, and economic systems that are more humane, inclusive, and participatory.

Social empathy The application of empathy to a larger context, making connections between personal troubles and structural issues; connecting the personal and the political can be very affirming to clients. By providing a social and political context, the facilitator reframes their issues outside the realm of personal failure, which can lead to empowerment.

Social gospel movement Movement directed towards a more socially oriented church among the Anglican, Methodist, Presbyterian, and Congregationalist churches that began in the 1880s. It advocated for improved living and working conditions and basic social justice.

Social insurance A type of income security program in which participants make regular payments into a fund from which they receive benefits if the risk covered by the insurance occurs. These programs follow the insurance principle of shared risk. Many contribute with the understanding that not all will necessarily need to access the benefits of the program.

Social planning An expert-driven approach to community work often found in social planning councils and city planning departments.

Social policies The rules and regulations, laws, and other administrative directives that set the framework for state social welfare activity.

Social programs The specific initiatives that implement social policy. A social program outlines the funds to be spent and the purposes for which they will be spent.

Social safety net The network of laws, policies, and programs currently in place around the country through which the Canadian state creates opportunities for individuals experiencing difficulties in their lives and helps them get back on their feet. In countries where the social safety net is weak or non-existent, there is little or no protection of this kind and individuals are often left to fend for themselves.

Social services Non-monetary personal or community services, such as daycare, housing, crisis intervention, and support groups, provided by the state and non-profit organizations for community members.

Social survey research An early method of research used during the late nineteenth century to highlight the extent of poverty and inequality in Canadian cities. Early studies by social researchers and reformers, such as J.J. Kelso in Toronto and J.S. Woodsworth in Winnipeg, contributed to an understanding of poverty and what to do about it. Royal Commissions also contributed to increased awareness and a growing interest in social service and social work.

Social systems theory Theory which places the individual within a series of interdependent systems. This theory is also sometimes referred to as the *ecological systems theory*, based on the scientific concept of the biological ecosystem, where every organism is affected by and influences the others within the system.

Social Union Framework Agreement (SUFA) The Social Union Agreement of 1999 between the Government of Canada and the provinces and territories is the umbrella under which governments concentrate their efforts to renew and modernize Canadian social policy. So far, several social welfare initiatives have been established under this framework: the National Child Benefit, the National Children's Agenda for Childcare, and services for persons with disabilities.

Social welfare Including both social services and income security, social welfare refers to the way people, communities, and institutions in a society take action to provide certain minimum standards and opportunities, and to help people face contingencies.

Social welfare model In the international context, this more conventional social welfare model is based on the notion that basic social welfare services should be developed in all countries to meet basic human needs. Social workers following this model of international practice are mainly concerned with the satisfaction of basic social and material needs of people (i.e., minimal standards of living, access to at least basic health, education, and other essential social services).

Social work practice Work consisting of a series or process of interventionist actions that is of benefit to those in need, especially work undertaken by trained staff. It may consist of social work with individuals, groups, or communities.

Social work theory An organized way of thinking about the world that guides the way we carry out social work practice.

Stereotype A set of beliefs or perceptions of groups of people, or ideas held by a number of people, often not based on fact.

Stonewall Rebellion A series of riots instigated by New York City's gay and lesbian communities in response to a police raid on the Stonewall Inn, a Greenwich Village gay bar in 1969. This is thought of as the unification of the gay and lesbian political movements of the time, as it represented the first significant collective uprising by these communities against state oppression. It also marked the beginning of a more public, large-scale movement for gay and lesbian rights.

Storming stage Second stage of group development, characterized by the emergence of conflict within the group; differences in understanding of the group's purpose and the group members' roles and expectations can lead to friction.

Strengths-based perspective Individual-level approach that focuses on personal strengths and assets rather than identifying and solving problems; recognizes that each person has unique strengths and abilities, and the capacity for growth and change.

Structural approach An approach to practice that focuses on the impact of wider social structures on personal problems and involves critical analysis of socio-economic structures that oppress and exploit people, whether based on class, race, age, gender, ability, or sexuality.

Structural-level theories Theories that emphasize social structures, processes, and systems and how they shape people's experiences; in contrast to individual-level theories.

Suffragette movement The suffragette movement is term applied to late nineteenth and early twentieth century campaigns run by women for the right to vote; the term comes from the word suffrage (the right to vote) and the traditional suffix "ette" used to feminize terms. A suffragette was a women who advocated for the right to vote. Some countries and jurisdictions granted suffrage early on (such as New Zealand in 1893) and much later (such as Switzerland in 1973). Full federal enfranchisement for women in Canada came in 1918; most provinces either preceded the federal legislation or quickly followed suit. Quebec did not grant suffrage to women until 1940.

Support/therapeutic groups Groups where the primary purpose is supporting people dealing with specific problems, such as victims of sexual abuse or people dealing with mental illnesses. These types of groups have a professional facilitator.

Sustainable development Development that meets the needs of the present without compromising the ability of future generations to meet their own needs, usually referring to environmental sustainability, but also includes notions of human resources.

Systemic discrimination The operating policies, structures, and functions of an ongoing system of normative patterns that subjugate, oppress, and force the dependence of individuals or groups. It involves establishing and sanctioning unequal rights, goals, and priorities and sanctioning inequality in status and access to goods and services.

Task-centred model A short-term therapy with a measurable outcome and proven effectiveness that is based on the assumption that people experiencing particular problems typically have the resources and motivation to resolve them.

Task groups Groups that have a particular established task to complete, such as a group that coordinates settlement services for newcomers in a community or a personnel committee charged with the task of hiring an executive director.

Termination Part of the final stage of the social work process, termination, or the ending of the client-worker relationship, occurs ideally when the action plan is completed and the client's goals have been met.

Third World The developing countries of Central and South America, Africa, and Asia. Also referred to as the global south or the developing world.

Transgender Transgender is inclusive of people who identify as bigender, gender benders, gender outlaws, cross-dressers, drag queens, drag-kings, transvestites, and transsexuals. Some intersexuals also identify as transgender. Some transgendered persons understand their experience in dimorphic absolutes (i.e., a man trapped in a female body), while others inhabit a more ambiguous zone "between" the sexes.

Transsexuals Transsexuals are people whose gender identity is at odds with their physical sex. Psychiatry still considers transsexualism a mental illness that requires treatment. Some transsexuals undergo gender reassignment surgery to have their anatomy coincide with their gender. Others use hormones to shape their body. Not everyone who identifies as transsexual uses medical interventions to change their physical appearance.

Undeserving poor Poor people were considered undeserving if they were perceived as being capable of working; undeserving poor were considered to lack good moral character. This historical conception ignored the idea that a person may be temporarily out of luck through no fault of their own. While part of the early Poor Laws, the public conception of undeserving poor still informs income security today.

Universal child care program This model aims to provide high-quality, affordable, regulated, childhood education and care to all families. A universal child care program is demonstrated in Quebec where accessible child care is provided to many families.

Universality One of five principles of medicare in Canada; requires that 100 percent of the insured persons of a province be entitled to insurance on uniform terms and conditions.

Universal programs Social welfare programs that are equally available to all citizens within a specific category such as age or disability, regardless of need or financial situation.

Universal public health care Publicly funded health care that is available to all who qualify (eligibility is determined by residence or citizenship status). Prior to the late 1940s, access to health care was based solely on one's ability to pay. Universal public health care for everyone in Canada took over five decades to evolve.

Visible minorities Within the Canadian context, this term (widely used in government statistics) refers to individuals who can be visibly identified and perceived as belonging to a minority group. Usually used in terms of racial groups other than those of European origin. Because it emphasizes physical difference from the "dominant" culture, it is a somewhat contentious term.

Voluntary clients People who have chosen to seek the services of a social worker.

Welfare state A system whereby the state ostensibly undertakes to protect the health and well-being of its citizens, especially those in financial need.

INDEX